SUICIDAL HONOR

General Nogi, following Emperor Meiji during the Great Military Parade in Nara, Fall 1908. Reproduced from Kuwahara and Sugawara, eds., *Nogi Maresuke no sekai* (Shinjinbutsu ōraisha, 1992), unnumbered plate following title page.

SUICIDAL HONOR

General Nogi and the Writings of Mori Ōgai and Natsume Sōseki

Doris G. Bargen

University of Hawai'i Press / Honolulu

Printed in the United States of America
11 10 09 08 07 06   6 5 4 3 2 1

Library of Congress Cataloging-in-Publication Data

Bargen, Doris G.
Suicidal honor : General Nogi and the writings of Mori Ōgai and Natsume Sōseki / Doris G. Bargen.
p. cm.
Includes bibliographical references and index.
ISBN-13: 978-0-8248-2998-8 (hardcover : alk. paper)
ISBN-10: 0-8248-2998-0 (hardcover : alk. paper)

1. Nogi, Maresuke, 1849–1912. 2. Seppuku. 3. Nogi, Maresuke, 1849–1912—In literature. 4. Mori, Ōgai, 1862–1922—Criticism and interpretation. 5. Natsume, Sōseki, 1867–1916—Criticism and interpretation. 6. Suicide in literature. 7. Japanese literature—1868—History and criticism. I. Title.
DS884.5.B37 2006
394'.880952—dc22

2006019423

University of Hawai‘i Press books are printed on acid-free paper and meet the guidelines for permanence and durability of the Council on Library Resources.

Designed by University of Hawai‘i Press production staff
Printed by The Maple-Vail Book Manufacturing Group

For

Carlin A. Barton

Liza Dalby

Fujikawa Teruko

CONTENTS

ACKNOWLEDGMENTS

In Natsume Sōseki's classic novel *Kokoro* (1914), Sensei reveals in his testament to a young friend his perplexity about a very peculiar self-assertive last gesture made by the scholar-painter Watanabe Kazan (1793–1841). Serving a life sentence commuted from death for his criticism of the shōgunal seclusion policy and a (false) charge of conspiracy, Kazan had postponed his death for one week in order to finish a painting. What complexities were involved in Kazan's act that it should resurface in the public memory in 1912 and become relevant to Sensei's own voluntary death? Should one respect or reject, despise or admire, Kazan for timing his death—suicide by the sword *(jijin)*—so supremely well for the sake of his artistic legacy? What fascinated Sensei about Kazan, or Sōseki about Sensei, is what fascinates me about General Nogi Maresuke (1849–1912), the historical figure at the heart of my study and the contemporary literature he inspired.

Many scholars, friends, and students have helped me in the effort to understand what leads a man like Nogi carefully to coordinate his purpose in life with his death, thereby conveying a message so intriguing that it becomes part of the cultural memory. My most severe and constructive critic has been my husband, Allen Guttmann, who helped me to clarify and organize my ideas. Carlin A. Barton inspired me with her study of honor, shame, and sacrifice in ancient Rome; and Liza Dalby, with her elegant, unorthodox research into Japanese culture. It is to them and to their Japanese kindred spirit, Fujikawa Teruko, that this book is dedicated.

In addition to the two anonymous readers for the University of Hawai'i Press, I am grateful to Christopher Benfey for his incisive comments on the entire manuscript, to Shion Kono for his suggestions about my chapter on Ōgai's "Sakai jiken," and to Karl Friday for his panel discussant's comments at the International Conference of Asia Scholars (ICAS) in Berlin 2001. I consider myself most fortunate to have in Patricia Crosby a superb executive editor who knows exactly what I am trying to say and has often said it better. Managing editor Ann Ludeman kept everything on track, and Barbara Folsom copyedited the manuscript meticulously and critically.

I also owe much to academics, curators, and librarians in America, Europe, and Japan. Our Five College East Asian Studies librarian, Sharon Domier, has long been an indefatigable resource in researching anything Japanese, and Shane Peters has provided professional computer and graphic-design assistance. In collaboration with Yamamoto Sanae of the Mori Ōgai Memorial Museum in Tsuwano, supervising librarian Inoue Makoto and reference librarian Andō Mamoru of Dōshisha University taught me more about family crests than I thought there was to know. Beate Weber, of the Mori-Ōgai-Gedenkstätte Berlin, provided bibliographical materials and other priceless bits of information. I gratefully accepted a loan of an American photographic stereocard of Nogi from Helen Hopper. William J. Tyler and Shigeru Shimozato shared with me their vivid photographs and remembrances of the Nogis' Akasaka residence in Tōkyō. My colleagues in Japanese at the University of Massachusetts Amherst, Stephen M. Forrest and Reiko Sono, have nourished my research with their finds and interest. One of our students, Mark E. Jolly, spurred my Nogi research with his honors thesis. Elizabeth A. Wilson (Mitchell) unearthed her University of Michigan thesis on "Sakai jiken" for my perusal. I thank Hartmut Grandel for primary materials by Germans in early Meiji Japan, Scott Sessions for stimulating discussions and secondary sources on Mesoamerican sacrifice, Andrea Rushing for information about sacrificial customs in Africa, and Wolfgang Decker for those of ancient Egypt.

My mentor for Heian Japan, Yoshikai Naoto, seemed unperturbed by my journey into the Meiji-Taishō period and surprised me with a rare source on Nogi's wife. Yoko Danno explored Sakai and Ōgai's story with me. Baba Minako, Higuchi Hideo and Fusako, Morita Masanori, and Takeda Masako sent me books and helped me decipher or understand what tends to escape foreigners. An expert on samurai and the Japanese military, Hiroaki Sato has tirelessly answered my questions and made me think differently by asking his own.

Dean Linda Slakey of Commonwealth College at the University of Massachusetts entrusted me with special funding for a year-long senior honors seminar on "Samurai and Rebels, Sacrifice and Martyrdom" that allowed me not only to test my ideas in the classroom but to hold a symposium on the related topic of assassination. Lee R. Edwards, Dean of the College of Humanities and Fine Arts, gave her generous support for research on this project. I could not have finished my book when I did without a year's sabbatical from the University of Massachusetts Amherst.

Finally, I thank my family and friends for their support in so many more ways than I can acknowledge here. Gridth and Steven L. Ablon, Akao Kimiko,

Kay Baker, Gwendolynne Barr, Rick Berger, Young-ah Chung, Dustin Cosentino, Douglas DaRif, Richard Freeland, Herwig and Bettina Friedl, Patricia J. Gorman, Erika Guttmann, Hugh Hawkins, Kodama Sanehide, Kuzuhara Yuki, Danika Medak-Saltzman, Nakano Aoi, Ross Nakatsuji, Elsa M. Nuñez, Halliday Piel, Walter Richards, Brian Sacawa, Sasaki Takashi and Noriko, and Uda Yoshitada—I cannot name them all.

A NOTE ON DATES, NAMES, AND CRESTS

Dates

On 1 January 1873 Japan changed from the lunar to the Gregorian calendar. Although references in my text and the texts I am quoting from will be to both calendars, I have converted lunar years to our Western calendar for the convenience of the reader. Thus, Nogi was born on 1849.XI.11, the eleventh day of the eleventh lunar month of Kaei 2 (1849), or 25 December 1849.

Names

According to Japanese convention, the surname is given first. I have followed this convention except when Japanese authors have themselves chosen to adopt the Western order of first and last name. It is also customary in many instances to refer to someone by a given or pen name rather than the family name; for example, Yoshitsune for Minamoto Yoshitsune, or Ōgai for Mori Ōgai (the given name is Rintarō). To avoid confusion about the custom of individual name changes, I have in some instances decided to use one name throughout rather than a series of historically accurate names; I have also eliminated the particle "no" between surname and given name (except in quotations).

Family crests *(kamon)*

Nogi Maresuke's crest belongs to the large category of *kamon* called "well curb" *(izutsu)*. According to Chikano Shigeru, president of the Association of Japanese Crests, the authentic Nogi crest is called "four joined well curbs" *(yotsu mochiai izutsu)*.[1] The Nogi Society (Chūō Nogi-kai) and Nogi Shrines (Nogi jinja) use a crest called "checkered four squares" *(ichimatsu yotsu me)*.[2] This crest heads my general chapters (1 and 2), and the authentic Nogi crest, from his tombstone, heads my Nogi chapters (3 and 4).

Mori Ōgai's extraordinary crest emerged from a family history complicated by adoptions. It belongs to the category of chrysanthemum *(kiku)* crests, but its pointedly unassuming variant, "a round crest with a torn chrysanthemum leaf" *(warisaki kiku no ha no maru mon),* is unidentified in crest directories.[3] By adopting a most inconspicuous chrysanthemum leaf crest from his mother's crested overcoat *(hifu),* Ōgai distanced himself from his maternal grandfather Hakusen's change of the family crest.[4] Hakusen undid the humility implied in the Mori crest of the fourth-generation Shūan (d. 1758) by turning Shūan's "*underside* [my emphasis] of a sixteen-petaled chrysanthemum inside a concave-sided hexagon" *(kikubasami ni jūrokuyō* ura *kikka mon)* on its face by inverting black and white. The crest that most resembles Ōgai's is that of the ninth-generation Shūan (d. 1831), who chose an "alternate round crest with a branch of bent chrysanthemum leaves" *(warisaki kiku no ha no eda maru no betsumon).*[5] Ōgai's crest decorates my Ōgai chapters (5 and 6).

Natsume Sōseki's family crest is called "boxed chrysanthemum or chrysanthemum in a well curb" *(mase kiku [igeta ni kiku]).* Unlike Ōgai, Sōseki never changed his crest because of changing family circumstances. Coming from a merchant rather than a samurai family, he lacked Ōgai's deep reserve about appropriating even a variant of the chrysanthemum emblem associated with the imperial house.[6] The undisputed Sōseki crest heads my chapter on Sōseki (7).

NOTES

1. Chikano Shigeru, *Nihon kamon sōkan* (Tōkyō: Kadokawa shoten, 1993), p. 46 (reproduction of crest no. 020-029); p. 47 (identification of Nogi Maresuke's crest from his tombstone in Tōkyō's Aoyama Cemetery *(reien).* See also Chikano Shigeru, *Tanbō Edo Meiji meishi no haka* (Tōkyō: Shinjinbutsu ōraisha, 1993), p. 14.

2. The Nogi Society uses the *ichimatsu yotsu me* crest for its home page http://www.nogijinja.or.jp, in fliers soliciting new members, and in its publications, such as the Nogi Shrine pamphlets and the journal *Senshin* (Cleansing the Heart). For name and illustration of the crest, see Itō Kōsaku, *Monshō: Chōjūgyo, katachi, shirushi, ji, gu,* 2 vols. (Tōkyō: Bijutsu shuppansha, 1969), 2:81.

3. I am grateful to Inoue Makoto of the Dōshisha University Library for making available to me reference librarian Andō Mamoru's communication of 4 July 2005 with Yamamoto Sanae of the Mori Ōgai Memorial Museum *(kinenkan)* in Tsuwano concerning the authenticity of the Ōgai crest.

4. Ōgai's mother, Mineko (d. 1916), was the only daughter of Hakusen, who had been adopted, after the mysterious banishment of his predecessor, from the Sasada family to restore the Mori line. See Shibata Mitsuhiko, "Kamon no hanashi: Natsume Sōseki to Mori Ōgai," in Yoshinari Isamu, ed., *Bessatsu rekishi tokuhon: Nihon 'kamon yurai' sōran* (Tōkyō: Shinjinbutsu ōraisha, 1997), p. 230.

5. The various Mori crests are reproduced in Shibata, "Kamon no hanashi," pp. 230–231.

6. See Shibata, "Kamon no hanashi," pp. 230–231.

INTRODUCTION
An Incomprehensible Act

The Meiji period officially began with the enthronement of Emperor Mutsuhito (1852–1912; r. 1867–1912) on 12 October 1868.[1] It ended with his death forty-four years later, on 30 July 1912. The funeral took place in Tōkyō on 13 September 1912. On that day, as the funeral procession departed from the imperial palace for the parade grounds of Aoyama, an extraordinary event occurred that shocked the nation. One of Japan's most famous and revered generals, Nogi Maresuke (1849–1912), committed ritual suicide by disembowelment *(seppuku)*. According to the autopsy report, he cut open his stomach from left to right and then from the bottom up, in the most difficult cross-line *(jūmonji)* form of seppuku.[2] Finally, with awesome willpower, he impaled himself on his military sword.[3] When informed of Nogi's act, those of his contemporaries who shared his familiarity with Japanese history realized that he had committed a traditional—but long outlawed—form of suicide called *junshi*. He had "followed his Lord into death."

Earlier that day, Nogi had dressed in the Western-style uniform of a modern military officer in order to have his photograph taken. He changed into traditional Japanese clothing in order to perform the anachronistic ritual that ended his life.[4] A change of dress may seem trivial by our standards, but to late Meiji men and women, who were adept at alternating between foreign and native forms of self-representation, it was highly significant. For Nogi, the difference between his Western military uniform and his samurai attire symbolized a deep split that ran not only through his psyche but also through the nation as a whole. His dramatic change of dress epitomized his renunciation of his official position as the emperor's modern general and his return to the ethical ideals of his samurai heritage. Although the philosopher Kuki Shūzō (1888–1941) describes a man whose *action gratuite* anticipated modern existentialist thought, he died the death of a samurai.[5]

Nogi committed seppuku in front of the late emperor's portrait *(goshin'ei)*. Other likenesses carefully chosen to be present at the scene as "witnesses" from the realm of the dead were photographs of his parents and of his two sons, both of whom had predeceased him.[6] Among the effects of immediate interest were his last writings. In his testament, written the previous day, Nogi emphasized in the very first clause that he had longed for death ever since he lost the imperial banner in the Satsuma Rebellion of 1877. By contrast, in the two poems he composed just before his death he focused solely on his indebtedness and gratitude to his Lord *(ōkimi)*, whom he was determined to follow into death. He did not die alone. That same day, his wife Shizuko (1859–1912) died with him by the sword.

Reactions to the Act

That Nogi felt honor-bound to take his own life in this way was—and still is—shockingly incomprehensible to Europeans and Americans unfamiliar with traditional Japanese conceptions of honor. As Nogi's contemporary, the novelist Tayama Katai (1871–1930), laconically commented, "I didn't think that General Nogi's attitude would be something that foreigners could understand."[7] In his memoirs, Stanley Washburn (1878–1950), an American correspondent who had been attached to Nogi's Third Army during the Russo-Japanese War (1904–1905), voiced a similar recognition of the cultural differences in responses to suicide: "To us, far off in England or America, the deed seems a dreadful one, but to those who knew Nogi and understood a little of his ideals and of his simple worship of his Emperor, the act seems not strange, but almost natural."[8] Washburn's colleague Richard Barry began his account by stating simply, "Volumes are required to explain Nogi." He then attempted to explain the inexplicable:

> Let us dismiss the common explanations of his remarkable act. It was not because he was remorseful over the 50,000 lives lost under his command. It was not because his two sons had been killed in battle, thus exterminating his line. It was for none of our Western motives whose existence we are almost bound to suspect: fear that under the new Emperor he would not have the position he enjoyed under the old, pique, melancholia, or the like.
>
> Nor yet was it inspired chiefly by that ancient samurai custom which required that a general should immolate himself on the grave of his Emperor. That but furnished him a convenient hinge on which to swing his real motive. . . . The quality that sinewed the basis of his act was that which a theosophist would call a mahatma's divination of the needs of his age. . . . He did not mean that others must die as he did, but that others must live as he did: live as he had that they might have the privilege of dying as he did should fate ever require of them that sacrifice. I feel the futility of explaining this to many. But some will understand.[9]

Barry and his contemporaries struggled to understand Nogi's act, not because it followed a peculiar Japanese custom too exotic to comprehend, but because it was meaningful to them even if that meaning was difficult to grasp. Scholars further removed in time have found that historical and cultural distance from the event does not necessarily lead to easier or better understanding. Writing in 1963, historian George Sansom described junshi as a "barbarous custom," a "ghastly habit."[10]

Westerners are not the only ones who have struggled to understand Nogi's junshi. The Japanese were, in fact, deeply divided about the act. By the end of the Meiji era, many Japanese considered seppuku an anachronism, an outdated custom that made no sense at all in a modernizing nation. Others were elated and profoundly moved by Nogi's sacrificial reassertion of honor and loyalty in an increasingly Westernized Japan.[11]

Although it would undoubtedly be interesting to undertake an extensive study of Nogi's place in Japanese popular culture, I have not attempted to document the contemporary reaction to Nogi's junshi as given in newspapers and magazines, letters, and memoirs,[12] nor to provide a historical survey of the use and misuse of Nogi's iconic figure through war and peace from 1912 to the present. I have chosen instead to concentrate upon Mori Ōgai (1862–1922) and Natsume Sōseki (1867–1916),[13] two internationally renowned writers of fiction whose work continues powerfully to resonate in the imagination of modern Japanese.

When Ōgai and Sōseki meditated upon Nogi's death in the form of several stories (Ōgai) and a classic novel (Sōseki), they were attempting to explain junshi to themselves as well as to their Taishō-era compatriots.[14] Among those with the finest antennae for a growing national unease about the rush to modernize were the literary elite. Ōgai and Sōseki, "national narrators par excellence" and "sensitive readers of the pulse of the nation,"[15] were both deeply involved in Japan's political affairs, the one as surgeon general for the army and the other as correspondent for the *Asahi Shinbun*. Both of them had lived in Europe, Ōgai in Germany and Sōseki in England. They knew better than most Japanese what might be gained, and what might be lost, from contact with foreign cultures. And both writers were seized by General Nogi's junshi in a way that profoundly inspired their writing. Questions about the meaning of violence in a society in transition moved these two writers to ponder Nogi's act and to probe deeply into its motivation. In their fictional representations of Nogi's junshi, they explored the connection of sacrificial death to the phenomenon of cultural transition.

Ōgai's response to Nogi's junshi took several forms, the most important of which consisted of a body of historical fiction set in the early Tokugawa period and a single historical novella set in the dawn to the Meiji era. Nogi's ghost, never explicitly mentioned in the fiction, haunts the stories. Looking forward rather than backward, Sōseki's novel *Kokoro* (1914) concentrated on the transition from the Meiji to the Taishō era. At a pivotal moment in *Kokoro,* General Nogi appears in fateful conjunction with Emperor Mutsuhito, better known by his posthumous name as Emperor Meiji. Reports of their linked deaths affect the consciousness and the behavior of the novel's characters. Taken together, Ōgai's stories and Sōseki's novel are among the most complex, profound, and intriguing interpretations of Nogi's junshi. In order to do justice to the complexities of their interpretations, I have purposefully refrained from forays into treatments of Nogi by a younger generation of authors, such as Shiga Naoya (1883–1971), Mushanokōji Saneatsu (1885–1976), and Akutagawa Ryūnosuke (1892–1927).

Approach and Overview

My effort to understand the significance of Nogi's junshi is resolutely interdisciplinary. I am convinced that acts of junshi, and General Nogi's junshi in particular, become meaningful as history and literature only if we understand them within the context of Japanese culture, from anthropological and religious as well as psychological perspectives. My study is intertextual and reflexive, in that historical events provided a stimulus for works of literature that, in turn, help us to understand historical events. Although I combine historical and literary interpretations, I did not set out to find new historical facts about Nogi, nor did I wish to enter the sophisticated debate among literary critics about Ōgai's genre of historical fiction and its truthfulness to facts. From first to last, my goal has been to understand the cultural significance of General Nogi's expiatory act of self-sacrifice in a time of reign change.

PART I, "Following One's Lord into Death," underscores the religious context of ritual suicide. It is divided into two chapters. Chapter 1, "Sacrifice and Self-Sacrifice," offers a workable definition of a universal custom and places its Japanese variant in context. To demonstrate the singularity of junshi, I explore selected instances of funerary sacrifice in Western and Eastern cultures—instances demonstrating that there have been many forms of ritual death that resemble junshi. Chapter 2, "The Japanese Custom of Junshi," outlines the history and specific features of junshi. In its purest, most distinctively Japanese form, junshi is self-sacrifice upon the death of a lord who has given his permission for the act and who is sacralized by it. Permission to demonstrate absolute devotion to one's lord by seppuku was by no means taken for granted. As in Nogi's case, there was often a battle of wills over the issue of permission.

Part II, "Nogi in History," underscores the political and military context of Nogi's junshi. It is a biographical study in two chapters, the first devoted to Nogi's life before his junshi and the second focused upon the day of his death. It is a "biographical study" rather than a "biography" because I have drawn from (and certainly not rivaled) the many detailed biographies published by Japanese scholars. Since General Nogi was an important actor upon the historical stage, my narrative must be, to some extent, a "life and times." In describing the "times" I have, for the most part, relied upon published sources, such as those dealing with the Satsuma Rebellion, the Sino-Japanese War, and the Russo-Japanese War, rather than undertaking extensive archival research into unpublished materials. In short, "Nogi in History" is a historically contextualized interpretation of a man's life written in order to explore the significance of his sacrificial death.

Chapter 3, "Nogi's Life Sentences," concentrates upon a series of crucial episodes in Nogi's life. As a young man, Nogi struggled to resolve the dilemma of vocation. Was he to be a man of the brush or the sword? Although his passion lay with the brush, family obligation led him, after initial fierce resistance, to take up the sword. Having become a soldier, Nogi experienced a series of crises in which he felt, acutely, that he had failed to meet the stringent obligations of the samurai's code of honor. Among the most important of these successive crises was the sense of shame that followed his unit's loss of the imperial flag during the Satsuma Rebellion in 1877. Prevented by command of the young Emperor Mutsuhito from atoning for his mistake by committing seppuku, Nogi carried his burden of guilt and obligation for the next thirty-five years. The burden became even heavier when his greatest military victory—the capture of Port Arthur in 1894—was accompanied by a massacre for which he felt a degree of responsibility. Nogi's sense of himself as a man "living as though dead" became still more intense a decade later when he was undeservedly honored, in Europe as well as in Japan, for the second capture of Port Arthur. (Nogi's anguish was intensified by the death of his two sons in the 1904 campaign that was actually brought to a successful conclusion by General Kodama Gentarō [1852–1906] rather than by Nogi.) Decades of moral travail were finally brought to an end in 1912, when Nogi, having at last obtained implicit permission from the emperor, followed his lord, a divine emperor, into death.

Chapter 4, "The Sword and the Brush," concentrates upon Nogi's junshi and that of his wife Shizuko. I discuss not only their actions but also their writing, including Nogi's testament, and the famous photographs taken of the two of them on the day of their death. (These are the photographs that intrigued the French postmodern theorist Roland Barthes.) This chapter concludes with my interpretation of Nogi's junshi as a potent symbol of the end of an era.

Part III, "Nogi in Literature," is subdivided into three chapters. Chapters 5 and 6 are devoted to five ventures into historical fiction that Mori Ōgai, Nogi's friend and military colleague, wrote in the sixteen months following Nogi's junshi. Chapter 7, "Natsume Sōseki," is devoted to an interpretation of this writer's greatest novel, *Kokoro,* published serially in the *Asahi Shinbun* between 20 April and 11 August 1914. Although any discussion of Ōgai's stories requires constant attentiveness to the actual historical facts, about which historians often disagree, his fictionalized renditions of the facts and his willful departures from the historical records available to him provide fascinating clues to the writer's crafting of a cultural memory about junshi.

The first version of Ōgai's "Okitsu Yagoemon no isho" (The last testament of Okitsu Yagoemon) was written in the five-day interval between Nogi's death and his funeral. It appeared in October 1912 and was subsequently revised and republished, in a considerably lengthened version, in June 1913. Based upon a seventeenth-century Hosokawa-clan retainer's journey to Nagasaki on an errand for Lord Tadaoki, the story dramatizes the deadly consequences of a quarrel between Yagoemon and another Hosokawa retainer, whom Yagoemon kills. Yagoemon's request for atonement by means of seppuku is denied by Lord Tadaoki. Delayed by thirty-four years, seppuku finally occurs as junshi.

"Abe ichizoku" (The Abe family), which appeared in the January 1913 issue of *Chūō Kōron,* is another narrative based on events involving the Hosokawa clan. More narrowly than in the previous story, the focus is on the crucial question of permission to commit junshi. The question of junshi *without* permission ("a dog's death") is examined from multiple perspectives: those of the retainers, their successive lords, and a relatively objective third-person narrator.

"Sahashi Jingorō," which appeared in the April 1913 issue of *Chūō Kōron,* resembles "Okitsu Yagoemon no isho" in that it, too, involves a deadly quarrel among retainers. In stark contrast to the first story, however, the eponymous hero does *not* choose atonement by means of seppuku. As if his moral choices were meant explicitly to represent an alternative to Nogi's, Jingorō evades rather than confronts the question of culpability. Honor does not dictate suicide. Instead of dying by his own hand in conformity with the samurai code, Jingorō chooses to vanish. His symbolic death by disappearance holds captive those who had hoped to lay matters to rest with Jingorō's dead body.

The last of the historical fictions Ōgai wrote in the months that followed Nogi's junshi is the most complex and revelatory. The "Incident at Sakai" referred to in the title, "Sakai jiken" (February 1914), occurred in 1868 when Japanese soldiers from Tosa, sent to guard the port city of Sakai (near Ōsaka), clashed with a group of French sailors who had come ashore in search of amusement. Eleven sailors were killed in the skirmish, and twenty of the men from Tosa were sentenced to death in order to satisfy the French government's demand for retribution. When nine of the twenty were unexpectedly spared, they reacted very much as Nogi did in 1877 when his desire to commit seppuku was frustrated. They were disheartened that they were compelled to live. In addition to the Japanese source drawn upon by Ōgai, Sasaki Kōzō's *Senshū: Sakai rekkyo shimatsu* (1893; rev. 1900; *An Account of the Circumstances at Sakai in Izumi*), we have a number of official and unofficial reports written by British, French, and German diplomatic personnel resident in Japan. These foreign sources document the incomprehension of the Europeans when the doomed soldiers welcomed the opportunity to die honorable deaths, by seppuku, as a statement of loyalty to their newly established sovereign. Although Ōgai did not have access to the full range of the European response to the incident at Sakai, Sasaki Kōzō's work provided enough information for Ōgai to underline the uniqueness of the Japanese version of ritual suicide. His fictionalized interpretation of this affair at the *beginning* of the Meiji era is—by implication—his last and most profound meditation on the *end* of that momentous era.

It is difficult in a few short paragraphs to communicate a sense of the complexity of Ōgai's historical fiction. It is even more difficult to suggest the inexhaustible profundity of Sōseki's *Kokoro,* a classic that has provoked generations of literary scholars to produce shelves of critical analysis. (My descent into cliché—"inexhaustible profundity"—testifies to my frustrating inability to produce a satisfactory introductory summary of *Kokoro.*)

My treatment of *Kokoro* begins with a survey of selected critical approaches to the novel, few of which do more than touch briefly upon the roles played within the novel by General Nogi and Emperor Meiji. Like most of those who have published comprehensive interpretations of *Kokoro,* I discuss the strangely intimate friendship between Sensei and the anonymous young friend who narrates the first half of the novel. Like nearly everyone who has commented on the novel, I also discuss at some length the motivations for K's suicide and for Sensei's. I do this with an eye to the many parallels between Sensei's suicide and Nogi's junshi. I discuss, for instance, the intimate male bonding between Sensei and the young narrator and between Sensei and K, bonding that reminds the historically informed reader of Nogi's devotion to Emperor Meiji. Like a small number of scholars, the most prominent of whom is Sharalyn Orbaugh,[16] I also attempt to explore and explicate the role of Sensei's wife, the major character about whom we are least well informed, the major actor to whom the fewest lines are given. Her name, Shizu, is hauntingly similar to the name of Nogi's wife, Shizuko. Was this merely accidental, or did Sōseki expect his readers to wonder if Shizu's fate was to Shizuko's as Sensei's was to Nogi's? I strongly suspect that the latter was, indeed, Sōseki's expectation. Like Nogi's junshi, Sensei's death marks the end of an era, but it also signals the dawn of a new age, an age in which, perhaps, women would tell their own stories or otherwise take matters into their own hands, whether to live or to die.

After having begun my study of Nogi's junshi and its literary ramifications with a brief commentary on non-Japanese royal mortuary customs in antiquity, I conclude with some further anthropological speculations about East–West similarities and dissimilarities. I do this in the form of a coda, "Last Stands in Ancient Rome and Modern Japan," a discussion of ritual suicide in classical antiquity, millennia before Nogi's junshi, and in post–World War II Japan, half a century after his momentous example. For antiquity, I have selected for comment—from many possible examples—the suicides of Marcus Porcius Cato Uticensis (95–46 B.C.E.), Marcus Tullius Cicero (106–43 B.C.E.), and Lucius Annaeus Seneca (c. 4 B.C.E.–65 C.E.). All three took their lives in a time of fundamental cultural transition. During the one hundred and eleven years separating Cato's death from that of Seneca, the Roman Republic was transformed into the Roman Empire. For postwar Japan, I have selected two examples: the "unreconcilables" of 1945, who committed seppuku rather than live with the shame of devastating military defeat; and the writer-activist Mishima Yukio (1925–1970), who chose death rather than life in a Japan that had turned its back on samurai tradition.

PART I

"Following One's Lord into Death"

CHAPTER 1

Sacrifice and Self-Sacrifice

Era Transitions

When Emperor Meiji died on 30 July 1912, after an eventful, remarkably long reign of forty-four years, his people were disoriented and inconsolable. The length of this reign and the close association of the emperor with his era made Meiji's death especially traumatic. His passing signaled the end of an era that—in encyclopedic compactness and formulaic generalization—"saw the transformation of feudal Japan into a modern industrialized state with a parliamentary form of government and its emergence as a world power through military adventures abroad."[1] The end of the era was also a pivotal religious moment.

Descended in an "unbroken" line of emperors from the sun goddess Amaterasu, Emperor Meiji was born in Kyōto, on 3 November 1852 (Kaei 5.IX.22), as the second son of Emperor Kōmei (1831–1866; r. 1846–1866) and Nakayama Yoshiko (1835–1907), daughter of major counselor Nakayama Tadayasu (1809–1888). His boyhood name was Sachinomiya. On 11 November 1860, Prince Sachi became crown prince and received his adult name, Mutsuhito, used largely for official functions. He succeeded his father on 13 February 1867, at age sixteen, and was formally enthroned on 12 October 1868. Ten days later he chose by lot the name of his era, the *nengō*, to be Meiji, or "Enlightened Rule."[2] His reign was so long that most Japanese, never having known any other ruler, preferred simply to speak of him as *tennō*, or emperor.[3] He received his posthumous name, Meiji Tennō, on 27 August 1912. This further strengthened the association of the man and the era, as it was "the first time in either Japan or China that the posthumous name of an emperor had been taken from the *nengō*."[4]

Fears about chaos in the wake of a divine ruler's death find universal expression in myths about a permanent eclipse of the sun, to which divine rulers are often likened. In the Japanese creation myths, as told in the *Kojiki* and *Nihongi*, brother–sister rivalries lead the sun goddess Amaterasu to withdraw into a cave in response to the wind god Susanowo's horrific assaults on her sovereignty and territory. The world is plunged into darkness. Unhampered by humans, the deities design an amazingly delightful solution. Their ritual laughter, inspired by a female deity's erotic dance on an overturned bucket, coaxes Amaterasu from her cave. As the dancer's performative feat is artfully concluded, a mirror playing upon Amaterasu's curiosity and vanity allows a powerful male deity to pull the sun from the cave. To avert another eclipse, Amaterasu's brother Susanowo is sacrificed by mutilation and "divine expulsion" from Takama no hara, the Plain of High Heaven.[5] Thus carefully shielded from her brother's taboo violations, henceforth Amaterasu reigns supreme. The symbolic mirror into which Amaterasu gazed became one of the three imperial regalia evoked in enthronement ceremonies.

The Japanese are not alone either in their fears of chaos or in the rituals designed to legitimize their ruler and avert catastrophe. Mesoamerican culture provides two dramatic examples of this. Like other Mesoamerican peoples,[6] the Aztecs recognized the importance of the sun to their livelihood and organized their lives around solar time. Anxious about the sun rising every morning, the Aztecs performed human sacrifice to keep it "moving" across the sky. Offerings to the sun occurred at regular intervals, most prominently at the awesome intersection between two calendrical cycles, every fifty-two years, or roughly one human life span. When the era of one Sun ended, the Aztecs entered a state of heightened frenzy and launched a new Sun on its course by offering it the still beating heart of carefully chosen and prepared human sacrifices. Only then could they rest assured of continuing to live by the power of the sun. Thus motivated by myth, the Aztecs practiced human sacrifice on a massive scale until the military conquest of Hernán Cortés in 1521.[7] Johanna Broda has argued that religious, state, and cosmic cults provide the context for human sacrifice: "According to Aztec religious theory, blood had to be spilled to make the cosmos continue to exist. The sun, in order to send its light to earth, needed to be fed on human hearts and blood. The ruler's obligation was to provide this nourishment to the sun; for this purpose he led his armies into the war and exacted tribute in victims for sacrifice."[8] In short, the sacrificial ritual was a religious offering to a divinity, an offering intended to mark—and pass through—the dangerous liminal moment of transition from the reign of one Sun to that of another. Aztec human sacrifice was designed to ensure the cosmic order represented by the daily rising of the sun.

Some Aztec sacrificial victims were treated royally before they climbed the steep stairs to have their chests cut open and their hearts ripped out for offering to the sun. In the yearly festival Toxcatl, dedicated to the multifaceted, omnipresent god Tezcatlipoca (Smoking Mirror), a captive warrior "was chosen for his perfect physical features" and "ritually changed into a *teotl ixiptla,* or image of the god, who paraded for one year throughout the Aztec city. At the end of the year the impersonator of Tezcatlipoca was sacrificed on top of a pyramid/ temple, where his heart was extracted and offered to the sun."[9] Before the moment of his sacrificial death the *teotl ixiptla* was adorned, loved, and venerated. Just when the captive was recognized as a perfect model, however, the former warrior broke the instruments of his domestication—flutes and whistles—and "reverted to the bellicose aspect."[10] Thus the god impersonator and warrior captive, who had "ascended by himself, [gone] up of his own free will, to where he was to die," was beheaded, his torso "not rolled down the stairs as was often done in other sacrifices" but "carried carefully away," and his head "displayed on the skull rack as a visual image of human destiny."[11] "This movement crossed not only geographical, domestic, and public space but also hierarchical space as the god's image joined with the office and person of kingship. In the adornment ceremony, the *teotl ixiptla* was transformed into the ruler's version of the god."[12]

Like Amaterasu's mirror, Tezcatlipoca's mirror was "used for divination," functioning as "a metaphor for rulership, for power."[13] The parallels between Emperor Meiji's general and Tezcatlipoca's *ixiptla* are striking. Like the Aztecs' captive warrior, Nogi too was lavishly decorated and frequently ordered to represent the imperial presence at home and abroad. His self-sacrifice upon the occasion of the emperor's death inspired such awe that Nogi was enshrined at the foot of his emperor's mausoleum (and in five other shrines solely dedicated to him).[14] Like the warrior who became Tezcatlipoca's impersonator, Nogi too reasserted his self just as he was surrendering it to his sovereign.

By reenacting an ancient pattern, Nogi recalled the half-forgotten past for his people. Like the Aztec *teotl ixiptla*'s heart sacrifice, Nogi's disembowelment regenerated imperial rule and inspired his deification.[15] As a metaphorical male way of giving birth, disembowelment can also be likened to the bloodletting rites in which "the Maya lords sought to experience a *totality*, even a divine totality, by imitating the capacity of women to menstruate (bleed from their genitals) and to give birth."[16] The death of a Maya sovereign required verification, or testimony, which was his blood.[17] If the sovereign himself did not shed the blood that bore testimony to his death, then the blood was shed vicariously, through ritual or impersonation, before the succession could occur. In an eerie analogue to Maya ritual, Nogi represented the emperor on the day of Meiji's funeral. Symbolically, his blood became one with Meiji's. It evoked Meiji's and absorbed its power at the same time that it was a donation, the sacrifice needed at the end of an era for the perpetuation of the imperial line. "The kind is dead. Long live the king."

"Following One's Lord into Death"

During Emperor Meiji's nocturnal funeral procession on 13 September 1912, the potentially unstable, even dangerous, hiatus between one reign and the next, the momentous transition from one avatar of the sun goddess Amaterasu to another, was virtually eclipsed by Nogi's ritual suicide. To fathom the cultural implications (and literary consequences) of Nogi's junshi as religious sacrifice we need to understand the concept of "following one's lord into death."

At its core, "following one's lord into death" is a form of suicide, and suicide is probably a cultural universal, abstractly defined as "the specific action of a human being that aims at ending his or her life prematurely or allowing it to end prematurely."[18] The study of suicide has been impeded, notes Georges Minois in his recent *History of Suicide* in the West, because the "silence and dissimulation that accompanied suicide surrounded it with a climate of discomfort."[19] Judgments of suicide vary from culture to culture and depend on numerous factors, including religion, class, gender, profession, and circumstances. Venerated by some and condemned by others, suicide is committed for every conceivable reason. Some may want to prevent capture and torture at the hands of an implacable enemy, and others to end the torment of incurable disease, escape the Shakespearean "pangs of unrequited love," or avoid the shame that follows the exposure of a loathsome act. "Following one's lord into death" is performed for none of these reasons.

When suicide takes the form of "following one's lord into death," it constitutes an act of self-inflicted human sacrifice. Although we, despite the headlines and news segments reporting "suicide bombers," are accustomed to thinking that sacrificed persons are unwilling to die, this has not always been the case. Following a sacred ruler into death, typically performed by seclusion in the sovereign's tomb or by live burial, has often been a willingly performed religious act. (For prehistoric times, the archaeological evidence of volition is seldom unambiguous.) In cultures where religious and secular spheres were not clearly separated, "following one's lord into death" was frequently based on the belief in an afterlife that mirrored the world of the living. The ritual sacrifice was intended to affirm the divinity of the deceased ruler and to be apotropaic in that the attendants would protect their ruler from the dangers of the afterlife. It was also intended to make endurable the anxieties concerning the succession that often characterized an interregnum period.

The Japanese Custom in Context

When and where did the custom of "following one's lord into death" arise and what were its earliest forms? The historical evidence indicates that junshi evolved over the centuries from a specific form of sacrifice to a specific form of self-sacrifice. Although the custom of junshi in its fully developed form was unique to Japanese culture, there were similar customs in other cultures that help us to understand and appreciate that uniqueness. Common to all of these customs was the religious belief that the needs of the dead are the same as those of the living, and that the living do well to pacify the spirit of their deceased.[20] It should perhaps be emphasized that these sacrifices, unlike those of the Aztecs and Maya, were funerary customs.

Evidence of these ancient practices is relatively new, as are the debates about them. Between the year of Nogi's victory at Port Arthur in 1894 and his junshi in 1912, archaeologists discovered large Egyptian royal tombs of the Archaic Period (c. 3000–2670) in Abydos and Saqqara that revealed an ancient custom of mass human sacrifice not previously associated with divine Egyptian kings and queens of the Old, Middle, or New Kingdoms. (These were also the years during which Jane Ellen Harrison and Friedrich Schwenn wrote their studies of sacrifice in ancient Greece and Rome.)[21] In the ethnocentric words of Walter Bryan Emery, the chief excavator at Saqqara, "this barbaric mortuary custom had died out in the more cultured North [of Egypt]" by the end of the First Dynasty.[22] As Emery catalogued the numbers of sacrificed men, women, and children in various tombs, he surmised that the Egyptian belief in life after death might have motivated whole retinues to continue serving their divine lord in the afterlife, "whether willingly or otherwise we do not know."[23] In the course of time, the sacrificial custom of following a ruler into death, as practiced by the royal retinue of the First Dynasty at Abydos and Saqqara, took a less bloody form. Humans and animals were replaced with mummiform figures known as *shabtis, shawabtis,* or *ushabtis.*[24]

Among the Yoruba who live in what is now Nigeria, the custom of funerary sacrifice at the death of a king survived into the twentieth century despite attempts of British colonial officers to end the custom. Those who were expected freely to offer their lives in order to accompany their ruler into the next world included the Master of the Horse, whose name in Yoruba—Ab'o̱baku—can be translated as "One who is to die with the king."[25] Wole Soyinka (b. 1934), winner of the 1986 Nobel Prize for Literature, dramatized this funerary custom in a powerful play entitled *Death and the King's Horseman* (1975). In Soyinka's play, the King's Horseman proclaims, as he prepares for his voluntary death, "Life is honour. It ends when honour ends."[26] Although it is explained to the British colonial administrator that the king cannot be buried until his horseman dies "so as to accompany him to heaven,"[27] the British are shocked and do their best to abort the ritual. Ironically, it is the horseman's son who returns home from England in order, not only to fulfill the religious custom of his people and thereby preserve Yoruba cosmology and social cohesion, but also to assert Yoruba "spiritual and cultural freedom against colonial intervention."[28]

Although the ancient Scyths, who ruled a realm between the Black Sea and the Caspian Sea, seem to have lacked a belief in an afterlife, "the Scythian sense of corporate identity" impelled them to perform "acts of limited self-sacrifice" during a forty-day cortège. Only those who had been especially close to the Scythian king followed him into death. The fifth-century Greek historian Herodotus described the sacrifices made by his Scythian contemporaries in vivid detail:

> In the open space around the body of the king they bury one of his concubines, first killing her by strangling, and also his cupbearer, his cook, his groom, his lackey, his messenger, some of his horses, firstlings of all his other possessions, and some golden cups; for they use neither silver nor brass. After this they set to work, and raise a vast mound above the grave, all of them vying with each other and seeking to make it as tall as possible. . . . When a year is gone by, further ceremonies take place. Fifty of the best of the late king's attendants are taken, all native Scythians. [They are] strangled, with fifty of the most beautiful horses.[29]

Religious historian Bruce Lincoln, writing of this Scythian custom in 1991, might have been referring to Nogi when he wrote of Scyths who felt, at the death of their rulers, that "their own lives . . . became unfocused, aimless, impossible."[30]

The earliest literary evidence of Greek parallels to Scythian rituals comes from the Homeric age. It was, according to Friedrich Schwenn, customary in the archaic period for a nobleman to be accompanied into the underworld by his attendants.[31] In Book XXIII of the *Iliad,* Achilles, before staging elaborate funeral games,[32] sacrificed twelve Trojans as a tribute to his dead friend Patroklos:

> and so he killed twelve noble sons of the great-hearted Trojans
> with the stroke of bronze, and evil were the thoughts in his heart against them,
> and let loose the iron fury of the fire to feed on them.
> Then he groaned, and called by name on his beloved companion:
> "Good-bye, Patroklos. I hail you even in the house of the death god
> For all that I promised you in time past I am accomplishing.
> Here are twelve noble sons of the great-hearted Trojans
> whom the fire feeds on, all, as it feeds on you. But I will not
> give Hektor, Priam's son, to the fire, but the dogs, to feast on."[33]

Achilles' choice of fire sacrifice is meant as a sign of respect for the Trojan youths. He has in mind more gruesome treatment for the man who slew Patroklos. Hektor's unaccompanied corpse he means to feed to the dogs.[34]

About Roman funerary customs we are far better informed. The historian Tacitus tells us that Emperor Otho (32–69 C.E.), when defeated at Bedriacum, committed suicide[35] and was followed in death by several of his loyal soldiers.[36] This episode was a textbook example of what the ancient Romans meant by *devotio,* a ritual that entailed a love of death exemplified by voluntary self-sacrifice. As L. F. Janssen explains: "True devotio cannot be brought about by pressure, but it has to be personal, self-imposed obligation."[37] Emperor Otho's followers resemble the Japanese warriors who followed their lord in death on the battlefield, especially when the motive was sheer devotion and loyalty, rather than a dishonorable fear of dying at the hands of the enemy.[38] The "devotus's charge into the midst of the enemy," not only "actively terrif[ies] the enemy, but the death that [the *devotus*] suffers ensures that they too will die."[39]

Gladiatorial games *(munera)* had their origins in something very like junshi. "Like the retainers who had in earlier times been buried with their masters in order to render posthumous service, gladiators acted in a bloody drama in which the *virtus* of the fighters symbolized a triumph over death."[40] Accordingly, as a form of human sacrifice, *munera* were first staged "at the funerals of prominent men."[41] Paul Plass points to the closure that such deaths were expected to bring: "At Rome death was originally brought under a measure of control by additional death staged at the dead man's tomb."[42]

Among the Germanic peoples to the north songs commemorated *Gefolgschaftsbestattungen* (burials with entourage). Archaeological evidence of this ritual has been found in Queen Asa's ninth-century tomb at Oseberg in Norway.[43] Among Slavic and Baltic peoples, those who followed their lord seem to have done so willingly and as a matter of course because they expected to live on in the aptly named "afterlife."[44]

A degree of uncertainty prevails in the discussion of the Chinese custom of *xunzang.* The term *xun* (J. *jun*) refers to "the killing of a person or persons to guard a dead man."[45] It has long been thought that the purpose of these human sacrifices was to provide the deceased sovereign with attendants in the afterlife or to feed the "potent spirits" of that threatening realm.[46] Jacques Gernet noted, in 1972, that the practice "required the prince's closest companions and his concubines to follow him in death." He added that "these human victims were to be replaced more and more often in the course of the first millennium by mannekins or figurines."[47] The practice continued well into the Han dynasty (206 B.C.E.–220 C.E.).

More recent scholarship has modified earlier interpretations of this Chinese practice. Evidence found near An-yang between 1927 and 1936 in royal tombs of the Shang or Yin dynasty (1765–1122 B.C.E., traditional dates), indicates that the accompanying bodies were not those of the Chinese sovereign's grief-stricken attendants.[48] Mark Edward Lewis has shown that the bodies were the results of "the mass execution of slaves and prisoners to 'accompany' the deceased Shang rulers. . . . The hundreds of bodies discovered in some royal tombs were probably prisoners taken in warfare, and it is even possible that some campaigns were fought solely for the purpose of obtaining these sacrificial victims."[49] In other words, the alleged Chinese prototype did not involve imperial attendants and was not a form of voluntary ritual suicide.[50]

The same can be said about the earliest forms of funerary sacrifice in Japan. The eighth-century compilation known as the *Nihon shoki* or *Nihongi* traces the custom of junshi back to the reign of the legendary Emperor Suinin (29 B.C.E.–70 C.E.). When Yamatohiko no mikoto, the emperor's younger brother, passed away, "his personal attendants were assembled, and were all buried alive upright in the precinct of the misasagi [imperial tomb]. For several days they died not, but wept and wailed day and night. At last they died and rotted. Dogs and crows gathered and ate them."[51] Whether or not the attendants died willingly is unclear. Were they weeping and bewailing their own fate, or Yamatohiko no mikoto's, or both?

The text is clearer about the emperor's response. "The Emperor, hearing the sound of their weeping and wailing, was grieved in heart, and commanded his high officers, saying:—'It is a very painful thing to force those whom one has loved in life to follow him in death. Though it be an ancient custom, why follow it, if it is bad? From this time forward, take counsel so as to put a stop to the following of the dead.' "[52]

Emperor Suinin's resolve to end the custom was put to the test when his consort died in the thirty-second year of his rule. He consulted with his ministers about the wisdom of his earlier decision. In the service of the emperor was one Nomi no Sukune, a great wrestler from Izumo, who proposed a brilliant solution: "Henceforward let it be the law for future ages to substitute things of clay for living men, and to set them up at tumuli."[53] These "things of clay" were, of course, the artistic figurines known as *haniwa.*

Doubts have been expressed about this episode, similar to those voiced in reference to the Chinese custom of *xunzang.* In an extensive note on the *Kojiki* (compiled in 712), referring specifically to the story of Emperor Suinin, Donald L. Philippi questioned "these dubious old narratives."[54] Paul Varley has also expressed skepticism. He maintains that the clay shapes were not originally meant to represent courtly attendants (as the *Nihon shoki* has it), nor were they "a human fence *[hito-gaki]* at the tomb"[55] (as the *Kojiki* states). According to Varley, the prototypes of the *haniwa* were merely "plain cylinders" meant "to reduce erosion or to mark off certain areas on the burial mound for ritual purposes."[56] Delmer Brown surmises that *haniwa* "may have been placed around a burial mound [built to pacify deceased rulers] in order to keep the soul from straying outside it."[57]

There are also doubts about the custom of junshi in the case of Queen Himiko (d. 248? C.E.) of Yamatai. The third-century Chinese contemporary compendium *Wei chih* (Record of Wei) chronicles Japanese events in a section called "Wajinden" (An account of the people of "Wa"). According to this text, when Himiko died, "a great mound was raised, more than a hundred paces in diameter. Over a hundred male and female attendants followed her to the grave."[58] The *Wei chih* does not indicate whether the attendants' deaths were voluntary or involuntary, but the text emphasizes that something went awfully wrong with the succession in the wake of these deaths: "Then a king was placed on the throne, but the people would not obey him. Assassination and murder followed; more than one thousand were thus slain. A relative of Pimiko named Iyo, a girl of thirteen, was [then] made queen and order was restored."[59] Joan R. Piggott concludes that archaeological evidence for this event is lacking, and Walter Edwards surmises that the Chinese compiler Chen Shou (233–297) might have projected onto Japan his own country's "practice of placing human sacrificial victims in royal tombs."[60]

The only ancient Japanese practice that seems symbolically close to that of entombing sacrificial victims with the dead king is the temporary enshrinement *(mogari no miya)* of a dead sovereign or a family member of the imperial house.[61] The *mogari no miya,* which lasted from less than one month to over six years, has been recorded from the time of the first legendary emperor, Jimmu (660–585 B.C.E.), to that of Empress Jitō (645–702; r. 690–697).[62] When Emperor Kōtoku unsuccessfully prohibited junshi in 646, he also tried to end the custom of *mogari no miya.*[63] Politics as well as religion often played a central role in *mogari no miya* because women who had been sexually intimate with the deceased emperor were secluded in his death chamber, often for an extended period of time, until the succession was decided.[64] Clearly, this practice stops short of accompanying one's lord into death, but it may be a relic of a more radical response to the loss of one's sovereign. The ritual practice of temporary enshrinement provided the occasion for an ordeal intended to ensure the imperial succession through a symbolic form of junshi.

CHAPTER 2

The Japanese Custom of Junshi

It is easy to understand that prisoners, captives, or slaves did not want to be sacrificed in order to serve the posthumous needs of a deceased ruler or to avert the cosmic uncertainties of an interregnum. Much harder to understand is a ritual sacrifice in which attendants—not captives—willingly followed their lord into death. Motivation was crucial. In its prototypical Japanese form, junshi is voluntary human sacrifice upon the death of a secular lord who is venerated like a deity. Junshi is performed by seppuku, an elaborate ritual usually requiring a second or a witness. Junshi expresses so strong a bond between lord and retainer that it cannot be severed by the lord's death. Junshi demonstrates the retainer's gratitude for the benefits and favors of the hierarchical lord–retainer relationship. It is a demonstration of absolute loyalty and devotion. It is a moral statement, a demonstration of suicidal honor.[1]

The etiquette of "following one's lord into death" reached such a level of refinement in Japan that perfect adherence to it enhanced the reputations of both the retainer and the lord. The most important aspect of etiquette, one that set junshi apart from the general custom of "following in death," was that junshi required prior permission from the lord in whose honor it was to be committed. Denial of permission presented the retainer with an ethical dilemma. Paradoxically, junshi committed without permission was sometimes considered the most glorious form of death. What made it so was a question of context and individual circumstances.

Junshi committed without the lord's permission was commonly described by the pejorative phrase "a dog's death" *(inujini)*. There were, however, exceptional circumstances. If there was reason to assume the existence of a "silent oath" or "tacit agreement" *(mokkei)* between lord and retainer, then the most despicable "dog's death" was actually proof of an uncanny inner identity of spirit. In fact, junshi with implicit rather than explicit permission was the most glorious death of all. Whether one deems Nogi's death honorable or contemptible therefore depends not only on one's attitude toward tradition but also on one's belief that a *mokkei* did or did not exist between Nogi and Emperor Meiji.

The motives for junshi varied. In the Tokugawa period, the prototypical motive for junshi was the retainer's need to atone for a failure or transgression. His willingness to atone for a failure or a transgression by committing seppuku was frustrated by his lord's insistence on forgiving him. His lord withheld permission to commit seppuku and in its stead bestowed the gift of life on him. No matter how reluctantly, the retainer postponed his seppuku. In exchange for the gift of life, he had now incurred a lifelong debt to his lord. The retainer's reluctant lease on life approached a critical moment when his lord's death became imminent. At this point, both lord and retainer faced some difficult choices. The dying lord might or might not grant his permission for junshi. The retainer might decide, after the death of his lord, to continue to live and to extend his gratitude for the gift of life to his deceased lord's successor(s). Or he might revert to his original desire to reclaim his honor by an act of self-sacrifice.

In ancient Japan, the custom of "following one's lord into death" was originally called *junsō* ("following into the grave"). With the gradual shift from religious toward secular motivations, *junsō* became less common than *junshi* ("following into death"), which was less fixed on the place than on the motivation for and manner of death. Nonetheless, the spatial trajectory of the sacrificial action—from inside the royal tomb, to the ground in front of it, to some other sacralized spot, and finally to the house of the sacrifice—is significant. This shift accompanied the shift from sacrifice to self-sacrifice.

Junshi, then, is marked by a specific sequence of interlocking acts. The movement from suicidal honor to devotional junshi involves three steps: first, the retainer's willingness to die for honor; second, his submission to his lord's will that he live in order to serve and affirm the lord–retainer relationship; and third, his desire to follow his lord into death in order to testify to his loyalty to the lord–retainer relationship.[2] Through exemplary self-sacrifice, the individual enters the chain of deified ancestors and becomes a focal point in cultural memory. In this way, junshi plays a crucial role in linking the high and the low, lord and retainer, religious and secular spheres. Most important of all, it links the past and the future. Nogi's junshi, occurring as it did at the end of an era, was a lament for what was gone and—perhaps—an affirmation of what was to come.

The first reasonably reliable historical evidence for junshi appears in the famous Edict of 646, in which Emperor Kōtoku (r. 645–654) regulated the burial systems in Japan.[3] Ironically, the first unambiguous reference to the existence of junshi appears in the form of its prohibition. Emperor Kōtoku "forbade, among other things, [both human sacrifice and self-sacrifice] in connection with funerals."[4] According to *Nihongi* XXV.31, which is presumably more credible about recent events than about episodes in the distant past, the deaths of important men had been marked by "strangling others by way of sacrifice, or of compelling the dead man's horse to be sacrificed, or of burying valuables in the grave in honour of the dead, or of cutting off the hair, and stabbing the thighs and pronouncing an *[sic]* eulogy on the dead (while in this condition)." Deaths had also been marked by "people sacrificing themselves by strangulation." Emperor Kōtoku decreed that these suicides were to be "entirely discontinued."[5]

The Kurayamada Mass Junshi of 649

The Edict of 646 failed to end the custom of junshi, however. In 649 a drama was staged that epitomized the shift from sacrifice to self-sacrifice.[6] The events[7] occurred despite the prohibition of only three years earlier and merit detailed attention because they reveal clearly the shift in motivation from forced sacrifice inspired by the belief in an afterlife in which the dead had the same needs as the living to self-sacrifice inspired by the desire to regain or preserve honor and to maintain or affirm the bond of loyalty between lord and retainer.

Nihongi XXV.42–45 tells the complicated story of a succession struggle for one of the two offices of Ōmi (Great Minister) when the death of the Ōmi Ahe no Kurahashi in 649.III.17 left a dangerous political vacuum. Not long after the mourning rites for the Ōmi Ahe, Himuka of the Soga clan[8] slandered the Ōmi Soga no Kurayamada Ishikawa Maro (a Soga collateral),[9] falsely accusing him of plotting to assassinate his (Kurayamada's) son-in-law, Naka no Ōe (626–671), then senior prince (*taishi;* later to become the emperor Tenji [r. 668–671]).[10] Unfortunately, Naka no Ōe, who had aspirations to the throne, believed Himuka's allegations.[11]

Emperor Kōtoku (Naka no Ōe's maternal uncle) acted on Naka no Ōe's fears of his father-in-law and sent his men to question Kurayamada about "the charge of treason."[12] His pride hurt, Kurayamada refused to answer and demanded, unsuccessfully, an audience with the emperor himself. Kurayamada then fled with his younger sons to the famous temple of Yamadadera at Asuka that he had founded in 641 to honor the emperor. There his oldest son Koshi was in residence. Koshi urged his father to rebel against the emperor.[13] To act on Koshi's aggressive impulses would, however, have given credence to Himuka's slander. Although Kurayamada had no desire to rebel, neither did he wish to appear a coward. Much as a lord in later centuries would test his retainer's seriousness before giving permission for junshi, so Kurayamada sounded out his dejected oldest son about his attachment to life. Koshi signaled his willingness to die by answering without hesitation, "I love it not." Thus father and son reached a tacit understanding on a deliberate course of action. In his last speech rallying his family, Kurayamada concluded that he could best demonstrate his loyalty and innocence by killing himself at this sacred site:

> Shall one who is in the position of vassal contrive treason against his Lord? Shall the duty of a son to a father be brought to nothing? This temple was originally built, not for me personally, but under a vow for the sake of the Emperor. I have now been slandered by Musashi [Himuka], and I fear that I shall be unjustly put to death. With so near a prospect of the yellow springs [underworld], I would withdraw (my life) still cherishing fidelity in my bosom, and the object of my coming to this Temple is that my last moments may be made easier.[14]

Renewing his vow of loyalty to the emperor, Kurayamada strangled himself at Yamadadera to prove his innocence to him, Naka no Ōe, and all who believed Himuka's slander.[15] Kurayamada's wife and children followed him in death, also by self-strangulation.[16] They were followed in turn by a large number of attendants. Kurayamada's suicide was a protest against a slander that dishonored him. The suicides of his wife and his children and numerous attendants were clearly instances of junshi, the term used in the *Nihongi,*[17] and can be understood as a collective effort to preserve the honor of Kurayamada's family and retinue.

Naka no Ōe's response to his father-in-law's death was brutal. Because of "Naka no Ōe's ruthless nature and his outrage at the alleged plot against him . . . the Ōmi's corpse was defiled by decapitation."[18] Kurayamada's self-strangulation had been especially provocative because it had set in motion the junshi of his family and attendants—an expression of their devotion to Kurayamada and a silent protest against Naka no Ōe's lack of faith in him.

But the story does not end with the attempt to dishonor Kurayamada. Naka no Ōe subsequently discovered that his father-in-law had been blameless. To add to his grief, his wife, Miyatsuko-hime, the daughter of the unjustly disgraced man, "died of a broken heart" (*Nihongi* XXV.45). She may even, as Gary L. Ebersole surmised, have committed suicide.[19] On the basis of two laments *(banka),* we can infer that Naka no Ōe was more than aggrieved over the loss of Miyatsuko-hime; he may well have been terrified at the *banka* poet's piercing question, "Who has taken her away?" If indeed Miyatsuko-hime committed junshi in its early form, she would by definition have followed the magic attraction of her father's sense of honor. Having already recognized his fatal error, Naka no Ōe must have been further shamed by his wife's decisive expression of loyalty to her father rather than to her husband.[20] The dramatic series of events concluded when the slanderer, Himuka, was banished to an appointment in faraway Tsukushi (an old term for Kyūshū).

The mass junshi of the family and attendants of Soga no Kurayamada was an important episode that shows the intricate interweaving of religious and political interests. It marked the transition from a sacrifice that may or may not have been voluntary to one that clearly was. This transition indicated an increasing awareness of the importance of protecting individual and family honor. The Kurayamada mass junshi at the sacred site of Yamadadera had far-reaching repercussions and became part of "living memory," as the "descendants of Naka no Ōe [later Emperor Tenji] found themselves continually trying to expiate this terrible tragedy in their family history."[21]

Junshi on the Battlefield

An episode from the Former Nine Years War (1056–1062) in northern Honshū exemplifies battlefield junshi. Appointed pacification general *(chinjufu shōgun)* of the Abe in Mutsu Province, Minamoto Yoriyoshi (988–1075) was hopelessly surrounded by the enemy, or so his vassal Saeki Tsunenori thought. According to the *Tale of Mutsu* (*Mutsu Waki*, 1062?), Tsunenori resolved to share his lord's fate: " 'For thirty years now I have been in Yoriyoshi's service . . . I am sixty and he is almost seventy. If he must die, I intend to share his fate and go with him to the underworld." Tsunenori's honorable resolve had a domino effect on his retainers' resolve: " 'Now that our lord [Tsunenori] is about to die honorably by sharing Yoriyoshi's fate, how can we stay alive? Although we are merely sub-vassals, we are men of principle too,' they said. . . . [A]ll fell in front of the enemy."[22] In later times, the voluntary deaths of these rear vassals *(baishin)* would be called secondary junshi *(mata junshi)*. Karl F. Friday maintains that the vassal and his subvassals were not self-destructive (except in a literal sense) by pursuing "their honor": "By choosing to die with Yoriyoshi . . . , Tsunenori and his men were not totally abandoning their self-interests; in a very real sense, they were actually furthering them."[23]

Interestingly, the type of junshi performed in response to Yoriyoshi's precarious situation took on a symbolic form destined to become popular in the Kamakura period (1185–1333). Assuming that Yoriyoshi had died in battle, Fujiwara Shigeyori decided to take the tonsure in order to "recover his body to give it proper burial."[24] Shigeyori's act of shaving his head, inspired by the apparent loss of his lord (who, it turns out, had in fact survived the battle), was a renunciation of the world not unlike death itself. The priest Jien (1155–1225) recorded a spectacular case of mass tonsure in the wake of the assassination of the third Kamakura shōgun, Minamoto Sanetomo (1192–1219), when almost one hundred of his followers took the tonsure.[25]

Junshi and Seppuku

Although the ways of following one's lord into death were many, it was the most highly ritualized violent form of seppuku that came to typify junshi. Among the samurai class of Japan, the most prestigious form of suicide was not self-strangulation but, rather, excruciatingly painful and meticulously executed disembowelment. According to a legend recorded in the *Harima no Kuni Fudoki* (compiled 715), this practice can be traced back to the goddess Ōmi no kami. Upon realizing the absence of her husband, Hananami no kami, she disemboweled herself with a sword in order to follow him.[26]

Although the earliest recorded cases of seppuku performed by humans rather than gods are not—strictly speaking—junshi, they are helpful in historicizing junshi as a form of seppuku. The earliest recorded legendary instance of seppuku occurred in 988, when a certain Hakamadare Yasuke committed seppuku in an effort to escape capture for theft; he died an agonizing death leaning against a pillar in his house.[27] The first great warrior to open his stomach in battle in order to avoid being killed by the enemy was Minamoto Tametomo (1139–1170).[28] He was then "literally invented and 'heroicized.'"[29]

Junshi seems, however, to have been infrequent during the unsettled centuries of nearly constant warfare. Men died in battle and their retainers perished with them at their side, or in their place, or ahead of them. Often their valor in battle was suicidal, setting an honorable example for those warriors who were undecided between devotional death and running away or defecting in hopeless battlefield situations. The most famous of all Japanese narratives of warfare, *The Tale of the Heike*, abounds in self-sacrificial deaths in the twelfth-century Genpei wars, but there are no clear references to junshi. Junshi occurred only when warriors, motivated by a debt of gratitude and a sense of loyalty, consciously resolved either "to follow" their lord *(oibara)* or "to accompany" him *(tomobara)*. This mentality was not fully established until the fourteenth century.

By the Genpei wars (1180–1185), men had perfected the form of falling on their swords, which soon developed into the more elaborate ritual of disembowelment that was then codified during the Kamakura period (1185–1333). Preparations for seppuku became increasingly elaborate, beginning with daily meditation on death for the purpose of eliminating fear by means of familiarization. By the time Nogi committed himself to the highest form of junshi—for a divine ruler—the custom had gone through many permutations. One of these was the addition of a *kaizoebara*, an assistant whose role required him to decapitate his disemboweled but still breathing master or companion. The *kaizoebara*, first instituted around the time of the Jōkyū disturbance (Jōkyū *no ran*, 1221), was later known as the *kaishakunin*, usually translated as "the second."

The first large wave of junshi by seppuku occurred in 1338, as described in the *Taiheiki,* a voluminous fourteenth-century warrior epic *(gunki monogatari).* Citing the mass suicide of six thousand followers of Hōjō Takatoki (1303–1333), Paul Varley asserts that "it is not until *Taiheiki* that the practice [of battlefield junshi] begins to assume the form of something that is expected of the loyal warrior or is part of the warrior's unwritten code."[30] Varley cautiously refrains from unreservedly assigning the term "junshi" to this "orgy of self-destruction" in a militarily hopeless situation. In fact, it is only when death is *not* inevitable that junshi, strictly defined, can occur. This precondition was met by Nitta Yoshisada (1301–1338). After Yoshisada had accomplished the incredible feat of decapitating himself, and after the enemy had made off with his head, his "lieutenants, who could easily escape with the remnants of their army, instead go to Yoshisada's corpse and, kneeling before it, commit *seppuku,* their bodies 'falling over one on top of another.'"[31] Another instance of junshi is documented for 189 warriors (432 warriors, according to the *Taiheiki*) who followed Hōjō Nakatoki (d. 1333) in death.[32] After hearing Nakatoki admit that he was unable to reward his men for their services in preserving the Kamakura shōgunate, and after witnessing Nakatoki's seppuku, Kasuya Saburō Muneaki took the lead in a mass ritual of junshi by committing seppuku with his lord's dagger and embracing his lord's knees:

> "How bitter it is that you have gone before me!" he said. "I thought to take my life first, to prepare a way for you in the nether regions. With all my heart I have served you in this world, nor will I break the bond now, saying, 'It must be so, since he has gone to the nether regions.' Wait a bit! I shall go with you to Mount Shide."[33]

Eiko Ikegami emphasizes that this junshi became possible for an extraordinary number of men because Nakatoki had acknowledged his failure to reciprocate his men's service with appropriate rewards and had given them the freedom to do as they pleased: "The general did not demand the death of his men, but rather asked them to go on living. The deaths of the four hundred men were honorable because they were voluntarily undergone. . . . Although the action of committing suicide together with the general appears to be the ultimate altruistic sacrifice, it symbolized the autonomy of the samurai at its core sentiment."[34]

Junshi in Peacetime

The earliest recorded case of a retainer committing junshi as seppuku after the natural death of his lord is that of Mishima Geki in 1392, for Hosokawa

Yoriyuki (1329–1392), the shōgun's deputy *(kanrei).*[35] It set an important precedent for the relatively peaceful Tokugawa period (1603–1868) when samurai felt themselves—in a sense—honor-bound to do for themselves what their opponents had, more often than not, done to them on the field of battle. This pattern had become the ideal by 1607, when three retainers committed junshi following the natural death of Matsudaira Tadayoshi (?–1607) and two others did the same for Yūki Hideyasu (1574–1607).[36]

In the half-century that followed, junshi reached epidemic proportions. This epidemic, which modern Japanese historians refer to as a junshi boom *(junshi būmu),* generated junshi upon junshi *(mata junshi),* which sometimes compelled the *kaishakunin* to follow his master.[37] The most spectacular *mata junshi* with the highest recorded numbers involved came in the wake of the death of Date Masamune (1567–1636), when fifteen of his retainers committed junshi and another five *mata junshi.*[38] The number of retainers committing junshi reached a peacetime peak in 1657 with the twenty-six retainers who followed Nabeshima Katsushige (1580–1657) in death.[39]

By this time, junshi had become a widely practiced "technique de corps" (in Michel Foucault's sense), one designed to ensure a safe political transition or to prove a point of honor. The role of junshi in "body politic" was beginning to be clearly recognized. According to a contemporary document, the *Meiryō kōhan,* junshi was classified into three "stomachs": of loyal obligation *(gibara);* of making the case in response to others *(ronbara);* and mercenary motivations *(shōbara).*[40] Well-established oaths of loyalty and house rules of the samurai were the foundation for Yamamoto Tsunetomo's (1659–1721) manifesto of the ethos and aesthetics of samurai death, the *Hagakure* (1710–1716; *Hidden Leaves*). Though not widely read in its own time, this conversational treatise came from a middle-ranking retainer who, frustrated by his inability to commit junshi for his lord Nabeshima Mitsushige (1632–1700), took religious vows instead.[41] By praying for his lord rather than following him in death Tsunetomo respected not only his domainal lord's ban but also the shōgun's. He transformed his disappointment over his lord's prohibition of junshi in 1661 into a philosophy of self-sacrifice predicated upon absolute devotion to one's lord, preparedness for death, and "death frenzy" *(shi ni gurui).* Eiko Ikegami sees in the *Hagakure* "the most dangerous part of the samurai ethos: a fusion of class honor and personal self-esteem in the crucible of an obsession with death."[42] At the same time, the *Hagakure*'s unconditional embrace of death, combined with devotion to one's lord as "secret love" *(shinobu koi),* reemerges in the debate over Nogi's junshi, which was most definitely not a frenzied rush into death and may be best understood as meeting the religiopolitical need for sacrifice in an interregnum world in limbo.[43]

By the mid-seventeenth century, junshi had become especially prominent in outlying domains *(tozama)* as a highly praised manifestation of loyalty and affection *(chōai)*. It was not always easy to say whether an act of junshi was motivated by honor or by love or by a combination of both. When junshi occurred as a result of male-male love *(nanshoku)*, the goal was for the retainer to become one body *(ittaika)* with his lord, much as in lovers' double suicide *(shinjū)*.[44] Like his contemporary Yamamoto Tsunetomo, the military strategist Daidōji Yūzan (1639–1730) favored this practice in his *Budō shoshin shū*.[45]

Not long after Nabeshima Mitsushige's prohibition of junshi in 1661, the practice was officially banned, in 1663, by the fourth Tokugawa shōgun, Ietsuna (1641–1680; r. 1651–1680), presumably for practical reasons.[46] In 1683, the fifth Tokugawa shōgun, Tsunayoshi (1646–1709), added a prohibition clause on junshi to the Laws for Military Houses (Buke shohatto), originally promulgated in 1615.[47] The shōgunate acted because junshi had acquired notoriety during the early Tokugawa period. Junshi increasingly appeared to be not only gratuitous, even impure, but also a threat to the Tokugawa shōguns. They seem to have feared rather than encouraged rituals that marked the transition from one lord to another.

The 1663 ban was frequently violated. In 1668, for instance, Sugiura Uemon committed junshi for Okudaira Tadamasa (1608–1668). Two sons of the former were executed, and the wealth of the latter was reduced and moved from one province to another.[48] Comments Eiko Ikegami, "Not surprisingly, enthusiasm for *junshi* waned considerably after this decisive action."[49] It is all the more surprising, then, that the custom did not die out. The suicides of the forty-seven *rōnin* in 1703 remain to this day one of the most famous events in Japanese history. These masterless samurai of the Akō domain (Akō *rōshi*) waited and waited and waited, for twenty-two long months, before they avenged their lord, Asano Naganori (1667–1701). Only then did they seek atonement for their unauthorized and therefore unlawful vendetta *(katakiuchi)* by obtaining permission from the shōgunate to commit mass seppuku. Their suicides were anomalous instances of junshi, because they were the consequence of a vendetta.[50] Nogi's anachronistic junshi was the last to reverberate through Japanese culture.

Although the "beautiful custom" *(bifū)*[51] of junshi had been undermined by impure motivations and outlawed in 1663 in order to deprive the daimyō and their samurai retainers of this singular access to honor, it remained a passionate topic of debate concerning the purity of motives whenever it was practiced. The shōgunal prohibition remained in effect after the Meiji Restoration. To Japan's new ruling elite, the Tokugawa-era prohibition seemed even more appropriate than when it was originally decreed. After all, there were no more samurai and no more lords among the modernizing Japanese, who eagerly looked to the West for inspiration and authority in matters ranging from the manufacture of coastal artillery to the design of an evening gown. The fact that the "barbaric" custom of junshi had been outlawed for centuries made Nogi, simultaneously, an anachronistic lawbreaker and a heroic upholder of Japanese tradition. Nogi must have been well aware of all this when he decided, with deep incisions of his samurai sword,[52] to make quite a few Japanese stop dead in their tracks.

PART II

Nogi in History

CHAPTER 3
Nogi's Life Sentences

The roots of Nogi Maresuke's junshi are deeply hidden in his personal history and intricately intertwined with the rebellious and reformist movements of the Bakumatsu period and the international politics of the Meiji period.

Nogi Genealogy and Early Training

The Nogi House traced its origins back to Atsuzane, the ninth son of Emperor Uda (867–931; r. 887–897). Prominent among the family's ancestors was Sasaki Shirō Takatsuna (?–1214), a grandson of Minamoto Tameyoshi (1096–1156). While Takatsuna was still a child, most of his family was destroyed in the Heiji Insurrection (Heiji *no ran*, 1159–1160), but he was spared—as was his future lord, Tameyoshi's grandson Minamoto Yoritomo (1147–1199), who became Japan's first shōgun. In 1184 Yoritomo appointed Takatsuna to be a member of his younger half-brother Yoshitsune's punitive force against their unruly cousin "Kiso" Yoshinaka (1154–1184). As a reward for his service in this successful expedition, Takatsuna was appointed military governor *(shugo)* of the old province of Nagato. His second child, Mitsutsuna, lived in Nogi (kanji: "field" and "tree") in the old province of Izumo, where the eponymous Nogi clan originated. The original surname Sasaki was changed to Nogi (kanji: possessive particle *no* and "tree") after a move to the old province of Tajima.[1] In his days as a warrior, Takatsuna's part in the internecine Minamoto warfare was important enough for him to figure in the great warrior epic, *The Tale of the Heike* (*Heike monogatari*, compiled by Kakuichi in 1371). As a child and as a man, Nogi Maresuke was mindful of his heroic ancestor's exploits.

Nogi Maresuke's father, Maretsugu (1803–1877), was born into a branch house. As a samurai official, he served the powerful Mōri clan of the Chōshū domain (Chōshū *han*). Maretsugu held hereditary rank[2] as one of his lord's mounted guards *(umamawari)*. As a direct vassal of the house of Mōri, Maretsugu was entitled to an income of 80 *koku*, which placed him in the third stratum[3] of the *ōgumi* group among upper samurai *(shi)*.[4] He served his lord as an expert in martial arts *(bujutsu)* and medical skills *(ten'i).*[5] An older brother was adopted into the family's main house *(honke)*, but, when he failed to produce an heir, Maretsugu was brought in to continue the line. Maretsugu married and then divorced Hide or Hideko,[6] the daughter of his adoptive father.[7] Nogi Maresuke, the third of his sons, was born to his later wife *(gosai)*, Hasegawa Hisako of Tsuchiura in the old province of Hitachi.[8] Maresuke was born in Edo, in the residence of the Mōri clan. His first ten years were spent in the capital.

The deaths of his two older brothers left Maresuke as heir of the Nogi main house. As such, he was expected, urged, and—finally—coerced to take up the "way" of the sword *(bushidō)*, a way of life unique to Japan. Had he been born a generation earlier, he might have been proud to follow in his father's footsteps, but he was fated to be among the last of those who were raised with the sword.

Sons tend to be rebellious, and Maretsugu's oldest son was more so than most. This did not seem to be the case at first. His childhood name *(yōmei)* was Nakito,[9] which has been written both as "crybaby"[10] and as "Nonexistent Person."[11] Since the word *nakito* appears neither in regular nor in name dictionaries, it may have been coined by the Nogi family. If *nakito* was meant as "crybaby," the nickname taunted Nogi for a tendency to break into tears. He was cruelly teased by playmates, who punned on his brother Makoto's name, which in another reading means "sincerity": "Nogi is truly a crybaby" (Nogi wa *makoto* ni nakito).[12] Physically frail, he often played with his sisters and seemed girlish *(joseiteki).*[13] If *nakito* meant "nonexistent person(s)," the nickname identified Nogi with the elder brothers lost before he was born.[14] In the Japanese tradition of coping with child loss, it is customary for the first surviving child to carry the burden of the previous losses. Young "Nakito," groomed to carry on the Nogi line, was expected to replace these two lost sons, whereas his younger brothers felt no such pressure to replace their lost siblings or to follow in their father's samurai footsteps. There is special poignancy in this, because Nogi himself was to lose two sons in the Russo-Japanese War, whom he categorically refused in his testament to have replaced through adoption in order to continue the Nogi House with another "Nakito."

Nogi Maresuke's indoctrination in *bushidō*[15] included the famous story of the forty-seven *rōnin.* Nogi Maretsugu did not fail to point out to his son that ten of these loyal retainers had committed junshi in the Edo residence of the Mōri clan. Young Nogi learned his lesson, and later became a model of waiting to die in extreme loyalty not to a domainal lord but to the emperor of Meiji Japan.

Takatsuna's Ancestral Lesson of Absolute Devotion

In November 1858 the Nogi family returned from Edo to their home in Chōfu, a branch domain of Chōshū *han* (at the western end of Honshū).[16] The town of Chōfu is closely associated with the legendary Emperor Chūai (r. 191–200), "who is said to have sojourned there with his consort [Empress Jingū Kōgō, r. 201–269] while on his way to quell rebellious Kyushu."[17] One of Chōfu's two principal Shintō shrines, Iminomiya jinja, is dedicated to the imperial couple's son, Emperor Ōjin (r. 269–310); the other commemorates General Nogi and his wife.

Chōfu lies only a few miles from Shimonoseki, the site of the Taira clan's demise at nearby Dannoura in the decisive battle that ended the Genpei War in 1185. No doubt the ten-year-old samurai-to-be heard stories of the defeated Heike warriors' spirits haunting the coastline. One of the most memorable of these tales concerned the exploits of Nogi's celebrated ancestor Sasaki Shirō Takatsuna, the warrior who had saved the life of Minamoto Yoritomo in the battle of Ishibashiyama.[18] Toward the end of his life, Nogi told this tale to his pupils at the Peers School (Gakushūin).[19] It was so important a part of Nogi family lore that it warrants retelling in some detail.

Minamoto Yoritomo's men stood on the banks of the raging Uji River that separated them from the Minamoto commander "Kiso" Yoshinaka, who had so ruthlessly conquered Kyōto that he was now facing his cousin Yoritomo's punitive force. Yoritomo concocted a scheme to intensify his men's ardor for battle. He possessed two extraordinary horses, Ikezuki and Surusumi. One of his retainers, Kajiwara Genda Kagesue (1162–1200), passionately coveted Ikezuki, but Yoritomo, claiming that he wanted to keep this horse for himself, gave him Surusumi instead. "Then, *for some reason,* he bestowed Ikezuki on Sasaki Shirō Takatsuna when Takatsuna came to request his leave to depart. 'Take the horse in the knowledge that many others have desired him,' he said." By thus favoring Takatsuna over Kagesue, Yoritomo made him a target of resentment. But Takatsuna was emboldened rather than intimidated. Moved by Yoritomo's unexpected generosity, Takatsuna made a pledge: "'I will be the first man across the Uji River on this horse.'"[20] As Paul Varley notes, the phenomenon of being "first in battle" *(sakigake; senjin)* was "the most conspicuous way in which warriors display their aggressiveness in the war tales."[21]

When Kagesue learned that the horse he desired had become Takatsuna's, his spirits rose in anger: "'I'll wrestle and sword-fight Sasaki right here: thanks to me, His Lordship [Yoritomo] will lose two valuable samurai.' He waited muttering." Rather than attacking Takatsuna outright, Kagesue needled him about his unearned gift horse: "'Well, Lord Sasaki! I see His Lordship has made you a present of Ikezuki.'"[22] To mollify Kagesue, Takatsuna fabricated a cock-and-bull story about having stolen the prized horse. "Kagesue's wrath evaporated. 'Confound it! I wish I'd stolen him myself.'"[23]

Kagesue was, for the moment, appeased, but his resentment quickly took the form anticipated by Yoritomo. He decided that he, not Takatsuna, would win the race across the river. "Although neither had let his intentions show, each had made a secret resolve to be the first man across the river." Takatsuna was clearly the more imaginative, nimble, and resourceful of the two men. Kagesue stopped when Takatsuna warned him from behind, "This is the biggest river in the west. Your saddle girth looks loose; tighten it up!" Trickery, combined with courage, works.[24] Triumphantly, Takatsuna announced his name: "'Sasaki Shirō Takatsuna, the fourth son of Sasaki Saburō Hideyoshi and a ninth-generation descendant of Emperor Uda, is the first man across the Uji River! If any here consider themselves my equals, let them grapple with me!'"[25] Takatsuna then charged into the battle against the forces of the enemy. After the defeat of Yoshinaka, Yoritomo asked anxiously about Takatsuna. Had he bet on the right man on the right horse?[26] He had.

What was it about this story that stayed with Nogi all his life and compelled him to retell it to his students? Yoritomo had singled out Takatsuna for a great favor that he had denied another man. The gift from lord to retainer was magnificent, and a strong bond between donor and recipient was created. The unsolicited gift of Yoritomo's prize horse created a debt of gratitude that required Takatsuna's absolute devotion to his lord. In accordance with family traditions of martial valor, Nogi Maresuke, who received much from Emperor Meiji, gave his all in return—just as Takatsuna had to his lord.

Pre-Revolutionary Years: 1858–1864

The Nogi family returned from Edo to the Mōri clan's domain in 1858. Five years later, young Nogi came of age and received the name Genzō at his coming-of-age ceremony *(genbuku)*.[27] The year of Nogi's *genbuku*, 1863, was memorable for a local political event that had momentous national consequences. Plans were laid in Chōshū for Emperor Kōmei's (Osahito; 1831–1866; r. 1846–1866) personal campaign against foreigners. Since the late 1850s the Chōshū domain had eagerly adopted the slogan "Revere the Emperor, Expel the Barbarians" *(sonnō jōi)*. The domain followed the strongly anti-Western and pro-emperor policy of Yoshida Shōin (1830–1859), an influential Chōshū reformer. On 25 June 1863, the domain's leaders moved from rhetoric to military action. They recklessly fired on Western warships in Shimonoseki Bay. It may well have been in anticipation of reprisal that one of Shōin's followers, Takasugi Shinsaku (1839–1867), formed a new military unit based on merit and competence rather than on inherited rank. This new unit, the Kiheitai, was organized "in the fashion of the Western-style rifle company."[28]

Emperor Kōmei must have realized that Chōshū's precipitous action was certain to bring retaliation. He abruptly withdrew his favor from Chōshū and turned to the rival domains of Satsuma and Aizu for support. In this anti-Chōshū coup of 30 September 1863, Chōshū's *han* representatives were expelled from court and replaced by new favorites from Satsuma and Aizu.[29] Chōshū faced a brief crisis of self-confidence, but disagreements between Satsuma and Aizu gave Kusaka Genzui (1840–1864) an opening. He rushed to Kyōto to exploit the quarrels at court to Chōshū's advantage. Sensing that Chōshū could regain access to court, he signaled on 28 May 1864 that "the time to march had come."[30]

In the midst of this political turmoil, the fifteen-year-old Nogi absconded to the residence of the scholar Tamaki Bunnoshin (1810–1876) in Hagi.[31] There were personal reasons for Nogi's desperate action. Feeling unloved by his relentlessly strict parents, drawn more to the brush than the sword, the young Nogi heir wanted to escape what his family assumed was his destined role as a samurai warrior. Frustrated by his father's refusal to allow him to become a scholar, Nogi sought emotional and intellectual refuge with Tamaki, who had already adopted Nogi's younger brother Makoto, renamed Masayoshi. Tamaki's wife persuaded her husband, initially reluctant to take in the runaway, to accept him. Nogi began to blossom in this new environment, finding there not only the opportunity to study but also the affection that his own parents had denied him. In his later recollections Nogi referred to his mentor with great awe and respect as "Tamaki-ō."[32] Although Masayoshi was to continue the Tamaki family line, it was Nogi who became Tamaki's spiritual heir.

By asking Tamaki to accept him as his disciple, Nogi was apprenticing himself to one of Japan's most distinguished scholars. Tamaki had founded the Shōka Sonjuku, a private school in Hagi whose alumni determined Chōshū's course during the Meiji Restoration. Yoshida Shōin, among the most famous and influential of these alumni, was Tamaki's nephew.[33]

Shōin has been called "one of the more brilliant political thinkers that Japanese society has ever produced."[34] When he was only ten, he had lectured on Yamaga Sokō's (1622–1685) treatise on military strategy to the domain's lord, Mōri Takachika (1819–1871), winning great praise from him.[35] Sokō, it should be noted, was one of the three great *rōnin* of the early Tokugawa period. He was also the military instructor of the leader of the Akō *rōshi*. He emphasized the union of sword and brush and issued "the first systematic exposition of what later became known as the Way of the Warrior *(bushidō)*."[36] In his treatise *The Truth about Our Realm* (*Chūchō jijitsu*, 1681), which expounds on the legendary continuity that distinguishes the Japanese imperial line from the changing dynasties in China, Sokō pointed "to the emperor as the focus of all loyalties [without] undermining the authority of the shogunate."[37] This treatise greatly influenced Chōshū leaders in the critical pre–Meiji Restoration years. Shōin and Nogi both heeded Sokō's conviction that Japanese culture was in no sense inferior to Chinese culture.

As an adult, Shōin alerted and engaged the "slender, almost impoverished educated service stratum of Chōshū society"[38] in a "primarily discursive and polemical"[39] fight for better social conditions and rewards based on merit rather than inherited ranks and stipends. He was critical of the shōgunate's authorities and plotted against them, always unsuccessfully. Instead, Shōin was devoted to the emperor, whom he saw as a sovereign able to support and legitimate his reforms. This put him increasingly at odds with the shōgunate. Opposition might have made little difference during the long years of Japan's isolation, but, as Albert M. Craig noted, "The arrival of Perry . . . forced attention on the country as a whole, and the previously innocuous emphasis on the Emperor suddenly became significant."[40] After several house arrests and imprisonments, Shōin was finally put to death during the Great Ansei purge (Ansei *no daigoku*) ordered by the *bakufu*-appointed Ii Naosuke (1815–1860), daimyō of Hikone and dictatorial senior statesman *(tairō)*.[41] Shōin's execution took place in Edo on 27 October 1859. It is likely that the eleven-year-old Nakito noticed people's reactions to the execution.

By introducing Nogi to the study of Shōin's revolutionary works, Tamaki initiated him, metaphorically, into the fraternity of those who venerated Shōin for his loyal support of the emperor and for his martyrdom at the hands of the shōgunate. Ironically, Tamaki's transmission of Shōin's legacy prepared Nogi to become the samurai his father had wanted him to be. And yet, as if out of lingering spite, in his late teens Nogi still preferred the study of literature to the pursuit of military science.

Young Nogi made Shōin's "The Seven Principles of a Gentleman" *(Shiki shichi soku)* his code.[42] This "thoughtful set of maxims" had been written in 1855 on the occasion of Tamaki's son Hikosuke's coming-of-age ceremony. Hikosuke had asked his cousin Shōin, then imprisoned for his revolutionary activities, for guidance.[43] It is important to note that Shōin envisioned the inclusion of non-samurai in the pursuit of these principles just as he "ignored samurai rank in the admission of students to his school."[44]

For many, Shōin was seen as having been ahead of his time and was worshiped as a martyr who had died for his beliefs. He had been instrumental in preparing a dramatic shift in loyalties from shōgun and daimyō to emperor. At the same time, he did not limit himself to the fanatic cry of "Revere the Emperor, Expel the Barbarians," as he "combined emperor-centered nationalism and samurai self-discipline with a pragmatic awareness of the superiority of Western technology."[45]

In the summer of 1864, Chōshū's fortunes took another turn for the worse. In the disastrous skirmish at the Forbidden Gate (Kinmon *no hen*),[46] Kusaka Genzui led the domain's troops in an attack on the Imperial Palace in Kyōto in order to regain access to the court. The storming troops were defeated at the palace gates. Later that year, the struggle between Chōshū and the shōgunate was complicated by the predictable intervention of a European-American punitive expedition. On 5 September 1864, American, British, Dutch, and French warships massively bombarded Shimonoseki in retaliation for the attack of the previous year.[47] This disaster was followed by the *bakufu*'s first military expedition against the insurgent reformers. The *bakufu* massed fifty thousand men at Chōshū's borders, ready to strike if the rebels persisted in their opposition to Tokugawa rule.[48] In order to save the day and prevent a punitive invasion, Sufu Masanosuke (1823–1864) decided to sacrifice three senior leaders in order to appease the *bakufu*. After making this difficult decision, Sufu felt honor-bound to take his own life, which he did on 25 October 1864. The three reformist leaders whom Sufu had designated as human sacrifices were ordered by the Hagi government's conservative Common Opinions Faction to commit seppuku. They complied on 9 December, and their heads were promptly delivered to *bakufu* representatives.[49] In addition, and quite gratuitously, four staff officers were executed on the twelfth.

The rebellion was not quelled. Having tried Shōin's "discursive and polemical" appeals for reform and Kusaka's foray at the gates of the Imperial Palace, Chōshū's leaders moved to "the massive military use of force."[50] Early in 1865, Takasugi Shinsaku (1839–1867), another alumnus of Shōin's Sonjuku, attacked and overwhelmed the Hagi government's forces. Takasugi then prepared for a major assault on the *bakufu* by purchasing eleven thousand Western rifles. At this point, in January 1866, Chōshū's leaders formed an alliance with their rivals from Satsuma (who had been among those who repelled them at the Forbidden Gate in 1864). The two domains were united in their determination to oppose the Tokugawa *bakufu* and restore the emperor to power. The Chōshū-Bakufu or Four-Sided War that began on 18 July 1866 ended a couple of months later with the flight of the *bakufu* forces.

During this phase of western Japan's fierce military resistance to the *bakufu*, Nogi first became actively engaged in preparations for armed conflict.

In February 1865, the sixteen-year-old Nogi organized a patriots' batallion *(hōkokutai)* to oppose the Tokugawa regime,[51] binding his peers with a remarkable pledge: "He who changes his mind will commit seppuku."[52] Nogi took this bold step at about the same time that Tamaki's only biological son, Hikosuke, also known as Masahiko (1841–1865), was "killed while serving as a shotai officer in the bitter fighting around Oda."[53] (The *shotai* were irregular troops who, although marginalized and from impoverished service backgrounds, were wholly dedicated to the reformist cause.)[54] The loss of Hikosuke was a severe blow. He died relatively young and apparently without offspring. Although the Nogi sons were not Tamaki's own, they must have been some comfort to the grieving parents.

Before Nogi's *hōkokutai* was able to engage the enemy, a war council, composed largely of alumni of the Shōka Sonjuku, was convened to end the Chōshū civil war of 1865. Thomas M. Huber's comment holds true for young Nogi as well as for his classmates. "Whereas the Sonjuku's struggle in the 1850's had been a struggle of ideas, each student now appeared in his capacity as the captain of a rifle company. The war of the brush had given way to warfare plain and simple."[55] In Nogi's case, the transition may not have been complete. When he became a young member of the Chōshū army, he was renamed Bunzō (lit. repository of letters).[56]

From the *Hōkokutai*, 1865, to the Imperial Army, 1871

In late 1864 the Satsuma leader Saigō Takamori (1827–1877) mediated between rebellious Chōshū and the Tokugawa shōgunate. At that time, he was able to prevent a clash, albeit at the cost of a purge of the emperor's supporters in Chōshū. Two years later, when political disagreement escalated into armed conflict, the Satsuma domain joined in the struggle to resist—but not to overthrow—the shōgunate. In late 1866, with Western arms supplied by Satsuma, the Chōshū forces, including Nogi's *hōkokutai* and a "mixed army" under Yamagata Kyōsuke (later known as Yamagata Aritomo [1838–1922]), defeated the shōgunate's forces.

Nogi's military career was interrupted when he was wounded by a bullet in the foot. He returned to the Meirinkan, the Chōshū domain's school in Hagi, and to the study of literature, his original passion. He was there, recovering from his wound, when the shōgunate lost the decisive battles of Toba and Fushimi on 27 January 1868 and when Edo castle was captured in May 1868. Sporadic fighting continued, and Nogi, despite his wound, left school without permission and rejoined his *hōkokutai.* He was caught, arrested, and returned to school. He soon managed to persuade the authorities to allow him to withdraw from school and return to his military unit—as "an assistant instructor of Chinese classics."[57] Having missed most of the fighting that had bonded the men of the unit and acting in the ambiguous role of soldier-teacher, Nogi felt like an intruder and was emotionally relieved, late in 1869, to be transferred to Kyōto as a member of the imperial guard. It was, of course, the *imperial* guard. The authority of the emperor had been—at least in theory—restored, and the terms of international relations were more favorable than under the shōgunate. Japanese were now free to learn from Western nations. In this sense, the dreams of Shōin and the other reformers had been realized.

Young Nogi's fate became increasingly entwined with that of the young emperor (who was only three years his junior). In 1871, the twenty-two-year-old Nogi was promoted to the rank of major in the newly formed Japanese Imperial Army. When the senior seventh court rank was conferred on him on 14 December 1871, his name was changed to Maresuke.[58] By taking the first of the two kanji in his father's given name of Maretsugu as part of his own, he officially succeeded his father. (*Mare* refers to "desire" and that which is "rare.") Ironically, it was only on the eve of the modernizers' abolition of the samurai class in 1872 that he seemed ready to accept his inherited status as Nogi Maretsugu's son. Although he officially assumed his responsibilities as family heir, Nogi's greatest affection continued to be for his mentor, Tamaki Bunnoshin. Nogi had an additional reason to feel close to Tamaki when Nogi's younger brother Makoto became Tamaki's adopted heir, legally replacing the fallen Hikosuke.

Ironically, Nogi became loyal to the Meiji government because it had released him from the obligation to become a samurai just when he had become one. By contrast, his younger brother and many of his friends, although they too had helped bring about the fall of the shōgunate, soon became disenchanted with the Meiji regime that deprived them of their hereditary samurai status: "Many samurai felt more than disoriented; they felt as if they were losing their souls."[59] The process of abolition was gradual. The cherished right to wear swords was curbed in the fall of 1868. The topknot and swords were made optional in 1871 *(sanpatsu dattō rei)*, and finally, the wearing of swords by *shizoku* was prohibited on 28 March 1876 *(taitō kinshi rei* or *haitō rei)*.[60] Between 1869 and 1871, in accordance with the egalitarian economic vision of leaders such as Shōin, the stipends of Chōshū samurai were reduced to 100 *koku* (although "stipends of less than 100 koku were left entirely untouched").[61] Since the Nogi family received a modest stipend of 80 *koku*, it was initially unaffected by the stipend cuts. As for the prohibition of the wearing of swords, Chōshū was better prepared than other domains because its soldiers had already made the transition to Western-style rifle companies.

Uprisings

Early in 1870 Chōshū was once again the site of rebellion, this time against the new "Meiji Restoration" government. Nogi was ordered to quell the disorder. Although he was extremely ambivalent about fighting against his own domain, he obeyed. After succeeding in this painful task, he was dispatched to garrison duty in Tōkyō, Nagoya, and Kanazawa. In 1873, for reasons that remain unclear, he resigned briefly from military service.[62] Presumably, the resignation was motivated by the identity crisis that had troubled Nogi for years and was to continue to plague him until the day of his dramatic death. Nogi had never wanted to be a samurai; he wanted to be a poet-scholar. He envisioned himself farming the land and reading and writing in a pastoral setting, but circumstances had forced him in his late teens to abandon his dream of scholarly tranquility. When that happened, he became a samurai with a vengeance. He did as he was told—for the most part. He oscillated between poetic solitude and the life of a soldier. In 1874–1875, he served as aide-de-camp to Yamagata Aritomo, another Shōka Sonjuku alumnus and one of Japan's top military officers. Nogi was not so ascetic that he shunned the Tōkyō nightlife. He visited the city's bars and geisha houses, often in the company of Yamagata. Debauchery may have helped Nogi to overcome his doubts about the military career that he—or circumstances—had chosen. His inability to resist sensual temptation, his "living it up" (Nogi *no gōyū*), may, on the other hand, have led to moments of self-revulsion.

Then came the crisis of the Hagi Rebellion (Hagi *no ran*), the last in a series of samurai uprisings *(shizoku ran)* in southwestern Japan that began with the Saga Rebellion (Saga *no ran*) of 1874 and culminated in that of the League of the Divine Wind (Shinpūren) in late 1876. For Nogi, the psychic toll of this new military crisis was immense.

In the winter of 1875, samurai disaffected with the young Meiji government once again became a source of trouble in Nogi's home domain of Chōshū. Nogi's appointment as commander of the Fourteenth Infantry Regiment at Kokura in northern Kyūshū (December 1875) brought him into conflict with Maebara Issei (1834–1876), a Chōshū samurai who had shifted his allegiance from membership in the Meiji government to involvement in armed opposition. Maebara Issei "raised the standard of revolt in Hagi and with a force of two hundred men came marching south into Kyushu."[63]

Aggravating the tension was a coincidence. The regimental officer whom Nogi replaced was Maebara's brother, Major Yamada Eitarō, who had also become a dissident.[64] Although Nogi was a Chōshū samurai himself, the appointment assumed that he, unlike the unreliable Maebara brothers, was loyal to the Meiji government and to the emperor. There was, however, dissonance within Nogi's own family. While Nogi assured Yamagata of his loyalty to the emperor, he was unable to vouch for his younger brother. Makoto, now known as Tamaki Masayoshi, was an advisor attached to the Maebara camp. He was, in fact, the "most active confederate"[65] of and a "major spokesman for . . . Maebara."[66] In other words, the civil war that sundered the nation was for Nogi, quite literally, a war between brothers. He pleaded with Masayoshi, but in vain. Unable to entice him to return to the loyalist side, Nogi reported matters to Yamagata, thus implicating Masayoshi in Maebara's preparations for rebellion.

Obliged to face his own brother in a civil uprising, Nogi procrastinated before sending his forces into battle. He did not engage Maebara's men until 28 October 1876, when he met and defeated them at Toyotsu (modern Fukuoka Prefecture).[67] Masayoshi died in battle three days later, while resisting the government's forces near the Chōshū castle town of Hagi. Having inadvertently followed the principle of *taigi messhin*, or sacrificing one's kin for the sake of nation or lord, Nogi was in a bind. He could not expiate the guilt felt over his rebel brother's death while continuing to pledge allegiance to the imperial banner. A few days later, on 6 November, Nogi's presumably traumatic sense of personal loss was intensified when Tamaki Bunnoshin, Nogi's mentor and his brother's adoptive father, committed seppuku (or *jijin*)[68] "to atone for the treason of his adopted son."[69] A most remarkable facet of his expiatory act was that Tamaki "had a woman, [Yoshida] Shōin's eldest sister, perform the *kaishaku* [role of second]."[70]

The anguish that Nogi must have felt was intensified when his superiors accused him of indecision, comparing him unfavorably with Kodama Gentarō (1852–1906).[71] Nogi defended himself by pointing out that he had provided valuable information about the enemy—even at the price of betraying his own brother. This defense did not save him from a deep sense of shame that he revealed even in enunciating his decision not to commit seppuku: "There is no greater shame than postponing the moment of death, but there are times when one does so from necessity."[72] Was this shame a result of having hesitated before acting upon orders, or was it a result of having been complicit in the death of his brother? Or was Nogi ashamed that he had not followed Tamaki's example of seppuku? All we can be certain of is that Nogi was deeply tormented. Mark R. Peattie convincingly argues that it was this tragic episode more than any other that triggered Nogi's death wish. He asks, "Was there indeed something reprehensible in his military conduct and had he considered atoning for it with his life?"[73] Clearly, Nogi wanted to atone for both his brother's and his mentor's deaths. Nogi neither fought the former as his enemy, as he was required to by his military role, nor did he follow his mentor in an act of junshi. In this liminal space, Nogi was to live for decades before committing junshi.[74]

Kumamoto, 1877, and the Imperial Flag

According to some anthropologists, human sacrifice can be a response to fratricide and civil war. The bloody cycle of retaliation and revenge can be halted—and averted—only by blood shed in sacrifice.[75] From this perspective, the origins of Nogi's quest for expiatory sacrifice through seppuku lay in the symbolic fratricide of his younger brother and the symbolic patricide of his mentor (who was also his chosen father figure) in civil war. From another widely held anthropological and religious perspective, ritual sacrifice can be understood as a way to appease the gods and to avert or end some catastrophe that afflicts a people. In Nogi's case, junshi served not only to *mark* catastrophe but also—for those who had taken Emperor Meiji as their divine ruler—to *avert* catastrophe and to ease the transition from one era to another.

The Satsuma Rebellion (Seinan *sensō*) of 1877 gave Nogi a chance, at least, to redeem himself for his indecisiveness in the Hagi Rebellion. The emperor may have been aware of Nogi's personal trauma when he appointed him to fight the Satsuma rebels. The emperor may, in fact, have recognized the price Nogi had had to pay for placing his devotion to him above his feelings for his brother and his mentor. It is conceivable—although this thought is quite speculative—that the emperor may not have minded Nogi's military failure as long as it produced unconditional devotion to him.

During the Hagi Rebellion, Nogi seems to have put aside whatever thoughts of redemptive suicide that he may have had. Unfortunately, in the campaign against Saigō Takamori, he suffered a second and even more public failure. Commanding the Kokura Fourteenth Regiment, he acted against orders in a reckless attempt to break the siege of Kumamoto Castle, which had been invested by Saigō Takamori and his rebel army from Kagoshima. This rash act exposed 240 of his men to an overwhelming Satsuma force.[76] Nogi lost not only a number of men but—more important—the imperial banner.[77]

The loss of the regimental banner on 22 February 1877 was a symbolic failure[78] of immense importance. The imperial flag was among the invented rites and symbols designed to legitimize the emperor as a human ruler as well as a living god *(ikigami)*. There had been no national flag before 1854;[79] the banners Japanese warriors had carried into battle had been the banners of their feudal lords and domains. The regimental banner was "the most symbolic link between the emperor and his army." It was "the repository for all the emotion and loyalty which formed the spirit of the regiment, and its loss represented [a] disgrace of disastrous proportions."[80] The loss became even more disgraceful when Saigō Takamori flaunted the captured banner in an effort to break the spirit of the imperial forces.[81]

Shattered by what he felt to be the unpardonable loss of the imperial banner, weeping in despair,[82] Nogi was impulsively about to commit seppuku when he was restrained by his men.[83] As he continued to brood over the fate of the flag, Nogi's sense of honor drove him formally to request the privilege of seppuku that had been denied him immediately after the battle. He appealed to the man—or god—whom he felt he had dishonored by losing the flag.

Accounts differ as to how his request was handled. Although General Yamagata had been on friendly terms with Nogi, his drinking partner, he seems to have felt that the loss of the imperial banner called for "extreme punishment." This reaction has been interpreted as granting Nogi his wish to die, but Yamagata cannot have issued an unambiguous order to that effect, because Major General Nozu Michitsura (1841–1908), commander-in-chief of the First Brigade in Kyūshū, pardoned Nogi "because of his battlefield successes."[84] (The siege of Kumamoto ended, after all, in an imperial victory.)[85] Leniency on the part of his superiors seems, however, only to have intensified Nogi's sense of shame—and this after he had barely been able to deal with the shame he felt as a result of having been complicit in the deaths of his brother and his mentor.

Nogi's appeal for the privilege of seppuku was forwarded to the emperor, who was then on an extended pilgrimage. (The pilgrimage, lasting from 24 January 1877 to 30 July 1877,[86] was to worship Emperor Kōmei at the imperial mausoleum in Kyōto, and the first legendary emperor, Jimmu [660–585], in Nara.) From this moment, if not earlier, Nogi's relationship with the emperor was, quite literally, a matter of life and death.

It is important to remember that the emperor was also in a liminal state. Officially divine, he was adopting many of the attributes of ordinary humans. To the Japanese it must have seemed nothing short of a miracle to have an emperor, a descendant of the sun goddess, step out into the broad daylight of the Meiji Restoration after centuries of feudal rule during which he had literally not been seen or heard except by the highest ranks of the court nobility.[87] For ordinary Japanese, the emperor had been "above the clouds" *(kumo no ue)*, and now he had returned to earth, not unlike the Amida Buddha in "descent on a cloud" *(raigō)* iconography. The emperor's subjects, who made sure that they were never spatially in a position literally to look down upon their descended-from-the-clouds ruler, must have been quite bewildered. There was even a folk belief that "if one looked up at the emperor one would be cursed, or . . . one's eyes would be crushed."[88] Takashi Fujitani speaks of the emperor's two bodies, one seen in pageants and on imperial excursions, and one unseen, reconstructed from a mythic past.[89] In their confusion, loyal subjects sometimes stripped naked at the sight of their divine emperor or ventured out to see him in transvestite dress.[90]

Nogi Maresuke was no ordinary Japanese, but he must have shared something of the awe that others felt in the presence of their divine ruler. While the emperor pondered Nogi's confession of guilt, Nogi in his shame dashed recklessly into combat in search of the punishment that no one seemed willing to grant him. He was wounded, but he again sought the front lines as soon as he could escape from the hospital.[91]

Nogi was not permitted to die. The young emperor was not yet sure of himself. He was trying forcefully to impress himself upon the people and had already embarked on the first two of his six Great Circuits.[92] Although this much travel and exposure to the people was utterly unprecedented for a Japanese emperor, there was still a sense of uncertainty on the emperor's part that did not permit the loss of loyal subjects to suicide. "Live!" the emperor admonished Nogi: *"'Iki yo,' to satosareta."*[93] Historians have rightly concluded that "Nogi lived on by order of the Emperor, 'suffering beyond death.'"[94]

Confirmation of this view came from Nogi himself. On New Year's Day, 1878, he expressed his extreme distress in a poem that culminates in the line: "My self is nothing but a person spared death" *(waga mi wa sunawachi kore shi shite tami o amasu).*[95] Postponement of death simply caused him additional pain. One thinks again of Nogi's heartfelt confession in the aftermath of the Hagi Rebellion: "There is no greater shame than postponing the moment of death, but there are times when one does so from necessity."[96] Both his request for punishment and the official pardon were found along with his testament and last poems on the day, thirty-five years later, that he finally committed his long-delayed seppuku.[97] Hauntingly similar to Nogi's plight was that of Akashi Gidayū, a sixteenth-century general who asked his lord Akechi Mitsuhide for permission to commit seppuku in order to expunge a stain on his honor. When Mitsuhide ordered him to live, Akashi disobeyed him and took his own life. In Yoshitoshi's famous woodblock print, produced in 1890, Gidayū stares at his death poem while the glowering tiger's dangling tail seems to transfer an ecstatic (*ekstasis,* "displacement") charge to the blade poised to deliver the lethal thrust.

Was Nogi's junshi a repudiation of the pardon and a belated self-sentencing or a last respectful bow to the imperial command broken only in the most excruciatingly painful way? Richard Michael Connaughton seems to opt for the latter interpretation, concluding that the denial of seppuku created "a fierce loyalty between soldier and Emperor, a loyalty that was

Yoshitoshi (1839–1892); ukiyo-e #83 (printed 1890) from the series *One Hundred Aspects of the Moon 1885–1892* (tsuki hyakushi); "As I am about to enter the ranks of those who disobey / ever more brightly shines / the moon of the summer night" *yumitori no / kazu ni irusa no / mi to nareba / terimasarikeri / natsu no yo no tsuki*—Akashi Gidayū. John Stevenson Collection.

reciprocated; it was a bond which lasted until the Emperor's death, and was to end for Nogi in tragic circumstances."[98]

Port Arthur, 1894: Victory and Massacre

In the seventeen years between the Satsuma Rebellion of 1877, Japan's last civil war, and the Sino-Japanese War of 1894–1895, Japan's first international war, Nogi reached full maturity. He lost his father in October 1877 and received his bride, Shizuko, from the Yuji family of a Satsuma samurai official in August of the following year. In his military career he was promoted to the rank of colonel in 1880 and major general in 1885. It was a sign of favor that he was sent to Germany where, for eighteen months, he studied warfare and military organization and became acquainted with high-ranking Prussian officers, including the Chief of the Prussian General Staff, General Graf von Moltke (1800–1891). While attached to the Imperial Guards Regiment in Berlin, he was profoundly impressed by German discipline and the Prussian officers' code of honor. These impressions went deeper than whatever knowledge of military tactics and strategy he acquired from the German lectures he had dutifully attended.[99]

Soon after his return in June of 1888 Nogi was given command of the Imperial Guards Regiment. In 1890 he commanded the Fifth Infantry Brigade, stationed in Nagoya. Early in 1892, he requested a leave of absence. Why he did this remains unclear. One theory is that his pride was offended by his having to obey a former inferior, Lieutenant General Katsura Tarō (1848–1913).[100] A more mundane theory has it that Nogi felt humiliated by the laughter of young officers when he lost his dentures and his horse stepped on them.[101] Whatever the case may be, for nine months, Nogi farmed the land at Nasu in Tochigi Prefecture that he had bought two years earlier from his wife's relatives. As if to make a spiteful point about his military dedication, he persisted in wearing "his uniform the entire time."[102]

Nogi seems to have intended to retire permanently from military duty, but Japan was building a modern national army at this time, and Nogi, having had the privilege of studying the Prussian model, was too valuable an asset for the government to lose. Offered a promotion to commanding officer of the First Infantry Brigade in Tōkyō in 1893, he agreed—like the Roman patrician-warrior Lucius Quinctius Cincinnatus—to abandon his plough and return to military duty.

Within a year, Japan was at war with China and Korea.[103] Having for decades observed with envy the expansion of British and French power and influence in Africa and Asia, Japan's leaders were determined to break into the circle of imperialist nations. Relations with China were strained by what the Japanese felt to be a lack of respect—perhaps even contempt—for Japan's achievements as a modern nation. In addition to Japanese imperial ambitions and a sense that the Chinese had somehow offended their "national honor," there were immediate political and economic reasons for war. The construction of Russia's Trans-Siberian Railway seemed to threaten Japan's interests in Korea.[104] Whatever the reasons, the emperor declared war on 1 August 1894.[105] The public's response was enthusiastic.

The First Army's Fifth Division under General Nozu began its march through Korea in early August 1894. P'yŏngyang fell on 15 September. As the Chinese were militarily unprepared to repel the approaching Japanese army, the Chinese government was reduced to posting warning signs, offering rewards for the capture of Japanese soldiers, and appealing to "heaven's warriors" *(tenpei)* to repel the aggressors.[106] General Nozu moved swiftly, but the road to Beijing was blocked by Port Arthur (Ch. Lüshun; J. Ryojun), the "Chinese Gibraltar," which, together with the strategic outpost of Weihaiwei on the opposite side, on the Shantung Peninsula, controlled the entrance to the Gulf of Bo-hai (J. Bokkai).[107]

Nogi's part in the drama of the Sino-Japanese War transformed him from an obscure brigade-level officer into a national hero. While the First Army moved through Korea, elements of the Second Army, commanded by Field Marshal Ōyama Iwao (1842–1916), landed on the Liaodong Peninsula. Nogi's First Infantry Brigade was among the units that landed on 24 October and began the march to Port Arthur. After the capture of Jinzhou (J. Kinshū) on 6 November, "Nogi's forces took Dalian [J. Dairen], the best anchorage on the peninsula, without firing a shot."[108] From there, it was not far to Port Arthur, which was reputed to be a virtually impenetrable fortress: "Before the war, a French admiral had declared it would take a fleet of more than fifty good ships with an army of 100,000 crack troops to break the fort, and they would still need half a year to finish the job."[109] No wonder, since the fortifications had taken sixteen years to build.

The capture of Port Arthur in a single day, on 21 November 1894, came as a stunning surprise. It was Nogi's most brilliant military success. Together with the Twenty-Second Mixed Brigade, Nogi's First Brigade had taken the fortress in a "lightning assault."[110] Nogi's achievement seems especially remarkable not only because of its amazing swiftness but also because everyone was convinced that capturing Port Arthur would require a tremendous sacrifice. No one had expected an easy victory.[111] The astonishing feat was made possible, in part, by the Japanese army's incorporation of the doctrines of Klemens Wilhelm Jakob Meckel (1842–1906), a Prussian military tactician who had served in Japan as an advisor from 1885 to 1888.[112] Boldly acting upon Meckel's doctrines, Nogi mounted the world's stage as an inspiring model of a successful modern military leader.[113]

On the heels of victory followed a massacre that has long been "either unknown or poorly understood in Japan or the West"[114] (despite the fact that it was, at the time, widely reported in the British and American press).[115] In retrospect, the massacre seems predictable. The Chinese army had committed many desperate acts of brutality.[116] The sight of their comrades' mutilated corpses lining the route to Port Arthur struck terror into the souls of the Japanese troops and, according to foreign observers, "was sufficient to excite revengeful feelings in the hearts of the best disciplined men."[117] And it did not bode well for the enemy that the Japanese troops were physically and mentally exhausted by the time they reached their destination.[118] Intoxicated by fear and anger, the conquering army turned the battle into a massacre that continued for days,[119] leaving about two thousand Chinese dead, many of them civilians, including women and children.[120] The massacre at Port Arthur was acknowledged by Japanese soldiers and civilians in their diaries[121] and subsequently rationalized in the Japanese press.[122] Field Marshal Ōyama's guidelines to his commanders had been based on advice from Ariga Nagao (1860–1921), the Second Army's legal advisor, who "justified the massacre on the grounds of provocation and reciprocity."[123]

Whether or not Nogi was implicated in the massacre is unclear. His troops were probably responsible for the deaths of 360 Chinese in the first wave of assault that led to victory,[124] but these deaths may have been simply the casualties of fierce combat. Immediately after the battle, the morning after the capture of Port Arthur, his brigade left for Jinzhou.[125] Evidence implicating Nogi comes from Shimana Masao, author of a critical study of what he calls the "Nogi myth." Shimana cites Japan's first war photographer, Kamei Koreaki (1861–1896), who claimed that Nogi, under great stress and sleep deprivation, commanded his troops, on their way to Jinzhou, to shoot four or five hundred Chinese troops whether they resisted or fled. (In addition to the six hundred photographs with which Kamei documented the war, he kept a diary from 25 September 1894 to 30 May 1895.)[126] Shimana also cites the official war record, *Kōkan senshi*, which states only that, as a result of a pincer movement, 560 out of 700 enemy soldiers died in the fighting that followed the fall of Port Arthur.[127]

Kamei's comments are especially significant because he had studied photography in Germany at the same time Ōgai and Nogi were there, the former to study hygiene, the latter to study military strategy.[128] At the time of the Port Arthur massacre, Ōgai was in Dalian (J. Dairen) as a medical communications officer in the Second Army. There, on 29 November 1894, he met with Kamei and discussed the events of the campaign. As Ōgai and Kamei were both from the town of Tsuwano and no longer inhibited by hierarchical constraints that had once ruled domainal relations, they might well have discussed the horrific matter of the massacre that had just occurred a few days earlier, but there is no trace in their diaries of the massacre having been a topic of conversation.[129] As for Nogi himself, his diary shows no entries between 13 July 1894 and 26 November 1899.[130]

Undisputed is the fact that, on 23 November, while the massacre was continuing, there was a tumultuous victory banquet in Port Arthur at which Nogi was not present. At the banquet, held to coincide with the Imperial Thanksgiving Day *(Niiname sai)*, Yamaji Motoharu, praising both the First and the Second Armies, boasted to Field Marshal Ōyama that these two armies would soon vie to enter Beijing. His speech was accompanied by howling laughter, followed by the tossing into the air of the military leaders to shouts of "Banzai."[131] On 9 December in Tōkyō, wealthy businessmen staged the "First Tokyo City Victory Celebration" for Port Arthur.[132]

The capture of Port Arthur did not end the war. In early 1895, Nogi had occasion to set an example of stoic endurance for his troops when he moved through snow and ice to aid his rival Katsura Tarō in the renewed battle for Hai-ch'eng (northeast of Port Arthur). "The suffering of the troops was intense," writes Peattie, "but Nogi drove them forward, setting them an example of dogged courage, sharing the limited rations and meager winter shelter. Within a week he had them before the walls of Kaiping [southwest of Hai-ch'eng] which he captured at bayonet point after four hours of close fighting."[133] Nogi's action relieved the pressure on Katsura.

Later that winter, after Admiral Itō Sukeyuki (1843–1914) had captured Weihaiwei (across the gulf from Port Arthur), he showed mercy to the enemy because the Chinese Admiral Ding Ruchang (1836–1895) had surrendered and then taken his own life with an overdose of opium. (Three of his captains followed his example.)[134] Writes Donald Keene, "The battle of Weihaiwei had ended not only in a Japanese victory but also with a vindication of the Japanese code of the samurai after the horrors of Port Arthur."[135] No doubt Nogi was among the many Japanese who admired the Chinese admiral for committing suicide to atone for his incompetence.

Japan had won the war with such formidable speed (even though resistance continued in Taiwan until 21 October 1895) that the Western powers were not only impressed but worried. The Treaty of Shimonoseki, signed on 17 April 1895, satisfied the victors, but a few days later, in their so-called Triple Intervention, Russia, Germany, and France "advised" Japan, in the name of peace, to retrocede one of the ceded territories, namely the Liaodong

Peninsula—including Port Arthur. With these three nations' military threat looming large, the government had no choice but to make concessions that deeply hurt Japanese pride. As a result, forty Japanese protested by committing seppuku.[136] Humiliation turned to outrage when the Russians later managed to lease Port Arthur from the Chinese. Japan's response to having been deprived of Port Arthur was to lay plans to take back the fortress from the Russians.[137] For this enormous task, Nogi would be called upon again in the Russo-Japanese War (1904–1905).

In the intervening years, in recognition of his achievement in the Sino-Japanese War, Nogi was promoted to the rank of lieutenant general and entered the middle rank of "Count" *(hakushaku)*[138] among the five ranks of the modern nobility *(kazoku)*.[139] The emperor must have congratulated himself for not having permitted Nogi to die in 1877.[140]

Between Wars

In the aftermath of the Sino-Japanese War, Nogi was needed to help pacify Taiwan, Asia's first, albeit short-lived, republic. He succeeded Admiral Kabayama Sukenori (1837–1922) and Lieutenant General Katsura Tarō as the island's third governor. This appointment was a great honor, even though Nogi could apparently not escape always being one step behind his fellow countryman from Chōshū, the ambitious Katsura.[141] Was he chosen because he was "apolitical" or because he was "serious, unassuming"?[142] Or was he considered ideal for the task because he had been successful at Port Arthur without being publicly implicated in the massacre that followed on the heels of victory?

Peattie characterizes Nogi's efforts to rule the Taiwanese as impractical but humane, and his control over "dishonest and insensitive Japanese officials" as firm but frustrating. " 'The brutality toward the natives by officers of this command must stop,' [Nogi] demanded. Such administrators not only provoked the Taiwanese into further resistance, he insisted, but were 'an insult to the Japanese nation.' "[143] Nogi's "extreme moral righteousness" did not endear him to those under his command and ultimately led him to confess, " 'I feel like biting and kicking my subordinates.' "[144] In November 1897 he begged his superiors to release him from a responsibility he considered himself unfit to bear, but it was not until February 1898 that he was able to retire, once again, from the military profession. In doing so, he disappointed the wishes of Yamagata Aritomo and the entire cabinet of Prime Minister Matsukata Masayoshi (1835–1924).[145]

Nine months later he returned to duty and was sent to command the Eleventh Division in Zentsūji (Kagawa Prefecture). There in Shikoku, where Nogi enjoyed training and bonding with his men, he agonized over some former subordinates who had been sent to China during the Boxer Rebellion and were charged with smuggling Chinese silver currency into Japan. Even though the battalion commander was cleared of these charges, Nogi resigned from the division commander's post.[146] Such a step, writes Peattie, underlined Nogi's belief in absolute individual responsibility within a larger military unit, a belief that became "an integral part of his moral dogma of the limitless responsibility of the officer, not only for his own conduct but for that of his subordinates."[147] His resignation was a sign of "his almost fanatic adherence to his own uncompromising code of honor."[148]

During the course of his eventful and controversial military career Nogi had now resigned from and rejoined the army four times. This behavior continues to be something of "a puzzle for his biographers."[149] The "suspensions" of his military career testify to his strong—perhaps excessive—sense of loyalty, pride, and honor. The offenses he believed he had committed were all magnified by his pride and high expectations of others' behavior. His first brief resignation, in 1873, was for uncertain reasons. The others were motivated, at least in part, by his sense of honor. In Nagoya in 1892, he had resigned in protest over having to serve a former inferior; in Taiwan in 1898, he had entertained unreasonable expectations about the conduct of an occupying army. In Kagawa in 1901, he felt shamed by the behavior of subordinate officers for whom he felt responsible.

During each of his three long "suspensions," Nogi sought relief in the countryside north of Tōkyō. His pastoral retreats lasted for nine months in the first and second "exiles," and nearly three years in the third. He farmed his plot of land at Nasu, wrote poetry, and read "about bushidō and military and general history."[150] He cleansed himself by returning to the ideals of his youth, by studying the seventeenth-century military thinker and nonconformist Yamaga Sokō. Nogi took note of Sokō's belief that Japanese culture was the equal of Chinese culture. In particular, Nogi admired Sokō's commitment to the ethics of Confucius and to the emperor. (Loyalty to the emperor was, of course, required by Confucian ethics.) Nogi's belief in the spirit of *bushidō* was strengthened by Sokō's conviction that the samurai could—or must—set an example in the fulfillment of his duty and in unflinching devotion to his lord. Each time Nogi returned to military duty from these self-imposed retreats, he rose in the esteem of his colleagues. The first and third major retreats led straight to his military engagements in the Sino-Japanese and the Russo-Japanese Wars. Whatever shortcoming had caused him to retire had been come to terms with and could now be overcome in determined leadership in battle. Nogi's retreats prepared him to serve his emperor with renewed devotion.

Port Arthur, 1904: Human Bullets

A decade after the Sino-Japanese War, incompatible imperialistic ambitions drove Russia and Japan to armed conflict. During the Russo-Japanese War, Nogi felt compelled for the second time to seek imperial permission for suicide, a desire that had its origins in the same painful combination of intolerable loss and triumphant victory. Whereas the scale of initial loss and final victory at Kumamoto in 1877 had been small, the magnitude of the loss and victory in the war with Russia was immense. Twenty-seven years lay between the siege of Kumamoto and the battle for Port Arthur, once again a coveted prize.

In order to be closer to the Sino-Japanese theater of war, the emperor had set up his imperial "tent" in Hiroshima. In the Russo-Japanese War, however, he seemed to distance himself symbolically from the forces converging on Port Arthur. As the entire nation expected Nogi to repeat his feat of 1894, the pressure on him must have been enormous.

The advance on Port Arthur went badly. It began on 5 May 1904, when the Japanese landed, unopposed, some sixty miles northeast of the fortress. En route to Port Arthur, the Japanese met Russian resistance at Nanshan, forty miles from the city. There, on 27 May, Nogi's son Katsusuke died of wounds received the day before.[151] His death presaged many thousands more.

Nogi, having received command of the Third Army in early May, was promoted to General (Taishō) on 6 June. He received this military assignment from the recently appointed chief of general staff, Yamagata Aritomo, the very officer who had "ordered Nogi to commit suicide in order to clear the name of his regiment in 1877."[152] Nogi had much greater difficulty in capturing the stronghold from the Russians in 1904 than from the Chinese a decade earlier. The siege began in June. Months passed, and the strain of the stalled campaign was beyond what Nogi was able to bear. He broke down and wept often during the long siege that squandered many lives by using men as "human bullets" *(nikudan)*. As Lieutenant Sakurai Tadayoshi (1879–1965) explained, "Strategically we needed to reduce the great fortress as quickly as possible, however great the damage to our army might be; so, therefore, the commanding general resolved with tears to offer the necessary sacrifice, and his subordinates willingly offered their lives and stormed the enemy with bullets of their own flesh."[153] Deeply impressed by the general's anguish and by his recovery of composure in the face of military disaster, the American war correspondent Stanley Washburn described Nogi's lonely hours spent looking at the moon from the roof of a haphazard pavilion he had had his men construct.[154]

As the months passed, the pressure on Nogi to capture Port Arthur mounted. He pored over military maps in search of a way out of the strategic

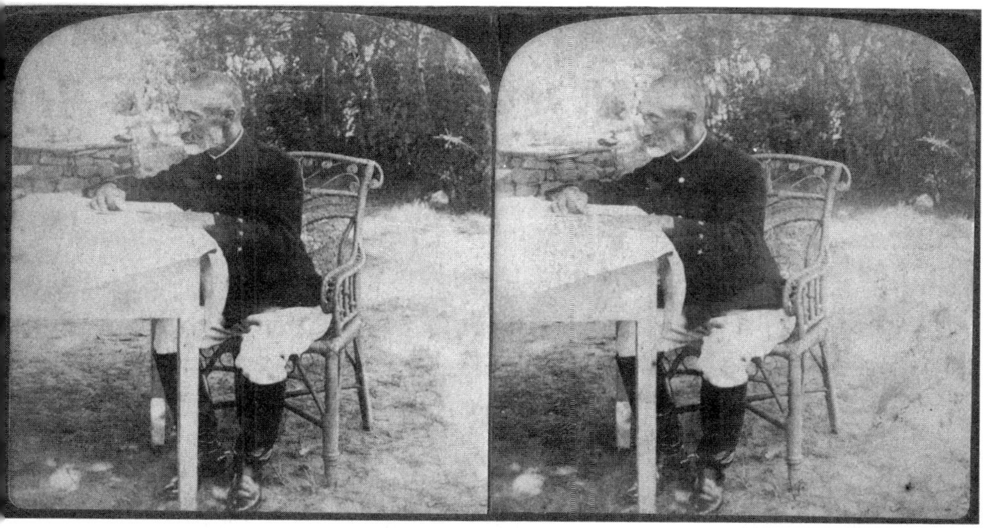

American photographic stereocard: "General Nogi, the indomitable fighter, at headquarters before Port Arthur, Manchuria." Underwood & Underwood, 1904. Loan to author from Helen Hopper.

impasse. Yamagata wrote to Nogi on 16 July 1904: "The speedy fall of Port Arthur is the most important element in the victory or defeat of our whole army."[155] Nogi launched a major assault on 22 August, but it was a disaster. The setback weighed so heavily on Yamagata that his sleep was disturbed. Yamagata biographer Roger F. Hackett writes: "After repeated failures to capture Port Arthur, Yamagata continued to rally Nogi's determination. In November 1904 he sent a verse of encouragement after he had imagined the fall of the port in a dream:

> With bombardments so numerous the heavens are frightened,
> for half a year you have laid siege and suffered countless casualties.
> Now with a spirit stronger than iron
> Port Arthur is captured with one blow.[156]

Alas, it was only a dream. On 28 November, Nogi launched his final attack on 203-Meter Hill, one of three strategic hills that constituted the defenses of Port Arthur. A Russian officer vividly described the bravery and the carnage on both sides. He related one breathtaking episode in which a raging Russian corporal tried to prevent the Japanese flag bearer from hoisting the Japanese flag on the hilltop by ripping the flag with his teeth and collapsing under a rain of bullets. As the Russians were retreating, another

Japanese collapsed while trying to raise the flag on the summit, only to be replaced by yet another who fell in a Russian fusillade. The pattern was repeated six times, and when the ninth man seized the flag to hoist it, the Russian officer shouted, "Don't shoot at the man with the flag; it will be hoisted anyway."[157] In retrospect the episode seems like a haunting commentary on Nogi's loss of the imperial banner in 1877.

After a siege of nearly six months and three disastrous frontal attacks that cost thousands of Japanese casualties, Nogi was replaced—despite the opposition of the emperor and unbeknownst to the general public—by General Kodama Gentarō (1852–1906), a kind of "shadow warrior" *(kagemusha).*[158] Kodama had been given a letter from General Ōyama removing Nogi from command, but he was reluctant to show the letter because he did not wish to "bring disgrace on the Third Army and on Nogi," and because he did not want to place Nogi in a position where he might "kill himself."[159] No doubt he was also aware of how much Nogi meant to the emperor.

The change of command occurred on 1 December. Nogi had almost taken Port Arthur the previous evening, when his men seized the strategically important 203-Meter Hill, but the Russians counterattacked and recaptured the bastion. In the midst of this reversal, Nogi's second son, Yasusuke, was killed.[160] Nogi's grief was expressed at the time in the form of a breakdown that left him, for the moment, unable to act. Nogi's grief found vicarious expression in a poem written a few days later by his friend Mori Ōgai (1862–1922). (Ōgai was, at the time, chief medical officer for the Second Army, commanded by General Oku Yasukata [1847–1930].) The undated poem, entitled "Nogi Shōgun," was probably written in December 1904 and is included in Ōgai's *Verse Diary* (*Uta nikki,* 1907). It dramatizes the general's battlefield response to his personal losses.[161] The poetic form of the poem is Ōgai's own invention; it consists of 6 stanzas, with 8 lines each, each 17-syllable line divided into a 5-7-5 rhythm. In Hiroaki Sato's fittingly staccato English translation, each line has two blank spaces to mark the division between sets of syllables and to produce an out-of-breath rhythm.[162] The first two stanzas describe the deadly combat on 203-Meter Hill.[163] Having concentrated his efforts on capturing "two rocky mounds" at the top of the fortified hill, the general is returning to his headquarters, the task still undone. In the twilight he encounters a soldier carrying a dead officer on his back.

The next three stanzas are triggered by the general's questions: "Who are you?——Where are you——carrying him?" The soldier does not care to identify himself and does not seem to recognize the general, which seems hardly possible, but he hastens to explain that General Nogi's first son, Katsusuke, had been killed earlier at Nanshan and now the second son, Yasusuke, whose body he is carrying, has fallen in battle over 203-Meter Hill. Is the soldier unaware of Nogi's identity or is he taking revenge for the suffering that Nogi has imposed on the men under his command? Despite the loss of one son, the soldier continues, the general had not seen fit to withdraw his younger son from battle to protect him, but had instead promised "that if/ he be killed,——a funeral be held——just once/ for the three of them,——himself included." The soldier is disoriented and asks the general directions to the hospital.

Like the first two stanzas, the last gives the perspective of an observer, perhaps the poet, who was close to Nogi during the campaign to capture Port Arthur. Initially, Ōgai's message is chilling, for the general does not acknowledge that he has recognized his son's body; he merely points the way to the hospital with his whip. Frustrated by the cold practicality of this gesture and desperate for a sign of raw grief, the poet-observer is reduced to recording what a cold "winter star" observed in the general's mien as night fell. Nothing. "The general——didn't even——move his eyelashes."[164]

Ōgai's poem captures the exact moment when the pain over the earlier death of one son turns to despair and utter loss of hope with the death of the only other son. The "two rocky mounds," symbolizing the general's "feeble——thread of hope" of capturing 203-Meter Hill, become metaphorical funeral mounds for the two sons. After his first son's death, Nogi had wanted to live on for the sake of the second son. Now both are gone and Nogi has lost the will to live.

Nogi's apathy seems to have been as clear to General Kodama as it was to Mori Ōgai. After initially suggesting that Nogi issue orders for a renewed assault, Kodama realized that he was too distraught to act on the suggestion. Kodama, still reluctant to humiliate Nogi by confronting him with Ōyama's letter of dismissal, suggested that Nogi step aside voluntarily: "Nogi thought about it for a moment and then agreed."[165] Thus Kodama took command and was able to recover control of 203-Meter Hill on 6 December. He continued the assault, and Port Arthur was taken on 1 January 1905. General Anatolii M. Stoessel (1848–1915), the Russian commander, who had in August curtly declined to hand over the fortress to Nogi,[166] now surrendered it[167]—not to Kodama but to Nogi. It was a photograph rather than "the traditional multicolored woodblock print or the newer lithograph [that] became a defining image of the Russo-Japanese War."[168]

After his entry into Port Arthur, Nogi conducted a ceremony on 14 January 1905, "bareheaded in the rain,"[169] for the repose of those who had died under his command.[170] He also expressed his sorrow in his poetry and letters.[171] In one poem-letter addressed to General Terauchi Masatake (1852–1919), the army minister, he spoke of inexpressible "anguish and humilia-

Generals Stoessel and Nogi. 1905. Unidentified photographer of the Mitsumura Toshimo Photographic Unit. Gelatin silver print. Japanese, taken 5 January 1905, printed after 27 January 1905. Collection of Jean S. and Frederic A. Sharf. Photograph © 2005 Museum of Fine Arts, Boston.

tion." There can be no question about his sense of guilt. "I have no excuse to offer to my sovereign and to my countrymen for this unscientific, unstrategical combat of brute force. . . ."[172]

Nogi did not return home after this nightmare of shameful victory. The fall of Port Arthur was a prelude to a long offensive by land and sea. In the decisive land battle of Mukden, Nogi and his Third Army played a supportive but not a major role. There was, of course, no role whatsoever for the army in the Japanese navy's destruction of the Russian fleet in the battle of Tsushima on 27–28 May 1905.

Tōkyō, 1906: Shameful Victory

During the ceremony that marked the surrender of Port Arthur, General Stoessel presented Nogi with a magnificent white Arabian horse, which Nogi accepted on behalf of the emperor.[173] Unlike his ancestor Sasaki Shirō Takatsuna, who was entrusted with his horse by his Lord Yoritomo before the battle had begun, Nogi received *his* horse after the battle had been won by another man. When Nogi returned home he was publicly celebrated as the hero of Port Arthur, sharing plaudits together with the "war god" of the Japanese navy, Admiral Tōgō Heihachirō (1847–1934). Nogi was unable to evade unwanted attention. Times were such that heroes had to be paraded in grand pageants for the edification of the masses. Takashi Fujitani has mapped the evolution of such "triumphal returns of military commanders at the head of their armies and naval forces."[174] In this, as in suicide committed for the sake of honor, the similarity to ancient Roman customs—triumphal processions and stoic suicides—is intriguing.

For his part, the emperor seemed pensive rather than jubilant in his reaction to the news of the fall of Port Arthur. He may have been saddened by the enormous losses on both sides. Donald Keene speculates that more than mere sadness may have been involved: "Perhaps the emperor, aware of the display of Japanese brutality at the time of the capture of Port Arthur from the Chinese ten years earlier, feared a recurrence."[175]

Whatever the emperor's mood, he had no objection to the honors heaped upon Nogi. The victorious general was sent to Europe, put on parade, and showered with effusive European admiration in letters, poems, and other laudatory documents that Mori Ōgai kindly translated for him.[176] Kaiser Wilhelm II awarded Prussia's "Pour le mérite" to both Port Arthur generals, the presumed Japanese winner and the actual Russian loser.[177] In short, Nogi became an official representative of Japan as a world power. It seems that the emperor needed a heroic Nogi as much as the humiliated Nogi needed the emperor—the one for life and the other for death. Yet there were limits to the pomp and glory that Nogi had to endure at home and abroad.[178] In the victory parade through Tōkyō in January of 1906, Nogi chose to ride an old nag in an inconspicuous position. The magnificent horse given him by Stoessel remained in its stable. At the emperor's reception that followed, Nogi stood out—to the dismay of the other dignitaries—for his battle-worn Port Arthur uniform. Normally quite attentive, if not obsessed, with his uniform,[179] Nogi seemed disoriented, presenting himself in shabby attire. Ironically, on this occasion, he appeared to emulate the emperor, who was notorious for appearing in a patched uniform.[180]

There were other signs of Nogi's extreme distress. As he read his report to the emperor on 14 January 1906, he choked up, sat on the floor, and wept.[181] He begged the emperor to allow him to die by seppuku,[182] but the emperor took his time, pondering the matter, and gave a reply overheard by a very few, who kept it secret until after Nogi's death: "I understand very well the feelings that make you want to apologize by committing seppuku, but this is not the time for you to die. If you insist on killing yourself, let it be after I have departed from this world."[183] No doubt Nogi came to interpret the emperor's words as permission for junshi, but at the time they must have had the ring of a life sentence in the prison of shame.

Robert Jay Lifton and his collaborators note that Nogi's "personalized relationship with the emperor . . . was not the norm in Meiji Japan but an aberration. His total identification with the emperor was an absolute loyalty not to an institution but to a person who transcended his own family and clan."[184] The option of disobedience seems not to have occurred to Nogi. He must have been in a state of despair when he composed a *kanshi* in which his poetic persona repudiated his military identity:

> Imperial troops, a million strong, conquered the arrogant enemy;
> But siege and field warfare left a mountain of corpses.
> Ashamed, what face can I show old parents?
> How many men have returned this day of triumphal song?[185]

The Emperor's Hand

That Nogi felt personally responsible for "a mountain of corpses" that included the body of his younger son is easy to understand. That his heavy sense of guilt was made even heavier by the burden of undeserved honors, bestowed by friend and foe alike, is also comprehensible. The emperor's reasons for denying Nogi's request to die are not as obvious as they seem at first glance. Did the emperor see that the pressures and demands on Nogi to take Port Arthur in 1904 as swiftly as he had in 1894 had exacted an immense human toll? Did he himself thus assume responsibility for his share in Nogi's military failures?

"If you insist on killing yourself, let it be after I have departed from the world." With these lapidary words Emperor Meiji not only explicitly imposed upon Nogi an excruciatingly long "life sentence";[186] he also, implicitly, called upon Nogi to perform what had long been an anachronistic ritual. Whether they intended to or not, the emperor and his general were reenacting junshi's classic pattern, whereby the supplicant asks permission to commit seppuku after his lord's death and the lord grants—or does not grant—that permission. But Nogi had not asked the emperor's permission to follow him in death. He asked only to be allowed to comply with the demands of honor, to die in order to atone for all the grief he had caused. Can it be that the emperor did not know what Nogi planned to do upon his demise? Permitting Nogi to commit seppuku only after his own death rather than when he wanted to was tantamount to ordering Nogi to commit junshi. The emperor's response was an aberration, an unseemly departure from tradition. Japanese lords did not command their vassals to postpone seppuku for cause x, y, or z so that they might, upon the death of their lord, commit junshi. Or did they? Such a scenario seems fit for a satire that we might envision in the Kabuki theater. After the fact, the scenario occasioned a mordant comment by the ultranationalist Tōyama Mitsuru (1855–1944). Noting that Komura Jutarō (1855–1911; minister of foreign affairs and plenipotentiary at the Portsmouth Peace Treaty) had died shortly before Emperor Meiji, Tōyama had quipped, "His Imperial Majesty must be pleased, for he is accompanied by Komura in the front and Nogi in the rear."[187]

Some serious questions remain. That Emperor Meiji had not allowed Nogi to die for intimately personal reasons denied Nogi freedom over his own body and enthralled him to his Imperial Highness (Tennō Heika). In his repeated denials of Nogi's wish the emperor staked a claim on Nogi's life. And in renouncing seppuku at the emperor's request, Nogi acknowledged this imperious claim. It was as if the renunciation were a promissory note to be redeemed at the moment of the emperor's death. It is in this sense that the emperor's unwritten will and Nogi's testament function together as a sacramental substitution for the emperor's explicit written permission to commit junshi. By not permitting him to die when he wished, the emperor—intentionally or not—contributed to Nogi's sense of lost honor; but the emperor's death was also the occasion for Nogi's redemption, his final atonement for the military disasters for which he felt he had been officially and undeservedly honored. In this sense, Nogi's junshi was also an act of restitution, replacing inauthentic with authentic honor.

Kindred Spirits

In *The Nobility of Failure* (1975), Ivan Morris argued that in Japan heroes are made not on the basis of their success but on the basis of their sincerity in the face of complete failure. Morris gives a fascinating account of Kusunoki Masashige (1294–1336), the hero of the Kenmu Restoration (1333–1336) that briefly restored imperial power. Masashige atoned for ultimate failure by sacrificing his life for Emperor Godaigo (1288–1339, r. 1318–1339). (In the popular imagination, his equestrian statue, erected in 1897 near the imperial palace in Tōkyō, has often been mistaken for a statue of General Nogi.)[188] Other great heroes fought not so much for the emperor as for what they believed was best for the country. Ōshio Heihachirō (1793–1837) was widely revered[189] for his failed Ōsaka uprising, the purpose of which was to save the people from starvation. For those attempting to understand Nogi's sense of suicidal honor, the most intriguing of the failures studied by Morris was that of Saigō Takamori (1827–1877), the leader of the Satsuma Rebellion and Nogi's immediate opponent in the fifty-day siege of Kumamoto castle.[190]

The Great Saigō (Dai Saigō) was posthumously celebrated as a national hero by the very powers he had opposed. The Meiji government he had helped create and then turned against eventually erected a monumental statue to him (and his dog) in Tōkyō's Ueno Park—this in honor of a man who never wanted his image reproduced in any shape or form and even refused the Emperor Meiji his request for a photograph.[191]

Nogi may well have been envious of the hero of the Satsuma Rebellion, not because Saigō led the last great national rebellion in Japanese history against what he felt to be a corrupt Meiji oligarchy, but because Saigō had wanted to die ever since the death of his lord Shimazu Nariakira in 1858. Saigō's first attempt at suicide was a farcical failure. He had agreed to join Gesshō (1813–1858), a priest of the Hossō sect at Kiyomizu-dera and an ardent imperial loyalist, in a double suicide (perhaps in the male-male erotic style of the Kagoshima warrior esprit [Kagoshima *shiki*]).[192] Gesshō, condemned to be executed by the *bakufu,* succeeded in drowning himself;[193] Saigō, like Nogi at Kumamoto, survived, neither able to accompany his friend Gesshō nor to follow his lord Nariakira into death.[194] A generation later, Saigō paid for his military failure in the Satsuma Rebellion by committing seppuku on 24 September 1877. This, at any rate, is the legend. In fact, it seems that Saigō, who had joined the rebellion reluctantly, was beheaded by Beppu Shinsuke (1847–1877) in an act of ritual kindness that spared Saigō a slow death from a mortal wound to the groin.[195] (In all likelihood, though, Nogi believed the legendary version of Saigō's death.)

The parallel here is even more striking than the parallel between Nogi's case and Masashige's. Nogi and Saigō shared a tendency to go into periodic retreat, sometimes in the form of self-imposed exile. Once drawn back into the world of politics, however, they engaged themselves with a vengeance, as if fiercely intent on destroying themselves and others. Saigō, for instance, was lured out of retreat in Kagoshima by the Korean dispute *(seikanron)* in 1873, which he wanted to solve single-handedly by undertaking an extremely dangerous diplomatic mission. (He insisted on serving as sole messenger in the hope of becoming a sacrifice, but his dream of martyrdom perished when the decision to despatch him as an envoy was rescinded.)[196] Nogi also oscillated between exile and frantic military engagement.

A more fateful point of comparison is that both Nogi and Saigō suffered from a death wish motivated by the deaths of the men closest to their hearts. They also shared a sense of having betrayed those closest to them. In addition to suffering the guilt of surviving a double suicide attempt, Saigō was distressed to find himself in deadly opposition to the Meiji leader Ōkubo Toshimichi (1830–1878), his former playmate, friend, and political ally.[197] Nogi was similarly aggrieved by the opposition of his brother in the Hagi Rebellion and suffered from a sense that he had betrayed him. In Nogi's case, the sense of betrayal was intensified when his mentor, Tamaki, testified to the sincerity of his political beliefs by committing seppuku. What most intriguingly distinguishes Nogi from Saigō is that Nogi's quest for suicidal honor was initially frustrated but eventually sponsored by none other than the emperor.

CHAPTER 4
The Sword and the Brush

Last Rites

Nogi intentionally timed his death on 13 September 1912 to coincide with the departure of Emperor Meiji's funeral cortege from the Imperial Palace at Nijūbashi in Tōkyō. Nogi was expected to be among the most esteemed of thousands of mourners. If the procession began at 8 p.m., the lineup must have begun quite some time before that. Ten thousand honor guards were part of the "massive funeral train" of over twenty thousand persons, and twenty-four thousand soldiers were positioned along the route.[1] (Some sources refer to seven thousand attending the funeral and three hundred thousand lining the streets.)[2] The concluding signal of the elaborate service came on 14 September, at 12:45 a.m., when the sound of cannon shook the capital, and "[s]ixty million people bowed in distant worship."[3]

Since he knew that a failure to appear at the palace for the cortege was certain to arouse suspicion, Nogi informed the authorities at noon on 13 September that he was ill.[4] His friend Mori Ōgai, the director of the Army Medical Corps, was present at the funeral. Ōgai's diary entry for 13 September somewhat laconically reads: "Was in attendance at the hearse on the way to Aoyama."[5] If Ōgai was there, it is inconceivable for Nogi's absence not to have been noted and discussed by the mourners. Nogi's sister-in-law found it "odd" that at 8 p.m. the general was still upstairs with his wife and had not yet departed for the funeral.[6]

To forestall discovery of the true reason behind his absence, Nogi had to begin his disembowelment before anyone could prevent him from his single-minded goal. If he began the procedure at 7:40 p.m., he might still have been alive at least to hear the cacophony of cannons, guns, and temple bells that announced the start of the funeral procession, but the exact timing of the Nogis' deaths is something of a puzzle. Carol Gluck maintains that Nogi and his wife committed ritual suicide at 7:40 p.m., "just as the funeral cortege was preparing to leave the palace."[7] Other scholars report that Shizuko's older sister did not hear strange noises from upstairs until after "the first cannon shot signaled the departure of the imperial hearse and the final passage of Emperor Meiji through the palace gates."[8] Nogi's home at 55 Shinzaka-machi in Akasaka-chō was two-thirds of the way toward the Aoyama Parade Grounds, the site of the funeral pavilion and the destination of the cortege. As they lay dying, Nogi and his wife may have heard the imperial carriage itself, drawn slowly by oxen, its wheels grinding gravel. It is more likely, however, since the four-kilometer-long cortege did not reach the Aoyama funeral hall until 10:56 p.m., that they heard only the distant booming of the cannonade of salutes that signaled the start of the procession and—in disconcerting disharmony—Buddhist temple bells tolling 108 times to mark the end of one era and the dawn of another.

Even if we cannot be sure about the position of the imperial cortege at the moment of Nogi's junshi, it is apparent that Nogi wanted his death to coincide with the emperor's funeral. After all, he could have committed junshi immediately after the emperor's death at 12:43 a.m. on 30 July 1912.[9] He had known for years that he had the emperor's implicit permission to follow him into death. He had certainly thought long enough about what he intended to do, but the exact time of the emperor's death was impossible to predict. Although the emperor had been ailing from diabetes and kidney failure since 1906, his death came unexpectedly and with relative speed, uremic poisoning having set in on 10 July. The first public statement of the emperor's serious condition was delayed until 20 July.[10] Knowing as we do how long Nogi had waited for his opportunity to commit seppuku, we can well imagine that he listened in his imagination to the critically ill emperor's every heartbeat as if it were his own, fully prepared to match his dying moment as precisely as possible.

Although the newspapers published the Imperial Household Ministry's medical bulletins that reported in unprecedented graphic detail the emperor's suffering from 20 July until his demise on 30 July, the emperor's death nonetheless left people in shock, for the medical bulletins that had stressed the emperor's "corporeality as never before" suddenly reversed the impression of imperial mortality by asserting that "his godly countenance remained in every respect unchanged from when he was alive."[11] Indeed, the emperor was treated as if he were still alive. High-ranking court ladies served the dead emperor his three meals a day until court ritualists took over the offering of foods on 13 August.[12] On that day, he was moved to the Throne Room, which was renamed *mogari no miya*[13] after the ancient temporary interment palace that housed deceased emperors for months or even years before the determination of the succession cleared the way for final burial.[14] The emperor's body remained in the *mogari no miya* for one month.

The emperor's paradox of life-in-death his general knew in reverse. Nogi realized that he could not resolve his own state of death-in-life before the

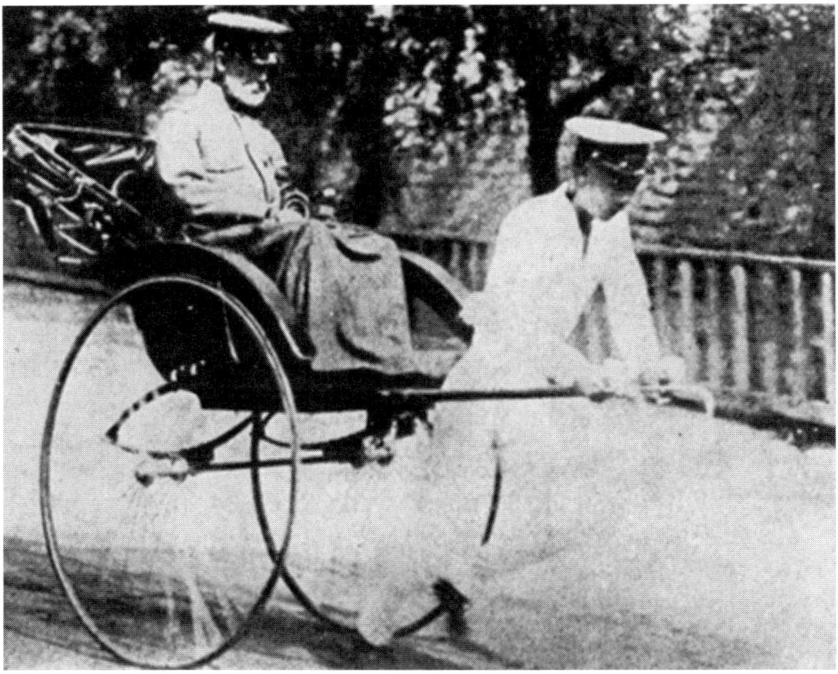

Snapshot of Nogi en route by *jinrikisha* to Emperor Meiji on 30 July 1912. Reproduced from Sasaki Hideaki, *Nogi Maresuke: yo wa shokun no shitei o koroshitari* (Kyōto: Mineruba shobō, 2005), p. 380.

emperor's paradox had been resolved. He had to make sure that his greatest moment carried precisely the right message. He solemnly situated that moment in the interval between the end of the emperor's lying-in-state and his Shintō funeral ceremony at the Aoyama Parade Grounds. As the emperor was transported in a spectacular pageant from one realm to the next, literally passing by Nogi's house, Nogi performed, in secrecy and without the customary second, the most violent spectacle of self-willed death known to the Japanese people. As rumors of the Nogis' junshi began to fly, even before the imperial ceremonies were over, it dawned on many that Nogi had eclipsed the Sun.

Nogi restored the practice of *mogari no miya* to its original meaning by performing actual junshi between imperial reigns. On the morning of the emperor's funeral, his spirit was installed "in the palace's Kiri Hall [where] his spirit would rest until a year later, when it would finally be enshrined along with the other imperial ancestors within the Kōreiden of the Palace Sanctuary."[15] While the emperor's spirit was enshrined in Tōkyō, his body was interred near the old capital. For his general, bodily separation, burial, and enshrinement occurred in the opposite direction, his body being buried in Tōkyō and his spirit enshrined at the foot of the emperor's mausoleum. It was as if each of these two separated selves—the emperor and the general—were reconstituted as part of one another.

Last Will

On 12 September, the night before the funeral, Nogi composed his testament.[16] It consists of ten articles[17] and is addressed to Yuji Sadamoto (his wife's older brother), Ōdate Shūsaku (Nogi's younger brother), Tamaki Masayuki (the son of Nogi's deceased younger brother, Makoto), and Shizuko (Nogi's wife). In this last document Nogi explains his complex motivations for suicide, arranges for the disposal of his property, including his own body, and decrees the entry of the Nogi family into the historical record. A last, unnumbered wish appoints Shizuko as executor of the testament and decrees that the Nogi line be extinguished with her death.

Nogi's directions for the disposal of his property were not at all unusual. The Ishibayashi house went to his brother Shūsaku, the Nakano house to his wife, Shizuko. Gifts from the emperor and the imperial family went to the Gakushūin in Tōkyō and the Chōfu Library in his hometown. These mundane stipulations provide no clues to the reasons for Nogi's junshi or to its significance. What stands out in the testament is Nogi's devotion to Emperor Meiji, his desire to preserve the written record of that devotion, and his determination that the Nogi line end with his death.

Nogi announces the reasons for his death in the first clause of his testament. He proclaims his intention to commit "suicide" *(jisatsu)* but at the same time he places this ordinary act within the context of "following in the wake of the emperor's death" *(jibun kono tabi miato o oitatematsuri jisatsu sōrō).* Nogi justifies his complex intentions by pointing to the sin *(tsumi)* of his losing the regimental flag *(gunki)* in 1877. Thwarted then in his desire to expiate his sin and recover his honor in an act of seppuku, he found himself "basking in the emperor's unending, overabundant favors to this day" *(kōon no atsuki ni yokushi konnichi made kabun no goyūgū o kōmuri).*[18] He acknowledges, in other words, that it was, symbolically, the emperor's horse he had received, just as Takatsuna had received Yoritomo's, and that he must honor the bond with the ultimate return gift of his life. Although he modestly refers to *"jisatsu,"* he knew that others would in fact regard his voluntary death as junshi.

Nogi's last will testifies that the dominating force throughout his adult life was fealty to Emperor Meiji. With the emperor's passing, Nogi was overwhelmed by a sense of purposelessness. It was the emperor who had ordered him to live when he wanted to die, and it was the emperor who had continued to honor him despite all his failures. Nogi's dedication to Meiji remained unwavering, too absolute and unique to be transferred to the emperor's successor. By not serving the future Emperor Taishō, Nogi followed the tradition exemplified by the seven retainers who committed junshi for the first Mōri daimyō, thereby demonstrating "their unwillingness to serve another master."[19] It was another striking indication of Nogi's dedication to Emperor Meiji that he valued the imperial gift of a gold watch above all else. He stipulated in his will that his nephew Tamaki Masayuki wear this gold watch only when in uniform, that is, only when visibly serving the Imperial State under Meiji's successor. Nogi's exact words were, "My gold watch, inscribed as a gift from the emperor, shall be given to Tamaki Masayuki. I would like to forbid him to carry it unless he wears military uniform" (onshi o wakatsu to kakitaru kindokei wa, Tamaki Masayuki ni tsukawashi sōrō hazu nari. Gunpuku igai no fukusō nite motsu o kinjitaku sōrō).[20] It is only fitting that the special Japanese term for "imperial gift" *(onshi)* should literally mean "bestowing an obligation."

Second only to Emperor Meiji in Nogi's consideration were his sons, both of whom had died in the Russo-Japanese War. It was their deaths in 1904 that transformed Nogi into the *"higeki no shōgun,"* the "tragic general."[21] Since Nogi planned to die the day after composing his testament, the only way to have extended his family line was to have availed himself of the respectable and frequently applied Japanese practice of adoption.[22] Adoption would have allowed him not only to preserve the high status of his family *(ie)* but also to ensure ancestor worship by his descendants. Yet he resolutely refused that option. He was no more able to adopt an heir than he was able to transfer his loyalty to the new emperor. Emperor Meiji and Nogi's sons, in their different ways, were equally irreplaceable. In his testament, Nogi specifically warns of the many difficulties associated with adoption. To underline his resistance not only to adoption but to any successor, he reveals his reluctance to appoint even an imaginary son to continue the line—although the *kazoku* status required him to do so. He asks only that his ancestral tombs be cared for by blood relatives.[23]

The government did not honor Nogi's wish to extinguish his line. Nogi's request "contradicted the state's hierarchical ideology" and "violated the Meiji state's policy of enshrining the family system, especially the nobility, as sacred extensions of the emperor."[24] The government overruled his testament and named an adoptive heir to the Nogi House. On 13 September 1915, despite public protest, the government elevated Mōri Motosato to the rank of count and appointed him to restore *(saikō)* the Nogi line.[25] By appointing a member of Chōshū's Mōri clan, a clan served by Nogi's father, to continue his line the government bestowed an explicitly abjured honor on Nogi.[26] Motosato resigned his nobility *(shaku-i)* in 1934.[27] Did he anticipate dark times for Japan and develop belated scruples about flouting the last will of Nogi Maresuke?

By abjuring adoption, Nogi seemed to have doomed himself to be one of Buddhism's unaffiliated dead *(muenbotoke)*, dependent for the appeasement of their souls on the goodwill of strangers willing to pray for them. Japanese religion, however, is a helix of Buddhism and Shintō. Although Nogi was literally a *muenbotoke*, his bond with Emperor Meiji virtually guaranteed him a place in the Shintō pantheon. In Chōfu and elsewhere, there are Nogi shrines built to honor him and his wife, his ancestors, and his two perished descendants. His blood sacrifice made him sacred, a *kami*, revered not by a limited number of descendants but rather by a nation. Junshi earned him the honor undeservedly bestowed upon him after the second capture of Port Arthur.

In the last numbered section of his testament, Nogi stipulates that his corpse be dissected to serve medical science and thus benefit the Japanese people. In a literal sense, Nogi intended nothing less than to offer himself as a sacrifice. It was as if he intended to inflict upon his own body all the battle wounds he had felt vicariously but not incurred physically. The dismemberment of his body in this unusual context bears eerie resemblance to the dissemination of Buddha relics. As René Girard and others have noted, violence often occurs in the context of a sacred ritual.[28] The violence done to Nogi's body by seppuku and by medical dissection was meant as a religious act intended, symbolically, to heal the wounds that his failures had inflicted upon the nation.[29] As Richard Barry argued in defense of Nogi's suicide, Shintō includes not only a belief in the materiality of the body but also a belief in the superiority of the spirit destined eventually to become a *kami*.[30]

Last Instructions

Traditionally, under special circumstances, a samurai's wife was expected to follow her lord (i.e., her husband) into death, just as her husband was expected to follow his lord into death. After she had witnessed her husband's disembowelment, she was to stab herself in the throat, piercing the carotid artery with a short dagger *(kaiken)*.[31] Nogi's wife, Shizuko, looms large in his testament, but there is no indication whatsoever that he expected her to act like a traditional samurai's wife. Rather, Nogi arranged for her future as his widow. He indicated how she was to live out her days, in which house, and in whose care. That he named her as executor of his testament is further evidence that he did not expect her to join him in junshi. Contrary to Nogi's expectations at the moment he signed his testament, Shizuko's dead body was found next to his. The common assumption is that she too committed junshi.

Kept ignorant of the details of the autopsy report, the public believed that double junshi had occurred in picture-book style, a belief passed on by the pioneers of Nogi scholarship in the West. In his study of Nogi's military career, Mark R. Peattie wrote that Shizuko looked on as Nogi "disemboweled himself in the manner prescribed by ancient ritual. A few moments afterward she picked up a dagger and, facing her husband, plunged it several times into her heart."[32] Ivan Morris wrote that "Madam Nogi, the perfect samurai wife, also killed herself."[33] To their account of Nogi's junshi, Robert Jay Lifton, Shūichi Katō, and Michael R. Reich added a footnote: "When Nogi composed his testament he evidently was unaware of his wife's intention to commit suicide with him."[34] Donald Keene observed laconically that Shizuko "stabbed her heart with a dagger."[35] A discord from Carol Gluck interrupted this chorus of agreement. She observed that Shizuko's death "received much less attention [than Nogi's]. Perhaps she might have expected this, having proved her loyalty to a man whom one eulogist described as disliking three things: priests, merchants, and women."[36] Noting that the imperial government suppressed "the full police medical report of the suicides," Gluck wondered if there were "clinical facts that might spoil the emerging heroic fiction."[37] There *was* at least one troublesome fact. The physician's report asserts that Nogi assisted his wife by guiding her daggered hand.[38] Toshiaki Kawahara went even further beyond the suspicion voiced by Gluck, suggesting that "Nogi had dealt her the fatal blow himself."[39]

The conflicting speculations about Shizuko's death raise a number of intriguing questions. Did Nogi falsify his testament in order to conceal from his wife his intent to murder her? This possibility sounds all too ghoulish and seems totally out of character. Did he falsify the testament because he intended, at the last moment, to request that she too commit junshi? This seems almost as unlikely. We are left with two possibilities. Was Shizuko's death a case of "assisted suicide" determined at the last moment by the two of them? Or did she decide, at the last moment, of her own uncoerced volition, to thrust the dagger into her heart (rather than into her throat), dying with her husband, although not quite in the prescribed manner of the traditional samurai wife? Before venturing an answer, we need to shift our focus from him to her.

Leaving aside for now the question of the exact degree of volition in her death, there can be no doubt that Shizuko had had a difficult life. Her husband had been living as though dead for the nearly thirty-five years that she had been married to him. In August 1878, the Satsuma bride was engaged to the Chōshū man in a marriage arranged by his mother.[40] Shizuko was from the distinguished Yuji family in Kagoshima.[41] The marriage came only a few months after Nogi had expressed his despair in the poem that ended with the line: "My self is nothing but a person spared death" *(waga mi wa sunawachi kore shi shite tami o amasu).*[42]

Although Nogi's mother had arranged the marriage, she disliked her daughter-in-law and treated her badly. As Nogi sought vainly to drown his sorrow in alcohol or to escape into sexual escapades, Shizuko fell into a depression that her unsympathetic mother-in-law did nothing to alleviate. It seems likely that Shizuko's life was cheered by the birth of her two sons, Katsusuke (August 1879) and Yasusuke (December 1881),[43] but she had to bear with her mother-in-law until her death in 1896.

As a woman bound to the customs of her time, Shizuko may never have had illusions about the role she played in her husband's life. One historian calls Nogi a "married misogynist."[44] The Nogis often "lived apart, he with his dominant and overpowering mother, his wife with the two sons of the marriage."[45] The 1904 campaign to capture Port Arthur brought additional distress. Just before her three men left for the Russo-Japanese War, Shizuko prepared a farewell dinner. "'Please show a smiling face at least for once,' she pleaded with her husband. Nogi looked sternly at her. 'This is not a smiling matter,' he said. . . . 'A father and two sons are going to the war,' he told her. 'None of us knows who will be killed first. There should be no funeral until all three are returned in coffins.'"[46] When the Nogis' eldest son died at Nanshan, Shizuko received a letter to that effect from her husband, even though he had told her earlier that she would hear nothing and that she should think of him "as if he did not exist." After Nogi's catastrophic losses at Port Arthur, followed by the death of their second son, she had to endure the public vilification of her husband and the stoning of their house.[47] If Shizuko had been able to feel her husband's pain as much as her own when their sons died, the tragedy might have knitted husband and wife more closely together. On the other hand, a troubling question may have distanced her from him even further. Could her husband, a general, not have prevented the loss of their sons?

Shizuko also suffered from Nogi's fanatical devotion to Emperor Meiji. What went on in Shizuko's mind between the emperor's death on 30 July 1912 and 13 September 1912 can only be conjectured. She apparently kept no diary. A document, "Haha no oshie" (A mother's instructions), emerged, however, that—if authentic—sheds some light on her views of the role of women at the end of the Meiji period.[48] Shizuko sent the document in a letter to her niece Teruko (1880–1950) giving her advice in marital matters. Teruko had lived in the Nogi household, but on account of her bad eyesight Nogi did not attempt to arrange for her marriage until 1912, when she was

Studio photograph of Nogi's wife Shizuko and the Nogis' two sons, Katsusuke and Yasusuke, taken in 1903, before the outbreak of the Russo-Japanese War. Collection of the Chōfu Municipal Museum, Shimonoseki.

already thirty-two years old. At that time, Shizuko accompanied her niece to Hokkaidō to be joined in marriage to the Ōmori family. Shizuko's letter of advice to Teruko was written only four months before her junshi and testifies to her belief in a woman's unflinching loyalty to her husband in sexual as in other matters. There is also an understanding that a Meiji woman should—gracefully—acquiesce in things that she might not feel like doing.

Sharalyn Orbaugh, commenting on Nogi's testament, notes with regret that Shizuko "left behind no testament to guide us in narrativizing her death."[49] Although Shizuko did not write an explanation of her actions, "Haha no oshie" suggests that she was resolved to die with her husband even if she might have preferred to live. Whether her husband confided in her or not, she must have wondered what he intended to do once the emperor was gone. Orbaugh assumes that Nogi let his wife know of his intentions and that she kept hers to herself: "although Shizuko was aware on September 12 of the General's intention to commit suicide the next day, he was not aware of hers (if indeed she had already formed the intention)."[50] Whatever he may have thought, it is difficult to believe that it was possible for her, in the wake of his junshi, to live on like an independent Taishō woman. How could Shizuko not fulfill her duty as the wife of a man so firmly grounded in the samurai ethos? What would people think if she did not follow him? What would she think of herself? Seeking fulfillment, Nogi did exactly what he had wanted to do since 1877. In all likelihood, Shizuko too sought fulfillment in death.

In short, whatever happened on 13 September 1912, it is difficult to see Nogi's assistance in his wife's junshi as anything other than consensual. And there is significance in the sequence of events. Unlike the samurai's wife who followed her husband into death after she had witnessed her husband's junshi, Shizuko was the first to die. For whom did she commit junshi? Women of her time were expected to observe the Confucian principle of serving men in the prescribed order of father, husband, son. Shizuko had no reason to die for members of her family of origin. Did she have reason to follow her husband in death? He was still alive. Was Shizuko's junshi intended for her two sons, or was it, most intriguingly, for the emperor, her great rival for Nogi's veneration and affection?

No matter how we answer the question of whom Shizuko intended to honor, the reversal of the normal order of double junshi casts her in unexpectedly unconventional roles. If it was her decision to die, which seems to be the case, then the reversal of order put Nogi in an odd position: it was as if she were honoring the emperor and he were, then, like a good samurai's wife, following her example.

There is still another, even more heroic, scenario imaginable for Shizuko. If Nogi had shown signs of hesitation, she might have gone first as a way to admonish and encourage him. This form of suicide, known technically as *kanshi*, also existed in ancient Rome, where it was much admired. A. Caecina Paetus, for example, had been condemned to death by the emperor Claudius for conspiracy in 42 C.E. His wife, Arria, stabbed herself, then handed him the dagger with words certain to shame him if he did not follow her example: "Paetus, it does not hurt" ("Paete, non dolet").[51]

Whether he intended it or not, Nogi had created exactly the kind of dilemma for Shizuko that Emperor Meiji had created for him. His testament arranged for her to survive him; the story of his life told her she should die.

Last Pictures

Clues to the thoughts of the fated couple may be found in the photographic record of their last days. Nogi wrote his testament on the evening of 12 September. The next morning he had himself photographed outside his home, in formal, even festive, attire. What was his purpose? Akutagawa Ryūnosuke (1892–1927) portrays, in his polemical story "Shōgun" (1922; The general, 1948), a young protagonist who suspects vanity, if not hubris, as a motive for Nogi's having his picture taken before committing suicide—with a sincerity no longer understood by younger generations.[52] To have one's picture taken is not only to affirm one's existence at a particular moment in time, but also to impose one's image upon posterity. Vanity, however, seems an implausible motive; Nogi's entire life was a protest against vanity and hubris.

Disagreeing with Akutagawa's young protagonist, we are nonetheless left with the task of interpreting the photographs. Despite claims to the contrary by Maurice Pinguet, the photographs do not present us with a pair of empty-eyed mannequins.[53] Nogi's face is covered by his white beard and moustache. In one of the photographs, made famous by Roland Barthes' classic study *L'empire des signes* (1970), the military hat shading his eyes half-conceals their expression.[54] If anything, there seems to be a hint of amusement in his almost jovial face. His posture is upright but relaxed, remarkably so considering that he is formally posed in a Western-style military uniform, encumbered by all his many military decorations. He holds white gloves in his right hand. Dangling from beneath his left hand, near his lower abdomen, is his long sword, its tip resting, cane-like, on the gravel. His headdress is three times as large as his head, which emphasizes his prominence as a public figure. He looks like a military man indisputably at ease with himself.

It is remarkable not only that Nogi had his photograph taken but that Shizuko's was taken as well, on the same site but not side by side. (Was the visual separation meant to signal the expectation that she was soon to live without her husband?) Her face is fully exposed, with hair flattened and drawn back. She is a woman without makeup, apparently without pretensions. Her full lips are tightly sealed and her small eyes stare straight ahead, without identifiable emotion. In contrast to her exposed face, her body is completely wrapped, as if in an archaic form of soft armor, in a formal wide-sleeved robe worn over a divided trouser skirt. Only the knuckles of her right hand, holding a folded fan tight against her stomach, protrude from beneath the cicada-shell robes. Husband and wife stand on the same graveled spot near the stone steps leading to their wooden house. In order to fit the general's military hat with its enormous white plume into the photograph, the photographer had to take Nogi's picture from a slightly greater distance than Shizuko's.[55] This creates the illusion that Shizuko is physically larger than her husband.

In *L'empire des signes* (1970), Barthes, who was totally ignorant of the Japanese language, sought to construct a fictive Japan through nonverbal materials. He was fascinated by these two enigmatic photographs. Barthes' caption reads: "They are going to die, they know it [for Nogi's photograph] and this is not seen [for Shizuko's photograph]." He interprets their poses as a denial of interpretation. Their facial expressions are blank, "as though emerged from water, rinsed of meaning." Him he sees as lost in his military uniform and decorations; her he sees as revealing her entire face yet remaining inscrutable, fittingly, because "Death was the meaning."[56] To come upon these apparently unremarkable photographs—as Barthes did—with knowledge of the acts that occurred only a few hours after the photographs were taken is awesome in the original sense of the word.

Sharalyn Orbaugh objects to Barthes' description of Shizuko's face as—in Orbaugh's paraphrase of Barthes—"frustatingly stupid, silent, uninformative." She interprets Barthes' reading as his obtuse "refusal" to see that "the death or madness of women" is "partly the result of modernism's specular fascination with woman-as-dead-body." In this critique of Barthes, Orbaugh expresses her fear that "a woman's own decision to die may be viewed by the world as just another death engendered, fantasized, romanticized, legislated, ultimately brought about by the needs and desires, the narratives of the patriarchy."[57] Orbaugh objects to the notion that Shizuko, like a piece in a row of upright dominoes, simply reacted to her husband's reaction to Emperor Meiji's death.

Orbaugh's feminist approach is a welcome correction to interpretations that have dismissed Shizuko as a mindless cipher, but we should give the pioneer of postmodernism his due. His language is poetic and suggestive rather than rational, analytic, and judgmental. The main point of his chapter on "The Written Face" is to remind us of the impossibility of adequately representing the meaning of death. Assuming that Shizuko had made up her mind to die, Barthes describes her face with provocative, questionable (he literally attaches question marks), and purposely contradictory adjectives: "impassive? stupid? dignified? peasant-like?"[58] It is the ultimate indescribability of death that he sees paradoxically inscribed upon Shizuko's face. He communi-

Nogi Maresuke. Photograph taken on the morning of 13 September 1912. Félicien Challaye, *Le Japon illustré* (Paris: Librairie Larousse, 1915), p. 29.

cates the conviction that Shizuko had a mind of her own, one that she was not willing to reveal. Her expression seems to be an accomplishment that asks for interpretation while Nogi, "lost in his beard, his kepi, his decorations, has almost no face at all."[59] He hides behind his facade while she stands out in bold relief, calmly interrogating death from behind her mask of dignified domesticity.

Nogi Shizuko. Photograph taken on the morning of 13 September 1912. Félicien Challaye, *Le Japon illustré* (Paris: Librairie Larousse, 1915), p. 29.

Last Words

To underline his purpose, a person committing seppuku or junshi customarily composes a farewell poem *(jisei)*, a literary counterpart to his more legalistic testament. Unlike the testament, which is usually written long before the day of death is known, the poem's composition is traditionally timed to coincide with one's death. These poignant circumstances demand the utmost self-control, and the stroke of the brush is intended to demonstrate just that. Even though the farewell poem is sometimes preceded by Buddha invocations or includes them *(geju)*, thus embedding last words and actions in a conventional religious context, *jisei* most forcefully constitutes a deliberate individual expression of the will to die. The scholar Nakanishi Susumu defines *jisei* as a poem on the discovery of one's genuine self at the point of death.[60]

Before committing junshi, Nogi wrote two *jisei*.[61] They highlight his lord as a *kami*, and himself as a revering subject. His first *jisei* begins with thick brushstrokes, the thickness repeated in lines three and five (my emphasis):

Kami agari	God-like
agarimashinuru	has he now ascended,
ōkimi no	our great lord,
mi-ato haruka ni	and his august traces, from afar,
orogami matsuru	do we humbly revere.[62]

In the second poem shown here, the calligrapher's flow of fresh ink links the central kanji—"ōkimi"—with the first character in the last line—"ware," or "I" (my emphasis):

Utsushi yo o	It is I who go,
kami sarimashishi	following the path
ōkimi no	of the great lord
mi-ato shitaite	who has departed
ware wa yuku nari	this transient world![63]

As Orbaugh noted, Shizuko left no testament and did not narrativize her death, but she did compose "one death poem (to his two)." In Orbaugh's translation:

Having heard that
once departed there is no
day of return,
how sad it is to encounter today
the royal procession![64]

In Shizuko's words:

Idemashite	I hear there is no
kaerimasu hi no	Sun to return,

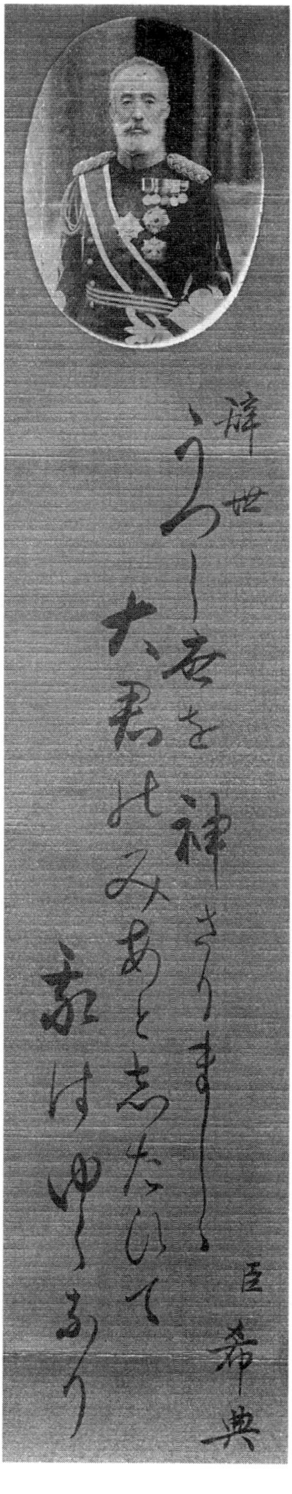

Narrow slip of paper (*tanzaku*). Taishō reproduction of Nogi Maresuke's photograph (half-length portrait, without hat), taken on 13 September 1912, with one of his two last poems, copied in his hand in ink on gold-colored paper with calligraphy rearranged to conform to the *tanzaku* format. Collection of the author.

nashi to kiku	as He departed—
kyō no miyuki ni	So sad to face
au zo kanashiki	the august procession today—

Shizuko's hand is uniformly delicate and devoid of emphasis.

Orbaugh sees only "anomie" in Shizuko's last poem and insists that, whatever action she might have taken upon learning of her husband's intentions, "None of these choices would be valorized (if even recognized as choices) by critics or historians looking for overt political activity, vocal resistance on the part of an autonomous individual to the institutionalized oppression of the state."[65] Orbaugh concludes that Shizuko's "refusal to narrativize her life and death may be seen as the only possible gesture of resistance to a hostile discursive economy."[66]

Yet it is only by today's ideals of gender equality that it has become possible to detect "anomie" in Meiji women's lives. In their own setting, however, Meiji women were not likely to have been without a degree of control of their situations. It is perfectly conceivable that Shizuko spoke her own mind in this poem and then freely committed suicide without following Nogi or anyone else in death. Whether Shizuko committed suicide despite or in agreement with Nogi's wishes, her act was antithetical to his. Her *jisei* can be read as a critique of her husband's junshi. At the center of her poem is, literally, an eclipse of the sun. She notes, symbolically, an irreversible imperial absence. Whereas Nogi's two farewell poems express his determination to follow his departed lord and, by implication, to join him in another world, Shizuko's poem is resigned to the reality of a death that permits no such reunions.[67] Despite the depth of her hopelessness, her *jisei* is an emblem of equanimity and resolution. Her image of a sun that will not return is more stoic than her husband's hopeful imagery of ascension and reunion. Her poem is—dare one say it?—closer than his to the way of the samurai.

The End of an Era

The Meiji Restoration of 1868 brought many changes to Japan. The emperor symbolically recovered—through his Meiji oligarchs—a measure of the political power the Tokugawa shōguns had exercised for more than two hundred and fifty years. With the centralization of the state in the person of the emperor, ancient customs and Shintō religious practices were revived in order to anchor the Japanese people more firmly to their past and to give them a stronger sense of indigenous tradition. Buddhism, the borrowed religion, was generally "associated with a decrepit bakufu."[68] It was driven into decline and fell into disfavor after the religious separation edict *(shinbutsu bunri rei)* of 1868. Although Buddhism had so thoroughly dominated the rituals of death that one speaks of "funeral Buddhism" *(sōshiki bukkyō)*, early Meiji ideologists decided to institute Shintō funerals, in the belief "that those who controlled death controlled life."[69] At the same time, the Meiji regime ushered in a new period of cultural borrowing, this time from the West rather than from China or Korea. The "invented traditions"[70] of a new nationalism based on ancient roots was a counter to the lure of Western tastes. It is no surprise that Emperor Meiji received a Shintō funeral, modeled on the Shintō funerary rites first performed in 1897 for Empress Dowager Eishō (1834–1897), the chief consort of his father, Emperor Kōmei.[71] Since Shintō abhors pollution and celebrates purification, such a funeral seems to be a contradiction in terms.[72] Only by resolutely denying that the emperor's corpse was impure was it possible to justify a Shintō funeral for the divine person of the emperor.[73]

Nogi exercised respectful restraint by waiting forty-five days beyond the thirty-five years he had waited to die. Between the onset of the emperor's illness and the day of the funeral, Nogi appeared at the palace to pay his respects 130 times in 56 days.[74] A dramatic turning point seems to have come on 20 August 1912, when Nogi, who had fasted and gone into an alarming physical decline, attended an imperial wake. He observed with disapproval and disdain the many high officials whose mourning seemed perfunctory and insincere. According to Togawa Yukio, Nogi's appearance then brightened, because he suddenly realized when and what to do to convey his last lesson to the whole nation.[75]

Emperor Meiji's final resting place was not the Aoyama Cemetery to which his funeral cortege took him on the day of Nogi's junshi. After a fifteen-hour ride by steam train, the symbol of modernity, he was interred in the imperial mausoleum *(goryō)* in Fushimi-Momoyama on the southeastern outskirts of Kyōto.[76] Four years later an impressive Nogi Shrine was erected at the foot of the grand approach to the emperor's Fushimi-Momoyama mausoleum. The Chinese cottage that Nogi had used as his headquarters during the 1904 siege of Port Arthur was brought there to serve as his memorial hall.[77] These symbolic placements—reminiscent of ancient *junsō*—testify to Nogi's lifelong and posthumous worship of Emperor Meiji, whom he followed into death.

PART III

Nogi in Literature

CHAPTER 5

Mori Ōgai's Junshi Stories

Among the mourners in Emperor Meiji's funeral procession on 13 September 1912 was Nogi's friend and military colleague, the writer and army surgeon general Mori Ōgai (1862–1922). When rumors of the Nogis' death reached Ōgai in the early morning hours of 14 September, he was shaken to the core and confessed in his diary that he "half believed, half doubted it" *(yo hanshin hangi su)*.[1] Ōgai had known Nogi as a military man and man of letters since the two of them had studied in Berlin in 1887.[2] Mori Oto (1889–1967)[3] noted his father's fondness for Nogi, which Yoshiyuki Nakai characterized as "a deep respect and admiration for this archetypal samurai born in the wrong century."[4] In his sublimated response to the emperor's death and Nogi's junshi, Ōgai became the curator of cultural memory.[5]

A significant change in the nature of Ōgai's writing occurred in the aftermath of the Nogis' death. Alan Wolfe, a literary critic who has explored the connections between Japan's modernization and suicidal narratives, clearly identifies Nogi's junshi as an "event that catalyzed a turn in Ōgai's own literary production. He shifted from his twenty years of writing fiction in modes inspired by Western naturalism and German romanticism and began a series of works of historical fiction."[6] In other words, Ōgai abandoned the sort of fiction that had made his reputation. Rather than seeking to repeat the success of his serialized novel *The Wild Goose (Gan)*, which appeared in *Subaru* from September 1911 to May 1913,[7] he turned to historical fiction. In writing about Nogi's junshi, Ōgai, unlike Sōseki, did not invent contemporary characters but seized upon historical figures whose plight resembled Nogi's.

"Okitsu Yagoemon no isho" (October 1912; The last testament of Okitsu Yagoemon) was Ōgai's immediate reaction to Nogi's death. Ōgai wrote the first version of this very short narrative on the spur of the moment, in the five-day interlude between Nogi's junshi and his funeral. This version of the story was submitted to *Chūō Kōron* on 19 September, the day after Ōgai accompanied Nogi's funeral bier. Almost as soon as this literary funeral offering appeared, Ōgai began to revise it. The second version was finished in early April 1913 and published in *Iji* on 15 June 1913. As if this were not evidence enough of his obsession with Nogi's junshi, Ōgai also wrote "Abe ichizoku" (The Abe family), completed in November 1912, published in the January 1913 issue of *Chūō Kōron,* and republished on 15 June 1913 in *Iji.* "Abe ichizoku" was quickly followed by a third historical novella, "Sahashi Jingorō," first published on 1 April 1913 in *Chūō Kōron.* The Nogi-inspired sequence of historical fiction concluded with "Sakai jiken" (February 1914; The incident at Sakai)—the story (discussed separately, in Chapter 6) that most profoundly dramatizes the vicissitudes of suicidal honor during Japan's transition from the Tokugawa to the Meiji era.

"Okitsu Yagoemon no isho" (First Version): Junshi Postponed

In the first version of "Okitsu Yagoemon no isho," Ōgai captures the rationale for junshi expressed by a retainer of the Hosokawa clan. While fulfilling a special request of his lord, this retainer finds himself responsible for the unintended death of another retainer. Because Yagoemon's request to commit seppuku to atone for this death is not granted, he decides to wait until his natural death is imminent before committing junshi for his Hosokawa lord.

According to Yagoemon's testament (first version), which Ōgai fabricated on the basis of two historical sources named in his appended note to the reader, Yagoemon committed junshi in 1658, on the thirteenth anniversary of his lord Tadaoki's death, but the two sources contradicted each other concerning two questions: when did Yagoemon make his fateful trip to Nagasaki and on which anniversary of Lord Tadaoki's death did he commit junshi? Since Ōgai hastened to finish the story by the day of Nogi's funeral as a tribute to his friend, he lacked time fully to research the historical facts. Instead, he decided to follow neither of his sources. He set the interval between Yagoemon's journey (1624) and his junshi (1658) at thirty-four years, thereby making it virtually the same as the interval between Nogi's initial trauma (1877) and his junshi (1912). At the time of their junshi, both Yagoemon and Nogi were about sixty-four years old.[8] That Ōgai was more intent, in this first version of the story, on creating parallels to Nogi than on eliminating errors of fact is apparent from Yagoemon's reference to committing junshi despite a law prohibiting it—even though the law was not passed until 1663.[9]

The Hosokawa clan is so important to Ōgai's story that it warrants a brief history. The Hosokawa came from a branch of the Ashikaga and helped Ashikaga Takauji (1305–1358) found the Muromachi shōgunate in the 1330s. The Hosokawa served as military governors *(shugo)* and shōgunal deputies *(kanrei).* They reached the height of their influence with Hosokawa Katsumoto (1430–1473), a man whose politics helped trigger the Ōnin War (Ōnin *no ran,* 1467–1477) and whose devotion to Zen inspired him to found Ryōan-ji in Kyōto. During a century of warfare (*sengoku jidai,* 1467–1570), the Hosokawa maintained their hold on power by associating themselves with Japan's three great unifiers. Hosokawa Yūsai Fujitaka (1534–1610) played a prominent role as poet and scholar under Oda Nobunaga (1534–1582) and Toyotomi Hideyoshi (1537–1598). His son Tadaoki (1563–1645) fought under Tokugawa Ieyasu (1542–1616) in the battle of Sekigahara (1600). By 1632 the Hosokawa had established themselves as one of the most important outer *(tozama)* daimyō of the Higo domain.[10]

Ōgai's story is set in the seventeenth century, when warriors were frustrated by the lack of opportunity to distinguish themselves in battle or to defend their honor in duels. In this constraining context, seppuku became more common, and there was a "sudden rise in the incidence of *junshi,*" which Eiko Ikegami sees as "a sign of . . . reflexive aggression."[11]

In Ōgai's story, the Hosokawa retainer Yagoemon is, at the time he tells his story and prepares to kill himself, concerned about his "posthumous reputation." As someone who took the tonsure five years earlier in order to pray for the heir of the Hosokawa clan, he knows he should be aloof from worldly concerns but admits, "at heart I am a warrior" (47; 2:379: konjō wa moto no bushi nareba, shigo no myōmon no mottomo taisetsu ni zonji). Yagoemon's suicide note is framed by defensive statements in anticipation of public reaction to junshi. He categorically rejects the anticipated charges of senility and derangement—charges that also haunted Nogi's junshi. He entrusts his last words to his intimate, the priest Seigan at Daitokuji, to be transmitted to his relatives in Kumamoto.

As in Nogi's case, Yagoemon desires that all traces of his physicality disappear, except for the obligatory "fingernail" to be sent as a memento to his family in Kumamoto. The trivial exception of the fingernail underlines his desire to spiritualize and sacralize his entire life and relationships not only by having his body cremated but also by burning the memorial tablets of the three Hosokawa lords (Tadaoki, Tadatoshi, and Mitsuhisa) under whom he had served.

The events that led to Yagoemon's junshi began in Kumamoto more than thirty years before the narrative present. (The place and time must have reverberated with Ōgai's readers, who were trying to come to terms with Nogi's 1912 junshi and with his loss of the imperial colors in Kumamoto thirty-five years earlier.) There it was that Yagoemon had served his Lord Shōkōji (Hosokawa Tadaoki's Buddhist name). Pursuant to his lord's command that he obtain a rare article for the tea ceremony, Yagoemon and one of his peers traveled to Nagasaki to meet a ship from Annam (part of modern

Vietnam) that happened to be carrying a tree of precious aloeswood, ideal for the manufacture of incense. Yagoemon spots this tree as just the sort of prize his lord might want him to bring back for the tea ceremony, and he is reinforced in his assessment of the wood by a retainer of Lord Date Masamune (1567–1636), who has come all the way from Sendai on a similar mission.

Yagoemon enters into a deadly debate with his companion, whom he expected to stand by him in outhaggling Lord Date's retainer. Yagoemon's practical companion does not consider a piece of wood worth the high sum that might be better spent on weapons. For Yagoemon, however, honoring his lord's wish is paramount, provided "it was not contrary to moral principles" (48; 2:381). The battle of words becomes vicious when Yagoemon's companion begins to ridicule Yagoemon's devotion to the way of tea. When Yagoemon responds by charging his companion with boorishness, the infuriated man reaches for his sword and swings at him "out of the blue" (49; 2:381). Caught by surprise, Yagoemon parries with a bronze vase used for ikebana (an artifact associated, ironically, with the tea ceremony). The skillful parry gives him time to retrieve his sword, with which he kills the aggressor. Although he has acted in self-defense, he is nonetheless guilty of killing one of his lord's retainers.

What did the military code of the time prescribe for such an offense? A century earlier, during the era of *sengoku daimyō* (warlords of a country at war), 1467–1570, the "practice of *jiriki kyūsai* (self-redress of grievances)" had prevailed among vassals, but the warlords of Yagoemon's time sought to curb the autonomy of the individual samurai and to enforce conformity. They adhered to the law of *kenka ryōseibai,* which dictated "equally severe punishment of all parties to a quarrel regardless of the reason behind the conflict."[12]

Yagoemon finds himself caught in a bind between these two codes. Although he is now free to purchase the bole of aloeswood for his lord, he can no longer rejoice in the accomplishment. He appears in front of his lord with a cultural prize greatly enhancing the Hosokawa reputation, and then quietly asks for "permission to commit *seppuku*" (49; 2:382). It is important to note that in Yagoemon's case, as in Nogi's, the original request is for seppuku, not junshi. In both cases, the request is denied because the authorities consider their subjects' display of loyalty and devotion more important than the illicitly violent act that occurred in the course of their doing their duty.

Ōgai deals here with a crucial point. What motive lies behind a daimyō's clemency? Not only has Yagoemon demonstrated unquestioning loyalty, he is also willing to die for his actions. His lord is understandably flattered by his devotion. Such men of "moral principle" (48; 2:381) can be trusted to remain loyal under duress. Such men one must keep in reserve for future service. In other words, the denial of Yagoemon's request to die is construed not only as a generous act of clemency but also as self-interested calculation. In addition, the recipient of clemency may well some day repay the favor by committing junshi, which would enhance the glory of his lord far more than mere seppuku.

The bole of aloeswood, transformed into incense, proves to be such a tremendous success only because it was purchased—metaphorically—with human blood. Lord Date of Sendai, who receives some of the incense from the aloeswood as a kind of consolation prize, calls it "Shibafune ['the firewood boat']" (51; 2:383).[13] When Lord Shōkōji's son Tadatoshi presents the incense at court, the emperor names it "Shiragiku [white chrysanthemum]" (50; 2:382), a poetic expression from an ancient poem. Yagoemon weeps with joy at the thought of the emperor's praise—but only, he hastens to inform readers of his testament, because he had "already decided to commit *seppuku* and secretly waited for an appropriate occasion" (50; 2:382). The analogy with Nogi is unmistakable.

There are other analogies—or associations—that are much less obvious. In Yagoemon's time, the way of tea, which plays such a central role in Ōgai's story, was intricately connected in people's minds with lord–retainer relationships and with seppuku. The great tea master Sen no Rikyū (1522–1591) was ordered by his lord and tea disciple, Toyotomi Hideyoshi, to commit seppuku after he and Rikyū differed on matters of state policy. Rikyū's disciple, Furuta Oribe (1543–1615), was ordered to commit suicide after he betrayed his lord, Tokugawa Ieyasu (1542–1616), during the 1615 siege of Ōsaka Castle.[14]

Ōgai's Yagoemon is given many important tasks by his retired lord's successor, Hosokawa Tadatoshi (1586–1641). In the 1637 campaign against Shimabara, Yagoemon hopes to die as a *hatamoto* (a direct vassal of the shōgun) but, like Nogi risking his life for the emperor at Kumamoto, this was not to be. He reverts to thoughts of seppuku. Having obeyed his emperor's order to live, Nogi waited only as long as the emperor's funeral before committing junshi. In contrast, Yagoemon serves several of his lord's successors. Then, in quick succession, those with the power to grant his wish begin to pass away. Yagoemon's younger lord (Tadatoshi) dies in 1641, followed by his lord's father (Tadaoki) in 1645. Tadatoshi's son Mitsuhisa (1619–1649)[15] dies four years later. These deaths, at remarkably regular four-year intervals, intensify Yagoemon's frustration. His lords are dying, and he is still denied the privilege of seppuku. He realizes the irony of his prolonged survival. If he does not act soon, he might simply die of old age. Which leaves him only the possibility of junshi. Only by subverting the will of the other and asserting his own can he ensure a posthumous tie to his lord.

It is not until 1653, when Mitsuhisa's eleven-year-old son Tsunatoshi[16] is appointed lord of Etchū, that Yagoemon begins to see the end of the tunnel. Even then, however, Yagoemon lives on for another five years, committing junshi—without permission—on the thirteenth anniversary of his lord's death. Waiting in excess allows Yagoemon to demonstrate to critics of his tardiness that he chose death by seppuku without regrets and refused to die a less painful, natural death from old age.

By the time Yagoemon finally decides to assert his will and commit junshi without permission, death has become for him such an anticipated reward that his feelings can only be described as ecstatic: "I secretly jumped for joy" (51; 2:383). On this, his last and greatest day, rivalled only by the day of mixed blessings when he obtained the bole of aloeswood, he can even be lightheaded and a little puckish: "I have been writing this note by the light of a candle which has just gone out. But there is no need to light another. There is sufficient reflection from the snow at the window to enable me to cut across my wrinkled stomach" (51; 2:383).

Apropos of Yagoemon's delayed seppuku, Richard Bowring asks "whether a suicide postponed for so long can really be justified."[17] This is a difficult question under any circumstance, but all the more so here because acts of junshi are no ordinary suicides. The answer to Bowring's question seems to be that Ōgai's complicated chronology serves to underline—and subvert—the apparent arbitrariness of our life spans. It is precisely in the face of such arbitrariness that Yagoemon, like the venerated Buddhist ascetics depicted in *ōjōden* (Buddhist accounts of rebirth in the Pure Land) or the Chan/ Zen masters, gains control over his own death. He can predict the day of his passing because he can set the date. His calculations are religiously inspired. Bernard Faure's comments on Buddhist techniques for controlling the time of death are relevant here: "The death of a Chan/ Zen master was dramatized as a ritual 'representation' of the Buddha's *parinirvâṇa*. The first duty of a master, and the proof that he had truly reached awakening, was to predict the day of his own death." If Yagoemon conferred on his community the benefits that the Buddhist masters conferred on theirs, then the act of dying "constitutes an apotheosis of his deeds and gestures, a ritualized and collective event determined in its slightest details by the *imaginaire* of the community."[18]

As far as Yagoemon is concerned, there was never any doubt about his intention to commit junshi—but later rather than sooner, after he had dutifully served all the lords whom he felt honor-bound to serve. His philosophy is to make his violent death coincide as closely as possible with his own natural death rather than his lord's. His point is that it is never too late for junshi.

Nogi, by contrast, concluded that Emperor Meiji's funeral was his necessary terminus ad quem. For him, his lord was a divinely awe-inspiring figure whom the lamentably inadequate Emperor Taishō could never replace. For Nogi, there simply could be no one quite like Emperor Meiji.[19] When *he* went, it was time for Nogi to follow him.

"Sahashi Jingorō": Anything But Seppuku

"Sahashi Jingorō," Ōgai's third historical novella,[20] stands in stark contrast to "Okitsu Yagoemon" in that the eponymous hero commits culpable—or at least morally questionable—actions and does *not* choose atonement by means of seppuku. The story, which fits neatly into the genre of the cautionary tale, was published on 1 April 1913 in *Chūō Kōron* and republished along with the revised "Okitsu Yagoemon no isho" and "Abe ichizoku" on 15 June 1913.[21] Ōgai originally named the collection *Itsujihen* (Collection of unknown matters), but was asked to change the title to *Iji* (Willpower).[22] The title alludes pointedly to such qualities of Japanese warrior culture as pride, backbone, iron will, and even an eccentric stubbornness. Ōgai himself described Sahashi Jingorō (1561?–?) as "a cross-grained man of tenacious *iji*" (my translation; 2:451: *iji tsuyoki sunemono*).[23]

"Sahashi Jingorō" differs pointedly from the first version of "Okitsu Yagoemon" in its treatment of the lord–retainer relationship. In this story, Ōgai portrays a retainer of Tokugawa Ieyasu, who is endowed with the same fine aesthetic sensibility that characterizes the Hosokawa retainer Yagoemon. While Yagoemon possessed an intuitive appreciation of incense as a tea artifact, Jingorō excels in the *bushi* arts of the flute and the sword. The two retainers part ways entirely in their degree of loyalty toward their lords. In comparing these two sets of main characters, it is important to bear in mind that "Sahashi Jingorō" takes place about half a century earlier than "Okitsu Yagoemon," "when the total subservience of servant to lord was not yet an established ethic."[24]

In these two stories, the retainers—who are driven by very different values—perform tremendous feats and thereby provoke the moral judgment of their lords. Whereas Lord Tadaoki understands—and sanctions—Yagoemon's killing of another retainer as an act of self-defense committed in the process of obtaining a most precious article for the lord's tea ceremony, Ieyasu, although impressed by Jingorō's skills, becomes wary of actions that appear to enhance the retainer's rather than his lord's reputation. As Ieyasu hints to one of Jingorō's defenders, "Your account seems to make Jingorō's motives and actions seem reasonable, although such is really not the case" (251; 2:93–94).

The Heron and the Wager

What does Jingorō do to make Tokugawa Ieyasu uneasy? He wins a wager and kills the welsher who balks at Jingorō's technically justified but ethically unacceptable demand for payment. This comes about after the sixteen-year-old Jingorō and several other youths in service to Ieyasu's oldest son, Matsudaira Nobuyasu (1559–1579), spot a heron in the distance. "One of the pages asked if the bird were in range. Most in the group seemed finally to agree the bird was too far off. Jingorō said nothing at first; *but after all the others concluded that the bird was impossible to shoot,* he spoke, *as if talking to himself,* 'I wouldn't say that it was entirely impossible . . .' " (my emphasis, 250; 2:91). Another page, Hachiya, calls him on this, betting that Jingorō cannot shoot the heron. Hachiya's stake is "betting anything he had with him at the time" (my translation; see 250; 2:91: *ima koko ni motte iru mono o nan de mo kakō*).[25] Jingorō proves his marksmanship by shooting the heron. Having won the wager, the stake he claims is the surrender of Hachiya's ancestral swords. Hachiya, of course, had never dreamed that anyone would make such an extravagant demand. When Hachiya refuses to comply, Jingorō immediately deals him a blow with such virtuosity that not a mark is found on the body.[26] Not waiting to see whether or not the blow was lethal, he then flees with Hachiya's swords. That he realizes he has transgressed by taking matters into his own hands—executing justice by exchanging Hachiya's heirloom swords with his own—is evident from his flight.

Unlike Yagoemon, who obtains and delivers the "prize" of aloeswood coveted by his lord, Jingorō acts in this episode in response to his own desire rather than that of his lord. While Yagoemon has carefully intuited his lord's wishes, Jingorō acts to please himself rather than his master. In Ieyasu's critical eyes, Jingorō acted on his own, without his lord's knowledge or approval. It is, moreover, in self-defense that Yagoemon kills his companion in their dispute over the worthiness, in *bushi* terms, of Lord Tadaoki's desire for incense. Whereas it is self-righteousness that compels Jingorō to strike Hachiya for not honoring their wager.

Tadaoki and Ieyasu evaluate their retainers' excesses quite differently. Tadaoki understands that Yagoemon selflessly responded to his request for a prized tea artifact. Ieyasu understands that Jingorō himself, while under his son Nobuyasu's command, turned the heron into a prize and placed a wager on killing it for personal gain. Both Yagoemon and Jingorō cause a death in their disputes over their respective "prizes," the first reluctantly, upon provocation by his companion, and the second at his own volition; but Jingorō is more culpable. Like his son Nobuyasu, with whose consent and rifle the heron was shot, Ieyasu understands that Jingorō had an indisputable right to profit from Hachiya's thoughtlessness; but Ieyasu cannot approve of the callously exorbitant demand for Hachiya's ancestral swords. In making that demand, Jingorō lacked respect for Hachiya and—by implication—for his lord. It becomes clear, as the fateful action unfolds, that the slain heron—a bird of majestic beauty—is symbolic of the samurai code of honor that Jingorō impetuously violates. Jingorō discovers that he must pay a price for his disregard of Hachiya's family honor and for his murderous response to Hachiya's balking. Rather than atonement by seppuku, he exiles himself, leaving behind his own presumably inferior swords.

Seeking Jingorō's reintegration into samurai society, his cousin[27]—whether of his own accord or at Jingorō's bidding—appeals to Ieyasu. The cousin provides extenuating details. He portrays Jingorō as a young man forced by the samurai code to take another man's life in the process of claiming his wager. His depiction of the incident characterizes it as a moral dilemma created by the clash of two forms of honor. Hachiya is honor-bound by an oath to fulfill the reckless terms of his wager and simultaneously to keep possession of his family's sacred ancestral swords. The cousin explains to Ieyasu that, at the height of their quarrel, Jingorō admonished Hachiya to follow the code of honor. The terms of the wager were the equivalent of an oath: "'The warrior who swears an oath will sacrifice even his life to keep it'" (my translation; see 251; 2:93: bushi wa seigon o shita kara wa, ichimei o mo suteru). An oath can, if violated, quickly turn into a "curse" (251; 2:93: *nonoshiru*). "You are a dog," Jingorō is reported to have told Hachiya, "to go back on your own promise" (251; 2:93: *seigon o hogo ni suru inuzamuraime*).

What is Ieyasu to make of the fact that Jingorō has treated Hachiya like "a dog"? What does it mean that Jingorō has left his own swords behind? Was Jingorō trying to demonstrate that pedigree can not guarantee a man's honor unless he is willing to fight for it? May the best man get the best swords? Were Jingorō's own abandoned swords a cynical replacement for Hachiya's allegedly irreplaceable heirlooms, or a token of remorse for having made Hachiya pay not only with his swords but also with his life? Hachiya was neither willing to give up his swords nor to trade them for Jingorō's. Although he considered them more valuable than his own life, he refused to sacrifice his life for them. He drew his sword only when insulted as "a dog." Although Hachiya paid with his life for his breach of promise to Jingorō, he was unable to defend his family treasure. While Hachiya was unsuccessful in appealing to Jingorō's respect for his family's honor, Jingorō himself ironically appeals to Ieyasu through a family member to take him back into service, dead or alive.

Amari

Jingorō's cousin asks either that Jingorō be spared or that he be permitted to die by his own hand and no one else's. Ieyasu carefully ponders the matter. He announces that he will spare Jingorō's life on condition that he alone kill Amari Shirōsaburō (dates unknown), a powerful vassal of Ieyasu's rival, Takeda Katsuyori (1546–1582). Seppuku looms large as an unspoken alternative (first suggested by the cousin). Jingorō chooses to become an assassin in order to be pardoned for murder—a heinous choice that his more honorable counterpart in "Okitsu" would not have made. As Yagoemon explains in the dispute with *his* aggressive companion, "So long as it was my master's orders, it was not for me to meddle or criticize; providing, of course, it was not contrary to moral principles" (48; 2:381). If given the choice offered Jingorō, Yagoemon would have unhesitatingly preferred seppuku.

As in Ōgai's other historical tales, the lord's motivation is as interesting as the retainer's. Some critics argue that Ieyasu sets an impossible task in asking for Amari's assassination[28] or that he is intent on "consolidating his position as Lord of Mikawa" when he "sends [Jingorō] on a dangerous mission, one on which he surely will die."[29] It is more likely, however, that Ieyasu fully expects Jingorō's success, especially after he has proved his martial skill (by killing the heron) and his ruthless will (by killing Hachiya). Leaving aside our ethical evaluation of Ieyasu's terms, we can consider them as tantamount to a second wager. If Jingorō "beats the odds" and successfully assassinates Amari, he will be readmitted to Ieyasu's service as a reward for having risked his life for his lord. Ieyasu will also profit through the elimination of an enemy, but this elimination comes at a price: Jingorō remains a potentially dangerous retainer.

The tense relationship that exists between Jingorō and Ieyasu is in sharp contrast to the devotion and trust between Yagoemon and Tadaoki. The latter relationship does not end with the death of the lord, for the retainer continues to serve the lord's family, waiting until his lords have died and he himself is on the verge of his natural death before atoning by seppuku for killing in self-defense. Although Jingorō has his lord's confidence in his abilities, he can neither regain his lord's trust, nor is he likely ever to win his respect and admiration. Considering Jingorō's stubborn will, his *iji*, Ieyasu would be foolish to rely on the loyalty of a man more likely to act in his own interest than in his lord's.

According to the terms of his wager, Jingorō must kill in order to live.[30] The scene in which Amari is killed is imbued with the same mysterious beauty as the scene in which the heron was shot. Whether such narrative aestheticization is designed to erase the brutal facticity of death, as Ogata

Tsutomu has argued, or, through cumulative effect, to enunciate the brutality all the more by making it stand out in relief, is not a question of Ōgai's intent so much as of his readers' responses.[31]

To underline his point, Ogata has also called attention to the fact that Jingorō's name does not appear in the scene of Amari's murder, making "the scene phantom-like" *(gensōteki na bamen)*.[32] Shortly after his arrival, Jingorō, described literally as "the newly arrived youth" (see 252; 2:94: *shinzan no wakashu*), wins Amari's trust. Using his flute to lull Amari, Jingorō inquires, in the manner of a loving page, "'Should you be cold, my lord?'" (252; 2:95). He is. Amari then exposes himself not only to the warm erotic touch of this *wakashu* but also to his icy blade. Jingorō is no gratuitously cruel butcher, but someone who dispatches his victims with expertise and with a minimum of pain and mutilation. What makes him brutal is not so much the physical violence he commits as his callous disregard for the heron's majestic beauty, for Hachiya's honor, and for the complete trust that Amari has placed in someone whom he gullibly took to be a *wakashu* lover.[33]

As when he claimed the stakes of Hachiya's wager, Jingorō now takes Amari's topknot as proof of having killed him and as a trophy. Does Jingorō's successful return please Ieyasu? Apparently not. Ieyasu takes Jingorō back into his service, but, in stark contrast to Tadaoki's response to *his* retainer's humble and contrite return from his mission to obtain a valuable tea artifact, Ieyasu neither rewards Jingorō for having killed Amari nor attempts to reconcile his ruthlessly ambitious retainer with Hachiya's family. Ieyasu keeps his distance from this unpredictable retainer who has proven himself, twice over, a killer.

Ieyasu

While his enemies are killing each other, Ieyasu is forced to order his son Nobuyasu to commit seppuku because Nobuyasu's father-in-law, Oda Nobunaga (1534–1582), suspects him of having secretly communicated with Takeda Katsuyori, at the time an enemy of both Ieyasu and Nobunaga.[34] It must be painfully ironic to Ieyasu that his eldest son must commit seppuku for the sake of honor while his retainer, formerly Nobuyasu's page, has not. (It is another small irony that Jingorō had used Nobuyasu's gun to kill the heron and that Ieyasu had commissioned Jingorō to assassinate Amari, Katsuyori's vassal.)

The moment of reckoning between lord and retainer arrives when all these painful events are almost forgotten. Ieyasu seeks reconciliation with his remaining enemies through the peaceful strategy of marriage politics, but he does not trust Jingorō to be a messenger for the proposed match of his second daughter with a member of the Hōjō family, against whom Jingorō has fought well. Knowing that Jingorō is listening to his conversation with his chief retainer, Ishikawa Yoshichirō Kazumasa (?–1592), Ieyasu cites rumors from his enemy-turned-ally to suggest that Jingorō, having served Amari as *wakashu* and received his affection, cruelly killed him in his sleep. Ieyasu does not lie, but he purposefully omits any mention of the heinous deal—to kill in order to live—that Jingorō accepted as the price for his readmission to Ieyasu's service. Ieyasu's criticism reveals a lord whose wager was in truth a test to see if Jingorō would do the honorable thing and redeem himself by committing seppuku instead of choosing life through murder. In other words, Ieyasu now implies that all along his preference concerning "some outstanding service" (251; 2:94: *nani ka hitokado no hōkō*) was for Jingorō to choose seppuku over assassination.

Why does Ieyasu wait so long to reveal his thinking? Having to confess distrust of his own retainer is a humiliating admission of unsound judgment. To salvage his pride, Ieyasu has waited for a propitious moment—reconciliation with his political rivals—before showing his true colors. Can his criticism, some six years after Hachiya's death and five years after Amari's, be considered fair and justified? Bowring argues that Ōgai portrays Jingorō sympathetically and Ieyasu as a villain: "Compared to his sources Ōgai goes out of his way to portray Jingorō in a good light, inventing the heron episode to give a plausible basis for the fight with Hachiya, writing the death scene [in which Amari dies] in a lyrical style, and making Ieyasu seem an unattractive and even vindictive man. When Jingorō leaves his lord it is seen as a reasonable act."[35] The difficulty with this argument is that the episodes that Bowring sees as portraying Jingorō "in a good light" seem rather to characterize him as arrogant, materialistic, and utterly lacking in compassion. One can be critical of Ieyasu without exonerating Jingorō.

Recognizing Ieyasu's contempt and, perhaps, feeling contempt on his part for Ieyasu, Jingorō simply vanishes—as he did after claiming Hachiya's swords—although this time not as an expression of fear or a bad conscience but rather as a recognition that the lord–retainer relationship, which he thought restored, has in fact been irreparably damaged. Noting this crucial lord–retainer antagonism *(kunshin kankei no sōkoku tairitsu no mondai)*, Ogata Tsutomu argues that the "involuntary snort" (254; 2:98: *fun*) that escapes Jingorō's lips when he overhears Ieyasu's calumny expresses his sense of betrayal in the lord–retainer relationship.[36] The question arises as to whether Jingorō's *iji*, or defiant obstinacy, bursts the frame of the feudal structure, as Ogata maintains,[37] or whether it is a revitalizing stress test built into an otherwise rigid feudal system. Despite his moral failures, which Ōgai seems determined to emphasize, Jingorō certainly makes his lord rethink a relationship that is locked into a rigid cage of loyalty, trust, and obligation. While Ieyasu is made to tremble at Jingorō's impulsiveness and unpredictability, Jingorō cannot rely on his lord's support and favor but must be prepared to survive on his own, if need be in foreign exile.

The Return of Jingorō

Ieyasu can be faulted for never openly and honestly discussing his expectations with Jingorō. Knowing that Jingorō can hear what he is saying to Kazumasa, Ieyasu gives him, once again, the chance to do what Ieyasu implicitly considers to be the honorable thing—commit seppuku. Having long expected the moment of truth that has now arrived, Jingorō responds to his lord's denigration by fleeing rather than by taking his own life. This leaves Ieyasu to wonder about and to fear, for the third time and more intensely than before, this unreliable retainer's possible return. It is important to note that Jingorō does not simply defect to Ieyasu's enemy as he might have done. Instead he moves to Korea, to the neutral ground that the historical Ieyasu's great rival, Toyotomi Hideyoshi (1536/37–1598), invaded in his Korean campaigns of 1592 and 1597.

Twenty-four years after Jingorō's third and final flight, a Korean mission visits Japan. Is it delusive paranoia or fear-inspired intuition that impels Ieyasu to identify one of the Korean high officials as Jingorō? This is the question that dominates the opening episode of the story. At the end of the story, the narrator repeats the question for readers themselves to answer, now that they can place it in context. At this point, in the first printed version of "Sahashi Jingorō," the narrator ends his story and the author attaches a postscript directly appealing to readers to provide him with further, reliable sources about Jingorō's life. (This marked break between narrator and author is omitted in the annotated editions.)[38] By placing his narrative among the documented sources available to him, Ōgai postulates a version of events that can compete with what these sources present as historical reality. In writing this story he practices what he preaches in his later essay "Rekishi sono mama to rekishibanare" (January 1915). In that essay, he depicts "history as it is and history aside from the facts"[39] (by which he seems to distinguish between positivist and interpretive historiography).

As for the verifiable historical facts, readers know that Ieyasu rose to power in this twenty-four-year period between Jingorō's disappearance from Ieyasu's Hamamatsu residence in 1583 and the Korean mission of 1607. Ieyasu had officially retired as first Tokugawa shōgun (r. 1603–1605) and handed over power to his third son, Hidetada (1579–1632; r. 1605–1623), but he was still in the process of completing his retirement. His Sunpu Castle was still under construction when the delegation from Korea arrived. Now past the zenith of his power, he was vulnerable to revenge from disaffected retainers and vassals.

In any case, Ōgai's Ieyasu is not unjustified in keeping a watchful eye on the Korean mission. How the diplomatic channels were reopened after Toyotomi Hideyoshi's disastrous Korean campaigns (1592–1598) the narrator explains at the beginning of the story. In 1599, Sō Yoshitoshi (1568–1615), the daimyō of Tsushima, sent "peace feelers to Korea."[40] According to Ōgai's story, Yoshitoshi was acting on orders from the Tokugawa family. Increasingly pressed by the Koreans for the return of their prisoners of war, Yoshitoshi arranged for a first exploratory visit of Korean priests to Kyōto and to Edo, where Ieyasu received them in 1604. Ieyasu at that time repatriated three thousand Koreans. Ōgai's story does not reveal, however, that Yoshitoshi then ordered a letter forged in Ieyasu's name that agreed to some bold Korean demands, which Yoshitoshi secretly fulfilled in order to make the 1607 Korean mission possible. The deception continued through 1607 and beyond. Was Ieyasu on edge because the Korean mission seemed to him just a little too good to be true?

The Korean envoys had been prepared to present all their gifts to the new shōgun at Edo Castle, but they decided to save some items to present to Ieyasu when they met him for an audience at Sunpu Castle. In transition from the height of his power to retirement, Ōgai's Ieyasu seems to experience a surge of anxiety that leads him, rightly or wrongly, to identify one of the three Korean higher officials as Jingorō. He hastily cuts the visit short.[41]

Did Jingorō indeed go over to the Koreans and is he playing a game of cat and mouse with his former lord? There is no evidence for this in the sources that Ōgai names at the end of his story, but Ōgai never restricted himself, in his historical fiction, to the bare facts. Jingorō is a force that lingers on as an endlessly sounding alarm within Ieyasu's consciousness; conversely, Ieyasu is the authority that Jingorō needs—or is magnetically drawn to—for the recognition of his feats. In this sense, Jingorō's return seems as poetically inevitable as Ieyasu's fear of it. Through his *iji*, Jingorō is such an awesome power in the mind of Ieyasu that Ieyasu, and Ieyasu alone, believes that he has in fact returned in the guise of one of the "Korean" officials: "'Does no one remember him? I am now sixty-six years old, but rarely do my eyes fail me. He was twenty-three when he fled from Hamamatsu in the eleventh year of Tenshō, and so he is forty-seven now. The brazen fellow! He's now posing as a Korean. That man is Sahashi Jingorō'" (248; 2:88).[42] Ieyasu keeps his anxious thoughts from the Korean envoys, however. No words are ever exchanged, face to face, between Jingorō and Ieyasu. Although Ieyasu explicitly rejects an interrogation of the Korean official he suspects of being Jingorō, his retainer Honda Masazumi (dates unknown), sensing his lord's hidden desire, carefully investigates at his own discretion: "Through Yoshitoshi, Honda inquired in a round-about-manner whether, among those [Korean officials] who had presented themselves that day, there might have been someone whom Ieyasu had known previously" (249; 2:89). The inquiry is fruitless. Ieyasu's problematic relationship with Jingorō remains unresolved. He orders Honda "to send these envoys away as soon as you can" (249; 2:89).

What looms larger than the majestic heron, Hachiya's heirloom swords, the flute that seduced and the blade that pierced Amari's chest is an action rather than an object—the seppuku that Jingorō evaded. By failing to commit seppuku, Jingorō disregards Ieyasu's hints that he follow what the samurai code defines as the honorable course. He chooses to live in exile—like a dog?—when he is given the option to die. His refusal of absolute loyalty to his lord contrasts sharply with Yagoemon's suicidal devotion (and, of course, with Nogi's). Whether a late-sixteenth-century retainer should be indulged, faulted, or despised for not preserving his honor by sacrificing his life is a question that the early-twentieth-century author refuses to answer unequivocally. That question was, presumably, what most intrigued Ōgai. He recognized that attitudes toward sacrificial honor had changed. He wanted to explore that change and help his readers understand it. Within half a year of Nogi's junshi, Ōgai had amassed materials for and was fully engaged in curating the modernizing nation's cultural memory.

"Okitsu Yagoemon no isho" (Second Version): A Spectacle for the Lord's Successor

Ōgai began revising the first version of "Okitsu Yagoemon no isho" in December 1912, finished the second version in early April 1913, and published it in June of that year. It was now a longer and much more complex narrative. The second fictional Okitsu Yagoemon is more distanced from his historical prototype than the first. This may be what the postmodernist Karatani Kōjin had in mind when he hinted that, while the first version of the story is Ōgai's "interpretation of Nogi's suicide," his revision not only makes the theme "ambiguous" but "tries to deny the theme itself."[43]

In Ōgai's revised story, Okitsu Yagoemon Kageyoshi (1594–1647) addresses his testament, written the day before his seppuku, to his son Saiemon Kazusada (?–1704), who had not appeared in the first version. By beginning his testament with a biographical sketch of his ancestors and by asking that the testament be preserved for his descendants, Yagoemon places himself firmly in a continuing male genealogy. This genealogy was not a part of the earlier version of the story.

Through this narrative technique, Ōgai overwhelms his readers with historical details that are held together solely by the genealogical line of the Okitsu family that his narrator Yagoemon is eager to pass on. We learn that Yagoemon's grandfather Kagemichi (1520–1560) was born in Okitsu (near today's Shimizu, Shizuoka Prefecture) and died in his prime in battle, pure and simple, with his Lord Imagawa Yoshimoto (1519–1560). Yagoemon's father, Kagekazu (1558–1641), had a more erratic, if not somewhat shady, career. He shifted allegiances from Sano Kanjūrō, a relative of his mother's line, to Lord Akamatsu (1562–1600). He then defected to the Hosokawa clan. There are hints that it was his intimacy with the poet Karasumaru Mitsuhiro (1579–1638),[44] whose son Mitsukata (1600–1638) was tied in marriage to Hosokawa Tadaoki's fourth daughter, Manhime (1598–1664), that first stirred Kagekazu's interest in the Hosokawa clan. Apparently, this interest was heightened during Lord Akamatsu's siege of the Hosokawa clan's Tanabe castle. As a member of the besieging force, Kagekazu was in a position either to block or to facilitate delivery of a vital message to the defenders from Hosokawa Tadaoki. The Hosokawa messenger, Mori Mitsuemon (dates unknown), happened to be Kagekazu's maternal cousin. Kagekazu betrayed his trust and allowed delivery of the message. This betrayal contributed to Lord Akamatsu's devastating defeat. It is unclear from Yagoemon's account whether Kagekazu was motivated more by his family connection to or by his growing fascination with the Hosokawa clan. Whatever the motives, there was a shift in allegiance. After Lord Akamatsu's defeat, Mitsuemon helped Kagekazu move to Buzen, where he became a retainer of the Hosokawa clan. In 1632 Kagekazu accompanied Hosokawa Tadatoshi (1586–1641) to Higo Province; both died in 1641, of illness.

Why did Ōgai insert all this intricate historical detail, which I have greatly simplified, into the second version of his story? A simple answer is that Kagekazu's shifts of allegiance provide a contrast to Yagoemon's loyalty to his lords. The accumulation of historical detail may also contribute to the illusion of historicity at which Ōgai seems to have been aiming.

In his genealogy, Yagoemon devotes only one concise paragraph to his older brother, Kurobē Kazutomo (?–1637), who accompanied Hosokawa Tadatoshi on the Shimabara campaign of 1637–1638 and is said to have died a glorious death on top of the wall of the besieged Hara Castle. (In contrast to the shōgunal forces' pathetically slow and ineffective quelling of this rebellion, the Hosokawa distinguished themselves in battle.[45] Yet, in the end, there was no glory in this massacre of starving peasants outraged over having to renounce their Christian faith.) Yagoemon's paragraph on this regrettable episode evokes Nogi's dilemma during the Satsuma Rebellion of 1877. The parallels are close. In both civil wars loyalists (Nogi for Emperor Meiji in 1877 and Hosokawa Tadatoshi for Tokugawa Iemitsu in 1638) faced and vanquished insurgents. The Okitsu brothers, Kurobē Kazutomo and Yagoemon Kageyoshi, both fought on the side of the shōgunate in the Shimabara Rebellion (Shimabara *no ran*), the former giving his life in battle for Hosokawa Tadatoshi and the latter receiving a wound in his left thigh as banner carrier for Tadatoshi's younger brother, Tatsutaka (1615–1645). One is reminded of Nogi's younger brother, who gave his life in the Hagi Rebellion, just prior to the Satsuma Rebellion in which Nogi lost the imperial colors and his flag carrier—the difference being that the Nogi brothers were on opposing sides.

What's in a Name?

Before the Shimabara Rebellion, however, came the crucial event in Yagoemon's life, one that profoundly shaped his desire to commit junshi twenty-three years later. This, of course, was the lethal quarrel over the aloeswood. In the first version of the story, Lord Tadaoki praises Yagoemon for having obtained a rare article for the tea ceremony, citing the poem that came to him as he tested the wood for its fragrance. As a sign of his appreciation he reveals that he has already named the wood "Hatsune" (First Song), from a phrase in the poem.

The symbolism of Lord Tadaoki's naming the wood is rich in meaning. The poetic name turns a utilitarian article into a work of art to be used in the tea ceremony. In its ritual meaning, "Hatsune" celebrates Yagoemon's triumphant victory in the contest with the Date and Hosokawa retainers for the aloeswood. By elevating a precious commodity to something still more precious, something that is worth the life of a man, Tadaoki not only excuses but sanctions Yagoemon's killing of Yokota Seibē (the unnamed companion of the first version). Bought with the blood of Yagoemon's companion, this "First Song" thus carries some dark overtones. The aloeswood symbolically represents the essence of sacrifice needed for the continuation of the Way of Tea that epitomizes the Hosokawa ethos.

In the revised version of the story, naming takes on a whole new dimension. Lord Tadaoki grants Yagoemon his personal name's second character *oki* (raise, call, awake, waken, build, launch, rise, stir, move, excite, provoke). Yagoemon obediently substitutes this character for the *oki* (offing, offshore, off) in the Okitsu family name that he had inherited. This renaming is like a baptism that detaches Yagoemon from his clan and binds him to the Hosokawa clan, and to Tadaoki in particular. In symbolic terms, part of Yagoemon's identity has been taken away and replaced by a new one, defined by his lord. This is not exactly what Yagoemon had asked for when he requested permission to commit seppuku. Instead of death, he has been granted a new life and a new identity. (Symbolically, he is now part of Tadaoki, so that killing himself —especially without permission—implies "killing" his lord.)

The gift Yagoemon has received is of the highest order; but, nonetheless, it is a gift that enthralls him to his Lord Tadaoki in ways he had not anticipated. Despite the fact that he gains his life instead of losing it, he feels that his life is no longer his own: it is a borrowed life to be returned when asked for. When Yagoemon undergoes the name change, he enters into a bond with his lord that is not reciprocal; after all, the lord's name remains unchanged. Although Yagoemon has presented his lord with a costly gift, the death of Yokota and Tadaoki's act of clemency mean that Yagoemon has actually incurred a debt. He now owes his life to his lord, and he is left with the heavy burden of paying for it. Seppuku is an obvious way to balance the moral books, but Tadaoki refuses to allow Yagoemon to exercise this option—which places Yagoemon in a box. Unable to exercise his own free will, he is no longer his own man. He is prevented, by the very person to whom he is indebted, from meeting the obligation to repay in this exchange of "gifts." As Marcel Mauss remarks in the classic anthropological study of gifts, "The person who cannot return a loan or potlatch loses his rank and even his status of a free man."[46]

Burdened with his debt, Yagoemon serves the Hosokawa clan, not only Tadaoki but also his sons, Tadatoshi and Tatsutaka.[47] Yagoemon lives through several Hosokawa deaths, but it is not until Tadaoki dies that he begins to wonder what to do with himself. At this point, Ōgai begins to plumb depths across which he had only skimmed in the first version of the story.

After having lived for years as if he were an extension of Tadaoki, Yagoemon suddenly awakens and begins to recover his autonomy. He contemplates the favors he and his relatives have received from the Hosokawa. It seems that the time has come to repay these favors and meet what he calls his "double obligation" (59; 2:12: *kono saizō no daion*). He refers, presumably, to the postponed obligation to pay for the death of Yokota and to Tadaoki's command that payment be deferred, but the translation "double obligation" does not do justice to the term *daion* (great debt), which alludes to Yagoemon's *saizō* (remaking). There is an element of the artificial, contrived, or crafted in Ōgai's choice of the term *saizō* as opposed to the quasi-religious term *saisei* (rebirth), which is given as a synonym in a note in the *Mori Ōgai zenshū*.[48]

Can Yagoemon recover the identity surrendered during all the years that he had lived as Tadaoki's loyal retainer? All this time Yagoemon has lived by the rules laid down for him by Tadaoki. Now the will of his lord has vanished with him and Yagoemon is suddenly on his own. Are the rules by which he has lived since the Annam episode of 1624 still valid after his lord's passing? Clearly, these are questions similar to those that must have haunted Nogi.

It is time to take another look at the samurai code of honor, not only from Yagoemon's perspective but also from Tadaoki's. Yagoemon had asked permission to commit seppuku for killing Tadaoki's retainer Yokota Seibē. He was denied the honorable way of atoning for this violent act because he had, in Tadaoki's view, done nothing dishonorable; he had merely done his duty. In fact, by knowing his lord's taste in tea and by firmly executing the lord's will when others interfered, Yagoemon did far more than his duty. His readiness to die in pursuit of his lord's interests exonerated him in the eyes of his lord and restored whatever honor he might have lost through an act of violence. From Tadaoki's point of view, Yagoemon needed only to continue his service. No doubt Tadaoki had his own best interests in mind, but he presumably saw his clemency as an act of noblesse oblige for which Yagoemon should be grateful.

For Yagoemon (of the second version), permission to live was hardly a favor, but he accepted his fate without complaint. Yet clearly something remained unresolved for Yagoemon, and his unease resurfaces with the death of the lord who willed him to live. How should he now repay the great debt of his reconstituted life? At first, the sudden freedom to make his own choices seems to overwhelm him. Was his lord's order to live only a temporary stay of life, or was he meant to live out his entire life until his natural death?

He had, it must be remembered, asked to commit seppuku, not junshi, but seppuku at this late date, after Tadaoki's death, would inevitably be interpreted as junshi. Conditions permitting, someone intending to commit junshi asks permission to do so when his lord's death is imminent. Yagoemon did not do so, since junshi had not been his original motivation for wanting to die. Now his frustrated intention to commit seppuku threatened to be transformed into junshi by default. As in Nogi's case, the original intent was virtually erased from public consciousness because the original intent was so far removed in time from the consummating act.

By way of searching for a solution to his peculiar circumstances, Yagoemon examines the four cases of junshi in the wake of Tadaoki's death in 1645. There had been even more cases—an extraordinary nineteen in all—and some of them quite controversial, upon the death of Hosokawa Tadatoshi in 1641, but Yagoemon examines only the four cases related to Tadaoki, whom he had directly served. It must also be noted that by the time he begins his research Yagoemon has already missed the most opportune moment for committing junshi for Tadaoki. Why, then, does he scrutinize the four cases of junshi for his lord as if they had special relevance for him?

The key may lie in the distinctions he draws in the course of his research. Not all cases of junshi deserve Yagoemon's scrutiny. For two of the four committed on behalf of Tadaoki, Yagoemon knows or reveals only the names of the suicides and nothing of the circumstances. It is the other two cases that interest him. What were the motives of these men? The first, Minota Heishichi Masamoto (1623–1645), was taken into the service of Tadaoki, probably because of his great-grandfather's distinguished death in battle with Sagara, lord of Tōtōmi. Heishichi must have been especially grateful to Tadaoki for retaining him, because his grandfather and father had been "wanderers" (59; 2:13). Perhaps Yagoemon, thinking of his own grandfather's death in battle for his lord, considered Heishichi a role model.

The most prominently featured junshi in Yagoemon's testament, however, is that of Ono Denbē Tomotsugu (1621–1645). It is the only junshi committed because of a transgression that left a stain on the family's honor. Denbē's father had disobeyed Tadaoki, and the son was assigned the cruel task of bringing his own father to justice. He had to find his absconded father or be executed in his place. For Yagoemon, Denbē's conflict of loyalty between his father and his lord seems to have mirrored his own dilemma. Denbē's solution is quite a creative one. He claims to have searched the whole country, everywhere, in vain. Impressed that Denbē has dared to return with a report that is his own death sentence, Tadaoki pardons him and spares his life. It is in order to repay this enormous, unsolicited favor that Denbē commits seppuku (see 59; 2:14) upon his lord's death. Denbē had no choice but to accept the gift of life received through the generosity of his lord. In this case, exactly as in Yagoemon's and in Nogi's, the lord was ready not only to tolerate but even to reward disobedience or failure if the transgressor demonstrated absolute loyalty; willingness to die expiated the moral transgression. The only difference between Denbē's case and those of Yagoemon and Nogi is that Denbē, facing a death sentence, never asked to commit seppuku.

It appears that the first version of "Okitsu Yagoemon no isho" attempted to have it both ways. In it Yagoemon tries to eat his cake and have it too. He follows his lord's order to live and refrains from seppuku immediately after delivering the aloeswood, but he refrains from junshi when it would have been appropriate—that is, soon after his lord's death. In fact, in order to avoid the appearance of committing junshi, he postpones his seppuku as long as possible, until just before dying from old age.

In the first version of the story, Yagoemon commits seppuku in 1658; in the second version, in 1647. The enormous difference of eleven years between the year of death for the two fictional Yagoemons in "Okitsu Yagoemon no isho" has been attributed to Mori Ōgai's attempt to correct a contradiction in his sources for the historical Yagoemon's year of death,[49] but thematic considerations are a more likely explanation. The year of death helps the reader understand whether or not each of the two fictional Yagoemons intended his seppuku to be understood as junshi. Although the answer seems to be negative for the first Yagoemon and positive for the second, both characters share an intense ambivalence that makes their ultimate intent impossible to determine with clarity. The first Yagoemon postpones his seppuku in order to make it coincide as nearly as possible with his natural death from old age and to avoid the appearance of junshi, but he also announces that he planned his seppuku to coincide with the thirteenth anniversary of his lord's death. If his seppuku is to be recognized as junshi at all, it is junshi in a most understated form, quite in contrast to the "spectacle" (60; 2:16: *haregamashiku*) of junshi that is the legacy of the second Yagoemon.

In contrast to the first Yagoemon, the second Yagoemon indicates in his testament a preoccupation with precedent as he contemplates the many junshi in the wake of both Tadatoshi and Tadaoki (in that chronological order). It is almost as if the nineteen cases of junshi for Tadatoshi, who preceded his father in death, must be matched to pay equal homage to Tadaoki. Contemplating the long delay between his transgression and its planned expiation, the second Yagoemon blames himself and becomes "envious" (59; 2:14) of those who already, namely, in a timely fashion, honored their lord with their lives. He is now so eager to prove himself that he feels compelled to give a perfunctory reason for the postponement of his seppuku: he had been posted by his lord to Edo, where he has no one who could help with the preparations for seppuku.

Meanwhile, Tadaoki's remains are cremated (1646.I.11) at the Taishōin in Yasushiro, and his bones transported to Kyōto, where they are deposited in the Kōtōin, the Hosokawa subtemple of the Daitokuji (1646.I.24). It is not until 1647.X.29, two years after Tadaoki's death, that Yagoemon can take leave of his present lord, Tadaoki's grandson Mitsuhisa, from whom he has finally extracted permission to commit junshi.

Yagoemon is now showered with favors and honors. In unwitting allusion to the tea ceremony that set off the chain of circumstances that altered the course of Yagoemon's life, Mitsuhisa makes tea for Yagoemon with his own hands. He then presents him with the nine-star Hosokawa crest *(kuyō no mon)*, a companion for the journey to Kyōto, and with farewell gifts of poetry from the eminent men of the day. Yagoemon accepts all these things, including the hospitality of his brother Matajirō. His return gift will consist of nothing less than his junshi. (Matajirō will receive the keepsake of his dagger and his son the testament.)

Yagoemon still humbly refers to his junshi as seppuku. His modesty stands in stark contrast to the pomp surrounding the event intended to elevate the prestige of the Hosokawa. At the foot of Mount Funaoka, a temporary hut *(kariya)* has been built for what Yagoemon considers a distasteful sensationalization of his death. (By contrast, the Yagoemon of the first version constructs a simple hut for his last rite.) Although the display pains him (60; 2:16: *kokorogurushiku*), Yagoemon resigns himself to what he takes to be the lord's will (2:16: *shūmei*). Yet whose lord's will is this? Yagoemon may feel uneasy because he obtained permission from the grandson of the lord whom he allegedly wants to follow into death. Yagoemon is also taken aback by the notion that *he* seems to be honored more than his lord, which turns the rite of junshi on its head.

There is another reason to be disturbed. Yagoemon is symbolically linked with Tadaoki by an extraordinary spread of 3,800 tatami mats that extend from the gate of Daitokuji, where Tadaoki's bones rest in his Kōtōin, to Yagoemon's temporary hut for the ritual of junshi. If this arrangement is not excessive in relation to Tadaoki, it certainly is in relation to Yagoemon's original intent, expiation of the wrong done to Yokota. Indeed, it is as if Yagoemon's original intention to commit seppuku had been completely appropriated by the Hosokawa to enhance their own prestige. The more show they make of Yagoemon's junshi, the more they can boast of his legendary loyalty to Tadaoki and to their entire clan.

In the first version of the story, Yagoemon had for years been "on intimate terms" (51; 2:383: *jikkon*) with the Abbot Seigan (1588–1661) of Daitokuji. Presumably, their relationship began after the death of Lord Mitsuhisa in 1649, when Yagoemon decided to retire from the world and become a Buddhist priest (47; 2:379: *sōmon*). He had built a rustic hut at the foot of Funaokayama, apparently for the purpose of his planned suicide, but Seigan seems to have invited him to the Kōtōin and to have initiated him into the Buddhist priesthood.[50] Yagoemon requested in his will that Seigan become the immediate recipient of his testament before sharing it with his family in Kumamoto. In Ōgai's second version of the story, Yagoemon directly addresses the testament to his son Saiemon, who is expected to be among the witnesses. The abbot is merely listed as another witness. To what degree the abbot may have been intimate with Tadaoki, or with Yagoemon for that matter, remains unclear.

In neither version is there a woman like Nogi Shizuko. One might argue that this omission is simply dictated by the historical sources, but Ōgai was willing, in other instances, to manipulate and adapt his historical sources. By omitting all references to a wife, Ōgai highlights male genealogy, especially in the second version, and with that, the matter of continuing the line. Ōgai has Yagoemon address his testament to his son Saemon in the hope that "son after son, grandson after grandson should pass it down, succeeding in their turns to my aim; they must excel in loyal devotion in service to our noble house" (61; 2:16).

As if to prove the sincerity of Yagoemon's hopes for the future of his line, Ōgai attached a genealogical chart within an appendix. This chart has tried the patience of some modern Western readers. William R. Wilson omitted it from his translation of the story (although he was not so intrusive as to delete the extensive genealogical material within the text). Omission of the chart was a mistake, but one that raises an important question: why exactly did Ōgai add the appendix to the testament of Okitsu Yagoemon Kageyoshi in his second version?

One prominent feature of the genealogical narrative that explains the chart is the appearance of adopted sons, who sooner or later become responsible for continuing the Okitsu line. General Nogi, it will be remembered, had refused this practice in order purposefully to extinguish his line. One wonders whether Ōgai's emphasis on adopted sons is meant to support or undercut Nogi's decision. At any rate, Ōgai traces the genealogy of the Okitsu house through adopted sons from the eighth and ninth generations all the way to the eleventh-generation namesake of the story's main protagonist. This Meiji-era Yagoemon, a member of a guard unit, was "skilled at the exercise of *shooting dogs* from horseback with bow and arrow" (62; 2:18: *inuoumono*).

What does Mori Ōgai, in his role as modern chronicler, mean to suggest about the status and prestige concerning this last known member of the Okitsu clan? To readers familiar with the (rather obscure) history of *inuoumono*, Ōgai has suggested something quite interesting. As a form of mounted archery, *inuoumono* had by the Meiji period become a "cultural relic" before it "died out completely."[51] In the Kamakura (1185–1333) and Muromachi (1333–1573) periods, however, *inuoumono* had been "immensely popular" as "the largest and most elaborate of the mounted archery contests."[52] During the century of warfare (1467–1570; *sengoku jidai*), when men were chasing each other rather than dogs, *inuoumono* seemed to have run its course, but it was occasionally revived until Tokugawa Iemochi (1846–1866; r. 1858–1866) officially banned it in 1862. The last known performance of the sport was for Emperor Meiji in 1881 at the old samurai stronghold of the Shimazu clan in the remote Satsuma domain.[53] Like the historical Yagoemon, who had committed junshi at a cultural watershed shortly before the custom was outlawed, so the Meiji-period Yagoemon participated in an anachronistic activity that had already been banned and was about to become extinct.

After tracing Kagemichi's descendants through his grandson Yagoemon Kageyoshi and down to the adopted Yagoemon at the middle of the Meiji period, Ōgai presents the Okitsu clan's genealogy from still another angle. He compares the genealogical destiny of Kagekazu's six sons to that of Yagoemon's second son, Yagoemon Kageyoshi. It appears that the lines of the first, third, and fifth son died out quickly. The fourth son was a maverick. He changed his family name to Teramoto after falling out of favor with Hosokawa Tadaoki during the Ōsaka campaign of 1615. He took service with Honda Toshitsugu (1595–1668) and then recovered the favor of the Hosokawa during the Shimabara Rebellion of 1637–1638. Showing the vicissitudes of fortune, the continuation of this fourth son's line into the early nineteenth century came also to depend on adopted sons, the last one featured in 1870 as "a ranking official in Kiku jail" (63; 2:21). Kagekazu's sixth son was the Matajirō who sheltered Yagoemon Kageyoshi before he committed seppuku. His line, too, was continued through an adopted son.

What then is left of the Okitsu line in the Meiji period? It had either died out—whether by death in battle (first son), through illness (third son), or after a long disability (fifth son)—or else the line was continued through adoption (fourth and sixth sons). What remained of the Okitsu clan, then, was nothing remarkable except for the memory of Yagoemon Kageyoshi's moment of glory when he committed junshi. Yagoemon's testament makes this memory possible. Even if there were no blood descendants left, there were those who bore his name and passed on his story. Thanks to Ōgai, the story has spread like a fan to include Japanese and foreign readers who can ask themselves whether or not they, in circumstances like Yagoemon's—or, by analogy, like Nogi's—would have acted as he did.

The two versions of "Okitsu Yagoemon no isho" represent Ōgai's struggle to come to terms with Nogi's suicide. Both versions imply that Yagoemon was not beyond criticism. In particular, Ōgai grapples with the issue of permission. Nogi did not verifiably receive it in the eyes of the public, yet he acted according to his understanding of the emperor's implied assent. The Yagoemon of Ōgai's first version also killed himself without permission—he hardly gave it a thought. He did, however, try to mitigate his final act of disobedience by delaying his suicide until the time of his expected natural death. By contrast, the second Yagoemon truly tortured himself over the question of permission. After studying the lives of men who had committed junshi, he decided to join their ranks. Since he found no case in which one of these men had explicitly been denied permission to commit seppuku for an act that only indirectly concerned his lord, he had to find his own solution to his special circumstances. Unlike the first Yagoemon, and unlike Nogi, he tried to avoid the appearance of disobedience to his late lord by asking for permission from his lord's heir. As an unhappy consequence of his punctiliousness, the second Yagoemon's junshi became a spectacle for the edification of the Hosokawa clan, which turned Yagoemon's original intent into a farce. While the suicide of Nogi and his wife took place in private, without witnesses, the second Yagoemon's junshi became a public circus that he had neither anticipated nor wanted. If the first version of "Okitsu Yagoemon no isho" implies that Nogi's act was premature, the second version seems to criticize him for not having secured explicit permission from Emperor Mutsuhito (Meiji) or Emperor Yoshihito (Taishō).

Interestingly, the *Mori Ōgai zenshū* prints the first version of the story[54] *after* the second, which is presented as the definitive version. The *Ōgai rekishi bungaku shū* also suggests that the prominently placed second version is to be preferred. Unlike the editors of these editions, Richard Bowring, the translator of the first version, saw the original version as "preferable," because the second Yagoemon's permission to die "serves to divorce the work from its first immediate inspiration—Nogi's death" and because there is a "sacrifice of intensity for factual emendation" in the revised version.[55] There is no compelling reason, however, to rank the two versions. Both stand to gain when they are read together.

"Abe ichizoku": The Perplexities of Permission

Between the two versions of "Okitsu Yagoemon no isho," Mori Ōgai explored Nogi's junshi in yet another story centering on the Hosokawa clan. He finished "Abe ichizoku" (The Abe family) on 29 November 1912 and *Chūō Kōron* published it the following January.[56] This masterpiece of short historical fiction also focuses on the vexing issue of permission, but "Abe ichizoku" is fundamentally different in form and content from the two versions of "Okitsu Yagoemon no isho" in that it is not the testament of someone about to commit junshi. Rather, it is a complicated examination of the crucial question of permission, not only before but also after the act of junshi. The examination involves multiple perspectives, those of the lord and those of the retainer. These perspectives are presented through the eyes of a narrator, a relatively objective third person, who poses both as a historian and as a contemporary eyewitness.

The narrator's meticulous eye for detail endows him with what seems to be incontestable objectivity. He provides precise dates, historic locations, and the genealogical background of nearly everyone involved in the epidemic of junshi that followed Hosokawa Tadatoshi's death on 1641.III.17[57] in the hour of the monkey (3–5 p.m.). Occasionally, however, he becomes skeptical about his facts and figures. His doubts become evident when he injects a note of disbelief, even cynicism, and perhaps a touch of the grotesque and the absurd. Most significantly, he asks some very critical questions about the ethics of junshi. The narrator's attitude of critical inquiry is best revealed in his abrupt shifts of perspective from retainer to lord. His pointed question—why do some men commit junshi while others do not?—forces him to examine not only the plain facts but also the hidden motivations and the idiosyncratic features both of the man who follows his lord into death and of the lord who encourages or discourages the act. Sometimes, by merely describing the scene, the narrator produces the kind of effect that anthropologists achieve when they tonelessly report exotic native customs. Only very occasionally does Ōgai's narrator correct a possible misperception in order to prevent misunderstanding due to the reader's unfamiliarity with the customs of the time. It is only in the poetic embellishment of certain episodes that the narrator hints where his own heart might lie.

By presenting multiple perspectives on junshi and its aftermath, Ōgai widens the reader's perceptual and emotional horizons. "Okitsu Yagoemon no isho" ends with Yagoemon's death, but the narrator of "Abe ichizoku" can also describe the effects of junshi on the family of the deceased and show how that act is perceived by the public. It is almost as if Ōgai were taking a "junshi poll" for Japanese readers who were still reeling from Nogi's suicide.

The matter of permission for junshi is carried ad absurdum in this novella. Of the many who commit junshi, some did and others did not receive permission; some then acted as instructed and others did not. The gamut of responses is quite unusual in a society that pays the utmost attention to following rules and obeying orders. The problem with permission for junshi in such a society is that there *are* no firm rules.

As an act of honor, junshi simultaneously demonstrates the bond of fealty between lord and retainer and the liberation of the latter's will, previously bound to his lord's. It is precisely this moment of the retainer's self-assertion—the reclamation of his own free will—that is problematic. Although junshi is primarily a matter between lord and retainer, it also concerns their families and their society. "Abe ichizoku" reveals that the expectations of family and others are important enough to change a man's mind as he ponders his response to permission granted or permission denied. In the case of Abe Yaichiemon Michinobu (?–1641), the original decision—not to commit junshi because permission was denied—is overturned by societal pressures, but honor is not lost. In other words, Abe Yaichiemon's case illustrates the dilemma between following his urge to serve his lord as requested and preserving his clan's honor. In the end, his family's honor takes precedence over his lord's last will.

While in "Okitsu Yagoemon no isho" Ōgai had emphasized the individual subject's determination, upon his lord's death, of exactly when and how to respond to his lord's explicit denial of permission to commit seppuku, in "Abe ichizoku" he demonstrated the sheer variety of responses to the call of honor through junshi, as if to advocate tolerance for Nogi's junshi in his own day and to reassure a public that felt uncertain about how to deal with it emotionally. By pointing to the roots of junshi in the past, he acknowledged that junshi was an old custom and simultaneously asked about its value in the present. At stake was whether or not Nogi and his wife had died in vain. By dramatizing the debate over junshi that had raged in the seventeenth century, Ōgai contributed to resolving the debate raging in the twentieth.

The Old Regime

The events of "Abe ichizoku" are dominated by the old regime of Hosokawa Tadatoshi (1586–1641) and the new regime of his son Mitsuhisa (1619–1649).[58] In the modern analogy that lay beneath the surface of Ōgai's text, Tadatoshi and Mitsuhisa's eras correspond to the eras of Emperor Meiji and Emperor Taishō. The stage for mass junshi is set by Tadatoshi's death in 1641. In the second version of "Okitsu Yagoemon no isho" we are told that nineteen retainers committed junshi for Tadatoshi. In "Abe ichizoku" we learn the details. Fifteen out of the nineteen committed junshi between Tadatoshi's death day on III.17 and his forty-ninth-day death rites on V.5. (These rites release the departed soul from limbo *[chū-u;* 2:30: *chū-in].*) Ōgai's narrator has chosen a representative number of these men to explain their rationale for performing junshi when they did.

The story begins with the end of the old regime. Lord Tadatoshi's death is sadly anticipated and watched over by none other than the shōgun himself, Tokugawa Iemitsu (1604–1651). To explain the devotion of Tadatoshi's retainers, their dying lord's virtues are extolled. The narrator takes great pains to establish the place of Tadatoshi within the Hosokawa clan. He tells of ancestors skillful with brush and sword, distinguished in both poetry and battle *(bunbu no itchi).*[59] He remarks on Tadatoshi's numerous offspring: four sons and two daughters. For these reasons, as well as for his personal virtues, Tadatoshi has earned his retainers' devotion. And he deserves an especially grand burial.

Tadatoshi dies and the matter-of-fact narrative is poignantly disrupted by a mysterious event. In the middle of Tadatoshi's cremation his two favorite hawks, Ariake and Akashi, plunge into a well shaded by the branches of the cherry trees of Shū'un-in. This is the first we hear of "junshi" committed not by retainers but rather by a daimyō's beloved hawks. Occurring as it does within the context of a funeral rite, the episode evokes the death scene of the historic Buddha surrounded by a weeping crowd of humans and animals. The narrator laconically concedes that an obsession with death was in the air and that people had no choice, under the circumstances, but to identify the hawks' last flight as junshi: "There was no room in their minds to doubt this judgment and try to find out some other cause" (S: 346; 2:30).[60]

Immediately following this account of ornithic devotion to a charismatic lord, the narrator mentions that a virtual tsunami of nine cases of junshi occurred just before Tadatoshi's cremation. A smaller wave of junshi occurs immediately before and after Tadatoshi's forty-ninth-day death rites marking the passage of his soul from limbo to the stabler realm of death. To the five retainers who committed junshi then, it must have seemed that time was of the essence if they still wanted to accompany their lord to the mountain of death and the river of three crossings (S: 346; 2:31: *shide no yama sanzu no kawa*).

With this last-minute frenzy in mind, the narrator raises the question of permission. He insists that there is no definite written rule but an "unstated" one about junshi that gradually evolved from the close bond between lords and retainers. Retainers followed their lord wherever he went—to Edo, to the battlefield, to "the mountain of heavenly death"[61]—provided that they had his permission to do so. The narrator warns that a retainer gains no honor by acting on his own volition. If permission is required to follow one's lord in life, it is even more necessary if one wishes to follow him in death: "A death without permission [is] a dog's death" (S: 346; 2:31: sono yurushi mo nai no ni shinde wa, sore wa inujini de aru). But then the narrator undermines what he has just explained by allowing for junshi without permission in cases of "tacit agreement" (S: 346; more literally, silent oath, 2:31: *mokkei*) between lord and retainer. Yet such an unspoken arrangement—"where the absence of permission did not mean anything" (S: 346–347; 2:31–32)—is so contrary to normal expectations that the narrator must turn to religion to find a precedent. Similar to junshi with tacit permission is the Buddha's sanctioning of the teachings of the Mahâyâna even though he had not given his permission for their distribution before he entered nirvana (see S: 347; 2:32: *butsu nehan*). In short, junshi without permission can be either the worst disgrace imaginable, a dog's death, or the exact opposite, the highest and most sanctified glory. Telling one from the other requires acute ethical discrimination. And it was just this sort of judgment that Ōgai was helping early Taishō Japanese to make about Nogi.

Chōjūrō

The narrator next turns to the question, "How, then, was permission obtained?" (S: 347; 2:32). One of the retainers who commits junshi under the old regime of Tadatoshi is the newly married seventeen-year-old Naitō Chōjūrō Mototsugu (1625–1641). He is an example of someone who, having received a very small favor, goes to extremes to secure permission for junshi. In his case, the small favor was granted when Tadatoshi attributed an unspecified "blunder" (S: 348; 2:34: *shissaku*) committed by Chōjūrō to the sake Chōjūrō was fond of drinking. This reattribution of his trivial misdeed to the spirits of rice wine leads to Chōjūrō's conviction that he can make up for his "blunder" and repay the lord's "generosity" (S: 348; 2:34: *on*) only by committing junshi.

Absurd as Chōjūrō's desire for junshi may be, it does not occur in a vacuum. The narrator makes a point of explaining the societal pressures that govern Chōjūrō's request for permission and his fear of "horrible humiliation" (S: 348; 2:34: *osoroshii kutsujoku*) if he fails to obtain it. Chōjūrō's youth excuses the folly of his wish to die for grossly inadequate reasons. He is a man still in the making, learning from his surroundings, the culture of seventeenth-century Japan. As he faces his dying lord, he is looking for guidance and receives it in the form of a scroll that Tadatoshi asks him to hang in the alcove just as he (Tadatoshi) is about to expire. The two large calligraphic characters on this scroll read *fuji,* or literally, "not two."[62] By entrusting Chōjūrō with the task of hanging this precious belonging just at the time of his death, Tadatoshi seems to be intimating to Chōjūrō that the two of them will be one in death—if his retainer follows his lord. That is, at any rate, how Chōjūrō interprets his master's request, for he makes his own request for junshi immediately after displaying the scroll.

The scene of his repeated entreaties for permission is comically absurd. As his lord lies dying, Chōjūrō is asked to massage his heavy legs, which he does. Chōjūrō then initiates further intimate physical contact by pressing his lord's foot on his forehead as he humbly asks permission for junshi. The retainer's gesture is twice met by the lord's gesture of denial, until finally, despite the disapproving comments of some attendants, Chōjūrō wins his lord's consent. The utter absurdity of Chōjūrō's grave request to die for a laughable offense is obvious. The sexual connotations of the scene are less so, but Japanese theatergoers may notice that the comic scene is reminiscent of the erotic playfulness of a scene in Chikamatsu's *Sonezaki shinjū* (1703; The love suicides at Sonezaki). In that famous scene, the "star-crossed" lovers Ohatsu and Tokubei agree by their elaborate foot play to commit suicide: "Narrator: She pretends to be talking to herself, but with her foot she questions him. He nods, and taking her ankle, passes it across his throat, to let her know that he is bent on suicide. . . . She taps with her foot, and Tokubei, weeping, takes it in his hands and reverently touches it to his forehead."[63]

To be sure, there is a world of difference between forbidden love and double suicide in the merchant-and-townsman culture *(chōnin)* of Tokugawa Japan and the intimate bonds between lord and retainer that affected decisions of junshi, but there are strong intimations that one reason for junshi was a bond of love so strong that it must not be broken by the lord's death. As Eiko Ikegami, a specialist on samurai culture, has noted about just such cases as Chōjūrō's, "the act of *junshi* represented the wedding of death and Eros, wrapped in the official ideology of samurai loyalty."[64]

Chōjūrō's resolve to commit junshi is tacitly approved by his family. His mother fully expects him to commit junshi on the day marking the first month after Lord Tadatoshi's death: "If he had told her that he would not do so, she would have been alarmed" (S: 349; 2:35). His young bride and his "younger brother," Saheiji (1629–?),[65] share these expectations, although the former has wept at the thought of losing him. When he makes up his mind about junshi, after Tadatoshi's death, Chōjūrō considers his family's unquestioning support and finds satisfaction in imagining the Hosokawa clan rewarding his family for his junshi: "He thought that he now had placed his family in a safe position, that he could die peacefully. With the thought, his face brightened" (S: 348; 2:35).[66]

When we consider that sake was the culprit responsible for Chōjūrō's deadly resolve, it seems ironic that his mother encourages him to become thoroughly drunk during the farewell ritual of passing sake cups among the four family members. Astonishingly, in light of the deadly task before him, he sleeps like a log. The narrator sounds a comic note in his reference to Chōjūrō's snoring: "The wind chime faintly tinkled from time to time, as if to remind itself of its job" (S: 350; 2:37). When Chōjūrō's second *(kaishakunin)*, Seki Koheiji (dates unknown), appears, Chōjūrō's bride wakes him, and they have a little lunch together. The deadpan narrator remarks simply, "Then Chōjūrō prepared himself calmly and went with Seki to his family temple, Tōkō-in, to disembowel himself" (S: 351; 2:39).

Tadatoshi's Deliberations

By way of a prelude to the long list of retainers who committed junshi, the narrator presents Tadatoshi's deliberations on permission, which are not unlike the Elder Seneca's (55 B.C.E.–41 C.E.) in *Suasoriae*, a work in which Seneca meditates on Cicero's fate. One suspects that similar thoughts crossed the minds of other responsible rulers, including Emperor Meiji, who were faced with such decisions. As a man of the old regime, Ōgai's Tadatoshi is torn between granting permission to these retainers in order to aggrandize his own glory and denying them permission so that they may live to serve his son, Mitsuhisa. He must choose between enhancing his personal reputation and transferring his retainers' loyalty and devotion to his successor, thereby assuring the new regime's stability. Although the choice seems clear enough, Tadatoshi's reasoning is full of contradictions. In the agony of his case-by-case granting or denial of permission, he attempts to rationalize his decisions. For example, he convinces himself that, although it was "*cruel* to have them die with him," his retainers "would be glad to offer their lives for him" (S: 351; 2:39: *zankoku*). When doubts nonetheless begin to assail him, he speculates about the effect of not granting permission—and how much worse that would be. His retainers would be stamped as "cowards" (S: 351; 2:40: *hikyōmono*) with "no sense of obligation" (S: 351; 2:40: *on shirazu*) and his reputation would be stained because he had kept such cowards in his service. And yet, if the retainers lived, they would have a good chance to redeem their honor by serving his successor bravely and well. Tadatoshi eventually granted permission to eighteen of the petitioners. He consoled himself with the argument that granting permission to the older retainers was "an act of mercy" (S: 352; 2:40: *jihi*). After all, there were plenty of younger ones to serve Mitsuhisa. Obviously, Emperor Meiji, if he deliberated in similar ways, faced the same dilemma of whether or not to grant permission to Nogi.

Genealogy

Now that the reader can fully appreciate the agony behind Tadatoshi's deliberations about whether or not to grant permission to this or that retainer, Ōgai's narrator turns genealogist and releases the impressive list of the eighteen retainers who did commit junshi. For almost every man, the narrator deems it necessary to catalogue a number of facts: his name and family history; his relationship to the lord; the nature of his service and special favors received; his wealth measured in *koku* and the number of retainers under his supervision; his *kaishakunin;* the time and place of his junshi; the issue of permission. The narrator does not slavishly follow this scheme but occasionally allows himself to digress with a telling anecdote. He explains, for instance, that Tadatoshi's poison taster, Hashitani Ichizō Shigetsugu (1611–1641), wanted to know what time it was when he disemboweled himself. Hashitani had a good last laugh, because the servant who was sent to count the drumbeats—then the equivalent of strokes of the clock—heard only the last four (2:42: shimai no yotsu dake wa kikimashita ga, sōtai no bachikazu wa wakarimasen). Aside from the absurdity of Hashitani's wanting to know the exact time of his death when he had to have been resigned, as poison taster, to the threat of death at every meal, the servant's words are hilarious because they contain an unintentional pun on *bachi* (drumbeats), which is homonymous with *bachi* (divine punishment).

In this passage, as in the genealogical appendix to the second version of Okitsu Yagoemon's testament, Ōgai indulges in a narrative device that resembles biblical genealogical lists or, more to the point, the lists of warriors recited in the oral tradition of warrior epics such as the *Heike monogatari.* A modern reader may grow impatient at the sight of these pages of names. Marvin Marcus has put it tactfully, "The weight of factual information, much of it genealogical, appears almost calculated to discourage the casual reader."[67] What, then, is the purpose of these lists and genealogies? Since the reader does not learn a great deal about the warriors or retainers mentioned, the lists may seem superfluous, but, as a form of narrative, ritual genealogical lists bear an uncanny resemblance to the ritual of junshi itself. They put each person in his proper place and establish his hierarchical position. They communicate and commemorate values held by those who died painful warriors' deaths for their nation, for their clan, or for their lord. If these values are to be perpetuated, they must be presented in impressive, excessive, incantatory abundance. As in warrior epics, the purpose here is to record the heroes' names for all posterity and to immortalize their fame. In his aptly titled study of Ōgai's biographies, *Paragons of the Ordinary,* Marcus also emphasizes the importance of genealogy within "the Confucian reckoning of things, [where] a name possessed iconic significance, and the proper recording of names for posterity was a meritorious act." Marcus comes close to attributing a sacred aspect to this activity: "It is as though the very act of naming—one is tempted to say the *sacrament* of naming—[were] sufficient unto itself, conferring identity, dignity, and perhaps even a degree of immortality upon those named."[68]

Gosuke

As in the warrior culture of ancient Rome, Japanese warrior culture had intricate ways of calibrating rank and honor. Of the Romans, Carlin A. Barton has unflinchingly observed, "Those with low status might feel keenly the contempt of the elite," but they could nonetheless "hiss you at the games or piss on your statue. They could kill you."[69] They could also, with their cheers or with their sacrificial offerings, exalt you. The same was true in Japan. As the example of young Chōjūrō demonstrates, the honor and glory conferred by junshi are not dependent on the rank and social status of the person who commits the ritual act. Another example of a lowly retainer exhibiting great boldness in asking permission for junshi is Tsuzaki Gosuke Nagasue (?–1641), the dog keeper, who sees himself as rivaled in Tadatoshi's affection only by the lord's falconers. Gosuke manages to coax permission from Tadatoshi. He leaves for Kōrinji, the temple of choice for his junshi, with his wife's approval, "'You're a man, too. Try not to be lesser in glory than those in senior positions'" (S: 355; 2:46). Before he can act, however, the clan elders intervene with the suggestion that he might better honor the lord by serving his successor.[70] The true reason for the administrators' objection may be that they are more concerned than Tadatoshi was about Gosuke's low rank. Can a daimyō be honored by his dog keeper's junshi? For Gosuke, the answer is an unequivocal yes. He feels dishonored by the sudden withdrawal of permission. "I'm a lowly retainer," he does not hesitate to admit to his dog, "but I'm no different from those of higher rank in having received a stipend to live from day to day" (S: 355–356; 2:46). Will his dog support him as his wife did? Will his dog die for him just as he plans to die for Tadatoshi? The dog lives up to his master's expectations by scorning the two rice balls Gosuke offers him just in case he prefers to live on as a kind of canine *rōnin*. Gosuke then provides the assistance necessary for the dog to commit junshi in anticipation of his master's death. The expression *inujini*, or dog's death, takes on a new meaning, since this dog's death is not at all shameful.

To the best of his ability, Gosuke observes all the formalities for the performance of junshi. It is precisely where he is awkward and unpracticed in the art of "the brush and the sword in accord" *(bunbu no itchi)* that he is most compelling. He writes the obligatory farewell poem *(jisei)*, even folding it the way he has seen it done, but it is pathetically unpoetic. No matter. Gosuke is sincere, and the more blunders he makes in proper protocol the more honorable his action becomes. The narrator describes his final brushstrokes *(zeppitsu)*: "The paper was not signed. He simply thought that because the poem already had his name, he didn't have to duplicate it by writing it again. In this he was faithful to the tradition without knowing it" (S: 356; 2:47).

Not surprisingly, Gosuke handles the sword as roughly as he handles the brush, but to the extent that he violates proper etiquette and procedure he moves the heart. Avoiding even the slightest hint of mournfulness, he asks his *kaishakunin* for assistance, then takes the sword, still dripping with his dog's blood and, with a triumphant verbal stab at the cowardly falconers, cuts his stomach crosswise, "laughing joyfully" (S: 356; 2:48).

The Interregnum

Despite Tadatoshi's careful deliberations about each request for permission, the narrator reveals that one request was not granted: that of Abe Yaichiemon Michinobu. Although the narrator, so meticulous about his details, leaves an incomplete record of the wealth of Tadatoshi's retainers, Yaichiemon appears to be the wealthiest, with 1,500 *koku.* He is a model retainer who never does anything wrong. He is annoyingly perfect. Perhaps he is *too* flawless—like Aristides the Just (d. c. 467 B.C.E.), whom the ancient Athenians exiled because they were bored by his perfection. Trying to induce an indiscretion, Tadatoshi had contradicted Yaichiemon again and again, but this ploy had merely "stiffened" Yaichiemon, which in turn caused his lord to "resent" him. Once the relationship had settled into this pattern, it seemed impossible to change it. The narrator sympathizes with Tadatoshi, who was not the only one who disliked Yaichiemon. Others, who praised the head of the Abe clan as an "outstanding samurai" (S: 358; 2:50: *rippa na samurai*), whispered, "'You can't get a crack at him'" (S: 358; 2:50: dōmo Abe ni wa tsukeiru hima ga nai).

And so Yaichiemon does not obtain the one favor he has ever asked for in his whole life. Instead he is told to transfer his impeccable loyalty to Mitsuhisa, of the future regime. After much deliberation during the interregnum, he intends to do exactly that, thereby avoiding a dog's death or becoming a *rōnin:* "But I am what I am. Let them think what they like. A samurai is no concubine" (S: 358; 2:51: Da ga ore wa ore da. Yoi wa. Bushi wa mekake to wa chigau.). His language is less a criticism of the common practice of male love *(nanshoku)* between lord and retainer, which is conducive to strengthening bonds of loyalty, than a criticism of the prostitution of this sanctioned practice.[71] Thus he continues to hold his head high while others, expecting him to die a dog's death, avert their eyes.

The rumors that begin to brew are fermented by Yaichiemon's continuing impeccable behavior, which some see as bordering on hubris. They needle him: "Abe stays alive, it appears, glad that he didn't get his permission. Even without it one could disembowel oneself if one wanted to. Abe's belly skin seems different from an ordinary man's. He should perhaps oil a gourd and cut his belly with it" (S: 359; 2:52). Here Ōgai may well be wondering whether someone like Nogi would have been hounded by rumors of cowardice if he had not committed seppuku. One can only speculate about those who might have pointed fingers at Nogi if he had chosen to live and serve the next emperor. Perhaps such rumors had already begun to fly in the days between Emperor Meiji's death and his funeral.

Yaichiemon decides, for the first and last time, to disobey his lord. He will commit junshi without Tadatoshi's permission. He summons his five sons to explain the why and the how. They are understanding and supportive. It is the oppressive rainy season, and the narrator notes the presence of a "single firefly" (S: 359; 2:53) that may, as often in Japanese poetry, symbolize a dead soul. Is it Tadatoshi's, posthumously witnessing and approving of Yaichiemon's disobedience?

The New Regime

The gruesome remainder of "Abe ichizoku" deals with the treatment of Yaichiemon's clan by the authorities of the new regime of Mitsuhisa. Although all the heirs of the eighteen retainers who committed junshi with Tadatoshi's permission are rewarded, the Abe heirs are not. Abe Yaichiemon's oldest son, Gonbē (?–1643), is barred from succeeding his father and the clan's domain is divided among the five sons, which leaves each one feeling rather inconsequential. The narrator becomes judgmental. He diverts the blame for this vindictive behavior on the part of the youthful and still inexperienced Mitsuhisa to his "inspector general" (S: 363; 2:57: *ōmetsuke*), one Hayashi Geki (?–1649), who had indeed recommended harsh treatment. The narrator notes that Mitsuhisa has accepted the inspector general's recommendation because it includes a clause favoring Mitsuhisa's new favorite, Ichidayū, the third Abe son. The narrator criticizes the government for not having treated Yaichiemon the same as the other eighteen retainers and for encouraging those who remained contemptuous of Yaichiemon even after he had responded with dignity to the malicious rumors about his soft belly.

The great tragedy to come is triggered when, at the first anniversary of Tadatoshi's death, on 1642.III.17, Gonbē stuns everybody by cutting off his topknot, symbol of his manhood and samurai status, and presenting it as an offering to Tadatoshi's memorial tablet. Gonbē's desperate act is his riposte to the gossipers' insult of his father's failure—an oiled gourd instead of a sword—to do what a man must do, permission or not. His violent gesture, however, is more than just a rebuke to those who sneered at his father for continuing to live as though nothing had changed when his lord died. He also protests the defilement of the Abe name by those who did not honor Yaichiemon's death by showing respect to his clan. Gonbē's protest is no ordinary protest. By cutting off his own topknot he evokes the horror of castration and makes a spectacle of his family's shame. He counters his family's shame by dishonoring the Hosokawa, an offense that is as horrendous and irreversible as his symbolic self-castration.

Provoked by Gonbē, Mitsuhisa admits that he is partly to blame for his behavior, but this admission does not deter him from punishing Gonbē. Regrettably, in the opinion of the narrator, Mitsuhisa lacks vision enough to overlook the provocation and meet resentment with generosity. Instead, he jails Gonbē and has him executed "like a common thief" (S: 366; 2:61).[72]

An escalation in the struggle for honor is now inevitable. The four remaining Abe sons barricade themselves in Gonbē's Yamazaki compound, together with their entire clan. It is clear to them that Gonbē's execution was not enough to satisfy Mitsuhisa's anger. A punitive force will be sent and they will all die. In the eyes of the authorities, the Abe clan has made an "*unpeaceful* move" (S: 366; 2:62: *odayaka naranu*) that cannot be tolerated. The Abe have become a threat to the new regime, which cannot allow its subjects to put the defense of their own honor above the interests of their lord. The government has no recourse other than to make them martyrs.

The Abe prepare to die honorably. They perform the rituals of purification. After a banquet, the older Abe men and the women kill themselves, and all the children are stabbed to death. As the young men prepare to die in defense of their honor, the narrator turns to the Abe neighbors and to the members of the punitive force. Among the neighbors, Tsukamoto Matashichirō (Sumoto, dates unknown) features most prominently. His family survived many struggles within the domain and Matashichirō has continued the tradition of serving the Hosokawa. Since his family is close to the Abe, he has been following the evolving drama with the anxiety of a relative. When the Abe first barricade themselves, he sends his wife over as a sign of friendship, a gesture that is deeply appreciated. Matashichirō's motives, however, are not entirely pure. He continually calculates the reception of his actions by the authorities. His divided loyalties are put to the test when the punitive force is about to attack. Should he obey official orders to refrain from interfering or should he stand by his Abe friends? While he cannot, as a loyal Hosokawa retainer, support the Abe, neither can he—a samurai—watch a massacre. He finds a compromise. He cuts the ropes of the bamboo fence between his house and that of the Abe to signal his true allegiance and then takes his spear to fight them: "Compassion is compassion, justice justice" (S: 369; 2:66: nasake wa nasake, gi wa gi de aru). Matashichirō's killing of any Abe, in particular his close friend Yagobē, is a labor of love resembling that of a *kaishakunin.*

Takenouchi Kazuma Nagamasa (1623–1643), a member of the punitive force, is an especially interesting case. Although he had fought ferociously for Tadatoshi and been rewarded with a precious sword and an increase in his stipend to 1,150 *koku,* he did not join the retainers who committed junshi for Tadatoshi. Not asking Tadatoshi for permission to die, the intriguing inspector general Geki accused him of having failed to behave honorably. Geki suggested that he absolve himself of the dishonor by sacrificing his life for his new lord, but Kazuma refused. He wants to die, but he refuses to ask Mitsuhisa for permission to commit junshi for Tadatoshi. A solution to the standoff comes when Geki advises Mitsuhisa to give Kazuma the deadly assignment of attacking the front gate of the Abe. In sending the young Kazuma into battle, Tadatoshi had said, "Don't get hurt!" (S: 370;

2:68: kega o suru na yo). In issuing his command, Mitsuhisa mimicks his father, "Try not to get wounded" (S: 371; 2:69: kega o senu yō ni). Although Kazuma wants to die, he is mortified by the mockery Mitsuhisa makes of Tadatoshi's lovingly protective words. His death in battle is simultaneously a protest against the new regime and a tribute to the old one. It is a form of junshi, after all. Kazuma himself humbly calls it "a dog's death" (S: 372; 2:71). Carrying an heirloom, the Shimabara sword, and the priceless "Hatsune" incense received from Tadatoshi, Kazuma goes in for the slaughter.

The assault is planned for daybreak on 1642.IV.21. All is quiet as the moment of truth approaches: "A swallow appeared from somewhere and swooped inside the fence" (S: 374; 2:74). Earlier it was a firefly that provided the spark for Abe's junshi; now it is a swallow that gives the signal for the first shot, simultaneously inciting the attackers and warning the defenders. The attack begins. Matashichirō enters the fray without authorization, wounding his friend Abe Yagobē. In response to Matashichirō's charge of cowardice, the retreating Yagobē explains his intent to commit seppuku. In a daze over what he has done to his fellow spearman, Matashichirō is stabbed in the thigh by the boy Shichinojō, whose older brother Ichidayū stabs Kazuma's page in the eye and then, together with Godayū, kills Kazuma. The violence and confusion mount. The narrator is hard put to find a metaphor to do justice to the chaos: "the main room was merely a thirty-mat space. Just as the horrors of a street fight are much greater than those of a battlefield, so the men fighting there, like a hundred worms piled up on a plate devouring each other, were a horrible sight indeed" (S: 375; 2:76).

Mori Ōgai's horrific image of "worms piled up on a plate devouring each other" has captivated his readers. Why is this image so shocking? So memorable? It is a feast or orgy so ghoulish that one does not wish to dwell on it, but there is more to the image than the mere desire to shock. All the worms look alike and all of them are involved in a fight to survive. The men in the thirty-mat room all have served the same master with the same purpose. In the confines of a thirty-mat room, friends and neighbors slaughter one another. Like worms confined to a single plate, they devour one another. In their last attempt to survive and acquire the charisma and strength of the others, they are like cannibals. In such combat there can be no winners and no losers.

Gon'emon lives to relate the tale of horror to Lord Mitsuhisa, the man whose lack of political acumen caused the needless massacre. Mitsuhisa does not quite know how to deal with the predictable outcome of his foolishness. And he learns nothing from the experience. There is little rhyme or reason to the rewards and punishments he metes out to the survivors. In the end, the vexing question of permission to commit junshi remains unresolved.

CHAPTER 6

Mori Ōgai's "Sakai jiken"

Rebellion and Martyrdom

One of Ōgai's responses to the national and personal trauma of 1912 was to write about an apparently unrelated incident that, like the deaths of Emperor Meiji and his general, marked Japan's transition from one era to another. This incident occurred at the apex of the political and social movements linking the revolutionary Bakumatsu period (1853–1867), the tumultuous interim of the Meiji Restoration (Meiji *ishin,* 1867–1868), and the Restoration War (Boshin *sensō,* 27 January 1868–27 June 1869).

On 8 March 1868, Tosa soldiers stationed in the port of Sakai, near Ōsaka, killed eleven French sailors, thus plunging the nation into an international crisis. The reaction in the United States mingled indignation with horror. "Some of the dead were horribly mutilated," reported the *New York Times,* "after the most approved method of the savages. Ears cut off, tongues removed, and eyes carried away as trophies."[1] War with the outraged Western powers was averted when the newly installed and still precarious imperial government submitted to their demands. Of the twenty Tosa men sentenced to be executed for their complicity in the deaths of the French, eleven were permitted to commit seppuku and nine were sent into exile. An imperial pardon, conspicuously timed, was issued for the exiles on the occasion of the enthronement of Emperor Meiji on 12 October 1868.[2] Ōgai seized upon these events and made them into a screened story that enabled him to express his complex feelings about Nogi and to meditate on the transition from one historical era to another.[3]

Mori Ōgai as Curator of Cultural Memory

Ōgai's "Sakai jiken" (February 1914; The incident at Sakai) is the last in the series of short junshi narratives *(junshi shōsetsu).*[4] The story features both actual seppuku and the unfulfilled desire for junshi. Of the stories in the sequence, this one is set most closely in time to Nogi's junshi. In addition, the divided fate of its main protagonists—like Nogi's watershed suicide—signalizes the problematic transition from one era to another. "Sakai jiken" reflects upon the meanings—private and public, national and international—of seppuku in general and Nogi's junshi in particular.

Written in only five days,[5] in a mood of great urgency, the story follows the documentary account *Senshū: Sakai rekkyo shimatsu* (1893; rev. 1900; An account of the circumstances at Sakai in Izumi). This account, based on the records of two survivors, Doi Hachinosuke and Yokota Tatsugorō,[6] was written by Sasaki Kōzō (1847–?), an official from Kōchi, the Tosa *han* capital.[7] Written at the request of Tosa men's families in order to add the eleven men who committed seppuku to the martyrs enshrined in the Yasukuni *jinja*,[8] this source is, not surprisingly, biased in favor of the Japanese version of the bloody skirmish. While some scholars have questioned the historical authenticity of Ōgai's fictionalized account, my concern is not the question of factual accuracy, nor am I concerned with Ōgai's neglect of other documents.[9] My emphasis is on his search for meaning in his source. As H. S. Versnel remarked of the deeply lamented death of the Roman general Germanicus (15 or 16 B.C.E.–19 C.E.): "the historicity of the picture is not essential or vital to the issue . . . : What interests me is the type of emotional reaction to a special traumatizing event and the forms in which it took shape."[10] That Ōgai approached history in a similar frame of mind is clear from his remarks about his "Ōshio Heihachirō" (January 1914; Ōshio Heihachirō), which tells the story of the Confucian philosopher who in 1837 led an uprising in Ōsaka. Originally inspired by a manuscript by the Kabuki scholar Suzuki Motojirō (1868–1927), Ōgai did extensive research that included the reading of a biographical study of Ōshio Heihachiro (1793–1837) by Kōda Shigetomo (1873–1954). But even here, Ōgai acknowledged the inadequacy of the historical record. In his "first-person postscript" to "Ōshio Heihachirō" he wrote, "As the manuscript [by Suzuki] was mainly composed of hearsay, I tried to extract the historical facts, but the haul was very meagre. In as much as the record was full of holes my imagination was spurred on."[11] In short, Ōgai oscillated between being faithful to his sources and creatively expanding on them, or—in his words—between writing "history as it is" and "history aside from the facts."[12]

Historical fiction about moments of transition marked by sacrificial death engages the reader's memory in special ways. In the context of defining "cultural memory," Jan Assmann has pointed out that "the term 'tradition' disguises the break that leads to the formation of the past and instead foregrounds the aspect of continuity." Assmann argues that it is essential to deal with the break that "tradition" disguises. After all, the archetypal experience of this break is death, the *Urszene* of the culture of memory, which compels us "to revive the dead" *(Akt der Belebung):* "Memorializing the dead [is] the most ancient and widespread form of cultural memory. . . . Remembrance of the dead is a matter of emotional bonding, cultural formation, and an attitude toward the past that consciously transcends the break."[13]

Ōgai chose to write about the Sakai Incident because he wanted to understand, not only the transition to the Meiji period, but also the less tumultuous but equally significant transition to the Taishō period. The spectacular deaths that followed the restoration of imperial rule under Emperor Mutsuhito on 3 January 1868 and his funeral as Meiji Tennō on 13 September 1912 form two incisive points between the past and the future. Whether the break with the past was marked by the deaths of ordinary soldiers and their commanders, as in the Sakai Incident of 1868, or by that of a famous general, as was the case in 1912, the break seemed to traumatize the nation. In the face of trauma that sharply increases the danger of repression, conscious efforts to memorialize—and control—the dead were monumental and multifaceted. The dead—the Tosa soldiers as well as General Nogi—were enshrined and worshiped. By retelling the soldiers' story directly and the general's indirectly, Ōgai dealt with his own and with the nation's trauma.

Ōgai's "Sakai jiken" puts the events of 1868 side by side with those of 1912, as if they were viewed through a stereoscope that reveals a three-dimensionality missing when one looks at a single image. Another way to describe Ōgai's narrative technique is to call it a palimpsest. The original text (the story of Nogi's junshi) has been overlaid by a new one (the Sakai Incident), thereby creating a third text in the mind of the reader.[14]

The palimpsest typically evokes layers of the past that have resurfaced in the present. As a curator of cultural memory rather than as a mere chronicler, Ōgai reversed the process by foregrounding the past in front of the present. He adapted the literary convention employed by Tokugawa authors and playwrights, who projected contemporary conflicts upon the screen of the past because they were forbidden by the government to write critically about the present.

What does Ōgai's rendering of the Sakai Incident reveal about Japanese ethical assumptions and conflicts with authorities in 1868 and in 1912? And what does Ōgai's particular rendition tell us about seppuku as a marker of political transition? Alan Wolfe has suggested one answer: "With the advent of modernity, seppuku took on the aura of a nationalistic narrative, one whose elaboration extends from one of Japan's first literary modernizationists, Mori Ōgai, and through to Mishima Yukio, whose own death in this manner is the most dramatic instance of an attempt to make suicide a part of Japan's distinctive national allegory."[15] And—beyond nationalism—we also find men, when pushed to the limits by the authorities, seeking nobility in honorable acts that allow them some measure of control over their own lives while still serving their country.

Historical Background to the Sakai Incident

Bakumatsu Incidents

The Sakai Incident of 8 March 1868[16] was the most serious instance of Japanese violence that took place during the Bakumatsu and Meiji Restoration periods against visiting or resident foreigners, but it was not the first. There had been many spontaneous outbursts of provoked or unprovoked violence. There had also been carefully planned assassinations, such as Henry Heusken's on 15 January 1861.[17] Many of these earlier attacks were led by "men of high purpose" *(shishi)* who bitterly resented the humiliatingly unequal treaties that the shōgunate had been pressured to sign with Western powers. By 1868, the mentality of resistance to foreigners shaped by *shishi* was shared by many ordinary people, including the soldiers involved in the Sakai Incident.

Many of the violent incidents were occasioned by the inability of Japanese and foreigners to understand each other's culture. Foreigners may not have been arrogant, but they seemed so to the Japanese. When their behavior violated Japanese standards of ethical behavior, their lives were endangered. On 14 September 1862, for instance, a British merchant Charles L. Richardson (1833–1862) and three of his companions failed to pay the proper respect to the daimyō of Satsuma, Shimazu Hisamitsu (1817–1887), as he passed through Namamugi near Yokohama. Richardson was killed and two of his companions injured in what came to be known as the Richardson Affair or the Namamugi jiken.[18] Hisamitsu protected the assailants, despite orders from the *bakufu.* Still rankling from an earlier incident that year in which a vassal of the Matsumoto domain had taken the lives of two British soldiers (and then committed suicide), the British were severe in their demands for retribution: an apology, indemnities, and the execution of Richardson's murderers in the presence of British observers.[19] After initial hesitation, the *bakufu* finally agreed to the British demands, but the Satsuma domain did not. A British squadron of seven warships then bombarded Satsuma's capital, Kagoshima, on 15 August 1863, in what is known as the Satsuei War (Satsuei *sensō*). Although the British succeeded in destroying much of Kagoshima with their new Armstrong guns, employed for the first time, they too suffered many casualties.[20] Memories of these events affected decisions taken in subsequent international incidents.

The Bizen Affair

Of all the many acts of violence against foreigners that preceded the Sakai Incident, the most relevant for understanding Ōgai's story was the international incident known as the Bizen Affair, or the Kōbe jiken. This affair, described by Gordon Daniels as "a turning point in the attitude of British towards the Meiji Restoration,"[21] occurred at an unusually sensitive time in Japan's relations with the West. The shōgun's forces had just been decisively defeated by their imperial opponents in the battle of Toba and Fushimi (27 January 1868), and it was unclear to the foreign powers whether or not the victors would recognize the treaties that had been imposed upon the shōgunate by the "barbarians." Max von Brandt (1835–1920), the Prussian attaché in 1867–1868,[22] identified the crux of the problem: "the bureaucrats of the shōgun had fled, and we had not yet established relations with those of the emperor."[23]

"Exact details of the incident are not clear," wrote Grace Fox, "as Japanese and Western sources differ."[24] There was, however, agreement on the basic facts. On 4 February 1868, Taki Zenzaburō (1837–1868), a retainer of the Bizen domain's senior retainer *(karō)*, Hiki Tatewaki (1829–1918), was accused of having ordered his men to fire on a group of Americans. Taki may have intended for the shots merely to hit the flags of the United States, Italy, and the North German Federation.[25] Even if that was the case, the assault on national honor was nonetheless quite serious. In any event, no one was killed, but two men were wounded. Prolonged and difficult negotiations were necessary to arrive at a just settlement, one that prevented war while at the same time preserving the honor of both sides.

On 8 February 1868, a group of foreign delegates met with an imperial delegation led by a man fresh out of a five-year exile, Higashikuze Michitomi (1834–1912). Settlement of the Bizen Affair was not the first item on the agenda. For the foreigners, the main purpose of the meeting was to obtain assurance that the emperor recognized the treaties imposed on Japan in the 1850s and 1860s.[26] For the Japanese, the main issue was whether the Western powers would revise the treaties to acknowledge that the emperor was now Japan's actual as well as nominal ruler. Agreement was reached on the treaties and on the need for the Bizen Affair to be settled in accordance with them, but a settlement was not reached. Confronted with the foreign delegates' demand for immediate retribution for the assault at Kōbe, the Japanese argued that the form of retribution should not be specified while the political situation in the aftermath of the *bakufu*'s collapse was still so volatile. In deciding the form of retribution, the new Japanese government had to satisfy not only the foreigners' demands but also those of its supporters in the Bizen domain who "expected the new government to carry out the isolationist policy and expel the barbarians."[27]

According to Sir Ernest Mason Satow (1843–1929), British diplomat and interpreter from 1862 to 1882 and minister plenipotentiary to Japan from 1895 to 1900, the Western representatives seeking retribution for the Bizen Affair singled out "the officer who gave the order to fire" for "capital punishment"—namely, Taki Zenzaburō. The imperial court had initially decided to order Hiki Tatewaki to accept responsibility for Taki's actions and to commit *harakiri.*[28] The "Mikado's government" then changed its mind,[29] acceding to the foreigners' demand for "the capital punishment of the officer who had given the order to fire on foreigners."[30] After weeks of delay, during which the foreign diplomats became skeptical about the imperial court's real intentions,[31] Taki was finally ordered to commit seppuku (referred to in Japanese sources as *kappuku,* "splitting the stomach").[32]

The Japanese government had modified in three ways its agreement to execute the man responsible for the order to fire. First, the imperial court stipulated that the execution was to be by seppuku. There seems to have been no protest, perhaps because the foreigners did not yet clearly understand that seppuku under these conditions was a form of self-sacrifice that elevated the condemned man to the status of a martyr.[33]

Second, the Japanese, by allowing Taki to die for his superior, Hiki, had recast the sentence in yet another way. For the Japanese, the substitution of Taki for Hiki was important because it transformed Taki's execution—in their eyes—into an expiatory sacrifice. Algernon Bertram Mitford (1837–1916), a member of the British Legation to Japan from 1866 to 1870, failed to comprehend what had happened, mistakenly assuming that "the dead man was indeed the officer who had committed the crime and no substitute."[34] Although Satow noticed the substitution[35] and requested an explanation from Saigō Takamori,[36] he failed in his memoirs to ponder its significance.

Third, there was a last-minute plea for mercy, suggesting that even though the Japanese had transformed Taki's execution into self-sacrifice through seppuku,[37] they still considered his death too high a price to pay, especially because they doubted that the foreigners understood the meaning of seppuku and could therefore not honor Taki's self-sacrifice. Although all the foreign delegates were extremely anxious to set a precedent for judicial action in response to offenses against them, they were divided in their response to the Japanese appeal. According to von Brandt, the plea was rejected by the foreign delegates after a five-hour discussion on 2 March, the very day of reckoning.[38] Von Brandt, who was one of the four to two majority, felt compelled to justify at length his vote against clemency by pointing to the contradiction between the Japanese willingness to comply with Western demands and their plea for mercy. The Japanese argument—that even in Europe life was not taken when no life was lost—was rebutted by von Brandt, who asserted that the Japanese soldiers had *intended* to kill (although this contradicts his earlier observation that the Japanese had aimed at flags rather than people). He explicitly rejected the argument advanced in the plea for clemency that violations of Japanese ceremonial processions justified the murder of foreigners.[39] It appears that von Brandt sensed a cultural pattern of maneuver and manipulation the key to which was inaccessible to the foreign delegates.

Mitford agreed with von Brandt in rejecting the appeal. He observed that "the Japanese petition for clemency was very half-hearted" and that some high-ranking Japanese "took the same view that I did, saying that clemency would be mistaken for cowardice."[40] As Mitford explained in a letter to his father (3 March 1868),

> that mercy, although it might have produced the desired effect among the more civilized clans, would have been mistaken for weakness and fear by those wilder people who have not yet a personal knowledge of foreigners. The offence—an attack upon the flags and subjects of all the Treaty Powers which lack of skill, not of will, alone prevented from ending in a universal massacre—was the gravest that has been committed upon foreigners since their residence in Japan. Death was undoubtedly deserved and the form chosen was in Japanese eyes merciful and yet judicial. The crime might have involved a war and cost hundreds of lives; it was wiped out by one.[41]

On the same day, Mitford filed a formal report to Sir Harry Parkes (1828–1885), British minister to Japan from 1865 to 1883.[42]

In his last speech, Taki "declared that he alone was the person who on the fourth of February had outrageously at Kobé ordered fire to be opened on foreigners as they were trying to escape."[43] Foreigners might have been less satisfied that justice was done if they had known that Taki received a stipend increase of 100 *koku* in return for his sacrifice. Ironically, this compensation, paid to his family, was soon nullified by the 1871 abolition of feudal domains and the establishment of a centralized prefectural system *(haihan chiken)*.[44]

The Sakai Incident in the Politics of Sakai and Tosa

The Sakai Incident occurred in a location of symbolic importance. The port city of Sakai (lit. "boundary"), just south of Ōsaka, straddled the boundaries of Kawachi, Izumi, and Settsu. It was once second only to Kyōto as a center of Japanese culture. At its economic peak in the sixteenth century,[45] its merchants had traded with Ming-dynasty China, and foreigners were so impressed by its commercial activity that the Jesuit visitor Gaspar Vilela (1525–1572) called the city "another Venice."[46] Poets gathered in Sakai, and the tea master Sen no Rikyū (1522–1591) was born there. It was not until the Tokugawa shōgunate instituted its seclusion policy *(sakokurei)* in 1639 that Sakai's broad horizon began to shrink. Nineteenth-century Sakai was a much diminished but still significant economic and cultural center.

The time of the Sakai Incident was as important as the place. It was a period in which political disorder threatened to become chaos. In the winter of 1867–1868, the shōgun's government was on the verge of extinction, fighting for its life against rebel forces loyal to the emperor. (Those who rebelled against the shōgunate are conventionally known, somewhat confusingly, as "loyalists.") Claiming that his troops had been defeated at Toba and Fushimi on 27 January by the sight of the imperial brocade pennant, the last shōgun, Tokugawa Yoshinobu (1837–1913),[47] abandoned Ōsaka Castle and fled by ship to Edo. His panicky flight triggered the dispersal of his officials, who now feared being branded "enemies of the court" *(chōteki)*. The area around Ōsaka fell into "a state of anarchy" (2:267: *museifu no jōkyō*).[48] The closed port of Sakai, which had been under the *bakufu*'s administrative authority, became, briefly, a lawless zone.[49] To restore order in the city, the imperial forces dispatched the Sixth and Eighth Infantry Divisions, comprised of men from Tosa Province.

Since these soldiers play a major role in Ōgai's story, it is important to understand the complicated politics of their domain in the years before the Sakai Incident. (Ōgai, of course, assumed that his readers were familiar with at least the broad outlines of the relationship between the politics of Tosa and the serial seppuku in Sakai.) Tosa was one of the four leading domains—with Chōshū, Satsuma, and Saga—that brought about the Meiji Restoration. Throughout the Tokugawa period, Tosa had been ruled by the Yamanouchi, a clan that owed its wealth to Tokugawa Ieyasu.

The Yamanouchi clan's long-standing alliance with the Tokugawa shōguns was challenged during the Bakumatsu period by a number of "country samurai" *(gōshi)*.[50] Rallying them to the slogan "Revere the Emperor, Expel the Barbarians" *(sonnō jōi)*, Takechi Zuizan (1829–1865)[51] sought a loyalist alliance with Satsuma and Chōshū. In 1861, Takechi and his followers swore a loyalist oath: "We swear by the deities that if the Imperial Flag is once raised we will go through fire and water to ease the Emperor's mind."[52] Failure to abide by the oath, signed in blood, required atonement by seppuku. This fateful oath placed Takechi on a collision course with the retired but highly influential Tosa daimyō Yamanouchi Toyoshige, better known as Yōdō (1827–1872; daimyō 1848–1859), who was then still committed to the Tokugawa shōgunate. The conflict between Yōdō and Takechi came to a head when the latter was implicated in the assassination of Yoshida Tōyō (1816–

1862), Yōdō's most trusted minister.[53] After three years of careful deliberation, Yōdō ordered Takechi to commit seppuku. Takechi, faithful to his loyalist oath, complied.[54] Ironically, in the short interval between Takechi's seppuku and the Sakai Incident, Lord Yōdō gradually shifted his allegiance from the collapsing Tokugawa shōgunate to the emerging imperial government.

Yōdō figured importantly in *bakumatsu* politics (and in Ōgai's story). In what now, in retrospect, looks like a prelude to the international crisis caused by the Sakai Incident,[55] Yōdō acted decisively to exonerate the Tosa men who were falsely accused of having murdered two British sailors from the warship *Icarus* on 5 August 1867.[56] More important, Yōdō persuaded the last shōgun to issue a memorial on 9 November 1867, calling for a return of imperial rule *(taisei hōkan)* and the creation of a bicameral parliamentary system.[57] Throughout this transitional period, Yōdō played the role of a negotiator, a middleman between the shōgunal and the imperial forces—in effect, a mediator between the old Japan and the new.[58]

Mitford, who was assigned to the Tosa clan at the time of the Sakai Incident, admired Yōdō and appreciated his mediating role. He characterized the Tosa daimyō's residence in Kyōto as "a hornets' nest," but he painted a very flattering portrait of the forty-one-year-old Yōdō, describing his political views as "statesmanlike" (although his personal life was that of "a very free liver" and "*viveur*").[59] Mitford was captivated by Yōdō's "magnetic attraction," which was only enhanced by a severe illness.[60] During the crisis of the Sakai Incident, Mitford placed his trust in Yōdō. Parkes, who feared that Mitford was in personal danger, ordered him to leave the Tosa domain's Kyōto residence, but Mitford took seriously Yōdō's solemn words of apology: "The act of violence which my retainers have committed has caused me to be deeply ashamed. I am aware that foreign nations must feel grievously incensed. It hurts me to think that my people should have interfered with the Mikado in his projects for civilizing the country. I pray that Tosa alone, and not the whole of Japan, may be rendered responsible for this deed."[61] Mitford decided to stay.[62]

Satow was more skeptical than Mitford about the efficacy of foreign diplomatic efforts. When he first received reports of the Sakai Incident, he immediately linked this newest outrage—even though he did not know its full extent—to the Bizen Affair: "It was evident to everybody that the execution of the Bizen officer had not had the effect of a warning. Confusion, despair; hopes dashed to the ground just on the point of fulfillment."[63]

Satow was an astute observer. The French reaction to the massacre at Sakai was predictably severe. Léon Roches (1809–1901),[64] who served as French minister to Japan from 1864 to 1868, issued five demands to the new imperial government: (1) the execution at Sakai of the officers and men responsible for the French deaths; (2) an indemnity of 150,000 Mexican silver dollars; (3) an apology in person by the principal minister of foreign affairs, a prince of the blood (Yamashina no miya), on board the French frigate *Vénus;* (4) an apology in person by the daimyō of Tosa on board the *Vénus;* (5) the exclusion of Tosa troops from open ports.[65] The Japanese were given four days to accept these demands, which were countersigned by the other foreign representatives on 12 March 1868. (In his story, Ōgai departs most notably from his source by omitting the demand for an apology from a prince of the blood.)[66]

Were the French demands reasonable? Meron Medzini thought not, accusing Roches of impetuousness in judging the Tosa soldiers' action, "Blinded by rage and the accumulation of frustrations and failures, Roches decided to teach the new regime a lesson."[67] Mark David Ericson differs, arguing that "Roches' response to this murderous incident was surprisingly prudent, cautious, and moderate, mainly because of the attitude of the imperial government and the support of his colleagues."[68] Whether or not the Japanese thought the French demands were reasonable, they sought above all to avert a military reprisal like the 1863 Satsuma bombardment (Satsuei *sensō*) that had followed the Richardson Affair. Devastating reprisal was a distinct possibility. As Roches reported on 11 March to the Ministre des affaires étrangères, "It would be easy for them [our troops] to burn Sakai and to spill torrents of blood to expiate French blood."[69] The imperial government had an additional motive to make amends quickly. The foreign delegates under Parkes' leadership had just agreed, while Roches was in Edo, to a neutrality pact that in effect stopped French assistance to the *bakufu,* hastening its demise.[70] The Japanese agreed to the French terms.

The harshest demand—execution of those responsible—required the Japanese to make some difficult choices (which became especially significant in Ōgai's story). As the French were in no position to identify those who had participated in killing the sailors, this task was left to the Japanese, in particular, the Tosa lords. Although Japanese officials reported to Parkes that "about twenty Tosa men and twenty townspeople armed with fire-hooks" had been involved in the Sakai Incident,[71] they decided to punish only the soldiers. Although the French had specified the execution of "the two officers in command at Sakai,"[72] twenty soldiers were condemned to die.[73]

In the course of preparing for the executions, events took some unanticipated turns. On 15 March, a representative of the imperial court, speaking for the condemned Tosa soldiers, requested that the men be allowed to preserve their honor by committing seppuku. Date Munenari (1818–1892), the Retired

Lord of Uwajima, obtained the consent of Roches, who seems not fully to have understood the importance of the request. (In Ōgai's story, which accentuates the shock and bewilderment of the French witnesses to the acts of seppuku, Roches' prior consent is not mentioned.)

On the appointed day, 16 March, the twenty condemned men began, one after the other, to commit seppuku. After the eleventh seppuku, Captain Bergasse du Petit Thouars (1832–1890), the commander of the corvette *Dupleix*, ordered that the suicides cease. *Le Moniteur Universel* asserted on 18 May 1868 that he did so "yielding to a humane inspiration,"[74] but the captain himself confided to Mitford that he stopped the bloody process after the first eleven men had committed ritual suicide because he could not bear the gory sight any longer.[75] He confessed his shock and revulsion: "His account of the scene to me," recalled Mitford, "was blood-curdling. Brave man as he was—one of the bravest—it nearly made him sick only to think of it, and his voice faltered as with difficulty he told the tale."[76] The captain's eyewitness account conveyed to von Brandt "a theatrical scene that sounded so unlikely as to require absolutely the entire credibility of the reporter in order not to appear unbelievable."[77]

Satow, who was not present on the day of the executions, attributed a different motive to du Petit Thouars. According to Satow, the captain stopped the bloody process after the eleventh man had performed ritual suicide because he had an Old Testament eye-for-an-eye sense of exact retribution.[78] Satow regretted the French interference, "for the twenty were all equally guilty." Stopping the process at the point where the Japanese dead were equal in number to the French dead "looked more like revenge than justice."[79] While condemning du Petit Thouars for not punishing *all* who had confessed their participation in the incident,[80] Satow nonetheless revealed his admiration of the dignity of the seppuku ceremony (as he had after witnessing Taki's seppuku two weeks earlier).[81]

Satow seems also to have doubted Mitford's description of du Petit Thouars as "one of the bravest." In Satow's opinion, the French had a second reason for stopping the acts of seppuku: they feared for their own lives as darkness approached. Von Brandt also thought, on the basis of what du Petit Thouars had told him, that the French had been deeply disturbed by the serial seppuku and had feared for their own lives as night fell. The captain had needed a pretext to leave and had decided to stop the seppuku after the eleventh Japanese had committed it since exactly that many Frenchmen had been killed at Sakai.[82]

In his official report to his superior, du Petit Thouars represented himself as a practical man who had had to deal with threatening weather and approaching darkness. He jotted down his impressions in a letter written on the night of the "executions."

> Meanwhile it was getting late; the weather was threatening, and I deemed it important to join the boats again, so that our men might be aboard before dark. To demand the postponement to the next day of the executions of the men that remained did not appear practicable. I determined, therefore, as soon as the eleventh head should have fallen, to inform Mr. Godoi [*sic;* Godai Tomoatsu (1835–1885)] that in view of the manner in which the engagement had been kept, I begged him to suspend the execution until I could have communicated with the minister of France, who I hoped would be pleased to consent that the men remaining should be placed at the disposal of the Japanese government, with the view of a commutation of sentence.[83]

Nowhere in this account did the captain acknowledge that each man had disembowelled himself before he was beheaded: "Soon the execution began; each man was beheaded on a place just opposite to us. Great excitement prevailed when the first two officers were executed; but this gradually calmed down, and then the most profound silence reigned in its stead." It was, of course, not the beheadings that were so time-consuming as to threaten the already weather-beaten time schedule; it was seppuku that delayed the "executions." The captain finished his self-portrayal as a compassionate witness concerned above all about the safety of his men: "You are aware that it was pitch dark and the sea quite rough when I arrived on board your ship in the steam launch." He took responsibility for "interrupting the course of reparation demanded by the minister of France." He did so out of "duty towards my country by assuring the return on board of all the men under my command, when the blood of the criminals had freely flown."[84]

None of the contemporary foreign commentators seems to have fully understood why the condemned men preferred seppuku to the much less painful death by execution. Satow was, in general, the most insightful of the foreigners who commented on the Sakai Incident, but even he, despite his appreciation of the dignity of ritual suicide, failed fully to explore its meaning. Parkes, who had advocated clemency to avoid Taki's seppuku in the Bizen Affair, came closer. He confided in a letter to his wife that the "*harakiri* which Roches mistakenly accepted in the Sakai affair makes heroes or martyrs of the men who undergo it, and rather encourages than deters from crime."[85]

Not surprisingly, on the Japanese side, the novelist Shimazaki Tōson (1872–1943) came closer still to understanding what du Petit Thouars seems uncomprehendingly to have witnessed. Of the Japanese who were present, says a character in *Before the Dawn* (*Yoake mae*, 1929–1935), "all . . . were men determined to uphold the honor of the nation." Before committing seppuku, each of the condemned men "recited a death verse." The imperial delegate Higashikuze is told that the men were "magnificent."[86] More intensely than Tōson, whom he may have influenced,[87] Ōgai concentrated on the acts of seppuku and what they meant for "the honor of the nation."

Mori Ōgai's "Sakai jiken" (1914)

Fated to Judge

The first episode of Ōgai's story begins with an unsettling confusion about rules and regulations that plagued Japanese officials in their relations with foreigners. With the collapse of the Tokugawa shōgunate, the chain of command has been disrupted, and local authorities are timid about acting on their own. They seem uncertain and indecisive. As he has not been officially informed that French soldiers have permission to travel across Yamato bridge from Ōsaka into Sakai, Censor General Sugi Kiheita feels compelled, even though he suspects that permission has been granted by Date Munenari, to demand a pass from the French. Admitting that they have not received permission, they turn back to Ōsaka. Later that same day French sailors land in Sakai and frolic through town in flagrant disregard of the inhabitants' sense of decency. Acting under Sugi's command to maintain order, the Tosa troops, who have no interpreter, try vainly to communicate with the French through gestures. As the Tosa men then attempt to make arrests, the foreigners flee, and one of them seizes an unguarded Tosa-division flag. Angered by the seizure of the banner, the man responsible for protecting it chases the thief, catches him, and splits his skull with an axe. This violent act provokes the French to open fire and the Tosa troops to return it. In Ōgai's rendition, thirteen of the French sailors are killed (rather than eleven).[88]

Immediately after the incident, Sugi takes the commanders of the two divisions to task for allowing their men to fire without orders, but they defend themselves. Their men had endured a series of provocations by the French, culminating in the theft of their flag,[89] a desecration that justified retaliation. And they were shot at first. Ōgai's narrator explains that the troops had borne ill feelings against the French for having, on a previous occasion, insulted their honor with the theft of a flag. While pretending to mediate between emperor and shōgun, the French had seized the precious imperial gold brocade pennant that symbolized the Tosa troops' authority to subdue the shōgunate's Matsuyama domain. What clearly emerges during Sugi's questioning is the Tosa soldiers' bold demonstration of their allegiance to the new imperial regime as symbolized by their regimental flag. They have come to think of the emperor as a samurai thinks of his lord.[90] They insist that their action was "meritorious, not sinful" (2:283: *kō wa atte tsumi wa nai*).

In his treatment of these two episodes in which foreigners dishonor symbolic flags, Ōgai may well have had in mind Nogi's loss of the imperial flag to the rebels in the Satsuma Rebellion of 1877. Just as Nogi asked to regain his honor by committing seppuku, so the leaders of the two Tosa divisions feel compelled to pay with their own lives for the bloodshed that followed the foreigner's theft of the Tosa flag. Yet neither in 1868 nor in 1877 was the decision about expiation left to those who felt the burden of guilt. The emperor refused Nogi's request to be permitted to commit seppuku. The fate of the Tosa men was also to be determined by others. Or so it seemed at the time.

After Censor General Sugi has done his part as "first responder," the Foreign Office commissions Yōdō, the Retired Lord of Tosa, to deal with the problem. On 11 March, he orders a simple interrogation rather than a full investigation. Why does Yōdō decide not to order a full investigation of the facts of the Sakai Incident? Why is he opposed to a thorough judicial inquiry? Seven months earlier,[91] when Tosa men were falsely accused of having murdered two British sailors from the warship *Icarus*, Yōdō had insisted on due process and justice for his men despite the fact that his Tokugawa patrons desperately wanted to placate the British in order to avoid an outbreak of hostilities like those of the Satsuei War. Thanks to Yōdō, the truth had been discovered and his men had been cleared of all charges. The difference in his responses to these similar events is a consequence of the intervening collapse of the Tokugawa *bakufu*. Yōdō's longtime patron, the shōgun, is no longer there to back him. The new government is insecure and not disposed to resist the demands of foreign powers.

Seventy-three men are questioned on 11 March about their participation in the assault upon the French sailors. The interrogation is conducted on the assumption that those who had taken part in the attack are honest enough freely to admit their complicity and to accept whatever punishment Lord Yōdō deems necessary. This assumption makes the interrogation "a test of bravery or cowardice" (2:276: *yūkyō o kokoromiru*). To the simple question Did you or did you not fire on the foreigners? twenty-nine men,[92] including the two division commanders and their lieutenants, answer in the affirmative.

The forty-four men[93] who deny involvement in the incident are taken at their word and returned to their domain. Having heard rumors of a possible death penalty and considering their actions to have been morally justified, the twenty-nine men who acknowledge firing on the French indicate that they prefer to die by their own hands rather than by the executioner's. This is true for the common soldiers as well as the officers. They debate their options.

Should they resist punishment by execution and fight to the death? Should they kill one another? Although they are suddenly deprived of their swords, the possibility of averting dishonor by resistance or by voluntary death remains, because one of the condemned men, Takeuchi Tamigorō, has secretly stashed away weapons. He writes "with his finger on the tatami, 'In my bag there are two short swords'" (see 2:277).

The swords are not used. The twenty-nine men who admitted their complicity in the attack seem reconciled to having others determine their fate. Then, on 15 March, they receive an order from Lord Yōdō that radically transforms the situation.[94] The imperial court, he explains, is under great pressure from the French. Twenty men, including the two division leaders and their lieutenants,[95] "should all offer their lives serenely" (2:278: *izure mo odayaka ni seimei o sashiageru yō to*). Yōdō's order is not merely that twenty of those who admitted their complicity must die, but that they should die as if they were choosing to perform a ritual act of atonement.[96] In asking twenty to die and leaving it to the men to decide who will be spared, Yōdō has created a situation in which execution can be reconceptualized as voluntary sacrifice rather than as a dishonorable execution unjustly imposed by a foreign power.[97] Yōdō's order is ingenious, because the act of seppuku combines elements of self-sacrifice (self-immolation by one's own sword) and execution (decapitation by the second's sword). There is, moreover, an important difference in the nature of the executioner: the *kaishakunin* whose sword completes the ritual of seppuku is a trusted friend. Yōdō's approach is also consistent with his earlier refusal to ask who among the twenty-nine actually killed the eleven French sailors.

A problem then arises that Yōdō might have anticipated. All twenty-nine of the men are willing to die. Yōdō, who is ailing, allows his son, the present Lord of Tosa, Yamanouchi Toyonori (1846–1886; daimyō 1859–1871), to solve the problem, which he does by ordering "drawing lots" (2:278: *kujibiki*) to determine which of the twenty-five common soldiers should die along with the four leaders (whose samurai status privileges them to commit seppuku). This solution treats all twenty-five men in a completely egalitarian fashion. As in the Roman practice of drawing lots to decimate units "guilty of cowardice in battle . . . or of sedition," it obviates "any suspicion of favoritism or animus in inflicting the punishment."[98]

The problem with Toyonori's solution is that selection by chance reduces the element of volition. Yōdō wanted his men to rethink the execution as self-sacrifice and thereby to change the meaning of their deaths. He might have simply allowed *all* of them to die willingly, but he felt bound by the arrangements for twenty to die that Date, presumably with his knowledge, was in the process of making with Roches.[99] He might also himself have chosen the ones to die. Instead, by asking the men to decide their own fates, he changed an imposed penalty into a privilege. Coincidentally, by asking for the sacrificial death of some but not all, he placed a greater charge[100] on those who were to die. They would be privileged, as others would not, to fulfill Lord Yōdō's will. At the same time, it would be precisely those excluded from the privilege of sacrificial death who would make the deaths of the others special by raising the charge on them. Insofar as they made sacrifice possible, they too would serve Lord Yōdō's purpose. The drawing of lots was necessary because no one wanted to serve in this ancillary way.

The lots are drawn at the Inari shrine and are taken to be the perfect expression of divine will. When humans cannot or will not make an excruciating life-or-death decision, they defer to the gods; in secular terms, they leave judgment to chance. In the case of the Tosa men, the discrepancy between the number of those who implicated themselves in the Sakai skirmish (twenty-nine) and the number of those needed to satisfy the demand for "reparations" (twenty)[101] prompts the ordeal. In day-to-day discourse, "ordeal" is used loosely to refer to any unusually painful experience, but an ordeal, whether by drawing lots or by fire or water or combat, is actually "a divinatory practice that has a judiciary function."[102] (The term derives from the ancient Teutonic mode of trial; the Gothic term *uzdailjan,* or "dealing out" judgment was latinized in 1599 as *ordalium.*) In this case, at the Inari shrine, there is an ironic twist. Instead of functioning as a device for determining guilt or innocence, the drawing of lots determines who is to be *excluded* from the privilege of self-sacrifice. By resorting to the expedient of sortition, Toyonori unwittingly undermines his father's appeal to the men to make a good sacrifice. While Lord Yōdō called for voluntary self-sacrifice, Lord Toyonori demands unconditional submission to the will of the gods.

But why does Toyonori arrange for the drawing of lots to be conducted at the Tosa Inari shrine attached to the domain's Nagabori compound in Ōsaka? The answer to this deceptively simple question is that the transfer to the shrine sacralizes the process. In 1770 Inari had been authorized by Fushimi Inari as the tutelary *kami* of the Tosa daimyō's residential storehouse *(kurayashiki).*[103] If the Tosa lords' symbolic presence at the Inari shrine was palpable, the imperial presence was there as well, especially since the decisive battle leading to the restoration of imperial rule had just been fought near the Fushimi Inari shrine. In the wake of the slogan "Revere the Emperor, Expel the Barbarians" *(sonnō jōi),* a series of "separation edicts" *(bunri rei)* was issued in 1868–1869 that emphasized the restoration of imperial rule *(ōsei fukko)* by recalling the emperor's divine authority.[104] Shintō shrines were intimately associated with the imperial house, whose lineage is from the sun goddess Amaterasu. Shintō shrines also had a long history of divination, sometimes involving the drawing of lots *(omikuji)* to determine the prospects for "marriage, schooling, travel, and business transactions."[105] In particular, Inari shrines were closely associated with Japan's rice-centered agriculture and were favored by the warrior class. In short, while Yōdō aims at voluntary self-sacrifice by soliciting the will to die of those who had admitted involvement in the Sakai Incident, Toyonori subverts the process, eliminates the element of volition, and substitutes divination in the form of a sacred Shintō ritual.

The drawing of lots at the Inari shrine is performed in a formal, ritualistic manner. Present are Tosa government officials as well as cannoneers and foot soldiers sent all the way from Kyōto, presumably to maintain order as well as to witness the reading of names and the correct drawing and recording of lots. Ordinary bystanders are bewildered and weep when they realize that this drawing of lots is a way to determine human sacrifice: "Those who had gathered at this time to worship at the shrine at first marvelled at whatever it was, only gradually realizing the meaning of drawing lots. All were intensely affected, and there were even those among them who wept" (see 2:279).

When the outcome of the *kujibiki* is known, the story takes another unexpected turn. The men—or at least some of them—attempt to reclaim their lost agency. Of the nine men who draw white life-granting lots, four petition, unsuccessfully, to receive the same punishment as the other five, "since they were *of one mind and the same flesh (dofuku isshin)* with them from the beginning" (2:280; my emphasis). This four-to-five division separates those actively determined to achieve martyrdom from those who are passively willing to accept it.[106] Not only do the four men protesting their "lucky" white lots desire to serve the imperial cause as transmitted by Lord Yōdō (even if it means opposing the divine will of the *kami*), they also desire to show their solidarity with those who are permitted to die. The ordeal at Sakai is creating a curious type of martyr, one who is forced to live. Here as elsewhere, etymology is an important clue to meaning. The Latin word *martyrium* ("blood testimony"), derived from the Greek *martyrion,* is translated into Japanese as *junnan,* whose first kanji is the "jun" of junshi. The combination *junnan,* which came into usage shortly after the Sakai Incident,[107] suggests self-sacrifice to a belief or nation in distress. In the trenchant words that Nogi applied to his own dilemma after the Satsuma Rebellion, the Tosa survivors will be "living as though dead."[108] Paradoxically, for them the freedom to go home is their punishment. At the same time, the protest of these "losers" against their exclusion has the effect of making the others appreciate their lot.

Fated to Die

The sixteen common soldiers permitted to die along with their officers prepare their last letters, with locks of hair included as final effects. Separately from their officers, the sixteen eat and drink—some to excess—then fall sound asleep, except for Doi Hachinosuke (1814–?), who suddenly shouts: "Hey there! The important day is tomorrow! In what way do you all intend to meet your death? It's all right with you if your heads are cut off?" (see 2:280). What possesses Doi to make such a blunt assault on the men's sensibilities?

Doi anticipates Ichi in Ōgai's "Saigo no ikku" (October 1915; The last sentence), a daughter who delivers her petition to die (together with her siblings) in lieu of her father, a man condemned to be executed. Neither Doi nor Ichi expresses what motivates them in a tempered, analytical vocabulary; both are possessed by the spirit of uncompromising urgency. Both have to overcome an initial resistance on the part of those whom they address. When the sixteen-year-old Ichi is heard at last, her resolve and sincerity are questioned (did she herself write the petition with such astonishing economy of words?). She counters by placing her complete trust in the authorities to do the right thing. Ichi's unpremeditated words stab at the magistrate's conscience and throw the authorities into turmoil. Ichi, like Doi, knows what she wants without knowing it. Her agency is half conscious and half unconscious. As every child knew, the obligation of a vassal to his lord was "as intensely personal as the behavior of a child toward his parent" and was conceived "in familial terms."[109] Within this lofty maxim and all the myths and stories about heroes lay a moral imperative for ordinary people to act in crises such as these.

Thus Ichi does not need to know the term "self-sacrifice" in order to act on the concept. Her grasp of the situation is intuitive. To underline her alertness to cultural memory, Ōgai's narrator adds that, even though the officials in mid-Tokugawa knew neither the Latin term *martyrium (maruchiriumu)* nor the equivalent of "self-sacrifice" *(kenshin),* terms that were imported or coined only in the Meiji period,[110] they fully recognized in Ichi's petition "the spearhead of resistance lurking at the core of self-sacrifice" *(kenshin no naka ni hisomu hankō no hokosaki).* They wince as they see Ichi's spirits soar, and even attribute her unshakable determination to "possession by a spirit" (3:239: *mono de mo tsuite*). Whether she has been seized by good or evil spirits can be divined only by Emperor Sakuramachi (1720–1750; r. 1735–1747), who is moved to commute Ichi's father's sentence from execution to exile, thereby simultaneously denying and honoring the girl's petition. Reminded by Ichi's unhesitating act of filial piety that he had been tarrying for three years before performing the *daijōsai* to legitimize his reign, the emperor may have issued the pardon to prevent soiling the imperial First Fruits Offering (Daijōe; 3:240) by permitting the execution of Ichi's father or Ichi and her siblings.

Where does Doi's Meiji spirit of rebellion take him? Since he is unable to evoke the response he wants from the sleeping men, he concentrates his efforts on Sugimoto Kōgorō (1835–1868): "Hey you! If anyone knows anything, it's probably you. How to die tomorrow—by beheading?" (see 2:281). It dawns on Sugimoto that their willingness to die is certain to be misunderstood if they are executed like common criminals. He suddenly realizes that what the sixteen ordinary soldiers have to give can be of value—can be honorable—only if they make "a special proposal" (2:282: *sekkaku no mōshiide*) to be allowed to die by seppuku. Rather than simply dying the "easy" way, by beheading, they spontaneously reach for the painful alternative of death by seppuku.

Ōgai describes this awareness in what may be the story's most significant sentences. "They must not die in shame and humiliation, though. And so they unanimously decided to request permission to commit seppuku at all costs" (2:281: shikashi chijoku o ukete shinde wa naranu. Soko de zehi seppuku sasete morō to iu koto ni, shūgi ikketsu shita). Unaware that they are living in a time of radical social change, they, common soldiers, request to die by seppuku.[111] The men are samurai at heart. They know what to do just when they have to do it because they have internalized a cultural imperative.[112]

WRITING ABOUT "Sakai jiken," Alan Wolfe noted "that not a few of the famous instances of seppuku of the last 300 years were essentially anachronistic. They were either against the law or at least against the prevailing ethic of the times, but in each instance they evoked some sense of a need for a spirituality thought to be lacking in the contemporaneous era. In this instance, the development of Ōgai's text makes clear that this resurrected spirituality is designed to assert Japanese superiority over the West."[113] Wolfe's astute conclusion about the nationalism of the Tosa men's seppuku can be extended. These men are concerned to assert themselves despite their lowly origins. They seek to demonstrate that commoners are able to live up to samurai ideals and to resist the authorities in order to sacrifice their lives for the imperial cause. As Thomas M. Huber noted, the "Meiji Restoration was in essence a blow struck at pervasive patterns of social injustice by a frustrated and ultimately embattled service intelligentsia. It was a domestic affair, in which the Western challenge figured only as a convenient instrumentality, used by the reformers to win broader approval for the basic structural changes they had long favored."[114] The Tosa men depicted in "Sakai jiken" are certainly not members of Huber's "service intelligentsia," which was comprised of "scholars, administrators, physicians, clerics, military technicians, and even a few poets,"[115] but they too are ready to strike a blow at social injustice as they go to their deaths. Their motivational "lineage" can be traced to the grassroots movements that began with those whom George M. Wilson classified as "patriots and redeemers."[116]

When confronted with dishonorable death, the Tosa men draw upon self-assertive pride *(iji)*. They are not content merely to submit to the authorities in order to avoid the shameful imputation of cowardice. They intend to gain honor for themselves and thereby for the imperial nation. What explains their uncanny ability to rise, step by step, above their ascribed status? How do they manage to become self-consciously engaged in matters of national honor that had only begun to be defined against Western values since Perry's arrival in 1853? Demonstrating that even ordinary people are prepared to transcend allegiance to their domainal lord and to serve the imperial nation, they imagine themselves as representatives of *Japanese* values as distinct from those of foreign peoples. They act as they do, not because they have been formally trained in the appropriate behavior, but because they are relying on mythic stories of Japanese heroism. Preserved in the imaginary storehouse of samurai culture, the values that drive the Tosa men to seppuku require visibility through ritual and etiquette. The men determine that their request must be embedded in a contract in which their vow of self-sacrifice will be honored, or sanctioned, by the highest authority. Doi's intuitive grasp of the heroic, even sacred, potential in the Tosa lords' orders becomes fully articulated in the petition of the sixteen to be allowed to commit seppuku.

The sixteen dress in their finest clothes in order solemnly to state their desires. When they are rebuffed by the guards, they protest in anger: "Tomorrow we will throw away our lives for the emperor!" (2:282: ware ware wa kōkoku no tame ni myōnichi ichimei o suteru monodomo ja). As they demand, successfully, to be heard by the guards' superiors, they elevate their rhetoric from "throwing away" their lives to "offering" them, as in a sacrificial act. "We are men who offer our lives in honor of the imperial command" (2:282: ware ware wa chōmei o omonjite ichimei o sashiageru mono de gozaimasu). Formerly speechless, the men have been transformed. Now they have a voice. Upon first hearing rumors of the death penalty and prior to their lords' orders, they had demonstrated their resistance to execution by considering fighting to the death or killing themselves. Now they are eager to follow their lords' orders, provided they can do so on their own proud terms.

Kominami Goroemon (1812–1882), the official entrusted to implement Toyonori's orders,[117] is initially hesitant to listen to the men's appeal. Even after he learns that his superiors have already decided to allow the men to commit seppuku, he seems reluctant to acknowledge the men's agency, for he informs them of the official consent as if the men had never asked for it. There is, however, no mention in the story of the fact that Roches, too, had consented to the act of *kappuku.*[118] Mention of French acquiescence would, of course, have lessened the ethical force of the men's act of *devotio,* or self-sacrifice, for the imperial nation.[119] Kominami reminds the men that, in any case, they owe their lives to their lords for the grief they caused them, and to Toyonori in particular, since he had to apologize—that day—to the French minister in person (in fact, he would do so only on the day after the seppuku).[120]

Kominami tells the men, unnecessarily, that, since both Japanese and foreign dignitaries will witness their seppuku, they "should be prepared to display the samurai spirit of the imperial nation" (2:284: *kōkoku no shiki o arawasu yō kakugo itase*). The presence of these witnesses further alters the moral equation. The men understand that their deaths are to be seen not only as a sacrifice to the emperor but also as a way to appease the foreigners' demand for retribution. This second order comes, like the first, with a catch. Ōgai's narrator notes that the men "could not suppress a smile" (2:285: *bishō o kinji enakatta*). Clearly, they do not smile simply because they have received permission to die honorably, but because the very strings attached to the privilege of seppuku and the authorities' admonition to behave as samurai prompts them to ask for samurai status.

Thus the men gradually come to realize the larger implications of their request to commit seppuku. Initially, they wanted merely to escape execution and die honorably; now they hear that they are on public display, and not only their honor but the nation's honor is at stake. Their lord's request to show the samurai spirit to the foreigners encourages them to ask for "samurai status" (2:285: *shibun*) from this time on. The men receive Kominami's immediate oral consent[121] followed by their lord's written confirmation. They are permitted to join the two division commanders and their two lieutenants, who are "now sad, now glad" (2:286: *yorokobi katsu kanashinda*)—sad because their men will die; glad that they have been permitted to perform seppuku and granted samurai status. All twenty men are now equally privileged to enter into the annals of those who—like Takechi Zuizan in the summer of 1865[122]—were ordered by Lord Yōdō to commit seppuku for the sake of Tosa's honor.

16 March 1868 (1868.II.23) is set as the day of reckoning. Unlike common criminals sentenced to death, the twenty men are neither shorn of their hair nor stripped of their clothes. They are not taken in shackles to their place of execution and spat upon by a crowd gleefully anticipating the flow of blood. Instead, dressed in white silk[123] and transported in individual palan-

quins, they are accorded the highest honors by the Hosokawa and Asano, two clans noted for their exemplary conduct of the rites of seppuku. It is a magnificent procession, and the twenty men are treated "with extraordinary reverence in everything" (see 2:288). The road is lined with people weeping and desperately trying to catch a glimpse of or even touch the men. The contrast to the contumely experienced by condemned murderers could hardly have been greater.

The executions were originally to take place at the site of the killings. The symbolic site now chosen for seppuku is a nearby Buddhist temple, Myōkokuji, by definition a sacred space. The temple becomes even more highly charged through the specific preparations for these men and the heroic act they are about to perform. At the temple gate is the imperial emblem. Displayed inside the precincts are the family crests of the Hosokawa and Asano. At the moment of their deaths the men will be able to fix their gaze upon curtains bearing the Yamanouchi crest *(mon)*.

No sooner do the men emerge from their palanquins than their last words are requested as "keepsakes" (2:290: *kinen*). This signals their imminent heroic immortalization. Minoura Inokichi (1844–1868),[124] leader of the Sixth Tosa Infantry Division, rises to his high rank and education by writing a poem in classical Chinese *(kanshi)*.[125] Defiant in tone, Minoura's *kanshi* defends the action taken at Sakai.[126] The third line of the poem expresses his desire to impart his noble cause to a thousand generations (see 2:290).

In a variant reading of Minoura's *kanshi*, Ōoka Shōhei (1909–1988) sees it as a protest against the Japanese authorities rather than the foreigners. He argues that Minoura may have ordered his men to fire on the French in order to demonstrate that foreigners could be expelled—if one did not accommodate them in the subservient manner of Lord Yōdō.[127] Ōoka also doubts that the sixteen ordinary soldiers were able to grasp the concept of an imperial nation *(kōkoku)*.[128]

Are Ōoka's doubts valid? Did Ōgai mean to imply that ordinary soldiers had already come to perceive a serious threat to their honor from Japanese authorities as well as from the barbarians? Even if the men were initially loyal only to their domain *(han)* in the ancient sense of province *(kuni)*, they were inspired by the injunction of their domainal lords to die willingly, not for Tosa, but in order to clear their own names and to relieve the emperor of foreign pressure. In Ōgai's fiction, if not in reality, Doi's impulse to petition seppuku is strong evidence of a new and larger commitment, first clearly articulated when the sixteen announced that they were giving their lives for the imperial nation (2:282: *kōkoku*).[129] When rebuffed, Takeuchi insisted on the right to pay homage to the "imperial command" (2:282: *chōmei*). Step by step their dedication is recognized, and they are initiated into the larger entity of the imperial nation by the combined symbols of the imperial emblem and the Asano, Hosokawa, and Yamanouchi crests. While Minoura's *kanshi* may carry overtones of bitterness about the authorities' suggestion of forced seppuku *(tsumebara)*, it leaves the men "a noble cause" *(taigi)* to die for. That cause is, definitely, the imperial nation.

Informed of a delay, the twenty men decide to pass the time by temple viewing before they begin to kill themselves. They discover that they are the objects of spectators who have come from the surrounding area. Realizing his inability to satisfy the crowd by writing poetry, one of the men decides to express his ecstatic sense of the extraordinary by trying to ring the temple bell.[130] (He is not allowed to do so for fear of a commotion.) Other Tosa men attempt to leave their marks by giving money to the monks, who will pray for them. With the naive curiosity of children, they explore the site designated for their seppuku as well as their prepared graves. At the former site they see the swords they will use. At the latter, they see their names already inscribed on the "large urns" (2:293: *ōgame*) that will contain their remains. They see and do not see. They combine nonchalant resignation with the thrill of breaking unknown ground. Playfully, Doi climbs into his urn, but finds it difficult to climb out again, eventually overturning the urn and crawling out. All of these antics, which would lead to moments of rapture in a *kyōgen* play, seem designed to make tolerable the liminal space between self-sacrifice and execution.

After this ramble through a temporal lacuna, the men are treated to a meal of fish and sake in the main hall, after which they engage in another round of poetry writing and the distribution of keepsakes to the hero-hungry spectators. The gifts exchanged between the condemned men and their hosts are tantamount to a kind of proleptic memorialization. The men must be well aware of the honors they are receiving and the obligation they are under. This exchange of gifts is part of their vow and their devotion.[131]

The time of the seppuku is set for noon and the *kaishakunin* take up their precise positions. The ceremony is meticulously arranged, with numerous Japanese and French officials and dignitaries in attendance. The name of the first to die, Minoura Inokichi, is about to be announced when the weather makes sport of it all: "At this moment, the sky abruptly filled with clouds and heavy rains came pouring down" (see 2:296). With the speed of lightning, lethal order turns to chaos. Then the rain stops at exactly 2 p.m. The preparations resume, and Minoura's name is finally called at 4 p.m.[132] He, the highest-ranking officer, steps up to the tatami, proclaims his defiance in the face of the foreign dignitaries, and proceeds with the gruesome self-immolation. His nervous *kaishakunin* twice fails to wield the decapitating sword properly, and each time the unperturbed Minoura urges him on, first gently, "'Baba-*kun,* what's getting you! Do it calmly!" and then shouting, "'I'm not dead yet, cut harder!'" (see 2:297). The third stroke lops off Minoura's head. Nishimura, Ikegami, and Ōishi follow, each performing his grisly task with apparent relish, each outperforming his tremulous *kaishakunin.*

Ōgai seems clearly to have intended that the blundering incompetence of the seconds have symbolic significance. Their role in the dramatic ritual most resembles that of an executioner, at least in the eyes of the foreigners, who are unaware that the *kaishakunin* performs an act of mercy for a man close to him. Here the part of the *kaishakunin* seems willfully botched.[133] By contrast, the voluntary self-sacrifice of seppuku is performed with virtuosity. No one who witnessed the oscillation between the inspiring and the grotesque, four times repeated in Ōgai's narrative, could have failed to note this contrast. The seconds' brutal butchering in fact helps demonstrate the men's unshakable determination to die by allowing them to repeat their call for decapitation. The command to cut again is intended to erase any doubts among the witnesses that the men committing seppuku were not acting of their own free will. In this they are like Cato Uticensis (95–46 B.C.E.) who, by intentionally botching his suicide and then "reseek[ing]" death,[134] paradoxically confirmed his will to die, thus achieving the feat of simultaneously comforting his family and friends and enraging Caesar.

Fated to Fear

The description of the individual acts of seppuku is such that the performers appear to be more gratified than the foreign witnesses. The Tosa men seem to be the masters of their fate, while the French observers grow increasingly uneasy. The commander of the French detachment, du Petit Thouars (whom Ōgai wrongly identified as the French minister), "seemed unable to endure it all, now standing up and now sitting down. . . . The posture [of the French witnesses] utterly disintegrated, and they began to whisper to each other, their hands trembling uncontrollably" (see 2:299). The French witnesses are deprived of their wits, shocked and shaken by behavior they seem unable to comprehend. They are beside themselves with fear.

How do the French understand what from their perspective is perverse behavior? They have no inkling of the implications of the Tosa lords' and men's changing the terms of the sentence.[135] They have come to Myōkokuji to witness punishment by execution only to find themselves confronted with the redemption of honor by a series of individual acts of self-sacrifice. Expecting to see criminals brought to justice, a routine procedure, they witness a totally unfamiliar performance of ecstatic self-immolation that revolts, confuses, and disturbs them. They are given no words to express their feelings, but their trembling bodies and their scrambling to the harbor speak volumes. The absurdity of the situation is rooted in cultural incompatibility. What was supposed to be the Tosa men's abasement and punishment becomes their moment of sacrificial glory. What greater contrast in conceptions of justice, what greater cultural dissonance in the ethos of honor could one imagine?

The French flee the scene in undignified disorder. Their flight from the stage of seppuku can be interpreted as a sign of a sudden rush of guilt for the Tosa dead—none of whom was formally convicted of a crime[136]—as well as simple fear for their own lives. They have not broken the cycle of violence, as they had hoped to do with their demands. Quite the contrary. The defiance symbolized by seppuku seems to promise a new round of retribution.[137] It is in this light that we can now more clearly see the implications of the historical du Petit Thouars' private confession of his fear at dusk and his decision to halt the series of seppuku as an expedient to relieve the paroxysms experienced by the French witnesses.

As Wolfe has noted, the story is "a self-conscious national allegory involving a reversal of the power situation." But the story does not stop with the flight of the foreigners. (French leave, indeed!) More is at stake than "spiritual resistance couched in nationalistic terms [through] the power of literary representation to assert a spiritual superiority even in the face of military weakness."[138] Approaching Ōgai's story from an anthropological perspective, one realizes that the men's seppuku is an activation—by unconventional actors—of a traditional habitus. It is a political strategy that enables the men to attain honor by drawing on the ancient ideal of "absolute self-sacrifice" *(kenshin)*.[139] The men's actions strike a deep chord in the Japanese psyche. Although they are too unsophisticated fully to understand the effect of their actions on the French, they must be aware that their seppuku underlines a moral difference between the Japanese and the foreign "barbarians."

It is not only the Tosa men's actions that strike terror into the hearts of the French; their words do as well. The historical du Petit Thouars related to Mitford vivid details that he omitted from his official report: "When the first condemned man came out he plunged the dirk into his stomach with such force that his entrails protruded; he held them up in his hand and began singing verses of hatred and revenge against the detested foreigners who were polluting the sacred soil of the Land of the Gods till death stopped his ghastly song."[140] Ōgai's rendition of Minoura's last words[141] makes clear that they enrapture the Japanese and chill the French. Minoura's "voice rolled like thunder: 'Frenchmen, listen! I am not dying for wretches like you! I am dying for our imperial nation. Watch closely *the seppuku of a Japanese man!*'" (2:296: *Nihon danshi no seppuku*). Willingness to die for the emperor and the imperial nation is obviously not something taken for granted by the French officers. (Two years later, in the Franco-Prussian war, French troops surrendered en masse rather than sacrifice their lives for Napoleon III.)

This moral drama of cultural difference remains largely opaque to the French, whose ability to decipher the Japanese cultural code is compromised by the terror that has gripped them. That the French observers remained obtuse in their grasp of the situation even after they had had time for reflection is rather a puzzle, because there were many similarities between the European and Japanese codes of honor. Roman history, which every educated Frenchman had studied, provided many instances of men—like Cato Uticensis—who chose death rather than dishonor. Educated Frenchmen were also familiar with the customs of the Indian tribes who were their allies or their adversaries in the struggle with the British for the control of North America. (Captured by the Hurons in 1637, a Seneca warrior "announced in a loud and confident voice, 'My brothers, I am going to die; amuse yourselves boldly around me—I fear neither tortures nor death.' He danced and sang up and down the cabin." And his Huron captors understood him and "wanted to see a stouthearted man with unconquerable self-control, maintaining defiance and self-respect to the bitter end, and the torture was a test of these qualities.")[142]

Incomprehension in the face of cultural difference is a two-way street. Although Ōgai was unusually well informed about European history and culture, he was probably unaware of the intriguing fact that ancient Roman ritual sacrifice included *devotio,* a phenomenon most likely to occur in anarchic situations like that prevailing in and around Sakai.[143] The Latin term referred not only to devotion and prayer but also to a curse, "the binding or fixing of one's enemy, the *defixio.*"[144] Without explicit use of the concept of *devotio,* Ōgai shows that this powerful combination of prayer and curse[145] rattles the French witnesses.[146] Sensing that the serial seppuku is an act of defiance (to them) as well as worship (of the emperor), the French lose their composure and terminate the ritual process. Uncomprehending, they fail to perceive that they are active participants in a sacrifice rather than mere passive witnesses to an execution. Unwittingly, they deprive themselves of an opportunity to be possessed by and ritually reconciled with their victims.[147] The French disruption of the Tosa men's seppuku constitutes nothing less than a violation of the sacrificial act.

According to Henri Hubert and Marcel Mauss, "[A]n essential characteristic of the sacrifice [is] the perfect continuity that is necessary to it. From the moment that it has begun, it must continue to the end without interruption and in the ritual order. All the operations of which it is composed must follow each other in turn without a break." The two scholars go on to warn, "The forces at work, if they are not directed in exactly the way prescribed, elude both sacrifier [the person for whom a sacrifice is performed] and priest and turn upon them in a terrible fashion."[148] By failing to understand what they saw and heard, by not accepting what they witnessed for what it was meant to be, the French excluded themselves from receiving the benefits of the sacrificial act. By insisting that they were dying for the emperor (their prayer) and not for the French (their curse), the Japanese leave the eleven French dead unatoned for. If the French witnesses had had their wits about them, they might have realized that their eleven dead remained unexpiated. Although there is no evidence that they feel haunted by them, their irrational fear expresses their failure to execute justice and an awareness that justice, as defined by them, has been appropriated by the Japanese. This fear does not allow them openly to admit their failure, as is evident in the French captain's misrepresentation of the seppuku as beheading in his official report.[149] (That he knew better is confimed by his all-but-hysterical confession to Mitford.) Repressing the fact that their demand for justice was turned against them at Myōkokuji, the French must continue to live in fear of the consequences of their failure to expiate French blood.

The hasty disruption of the ritual also presents a new challenge to the Japanese. The French have not only ruined their chance to be empowered by the collective sacrifice that, in the prescribed pattern, "regenerates the sacrifier and gives him a new power,"[150] they have also interfered with the Japanese effort to seize this power for themselves. Although the eleven Tosa men who died by seppuku were proud and honored to do so, there is now a strong sense among the survivors that their collective sacrifice has been tarnished by the abrupt termination of the ritual process.

The Japanese cannot allow the nine men who were deprived of their chance to commit seppuku simply to go home as if they had never vowed to die. The disruption of the ritual process has created a phenomenon that anthropologists refer to as "angry spirits" *(onryō)*. These angry spirits do not appear because the dead themselves feel anger, but rather because those who were intimately bonded to the dead do. They—the survivors of an intense relationship—project their sense of guilt and imagine the resentment of the dead. The Tosa men, bound to death as if they had sworn an oath, are forced to sunder into eleven dead and nine who are still alive. The latter are not resentful of the French who have excluded them. They focus instead on their companions whom they wish to follow into death: as long as they are not permitted to join them, they must fear that they have failed and betrayed them.

The nine men are eager to endure maximum pain, if need be short of death itself, in order to pacify the "angry spirits."

Who is responsible for the fact that there are nine frustrated and haunted survivors? The answer points to the mismatched intentions of the Japanese and the French. Fear aroused by witnessing something larger than executions—sacrifice—made the French recoil from receiving more retribution than they deserved. By refusing to let more Japanese blood flow than French blood had been spilled, they foiled the reconciliation through the sacrificial ritual that the Japanese had carefully constructed to bind the French to them through mutual obligations. The two sides were at cross-purposes from the start.

Fated to Live

After the seppuku of the first eleven men, how can the remaining nine be consoled and anger born from a disrupted ritual process be quelled? As the twelfth man, Hashizume Aihei (?–1889), simply ignores the panicky departure of the French and prepares to proceed with his seppuku, he is ordered to wait. This is the last thing he and the remaining men want to hear. In a state of ecstasy, they clamor to die: "Since die they must, the nine men were all obsessed with wishing themselves dead" (see 2:299). They are told by the seven elders, three of whom "draw near on their knees," that "the French minister [in reality, Captain du Petit Thouars] had admired the dedication with which the Tosa men made light of their own lives in public, but since he could no longer stand to witness any part of this gruesome spectacle, he would appeal to the Japanese government to spare the remaining men's lives" (see 2:300).

Readers of "Sakai jiken" can hardly overlook a numerical coincidence: whereas the first group of nine men was spared by the divine will of the *kami* who determined the outcome of the fateful lottery, the second group of nine is spared at the behest of the "barbarians." To the second group of nine survivors, French mercy is unwelcome, even hateful. This ironic twist of fate is so intolerable, in fact, that the tilted urns of these nine spared men are subsequently engraved with the words "those fated to live" (2:306: *ikiun-sama*).

The nine who are fated to live are nonetheless treated by their countrymen as if they were the honorable seppuku suicides that they intended to become. They are divided into two groups: three men are taken into custody by the Asano clan and six by the Hosokawa clan. They are to be returned to the Tosa *han*'s Nagabori mansion in Ōsaka. Hashizume, the man whose attempt to commit seppuku was halted, resists. In a last attempt to make good on his pledge to die, he bites his tongue, thereby signaling his protest against the imminent subversion of Japanese culture by foreign influence: "He regretted that an objection was raised when it was his turn, after his comrades had died gallantly" (see 2:301). Quick medical treatment frustrates Hashizume's attempt to perish by bleeding to death.

It is important to recognize Hashizume's motives. Whereas the eleven men who successfully committed seppuku died for the emperor (rather than for the French), Hashizume conceived of an abbreviated form of junshi. Sasaki Kōzō, whose account is Ōgai's source, refers to Hashizume's attempt at sacrificial death as *gishi.*[151] This term is homophonous with the characters for "loyal retainer," "righteous person," "martyr" *(gishi)*. Hashizume's desire to die was well understood by the Japanese. Among the foreigners, Satow was not only curious about the fate of those spared but able to recognize their pain: "The nine whose lives were spared were grievously hurt, we were afterwards told, and no wonder, considering what the spirit of the Japanese *samurai* was."[152]

In a preliminary effort to honor the nine disconsolate survivors, the two clans bestow the grandest luxuries upon them. That six of the nine are entrusted to the Hosokawa is considered by them as the third greatest honor their clan has ever received. (The other honors were taking custody of the forty-seven *rōnin* in 1702 and of the assassins of the tyrannical Ii Naosuke in 1860.) Both the Hosokawa and Asano clans provide lavish feasts meant to assuage the men's extreme frustration over their inability to commit seppuku. Having in some sense departed from the realm of the living without having entered the realm of the dead, they acquire a special aura, a kind of liminal glow. They are, in Ōgai's rendering, treated like royalty, like living national treasures, almost like gods (see 2:302):

> The Hosokawa and Asano houses treated the nine men with extreme generosity. . . . For night robes they supplied brand new striped lined kimono. Every night, for bedding, foot soldiers spread triple futon on the tatami. Every other day they heated water in wooden bathtubs. They handed the men towels and white tissue paper. Each of the three daily meals included, without fail, broiled fish, which was first tasted by the hosts' leaders. In the afternoon tea was served with sweets in lacquered boxes. Fruits were offered from time to time. Two or three foot soldiers took up prominent positions on the board walk of the privy. Retainers ladled out water for them to wash their hands. At night guards watched over them while they slept. Visitors who came to pay their respects placed their foreheads on the veranda. The men were given books to read. When they were sick, doctors were dispatched who mixed medicines and prepared infusions right in front of their eyes.

In this elaborate manner, the nine are simultaneously de- and resacralized at the same time that those who have already committed seppuku are recalled and venerated.

In reality and in Ōgai's imaginative reconstruction, their story, which has already taken a number of wholly unanticipated turns, takes another when the Japanese court grants the request of the French minister to spare the lives of the nine whose self-sacrifice had been stopped. For the moment, the question of the ultimate fate of the men is left unanswered. Rather than rejoicing at their escape from an excruciatingly painful death, the men are as regretful as the four who had earlier protested the white lots drawn at the Tosa Inari shrine.[153]

The Hosokawa and Asano commemorate the men's unwanted reprieve by staging a lavish farewell feast, after which they send them off to Tosa. The journey home becomes a festive procession. Worshiping onlookers line the road into Kōchi, the capital of Tosa. The nine survivors are now and ever after "the men of the Sakai Incident."

Like soldiers coming home from battle, the nine are placed in the custody of their families for about three months. In the seductive warmth of the family hearth, their resolution to die recedes into the backs of their minds. As they contemplate the possibility of living, they begin to think that adulation and the rites of comfort are a form of betrayal. All this honor and glory, when their comrades are dead? To fight their darkest thoughts, the nine struggle to hold on to their resolution to follow the path of their eleven comrades.

On 9 July 1868 the new sentence is revealed. The nine Tosa men discover that the commutation comes with some puzzling conditions. First, they are to be stripped of their stipends and exiled to the remote western part of Tosa Province. Second, their firstborn sons are to become enlisted soldiers (with double stipends). Third, those who are heirless will be assigned double stipends in exile. There is no mention of seppuku.

Who has issued these specific orders? Ōgai's story provides no answers. Ōoka Shōhei has criticized Ōgai for omitting an important piece of information given in his source, namely, that the imperial court issued these orders.[154] Responding to Ōoka's harsh criticism, Ogata Tsutomu warns against interpreting Ōgai's omissions as falsifications.[155] After all, this omission in no way implies that the court was not the ultimate source of this as of all previous orders concerning the Sakai Incident. Ōgai's silence leaves it to his readers to assume that these orders, like the others, made their way down the chain of command. In this chain, the Tosa lords served as an important link[156] and shared the responsibility for the orders with the imperial court.[157]

The nine men's first response to the orders is fierce resistance. Their persistent desire to follow their comrades into death motivates them to protest against the authorities—now with words rather than deeds. Hashizume, the man who attempted to commit suicide by biting his tongue, becomes the men's spokesman. He challenges not punishment as such but the lack of explanation of its terms: "we are not given any reason for now being sentenced to exile" (see 2:304). At a loss to explain, the nameless censor-inspector *(metsuke)* who communicated the details of their sentence to them speculates that "exile" (2:304: *rukei)* must be a way to dispose of their case while bearing in mind the suffering of the eleven who died.

It is significant that the censor, who is, after all, a specialist in punishments, can only speculate on the reasons for commutation to exile. He, like Kominami earlier, when the men petitioned to die by seppuku, is perplexed by the Tosa men's "unprecedented" (2:304: *senrei no nai)* situation. As Elizabeth Wilson (Mitchell) has astutely observed: "They are caught at the mercy of a system in transition and bewildered by a set of shifting, conflicting discourses. In this situation, they are sacrificed as those in charge of the system strive to find some coherent course of action."[158]

As a matter of historical fact, the authorities were resorting intuitively to some deep, cultural pattern. In the Bakumatsu period, punishment by exile was often used as a way to remove prominent rebels such as Saigō Takamori or court nobles such as Higashikuze Michitomi from the political scene. Later in the Meiji period, Nogi repeatedly inflicted exile on himself. Banishment almost ended the Mori family in the eleventh generation, and the experience had special resonance for Ōgai.[159] Resented by his colleagues for his attempts to introduce modern German scientific methods to Japan, he was demoted in rank in 1899 and sent to head the medical corps of the twelfth division in Kokura, Kyūshū.[160] He experienced his transfer as a banishment,[161] even as the death of his literary persona, and referred to the period until 1902 as "those silent 'years of exile.'"[162] (Among the few who gathered to see him off to Kokura from Shinbashi station was Nogi Maresuke.)[163]

It is also significant that the censor uses the word "suicide" *(jisatsu)* or "self-killing" rather than "seppuku." In response, the nine refer to the seppuku of the eleven with the morally neutral term "death" *(shi).* Was this an attempt on their part to devalue a spectacularly dramatic act that they were not allowed to emulate? Did their word choice betray their fears of becoming jealous epigones? Although the nine accept the new verdict with "wry smiles" (2:304: *kushō*), their unconcealed repugnance at the thought of exile reveals that they are now unwilling victims. In such circumstances, warn Hubert and Mauss, "the spirit of the unwilling victim of sacrifice would seek vengeance; the sacrifice, instead of promoting the health of the community, would threaten it."[164] It was to forestall this threat that the Hosokawa and Asano clans had sought to instill in the nine Tosa men a sense of pride.

But why exile rather than the deaths desired by the nine survivors? Should they now be condemned to live because their foreign accusers have disappeared and dropped their demand for the death penalty? Hashizume argues that the nine men were ready to give their lives for the emperor and the nation when the French had tried to stifle their fierce samurai spirit by commuting death to life. The life sentence imposed by the French was, for the reprieved men, a punishment worse than death. For them, to suffer the additional indignity of exile adds insult to injury. The imperial and domainal authorities, however, are acting in conformity with *their* sense of justice rather than that of the foreigners. What do they have in mind? To them, the nine men's family custody represented a temporary measure designed to deal with the unfinished business left by the French. Now they feel compelled to reclaim control over the matter and to issue a life sentence of their own, which they choose to be exile.

The nine men cannot understand what they perceive as a humiliation. The Tosa lords in particular appear cruel, as they had in their first order of sacrifice and sortition, but they are in fact shrewd politicians acting in concert with the court to cauterize, through collective pain, the psychic wounds inflicted on the nine men, the domain, and the nation. The new order releases the nine men from their indebtedness to the French for their lives. Most important in the long term, the imperial court will respond to increasing pressure to eradicate the disgrace of living in exile, to issue a pardon, and to reconcile the surviving men to life. This is the lesson that the men do not yet understand but that exile will teach them.

The authorities have other reasons still. In the words of the censor dispatched to communicate their will to the nine survivors, the emphasis is no longer on the foreigners and their grievances but rather on "approximating the pain of the eleven men who had killed themselves" (2:304: *jisatsu shita jūichinin no kutsū ni junzuru*). The word *junzuru*, "correspond to, conform to" is conspicuously homophonous with *junzuru*, "to sacrifice [immolate] oneself, to die as a martyr; to follow [one's master] to the grave." What Ōgai wrote may or may not be what the men heard the censor say. The double entendre is nonetheless provocative. The commutation of the sentence to exile seems to indicate that the authorities, who were willing to grant the men samurai status, are unwilling to allow seppuku that could be interpreted as junshi. Approximating the pain of their eleven comrades is one thing; performing junshi in their honor, as if the dead had been lords, is quite another. Whether the men intend it or not, they threaten the authorities, foreign and domestic, with their understanding of the situation, their response, and their demands. Exile will silence them.

In general terms, the reason for exile is a transgression, which may be defined by a wide range of forbidden activities (insubordination, conspiracy, treason, illicit affairs, murder). The purpose of exile is atonement for transgressions that do not require a sentence of death. As Karl Meuli has pointed out in his classic study of ancient Greek ritual, the purpose of exile is to protect the transgressor's family, community, or nation from the haunting pursuit of the angry dead.[165] In the case of the nine Tosa exiles the angry dead are, presumably, the eleven Tosa men who sacrificed their lives to atone for the eleven Frenchmen who died at Sakai. In this second round of punishment, then, the sentence of exile protects all surviving Japanese from the spirits of the eleven men who sacrificed themselves on their behalf.

But why exile rather than imprisonment? Unlike the prison sentence for common criminals, exile is reserved, according to Japanese tradition, for noble persons who most acutely feel the pain of absence from the capital. Ivan Morris has, in all seriousness, referred to the exile of Heian nobles as "the kiss of death."[166] (Morris had in mind the example of the great scholar-statesman Sugawara no Michizane [845–903], who died in exile.) What lies behind the provocative conflation of love and death in Morris' expression? It is easy to understand why exile is likened to death. After all, one of the Japanese terms for "exile" is *bōmeisha,* which literally means "a person whose life is lost" or expunged from the "family register" *(mei).* For one's name to be removed from the family register suggests extinction. This type of erasure from the memory of the living seems even worse than death, for the names of the dead are not removed from the family register. In reality, however, even the most radical attempt at erasure of an existence would leave a remnant in the form of a ghost, as in the case of Michizane's august spirit *(goryō).* But exile can also be an act of mercy since it is not death itself. Bloodshed is avoided. The exile, moreover, carries the potential of yet performing a service to the community or nation and is often recalled—both in a figurative and a literal sense, which is precisely how the Sakai Incident will be resolved.

What next happens to the nine Tosa exiles is briefly described by Ōgai, who imparts a religious quality to their experience of wandering.[167] The road to exile leads to the village of Nyūta in the district of Hata in the Tosa domain. Despite the humiliation of their new sentence, the men attempt to maintain their dignity as they set out as *rōnin.* As if on a pilgrimage to a sacred site, they walk until they are too weak to continue. They must then be carried, as before, in palanquins. When they reach their place of exile they are taken in by the villagers and then lodged together in a separate house (except for one man, who enters the Buddhist temple Shinseiji). Do the villagers shun them as outcasts or honor them as heroes? Are they idolized or ostracized? Ōgai does not tell us what to think. In the classic topos of the noble exile there is often some decisive event that allows the banished hero to return home in glory. To what extent can this classic paradigm, noted by the folklorist Orikuchi Shinobu (1887–1953), be detected in "Sakai jiken"? On this, Ōgai eventually breaks his silence.

Ōgai first tells us that the nine Tosa men lead admirable lives in their exile, conducting memorial rites for their eleven companions and teaching, in true samurai fashion, the martial arts and the Confucian classics. That simple soldiers can meet the obligations of samurai must be attributed to the Hosokawa and Asano clans that instructed them in the samurai code of honor. The treatment of the exiled men serves, as Carlin A. Barton has noted in her analysis of ancient Roman sacrificial culture, as "heightening the [moral] charge," as a tapping of energy "for the enhanced well-being of the city and its inhabitants. The charge or energy within a person or animal or thing could be immediately released, as at the slaying of the sacrificial animal, or it could be 'banked' in a temple, tomb, or other monument."[168] In the case of the Tosa men, the energy is banked in their place of exile. They have learned to bear their condition with dignity, so that the energy from the negative charge they carried into exile can be converted to a positive charge to flow back into the imperial nation. Indeed, their highly productive activities in exile demonstrate just that.

Those activities can be understood as a form of therapy. The nine were removed from the scene of their traumatic confrontation with their own deaths at Myōkokuji. Although they were first returned to their individual homes (sharpening the denial of the punishment they were craving and gnawing at their sense of honor), they were then sent to unfamiliar surroundings within their home province, thus incrementally increasing their distance from the eleven whom they had so desperately wanted to emulate. Exile is meant to help not only the nine survivors but all Japanese to forget the trauma of the Sakai Incident; but forgetting a traumatic event is clearly not the same as coming to terms with it. Exile is a state of remission.[169]

In still another metaphorical frame, exile can be likened to the drawing of lots—a test determined, ultimately, by divine will. It may well have been that the Tosa lords, as uncertain what to do with the nine as Yōdō had been before with the original twenty-five, resorted to the idea of exile as Toyonori had resorted to the drawing of lots—because they wanted to transfer responsibility for the final outcome to "higher authority"—that is, to the *kami* (in the first instance) or to the emperor (in the second). Once again, they thrust the Tosa men into a state of uncertainty, leaving them not knowing whether they are to live or die. The authorities act as they do in order to avert a greater calamity from befalling their people, be it a war with Western powers or assaults by the angry spirits of the Tosa dead. Yet having done what they did or had to do, they are unable to rest.

To the degree that the surviving Tosa men are representatives of all Japanese, their languishing in exile means that the entire nation remains in limbo and cannot truly be at peace with itself. Resolution comes, ironically, in the wake of a plague that devastates the region. One of the exiles—Kawatani Gintarō—is stricken and dies (on 19 October 1868).[170] Kawatani's death is a reminder that eleven men had committed seppuku for the emperor and that nine other men who wanted to do so are lingering in exile. Mutsuhito, enthroned on 12 October 1868, celebrates his accession with an amnesty designed to cleanse the nation of shame and to pacify vengeful spirits. It is uncertain when the imperial pardon is issued, but the emperor's enthronement is clearly the occasion for it. In any event, the Tosa censor receives the imperial pardon on 30 December 1868 and the eight surviving men arrive in the Tosa capital of Kōchi on 9 January 1869. Having been denied the opportunity to fulfill the original terms of their contract with the new government—samurai status in exchange for seppuku—the eight are now honorably reintegrated into society. The price of reintegration is the surrender of their samurai status. It is what they must sacrifice in lieu of their lives.

Their eleven companions had achieved honor in the traditional way, through self-sacrifice by means of seppuku. To argue, as did Eric W. Johnson, that their deaths were "cheapened" and "absolutely meaningless," and to describe the men as "sacrificial goats,"[171] is to deny the Tosa men the very thing they sought—honor. Johnson discerned an "antagonistic attitude on Ōgai's part toward high authority" in "the ritual of suicide [that] was in this case their country's first line of defense."[172] Another take on this, however, is to see the Tosa men's critical self-assertion in the face of authority as the greatest form of service to their country.

The surviving eight Tosa men find themselves on the far side of the historic watershed known as the Meiji Restoration. The moment of glory was in sight when they grasped their swords, when the opportunity for seppuku was at hand. Although they were denied the chance to lay down their lives for the new imperial nation, they were given an opportunity to show their devotion to their comrades who had done so. The novel forms of heroism allowed them—the biting of the tongue, the grim smiles about exile, the endurance of the plague—were never codified into the equivalent of *bushidō.* Their fate as exiles, defined by ancient forms of expiatory sacrifice and repentance, was to live. Their lives—like the sacrificial deaths of their comrades

—testify that in a nation undergoing radical change the deep reservoir of Japanese values can be tapped at any moment to redefine identity and to save the nation's honor.

Postscript

On the final page of Ōgai's story the Tosa men's gravesite turns into an attraction for pilgrims. The reader's curiosity about the Tosa men's posthumous history can be satisfied only to the extent that Ōgai extracted information from his source, which largely concerns the lives of the two division commanders. Although Minoura's family line is terminated because he had no son, it was revived through a man with the same family name. Nishimura's family line also continues through adoption. These developments stand in contrast to Nogi's last wish to terminate his line and the government's ultimately unsuccessful revival of the Nogi family through adoption.

Although American diplomats were particularly distressed by the canonization of the eleven Tosa men who had committed seppuku,[173] all twenty were memorialized, not only in the writings of Ōgai and others, but also in the form of physical monuments: a commemorative pillar on the site of seppuku at Myōkokuji in Sakai; tombs (with the graves of the eleven) and the nine tilted urns at Hōjuin in Sakai. In his memoirs (1901), von Brandt made a point of acknowledging the Japanese efforts to sacralize the Tosa men's deaths: "Soon images of the graves surfaced that were venerated as those of especially brave and loyal men. Numerous copies of these images were distributed throughout the country, largely at the behest of priests hoping to attract visitors to their temple. Typical of the ways that such events were and still are understood in Japan, however, was a retired general's petition to the legislature in 1894 to build a monument to the executed men as defenders of the country's independence and as curators of its honor."[174] In a mood of reconciliation, the dead from both countries were honored by the erection of a monument at Myōkokuji in 1919.[175] An early Shōwa reprint of Sasaki's account of the Sakai Incident, titled *Rekkyo: Meiji Ishin Senshū Sakai Tosa hanshi kappuku jiken jikki* (1929), contains a loose foldout of the architectural plan for a new eagle-topped memorial to the eleven Tosa men's "sacrifice" *(gisei)*.[176] The account contains photographs of the men's mortuary tablets *(ihai)* and of their equipment: helmets, weapons, and—most important of all—the blood-stained regimental flags of the two Tosa regiments. There is also the reproduction of an unidentified painting or print of the eleven and Doi Hachinosuke (a later addition) in three rows of four.[177] Formally dressed in *hakama* and crested *haori* and wearing the samurai topknot, the eleven are shown in the process of memorializing themselves by writing farewell poems *(jisei)*. Photographs of the site of *kappuku* at Myōkokuji and the Shintō torii and graves of the eleven at Hōjuin conclude the visual set.[178]

The French, though not as gratified by the "executions" as they had hoped, were satisfied that their five demands had been fulfilled.[179] They too were eager to bring forth heroes and to honor and commemorate their dead. As early as 10 March 1868, Captain du Petit Thouars recommended a courageous noncommissioned officer for the Cross of the Legion of Honor. Others who had helped save the wounded and bring back the dead in the Sakai Incident could expect to receive lesser military medals.[180]

For Ōgai, the Sakai Incident epitomized all the anarchy, chaos, and confusion accompanying era change. Having just experienced the emotionally wrenching transition from Meiji to Taishō, he saw the events of March 1868 as an adumbration of the events of September 1912. Nogi's junshi marked the end of an era, just as the seppuku of the eleven and the desire for junshi of the exiled nine Tosa men marked the end of theirs.

When the emperor died, Nogi was free to commit junshi, and Ōgai was, in a sense, liberated to write history in the selective mode of the creative artist, using the past to recontextualize and reinterpret the present. Nogi's junshi motivated Ōgai to explore the roots of Japanese values, their distinct cultural features, and their potential for survival in the modern world. In their different yet concerted ways, Nogi and Ōgai each launched a new era, in which their values were questioned much as were those of the eleven Tosa men who committed seppuku and the nine who were denied the singular honor of following them.

CHAPTER 7

Natsume Sōseki's *Kokoro*

Living as Though Dead

In Ōgai's historical fiction, Nogi does not appear. Yet Ōgai was obsessed, from the moment he heard about Nogi's junshi, with coming to grips with a man he thought he knew. Like many, he was uneasy; and like many, he was moved. Nogi had committed an act both anachronistic for the new Japan and eminently suited to his personality. With the fervor of Heinrich von Kleist (1777–1811), some of whose historical fiction he had translated from German into Japanese,[1] Ōgai set out in his historical fiction to uncover the mysteries of junshi. Swooping down like the swallow in "Abe ichizoku," he seized upon incidents in Tokugawa and Meiji Japan and used them to meditate on the significance of Nogi's dramatic life and even more dramatic death. For those among Ōgai's contemporaries who were capable of reading between the lines the stories were a revelation.

There is no need to read between Natsume Sōseki's lines because Nogi makes a cameo appearance in one of *Kokoro*'s climactic episodes. For good reason. Sōseki was fascinated by Nogi's junshi and its momentous effect. The most important event in *Kokoro* is a suicide inspired by his example. Sōseki's characters experience the Nogis' junshi as a historical event that matters to them. Whereas Nogi's junshi inspired Ōgai, looking to the past, to become a curator of historical custom, it provided Sōseki with the occasion to create a complex template that seemed, with uncanny precision, to forecast future patterns of behavior. Small wonder that *Kokoro* became one of the most widely read of twentieth-century novels. As Sōseki realized, Nogi's legacy, although deeply rooted in the customs of the past, speaks to modern sensibilities.

Selected Critical Approaches

Figuratively, Sōseki took up the pen to write about Nogi when Ōgai put his aside. Unlike Ōgai, Sōseki did not radically alter the kind of fiction he had written before the shock of Nogi's junshi. *Kokoro,* which appeared in the *Asahi Shinbun* in 110 installments from 20 April to 11 August 1914, was the climax of Sōseki's career rather than a new departure.[2] In their discussions of *Kokoro*, literary critics have without fail mentioned the historical backdrop of Emperor Meiji's death and Nogi's junshi, but they have, for the most part, limited themselves to dissecting the novel in terms of its complex narrative structure and its fictional characters' intertwined personal relationships. With the notable exception of Isamu Fukuchi, who explored "the Spirit of Meiji" (Meiji *no seishin*) as the ultimate key to the novel,[3] critics have rarely dwelled on *Kokoro* as a marker of Japan's transition from the Meiji to the Taishō era.

There can be no doubt that Sōseki wrote, and his contemporaries read, *Kokoro* with the Nogis' junshi very much on their minds, but the capacity for a historically engaged reading of *Kokoro* has faded with time. Although the characters of the novel speak of junshi in conjunction with "the spirit of the Meiji era" (245/297: *Meiji no seishin ni junshi suru*),[4] modern readers have only a vague idea of the relationship between junshi and "the spirit of Meiji," which is, in any event, a complex and abstract concept. Fukuchi's discussion of the various critics who have speculated (and differed) about the meaning of *Meiji no seishin* is helpful, especially for his comments on Etō Jun, who interprets that spirit as Emperor Meiji himself, the living symbol of a "traditional morality" that serves to control "ugly" modern egotism. Fukuchi goes on to argue that Meij-era confusion about traditional and modern moralities created *Kokoro*'s tragic "sense of loneliness."[5]

Writing about Sōseki's 1914 lecture on individualism ("Watakushi no kojinshugi"), which was delivered at Gakushūin, where Nogi had been president from 1907 until his death, Jay Rubin and Karatani Kōjin suggest more direct connections between the "spirit of Meiji" and junshi. Rubin maintains that Nogi's anachronistic act "opened up wellsprings of emotion in Sensei [*Kokoro*'s protagonist] that he had assumed to be long since dried up, thanks to his education in 'this modern age, so full of freedom, independence, and our own egotistical selves.'"[6] Karatani, although he describes himself as critical of "periodizing history according to era names," wonders if Sōseki associated the "spirit of Meiji" with the entire so-called Meiji period[7] or only with the earlier, formative part, when a "multiplicity of possibilities . . . existed prior to the rapidly consolidating modern nation-state of the Meiji 20s."[8]

> What Soseki referred to as the "spirit of Meiji" was not the spirit of the entire age of Meiji, which he detested. He felt no sympathy for General Nogi's thinking. Rather, what Nogi's suicide recalled for Soseki was the repressed and forgotten revolution represented by Saigo Takamori, who died as rebel leader of the Seinan War in which Nogi had taken part on the side of the government.[9]

Finally, however, a Zeitgeist approach to *Kokoro* via the "spirit of Meiji" leads to rather than answers the questions raised by Sōseki's startling references to Nogi's junshi.

As Rubin frankly conceded, "Critics have had difficulty explaining exactly how the suicide of General Nogi is related to the suicide of Sōseki's protagonist."[10] Japanese contributions to the "*Kokoro* debates" *(Kokoro ronsō)* of the 1980s did little to answer Rubin's call for an explanation of "how exactly" Sensei's suicide is related to General Nogi's.[11] In the 1990s, however, when a number of Western critics responded to the Sōseki boom in Japan and began contributing significantly to the *Kokoro* debates, Sōseki's references to Nogi and Emperor Meiji were subjected to closer scrutiny. David Pollack mentioned them only to conclude, disappointingly, that they lie "entirely outside the novel's fictional framework." He acknowledged that "their story stands as the solid, permanent frame within which the more mutable fiction of modern life takes place,"[12] but he was concerned less with the immediate historical context than with the influence of Chinese thought on *Kokoro.* Pollack, exploring the history of ideas, saw Sōseki as engaged in a despairing struggle with the opposed ideals of Mengzi, known in the West as Mencius (371–289 B.C.E.), and Xunzi (c. 293–235 B.C.E.), two Chinese philosophers who differed over the question of whether man is inherently good or evil. Pollack noted that the latter's name is pronounced "junshi" in Japanese.[13] The accidental homonym of the Japanese form of Xunzi's name seems, in my view, to distract attention from Sōseki's focus on Nogi's shocking and, for Sensei, exemplary act of anachronistic junshi.

Mundane history does figure, briefly, in some critiques. Concerned with the difficulties of cultural transition to modernity, Dennis C. Washburn concentrates on the weight of the past on Sensei—as exemplified by Emperor Meiji's death and Nogi's junshi—and on the formation of an "apocalyptic sense of the self" and "relativistic individualism."[14] James A. Fujii sees the general and the emperor as historical representations "whose much-larger-than-life dimensions had been created by a commodified print culture." Joining those who are sharply critical of Nogi's ineptness as a military man, Fujii observes that Sōseki, despite his "ambivalence" about Nogi's "anachronistic suicide," nonetheless "appropriates an image of General Nogi associated with military valor, moral rectitude, and unflinching loyalty." This appropriation—or misappropriation—allows "the text's complicit silence concerning Japanese adventurism on the continent."[15]

Among the historically oriented critics of *Kokoro,* Nishi Masahiko stands out for his nuanced comments comparing Ōgai's treatment of suicidal death with Sōseki's. He points out that death in Ōgai's "Abe ichizoku" and in *Kokoro* does not occur at random but rather as a "chain reaction" *(rensa hannō)* intrinsic to junshi.[16] After touching briefly on the postmodernist concept of "assujetissement,"[17] Nishi clarifies some aspects of the two Japanese authors' different literary adaptations of the ritual features of historical junshi. He considers Ōgai's "Okitsu Yagoemon no isho" as the prototype for superimposing Nogi's junshi on another event in a technique Nishi calls "layering and matching" *(kasane awase).*[18] (Since Ōgai does not actually mention Nogi in his historical fiction, the term "palimpsest" seems more accurate than *kasane awase.*) Ōgai uses historical material that can only evoke, not literally incorporate, the later event of Nogi's junshi. By contrast, Sōseki weaves into his literary fabric Nogi's historical junshi as a coeval event that directly affects the actions of his fictional characters.[19] While Ōgai's fictionalized historical characters from generations past powerfully evoke Nogi's junshi in the mind of the reader, Sōseki's characters deal directly with Nogi's junshi as a contemporary historical event. Ōgai asks the reader to make an interpretive leap from the past to the present. Sōseki, by contrast, asks the reader to step from a fictional private conflict to a simultaneous historical public conflict.

These varied approaches by Japanese and Western scholars are helpful, but history plays a larger role than all but Nishi's critical appraisals seem to allow, serving Sōseki as a palimpsest, a kind of mortuary tablet he erased in order to inscribe a new text. General Nogi and Emperor Meiji are not simply passing guests in Sōseki's house of fiction. They are its ever-present ghosts.

Betrayal

Sensei and Nogi

What might a reconstruction of the multilayered parallels between fiction and history reveal? It is generally understood that Nogi provided the blueprint for the character known only as Sensei ("mentor").[20] Sōseki's analogy for Nogi's traumatic loss of his brother, his mentor, and the imperial banner is a triangular romance resulting in the death of Sensei's friend K. Sensei and K both die by their own hand in atonement for their complicity in the deaths of those of paramount importance to them. For Sensei, that someone of paramount importance was K, whose suicide resulted from an intense rivalry in their student years over a young woman known then as Ojōsan ("young lady"). Sensei's subsequent resolve "to live as if I were dead" (243/294: *shinda tsumori de ikite ikō to kesshin shita*) uncannily resembles Nogi's sentiment expressed in the fourth, and last, line of a Chinese verse *(zekku)* he composed on New Year's Day of 1878: "My body is nothing but a subject spared death" (waga mi wa sunawachi kore shi shite tami o amasu).[21]

The literary palimpsest in which "Sensei" effaces "Nogi" is a displacement in which the original outlines, here the historic model's traumatic experiences, remain detectable within the psychic struggle of his fictional counterpart. Sōseki contrived for the historic event of Nogi's junshi to reach deep into the private life of his similarly troubled character. It generates Sensei's story in the form of a lengthy testament that takes Sensei ten days to complete, a rather long-winded span compared to the single evening it took the laconic general to compose *his* testament. Sensei's testament reveals unmistakably what attentive readers have already guessed.

Nogi's suicide clears the way for Sensei's, just as Emperor Meiji's death removed the barrier that had for decades prevented Nogi's suicide. Both Nogi and Sensei decide to die in an immediate response to a public, triggering event (the deaths of Emperor Meiji and Nogi, respectively) even though their ultimate motives for suicide lie in the more distant past. As Sensei meticulously notes when he reads Nogi's testament in the newspaper,[22] the general had been longing to die for thirty-five years (see 246/298). Pondering Nogi's junshi, Sensei asks himself: "'When did he suffer greater agony—during those thirty-five years, or the moment when the sword entered his bowels?'" (246/298). Although his own wait was probably less than a third as long, Sensei can empathize fully with Nogi's protracted agony. It was years before the novel's present that Sensei's friend K had killed himself in the house where the two of them were boarding as university students and courting the landlady's daughter.

No analogy can be perfect. Whereas Nogi carefully composed his testament the day before the funeral of Emperor Meiji, Sensei acted impulsively, as if he had not anticipated the kind of event that would permit him to stop "living as though he were dead." Nogi acted as if he had always known that he would die when the emperor did. Sensei, in contrast, had not been waiting for the death of anyone specific in order to end his life. In lieu of such a person, there was, however, someone on whom he depended to release him from the "dark shadow" (245/296: *kuroi kage*) hovering over his life, thereby prompting him to commit suicide. In order to identify that person, readers must work through the issues debated among the characters and understand their relationship to the historical models that lay behind them.

The historical Nogi's original trauma was, as we have seen, a consequence of a civil war in which he not only opposed his brother and his mentor but also felt shamed by his part in the loss of the imperial colors. In his testament, Nogi referred to his seppuku as suicide *(jisatsu)*, not as junshi. His choice of terms has generally been rejected or simply ignored. There is, however, significance in the fact that he abstained from claiming to follow the emperor into death and instead emphasized his military disgrace at Kumamoto in 1877, which, in turn, was caused by his distress over his rift with his brother and his mentor. From this perspective, Nogi humbly distanced his act of disembowelment from the emperor's death, which provided the occasion but not the motive of his act. The same can be said of Sensei, whose suicide is most intimately linked to K's; within the novel, Nogi's suicide is a compelling example, the proximate but not the ultimate cause.[23] Although Nishi Masahiko suspects "parody" in the "big difference" *(ōki na zure)* between Nogi's junshi and Sensei's suicide,[24] it seems more likely that Sōseki wrote in earnest, intending Sensei's act to be a modern adaptation of Nogi's anachronistic junshi. The two deaths are accomplished through different ritual performances grounded in different eras and different customs, but neither is less serious than the other. Junshi figures centrally as a metaphor in that both men's violent deaths, so differently executed, are motivated by a more intimate, private desire to join those for whose deaths they feel responsible. For Nogi, this is not Emperor Meiji; and for Sensei, this is not Nogi.

Sensei and K

Sensei follows K in death. Two related questions immediately arise: why did K kill himself and why did Sensei want to follow him in death? In order to give adequate answers one must first explore the sources of conflict and the personalities of the two main male protagonists of *Kokoro*'s narrative past.

Sensei's bond to K derives in large part from the fact that both of them experienced the trauma of a "family drama," although of a different sort than the one postulated by Freud. Both of them had to struggle against plots to disinherit them. It is important to recognize that neither K's nor Sensei's traumatic disinheritance was merely a matter of money. Personal integrity and family pride were also at stake. Sensei reveals in his testament what he had often hinted at in his advice to Watakushi ("I"), the young narrator of the first half of *Kokoro.* Sensei had been deprived of his rightful inheritance by the machinations of his uncle, whom he seems to have alienated by refusing to marry his daughter (who is, of course, Sensei's cousin). K suffered a similar injustice. Behind Sensei's detailed comments on K's mistreatment one can detect the pain felt by Sensei himself as he recalls his own mistreatment at the hands of his relatives.

K is the second son of a Buddhist priest of the Jōdo Shinshū (True Pure Land) sect. Although his family is described (by Sensei) as living "comfortably" (165/200), his father sends him out for adoption into a doctor's family. K, who has no desire to become a doctor, perceives the adoption as a hostile scheme concocted by the husband of his beloved older sister, about whom Sensei speculates that "she must have seemed more of a mother [to K] than his stepmother ever did" (172/208). K responds rebelliously. He enrolls at the university, but instead of studying medicine, he uses the money his adoptive parents send him to follow the "true way" (166/202: *michi*) of religious study. When he confesses his deception, the adoption is revoked. Although his father repays the misused money, he punishes him by barring him from returning home. This "later expulsion" (175/212) intensifies K's distrust of, disillusionment with, and contempt for the world. Disillusioned by his own family, Sensei is drawn to and stands by his similarly disillusioned friend despite his disapproval of K's having deceived his adoptive parents.

While both K and Sensei lose their inheritance, there is a significant difference between their grievances. K's is greater. His father not only sent him off to be adopted; he also irrevocably expelled him from the family. It is true that K, by deceiving his adoptive family, provided the reason—or pretext—for his punishment, but K is nonetheless shocked to find that his biological family wants to "wash . . . their hands of him" (171/207: *katte ni shiro*). Sensei, by contrast, loses his parents, who seemed to have loved him, to sudden illness. Only then does he become ensnared in his uncle's schemes. Comparing the two cases, one realizes that K's was more hurtful.

Initially, Sensei welcomes K into his life as a person who can restore the trust that Sensei's uncle had destroyed. The two young men form a friendship based on their painful past experiences. When Sensei asks K to move in with him in a boardinghouse in Tōkyō, he does so in order to gain an ally in combatting family discord, but he is risking—perhaps even calling for—a different sort of trouble. The young men believe that their commitment to each other is unassailable, but serious discord occurs when both of them fall in love with the same woman (whom they refer to simply as Ojōsan). The imbroglio comes about when Sensei, who has begun courting Ojōsan, sees her relationship with K as a test of the sincerity and strength of K's friendship for him. He does this at a time when he is confident that "K seemed totally unaware of my love for Ojosan" (187). Sensei's urging Ojōsan and her mother "to talk to K as much as possible" (178) may have been merely an effort to combat K's reclusive tendencies, but it is tantamount to baiting a trap. Will K and Ojōsan turn to each other and away from him? It is impossible to know whether Ojōsan merely enjoys K's company, whether she is flirting with him, or whether she is shifting her romantic interest from Sensei to K, but it is clear that K does indeed become enamored of Ojōsan. It is also clear that Sensei does not know how to interpret Ojōsan's laughter when he observes her with K. Sensei becomes tormented by irrational "jealousy" (199/240: *shitto*) over K's having taken the bait and become involved with Ojōsan. Obviously, the young men cannot remain the friends they have been if one of them—even if unwittingly—takes away the other's prize.

Confession

Deceit and disinheritance breed both sympathy and distrust. In order to save their friendship, the two men need to confide in one another. The process is difficult. While one struggles to confess and finally succeeds, the other wrestles with himself but fails to disclose his heart.

Unaware that Sensei has been courting Ojōsan, K assumes that Sensei's display of jealousy is simply a response to his—K's—shift of affection from their male friendship to a conventional romantic attachment. K seems to have learned from his traumatic conflict with his adoptive and biological families that there is always a price to pay for deception. K confesses to Sensei his love for Ojōsan and offers to sacrifice it on the altar of their friendship. The confession seems designed to cleanse their male friendship from the impurity of deception. Although K could have reminded Sensei that he had encouraged him to court Ojōsan, he does not.

If K hopes for a reciprocal gesture from Sensei—that he was disturbed by the redirection of K's affections from him to a woman or that he himself is interested in Ojōsan—he is disappointed. Sensei might have said, "I, too, have a confession. I, too, have become emotionally involved with a woman. And, sadly, it is the same woman." But Sensei initially remains silent, hiding his feelings and thereby betraying his friendship with K. Sensei's silence contributes to K's distress. When Sensei does break his silence, he mocks K's confession rather than responding to it with his own. In an earlier discussion, K had said, "Anyone who has no spiritual aspirations is an idiot" (214/258: seishinteki ni kōjōshin no nai mono wa baka da). Now that K has confessed that he is sexually attracted to a woman, Sensei taunts him by quoting his own words back to him.

All that K seems to want—and he is begging and pleading—is peace with Sensei: "Let us not talk about it any more" (216/261). Sensei is implacable. Of himself at that time, he writes, "The wolf jumped at the lamb's throat" (216/261: ōkami ga suki o mite hitsuji no nodobue e kuraitsuku yō ni). Sensei asks K whether he can "will [himself] to stop thinking about it [and whether he is] prepared to do that" (217/261). Unclear as Sensei's question is, K meekly acknowledges that he has done grave harm to their friendship. In the aftermath of this tense conversation, K awakens Sensei in the middle of the night and attempts, vainly, to initiate a conversation. Shortly after this, he asks a question that seems to imply that Sensei has a bad conscience, "Have you been sleeping well lately?" (219/265).

Although it is clear to Sensei that K would gladly resume his courtship of Ojōsan if he—Sensei—were not opposed to it, he refuses to give K any such reassurance and instead continues to act in secret by asking Ojōsan's mother for her daughter's hand. In the process he lies about K's involvement with Ojōsan and asks her mother to inform her daughter of his love. In retrospect, Sensei wonders, "where was my *conscience?*" (224/271: *ryōshin*). When K inquires about his health, Sensei misses another chance to be honest with him. He comes close to asking K's forgiveness but blames the social context for his failure to do so: "I think that had K and I been alone *in some wilderness,* I would have listened to the cry of my conscience. But there were others in the house" (225/272: *kōya no mannaka*). Sensei realizes that he is a "cowardly soul" (226/273: *hikyō na watakushi*). It is left to Ojōsan's mother to break the news to K of Sensei's marriage proposal to her daughter. That K takes the news stoically weighs heavily on Sensei's conscience. He interprets K's behavior as a withdrawal from their friendship and a sign of his ultimate withdrawal from the world.

The motivation for K's confession is clear. It is meant to prevent the loss of his friendship with Sensei. It reaffirms his loyalty to Sensei. The subtext of the confession, however, is an unspoken request for forgiveness, perhaps even for assurance that there was no need to confess. K's confession may thus contain, subliminally, his hope for permission to continue his courtship of Ojōsan without risking the loss of Sensei's friendship. It is also possible that he confesses because he values male over female liaisons. If this was the case, then K's confession and his renunciation of Ojōsan hardly qualify as a noble sacrifice.

Sensei's motives are even less clear. Why does he betray K's trust by not telling him earlier of his intentions concerning Ojōsan? One reason for Sensei's lack of candor may be his sense of inferiority to K and his fear that this admired friend might ridicule or despise him. It might also be that Sensei is ashamed to admit that K is no longer the main focus of his affections. More than that. In his testament, Sensei admits to Watakushi that he wanted not merely to test but actually to destroy his rival: "I confess to you that what I was trying to do was far more cruel than mere revenge. I wanted to destroy whatever hope there might have been in his love for Ojosan" (214/258). Sensei explains to Watakushi that K's confession affected him in several ways. Although it told him that K respected him enough to confide in him, it also revealed that K had not only chosen to prefer a woman over Sensei but also to abandon his claims to "the true way" of spirituality and thus to betray his own moral self.[25] Sensei, in turn, was "demoralized" (215/260: *omowazu gyotto*) by K's change of heart because he had tried so hard to emulate him that now he feels his efforts mocked. His attempt to be like K may well have led to his withholding from K the truth about his own intentions regarding Ojōsan. Whatever the reasons, Sensei's failure to be honest with K has disastrous consequences. After confessing to Sensei, waiting vainly for his reciprocal confession, and hearing of his engagement to Ojōsan, K confirms Sensei's worst fears by committing suicide. He shows Sensei the blood that he wanted to see.

What did K intend his suicide to mean? The answer to that question can never be certain, as Sensei discovers in his struggle to cope with his friend's dramatic death. The suicide seems at first to have been directly motivated by Ojōsan's engagement to Sensei, a typically romantic Werther-like response to unrequited love. Evidence for this is the fact that his death weighs heavily on the engaged couple, each of whom feels a measure of guilt for the anguish they have—wittingly or unwittingly—caused. This cause-and-effect equation is, however, too simple. K's behavior emitted signs of suicidal thoughts even before Ojōsan's mother told him of her daughter's marriage plans. K may have wanted simply to atone for his lack of total commitment to his male friend; news of Ojōsan's engagement may have been merely the last straw. By self-sacrificingly eliminating himself from what he now must recognize as a fateful love triangle, K may have hoped to ensure the respect of both Sensei and Ojōsan. Or perhaps K acted as he did in order to punish Sensei and Ojōsan by afflicting them with a sense of guilt. Motivations can be as mixed in fiction as they are in our everyday lives. It is not impossible for all these somewhat inconsistent motivations to have played a role in K's decision to kill himself.

K's farewell letter is addressed to Sensei, the man who betrayed him. It is a remarkably pacific letter, quite without the implicit demands of his earlier confession. Instead, the overwhelming sentiments of the letter are regret and apology. Although Sensei is relieved that K did not accuse him of selfish and dishonorable conduct, he is acutely affected by a question that K apparently appended spontaneously: "Why did I wait so long to die?" (230/278: motto hayaku shinubeki da no ni naze ima made ikite ita no darō). This question implies that, had it not been for Sensei's friendship, K might have killed himself earlier, perhaps after the adoption fiasco in which K's father not only failed to forgive his deception of his adoptive parents but rejected him. K's question relieves Sensei of some of the burden of his sense of complicity in K's suicide, although that relief may come at a price: to the extent that K allows Sensei's guilt to diminish, he is denying the importance of their bond of friendship. In other words, K hints that his death is not solely attributable to the unendurable stress on their male friendship because of a woman, but that it has causes predating the complications arising from the fateful love triangle.

Loyalties

Male-Male Intimacy

Nishi Masahiko deduces from the prominence of confession *(kokuhaku)* in *Kokoro* and its tie to exclusively male intimacy *(shinmitsusa)* that Sensei's testament, addressed to Watakushi, can be compared to a love letter *(koibumi)*. Episodes such as the beach scenes—picturing Watakushi and Sensei at Enoshima and K and Sensei at Bōsō—underscore the aptness of the term.[26] Nishi is not the first to note the homosexual aura of *Kokoro*'s highly charged male friendship.

The friendship between Sensei and K is problematized by the male-male intimacy that seems to interfere with their erotic interest in the woman they both attempt—or pretend—to court. Anticipating Eve Kosofsky Sedgwick's *Between Men* (1985), which asserts that two men overtly courting one woman are actually covertly attracted to each other, the psychiatrist Doi Takeo maintained in 1969 that Sensei and K were motivated by homosexual as well as heterosexual impulses.

The strongest evidence for Doi's thesis occurs during the excursion to Bōsō, which follows Sensei's discovery of Ojōsan and K together in K's room. Sitting on rocks by the sea and thinking of Ojōsan Sensei wonders "whether K was not sitting there indulging in *exactly the same reverie*" (186/225: *onaji yō na kibō*). Overcome by jealous rage, Sensei seizes K's neck: "I shouted as an uncontrolled savage might have done. Once, I grabbed [him] from behind. 'What would you do,' I said, 'if I pushed you into the sea?' K did not move." Reacting as if the sudden physical assault were an embrace, K responds, "'That would be pleasant. Please do.'" K's response can be seen either as receptivity to a sexual advance or as willingness to die. It may, in fact, be both. That it cannot be glossed as a mere jest is clear from Sensei's reaction to K's compliant words. "Quickly, I withdrew the hand that had been holding his neck" (186/225). Repressed homosexual impulses certainly seem to contribute to the unbearable tensions within the love triangle that cause K to abandon his courtship of Ojōsan and to kill himself. Sensei is left with Ojōsan and a sense of profound guilt about his role in K's suicide. He may, in fact, have fulfilled Oscar Wilde's frightening prophecy: "Yet each man kills the thing he loves."[27]

Doi attributed Sensei's suicide to his inability to admit his conflicted feelings, after K's death, either to his wife or to the anonymous addressee of his testament: "More likely than not, Sensei prefers to have his suicide understood as a sacrifice to a passing age than as loyalty arising from homosexual feelings for K." Doi goes on to speculate that Sensei's behavior may be a warning to Watakushi not to do as he did: "He [Sensei] does not want the boy tied to him as he had been tied to K; and he presents his past as a final admonition."[28] Speculation need not stop at this. Sensei is a mystery, not only to Watakushi but also to his wife, because he periodically rejects her love as well. What can motivate this flight from affection if not a jealous determination to guard the precious bond with K (whose grave he compulsively visits)?

Sensei does, however, leave Watakushi (but not his wife) with the freedom to interpret his testament, either as a warning or as an invitation eventually to follow him in death.

Doi's controversial interpretation of *Kokoro*'s erotic intricacies gains plausibility when we consider the historical context. The Meiji period coincided with the crest of the Victorian era. For earlier generations, expressions of intimate male friendship were considered quite normal, but as Japan opened itself to Western influences, respectable middle-class Europeans and Americans—people like Sensei—were experiencing a period of sexual repression. In Japan as in Europe and America, overt expressions of intimate male friendship became taboo. As Stephen Dodd has noted, the "new libidinal economy" of the Meiji period came to reflect this strong influence of Western codes of sexuality. The traditional terms—celebratory (*nanshoku;* lit. "male colors") and bold (*keikan;* lit. "wicked cocks")—were replaced by the newly coined term *dōsei*—that is, "same sex," a literal translation of "homosexuality."[29]

During the Meiji period, young men still formed strong male bonds. As they became increasingly wary about acting upon sexual impulses condemned in the West, some of them discharged the sexual energy generated by male-male bonds in the form of political action. Komori Yōichi observed in 1995 "that 'homosexual energy' *(nanshokuteki enerugī)* centered upon the young Meiji emperor at the time of the Restoration was an important motivation among the groupings of young men known as *shishi* (men of action)."[30] While the *shishi* of Nogi's generation were inclined to sublimate their homosexual energy into devotion to Emperor Meiji, this outlet is blocked for Sōseki's Sensei and K, neither of whom has the slightest interest in politics. Squarely within the generation that Dodd and Komori have characterized as full of ambivalences concerning sexual preferences, Sensei and K are inhibited in the physical expression of their intensely passionate friendship.

Komori surmises that this generational shift in attitudes toward male-male sexuality was concurrent with the Satsuma Rebellion and the defeat of Saigō Takamori and his band of young men in 1877,[31] a time that was, as we have seen, crucial for Nogi's increasingly close bond to Emperor Meiji. The fact that Sōseki's psychically conflicted characters are of his own generation, not Nogi's, suggests that Sōseki may also have struggled with the shifting social discourse on intimate same-sex friendships.[32]

Watakushi and His Parental Figures

From the anonymous narrator's account of Sensei's bespectacled appearance and subdued behavior, readers receive the impression that he is a middle-aged man, yet Sensei is in his prime when Watakushi, then a student about to enter his last year in secondary school, first meets him on the beach at Kamakura. The misleading impression that Sensei is middle-aged if not elderly can be attributed to Watakushi's youth and inexperience. It may even be that Watakushi seeks to rationalize his attraction to Sensei by thinking of him as a father figure and a *sensei*. In reality, the age difference between them is only thirteen to fifteen years, enough to make the older man a "mentor" of the younger but hardly sufficient to cast Sensei into the role of father. As for Sensei, his doubts about his role as a father figure explain his repeated references to Watakushi's duty to pay closer attention to his ailing biological father. Sensei attempts to prepare him for his father's death by discussing with his wife, in Watakushi's presence, the question of his own demise. Who will die first and leave the other behind?

In fact, Sensei's appearance in Watakushi's life problematizes rather than clarifies his relationship with his father. Sensei alerts him to his financial dependence on his father and to the importance of settling matters of inheritance in order to avoid the kind of betrayal by relatives that befell Sensei upon the death of his parents. It so happens that the closer Watakushi comes to knowing Sensei, the greater the emotional distance from his biological father.

When Watakushi returns to his parents' home after graduating in the spring of 1912, he realizes with sorrow that his father does not have long to live. At the same time, he is annoyed by his parents' provinciality. He is taken aback at his father's speaking of his son's diploma as if it were his own. Watakushi abhors self-congratulatory compliments and refuses to be paraded trophy-like around the rural neighborhood. He finds his father's display of pride repugnant because his father cannot appreciate his accomplishment except as a vocational prerequisite. His parents' pressure on him to find a suitable job is intolerable to Watakushi, who wants only to follow Sensei's example of idleness. He is increasingly alienated from what he takes to be his parents' opportunism and materialism. Although his parents become increasingly critical of Sensei's ways, they have no scruples about urging their son to use Sensei to find a job. Watakushi resents this pressure, but he does his mother the favor of writing to Sensei, even at the risk of losing Sensei's respect. (Sensei does not reply.) Watakushi craves a different sort of acknowledgment and respect from Sensei, who lives a cosmopolitan life in Tōkyō and does not put much stock in such things as a university diploma. The truth is that Watakushi, since the deepening of his relationship with Sensei, has become ashamed of his parents. They seem unsophisticated and naive in comparison to Sensei and his wife. The very first time that Watakushi noticed Sensei on the beach at Kamakura he was in exotic Western company of the sort his parents would be scarcely able to imagine. His mother's provincial idea of a present for Sensei is dried shiitake. In contrast, Sensei's wife offers Watakushi black tea and Western cakes.

More important, Watakushi takes his parents for granted and is under the impression that he need not make any effort to win their unconditional love. What intrigues him about Sensei and his wife is precisely that he has to work hard to earn their trust, affection, and admiration. Although they admonish him to care more about his parents, Watakushi postpones acting on his good intentions because what really matters to him is his attachment to Sensei (and Sensei's wife). Later, he will learn, from Sensei's testament, that after deceit or betrayal of the kind that K committed and endured one may not be allowed to return to one's parents.

Contemptuous of his parents' pride in his success, Watakushi is glad when news of the emperor's illness causes his father to cancel the celebration for his diploma. He takes his father's decision to mean that there can be figures outside the family, "significant others," who are far more important than the family's newly graduated son. Watakushi certainly does not consider himself to be in competition with the emperor for his father's respect, but his father's priorities allow him to feel justified in seeking to tighten his bond with Sensei. His father's obsession with the emperor's illness and his own releases Watakushi from the shackles of unwanted attention. When the emperor dies, Watakushi longs, above all, for a letter from Sensei.

Although the lesson that Sensei tries to teach Watakushi about safeguarding his inheritance does not go entirely unheeded, Watakushi finds it difficult to act while his father is dying. His father is already too far gone to deal with the matter, and Watakushi's uncle arrives on the scene as if to make Sensei's warning come true. Watakushi brings up the matter of inheritance with his older brother, whom he trusts, but we never learn how the inheritance claims are settled. (Such events fall outside the temporal frame of the story.) As his father's condition grows critical, Watakushi continues to refuse to pester Sensei about such a trivial matter as a job, thus putting his relationship with Sensei above satisfying his parents' wish for his financial independence.

Death and Loyalty

It is at this moment in the story that news of General Nogi's suicide arrives, "like the bitter wind which awakens the trees and the grass sleeping in the remotest corners of the countryside" (109/136: *hitsū na kaze ga inaka no sumi made fuite kite, nemutasō na ki ya kusa o furuwasete iru saichū ni*). The imagery that captures the effect of Nogi's death stands in sharp contrast to the paralyzing, nullifying effect of the earlier news about the emperor's illness, which, Watakushi writes, "puffed away like dust my graduation party" (my translation/112: *watakushi no sotsugyō iwai o, chiri no gotoku ni fukiharatta*). Although Watakushi had denied the connection his mother made between his father's depression and the emperor's illness by the symbolic act of blowing off the "dust" (89, 90/114, 115: *hokori*) on his father's chessboard, he must acknowledge that his father's response to the emperor's death does, indeed, indicate close identification. His father envisions himself following his emperor in death as he had in illness: "I too" (91/116: *ore mo*). When General Nogi commits junshi, Watakushi's father, as we have seen, wishes to follow his example, much for the same reason that Sensei cites for committing junshi—to follow the spirit of the Meiji era, which Nogi most spectacularly embodied. Unlike Sensei, Watakushi's father has no motive that we are told of for following anyone in death. Yet his anticipated death becomes meaningful to him because he passionately associates himself with both historical figures—Emperor Meiji for his illness, General Nogi for representing the fast-fading spirit of loyalty in modern Japan. Watakushi's father's death is not junshi in any traditional sense, but it surely has a psychic affinity to junshi proper.

Closest to the imagery of the "bitter wind" that Nogi's suicide brings to Watakushi's family, however, is "the sudden gust of wind" (229/277: *shippū*) that hit Sensei when he found K's dead body. For Sensei, the concomitant of that wind is "a black light" (my translation/277: *kuroi hikari*) that will stay with him to the day of his own death. For Watakushi, the turbulence caused by Nogi's death results in some uncoordinated communications with Sensei, not unlike the last disjointed conversations between K and Sensei. In each case, the attempts at communication fail. Watakushi, like Sensei in his struggle with K over Ojōsan, cannot decide whether or not to reveal—and act on—his sincere intentions. It was when the emperor died that he had first noted his acute desire to return to Sensei in the mourning metropolis of Tōkyō: "There was but one light shining, and that came from Sensei's house" (92/117: itten no tōka no gotoku ni sensei no ie o mita). Watakushi's desire surges once again after Nogi's suicide precipitates a new crisis in his father's illness. From reading only snippets of Sensei's last letter, Watakushi surmises that Sensei too is close to death. Rushing to Sensei's side means abandoning his father, but off he goes to Tōkyō.

Watakushi's abandonment of his father seems so deplorable because it is unfilial. It denies his responsibility for taking care of his father's physical and emotional needs. Although Watakushi makes no attempt to justify himself, he acts as he does because of the circumstances in which he finds himself. In those critical days after General Nogi's passing, Watakushi allows his mother to make him an accomplice in a scheme to boost his father's morale. His mother tells her husband that Watakushi has obtained a job through Sensei's help. Worse than the untruth is the misuse of Watakushi's relationship with Sensei. At just this time, Watakushi has been reminded of Sensei and his estrangement from the world by one Saku-san, an old friend of Watakushi's father. In what may be just a desperate attempt to cheer Watakushi's father by means of a depressing contrast, Saku-san protests that it is he, Saku-san, who is spiritually dead: "Look at me. My wife is dead, and I have no children. I am leading a meaningless existence. I may be healthy, but what have I to look forward to?" (111/139). Saku-san's words remind Watakushi of Sensei's childlessness. For Watakushi, the bizarre words with which his father greets Saku-san signal that there is nothing more to be done for him: "I am finished" (111/139: ore wa mō dame da). Saku-san's glum words, however, paradoxically suggest to Watakushi that he may be able to do something about Sensei's "meaningless existence." He is young and innocent enough to think that maladies of the soul are more easily cured than physical illness.

Unmistakably, what Emperor Meiji was to Nogi, Nogi is to Watakushi's father, who wonders in his delirium, "Will General Nogi ever forgive me? . . . How can I ever face him without shame? Yes, General, I will be with you very soon" (117/145: Nogi taishō ni sumanai. Jitsu ni menboku shidai ga nai. Ie watakushi mo sugu oato kara).

At this juncture, Watakushi receives two telegraphed messages from Sensei, the first telling him to come to Tōkyō and the second, not to come. Watakushi responds to the first message by sending a telegram of refusal followed by a letter explaining that he cannot leave his dying father. Watakushi's family is understandably relieved and gratified by his demonstration of his loyalty to them. Although Sensei admits in his testament that at first he was "deeply disappointed" (126/155: *watakushi wa shitsubō shite*) that Watakushi did not accede to his summons, he came to realize from Watakushi's explanatory letter that there was a legitimate reason for his refusal.

Sensei's decision finally to commit the act of suicide that he had contemplated for years is motivated more by Nogi's exemplary junshi than by disappointment over Watakushi's refusal to leave his dying father, but Sensei's "testament," which he mails to Watakushi, does include an ominous sentence: "I myself am about to cut open my . . . heart, and drench your face with my blood"(129/158: watakushi wa ima jibun de jibun no shinzō o yabutte, sono chi o anata no kao ni abisekakeyō to shite iru no desu). Watakushi, with his father's confession of shame to General Nogi still reverberating in his mind, rushes to Tōkyō, hoping no doubt to dissuade Sensei from *his* suicidal act of expiation.

The Narrative Gap and Death

Watakushi's narrative ends with his train ride to Tōkyō. Sōseki's technique creates the illusion of a seamless transition between Watakushi's story and Sensei's (even though any narrative carries the potential of events that are anticipated to have already occurred by the time they are narrated). By terminating his story when he does, Watakushi entices readers to take over his earlier detective-like role vis-à-vis the mystery of Sensei's past. Readers are now challenged to reconstruct Watakushi's future as he had tried to reconstruct Sensei's past.

Sōseki leaves his readers wondering whether Watakushi finds Sensei alive, dying, or already dead. Although we are told early on in Watakushi's narrative that Sensei is dead, we are not told exactly when he died. Nor are we told whether or not Watakushi returns home to attend his dying father or to be among the mourners at his father's funeral. Nor do we learn the fate of Sensei's widowed wife. Finally, we are left to wonder, what happens to Watakushi?[33] Are we to imagine him liberated or orphaned by the deaths of his biological and his symbolic fathers? If the latter, which seems more likely, are we also meant to imagine him committing junshi and following his fathers into death? The pattern for such drastic action is discernably at hand in the historic example of Nogi's junshi, which, aside from following his emperor in death, simultaneously served his need to atone for a variety of military failures and personal betrayals. This same pattern also emerges in Sensei's following both Nogi and K in death—the one as a symbol of the Meiji era and the other as atonement for his betrayal of their friendship.

Linked Death

In order fully to understand the relationship between Nogi's junshi and Sensei's suicide, it is important to achieve some conceptual clarity about the different categories of death mentioned in *Kokoro*. There are several instances of natural and unnatural death, historical and fictional, anticipated or accomplished. The historical paradigm is Emperor Meiji's natural death from illness, followed by the junshi of Nogi Maresuke and his wife. Among Sōseki's fictional characters, K is the first to die, choosing suicide as atonement for the betrayal of his principles. His death, therefore, marks the starting point of the lethal "chain reaction." Chronologically, K's death is followed by that of Emperor Meiji and then by Nogi's.[34]

The fact that K's death is a suicide that implicates Sensei seems to demand a response from the survivor of their friendship. K's suicide thus creates a novel variant on the traditional pattern of junshi in which a person commits seppuku to follow a lord or superior who gave his loyal subject permission to do so before his own demise. In contrast, motivated by a fateful combination of obligation, indebtedness, and guilt, Sensei's desire to follow K is not dictated by a hierarchical lord–vassal relationship that requires permission for junshi. He and K are equals who have destroyed their friendship through mutual betrayal. Offering his own life, K pays for his violation of male friendship; but Sensei feels condemned to live and obliged to endure his guilt in order to meet his obligations to the memory of K and to the woman both men courted. His sense of inescapable obligation ends when he finds someone he can trust sincerely to care for K's memory, for his own memory, and—perhaps—for his wife. It is only then, after General Nogi's junshi provides the classic example of a man who patiently waited until the proper time to commit junshi without official permission but with tacit consent *(mokkei)*,[35] that Sensei can follow K in a modern variant of junshi—without permission or tacit consent from K.

Whether Sensei has or thinks he has Watakushi's consent is a matter for conjecture, but his words and behavior strongly suggest that he feels his death to be a sacrifice offered to Watakushi. Just as Nogi had cut open his stomach to expiate his sense of guilt, so Sensei—displacing the incision from (traditional) stomach to (modern) heart—tells Watakushi in his testament that he wishes to "cut open my own *heart,* and drench your face with my blood. And I shall be satisfied if, when my heart stops beating, a new life lodges itself in your breast" (129/158: *shinzō*). Sensei is ready to sacrifice himself on the altar of K so that Watakushi can live on, feeding on his sacrifice, having at last obtained the knowledge that Sensei had earlier been reluctant to impart.

It is the relentlessness of Watakushi's desire to know Sensei that causes Sensei not only to share his most intimate secret (his complicity in K's death) but to do what that secret demanded (to follow K in death and to anoint, with his own blood, Watakushi as his successor): "I was moved by your decision, albeit discourteous in expression, to grasp something that was alive within my *soul.* You wished to cut open my *heart* and see the blood flow" (129/158: *hara,* stomach; *shinzō,* heart). It is important to recognize that the language here is the language of ritual sacrifice. Sensei describes Watakushi as if he—Watakushi—were an Aztec priest sacrificing to the gods in order to ensure that the sun will rise every morning.

Telling Watakushi of K's death, Sensei attributes an almost seminal power to the "tremendous spurt" (233/282) K's blood made as he cut open his carotid artery.[36] Watakushi's desire to know Sensei is not unlike Sensei's desire to know K, and in each instance that desire carries carnal overtones. It is, moreover, a desire so intense that it approximates killing the other, whether by Sensei's pushing K into the sea or by Watakushi's cutting open Sensei's heart. Not surprisingly, Sensei does not want to reveal himself to his wife: "I intend to die in such a way that she will be spared *the sight of my blood*" (246–247/298: *chi no iro* [lit. *iro:* color; metaphorically, passion]). The sacrificial blood, it will be noted, excludes the woman (Ojōsan) and connects the men (K, Sensei, and Watakushi). Rather than adopting the utilitarian gift theory of sacrifice inherent in strict hierarchical relationships that peak in junshi and create an idealized " 'eternal' male intergenerational continuity," Sōseki establishes intergenerational sacrifice in *Kokoro* in order to "create and maintain kinship between men and men."[37]

Although Watakushi's reaction to Sensei's death is adumbrated rather than illuminated, it is crucially important. While Emperor Meiji and General Nogi are being publicly mourned, Watakushi expects soon to mourn in private both Sensei and his father. As we have seen, Watakushi's loyalties are not in question until he discovers from snippets of Sensei's testament that he might still be able to prevent Sensei's suicide (as contrasted to merely standing by helplessly while his father is dying). That this effort to rescue Sensei must have been in vain the reader already knows because Watakushi revealed the fact of Sensei's death early on in his narration. As readers make the transition from Watakushi's account to Sensei's testament, they become so engrossed in Sensei's past that Watakushi's father's fate is likely to be all but forgotten by the end of *Kokoro,* and with it Watakushi's silence about it.

In addition to the deaths of K, Emperor Meiji, General Nogi and his wife, Sensei, and Watakushi's father, there are the unknown fates of Watakushi and Sensei's wife. Because in *Kokoro* Natsume Sōseki developed a mechanism of analogies with missing terms, he forces the reader to become engaged not only in filling in the narrative blanks but also in searching for the second terms of incomplete analogies.

Has Watakushi, in the manner of K and Sensei, accumulated enough guilt to commit suicide? If there is guilt, acknowledged or not, what motivates it? In all probability, as was the case with K and Sensei, Watakushi's guilt, if it exists, has multiple causes, all rooted in relationships gone awry. Each of these relationships about which Watakushi feels guilty has parallels in the troubled relationships of other characters—and often with those of Nogi as well. There is the betrayal and abandonment of his family (paralleled in K's estrangement from his parents and Sensei's resentment against his uncle). There is the betrayal of an intimate male friend (paralleled in the mutual betrayal of K and Sensei). Finally, as recent Japanese critics have speculated, there is romantic engagement with the male friend's wife (paralleled in K's and Sensei's rivalry in pursuit of Ojōsan's affections). That Watakushi feels guilty about abandoning his family during the crisis of his dying father is evident from the notes his sends to his mother and brother as he boards the train to Tōkyō. Since it was Watakushi's telegram denying Sensei the chance to confess his past to him that contributed to Sensei's decision to die, Watakushi must also feel himself at least partially culpable for the very crisis that he is relying on to exculpate him from blame for abandoning his dying father. And then, when Watakushi arrives in Tōkyō, he discovers that his delay has caused him to arrive too late to save Sensei from suicide.[38] There is no way of knowing if Watakushi also feels guilty about concealing romantic feelings for Sensei's wife, but it is not unreasonable to conjecture that he does.

The difference between Watakushi and his historic and fictional predecessors may well be that he seems able to rationalize his guilt to himself instead of coming to confess it, as did Nogi, K, and Sensei. Or are we to assume that Watakushi's account of his relationship with Sensei is intended to be a confessional testament written in anguish as Watakushi prepares for his own act of junshi? Watakushi may have been inspired by Sensei's suicide to follow him into death in atonement for his shortcomings with respect to him as well as his father.[39] If it took Sensei a mere ten days to write his confessional testament, it might not have taken Watakushi any longer to write his memoir of their relationship. If this conjecture is true, it would explain why there is no word in *Kokoro* about Watakushi's father's death and no mention of the fate of Sensei's wife.[40]

Secret Knowledge

Enter Shizu

The least developed and most puzzling of *Kokoro*'s four characters is Sensei's wife, Shizu. She is a pivotal figure who holds the key to the mysteries of the past, present, and future.

In a conversation that reveals Sensei's deepening interest in Watakushi and his fear of losing his friendship as he had lost K's, Sensei tells Watakushi that he will sooner or later discover a woman and quickly forget him: "'The friendship that you sought in me is in reality a preparation for the love that you will seek in a woman. . . . That you will eventually go elsewhere for consolation is a fact I must accept. Indeed, I even hope that you will. But . . .'" (27/36; 37: isei to dakiau junjo to shite, mazu dōsei no watakushi no tokoro e ugoite kita no desu. . . . Anata ga watakushi kara yoso e ugoite yuku no wa shikata ga nai. Watakushi wa mushiro sore o kibō shite iru no desu. Shikashi . . .). Sensing that the depth of his affection has been questioned, Watakushi asserts that such a thing could not possibly happen: "'Sensei, if you really think that I shall drift away from you, there is nothing I can do about it. But such a thought has so far never crossed my mind'" (27/37: Watakushi ga Sensei kara hanarete yuku yō ni oomoi ni nareba shikata ga arimasen ga, watakushi ni sonna ki no okotta koto wa mada arimasen). There is, however, a woman who has already begun to complicate the men's relationship simply by her existence, and she is, of course, Sensei's wife, Shizu (17/24). Watakushi may not conceive of her as the woman who will make him forget his Sensei, but Sensei cannot avoid recalling her role in the traumatic experience that has haunted him for a decade.

It can hardly be coincidental that this key figure bears the name of General Nogi's wife, Shizuko, lacking only the diminutive "child" *(ko)*, omitted as if to stress her maturity and suggest gender equality. She is, of course, the Ojōsan courted more than a decade before by K and Sensei. It is unlikely that she is older than her husband. If Sensei's version of "divine punishment" (17/24: *tenbatsu*) is that he must live with the heavy burden of his sense of guilt, Shizu's is that she is childless and longs to become a mother. Although the reason for the couple's childlessness—infertility, impotence, abstinence?—is never stated, it is clear that Sensei does not want to father a child, because he feels that doing so with Shizu would be tantamount to betraying K once again. Nogi, refusing to replace his lost sons with an adopted heir, accepted the extinction of his line as a partial atonement for his failures. Sensei, by contrast, *is* willing to adopt a son, but Shizu is as opposed to adoption as she is to Sensei's monthly "pilgrimage" (13/18) to K's grave, which she seems to consider morbid (judging from the radical change she observed in her husband after his friend's unnatural death).[41]

Shizu's rejection of Sensei's suggestion that they adopt an heir is adamant because it is clear to her that Sensei has Watakushi in mind. In fact, Sensei communicates his wish to adopt him so emphatically that Watakushi feels "that Sensei's strength had entered my body, and that his very life was flowing in my veins" (50/65). Watakushi, who from the first days of their encounters on the beach of Kamakura, has actively sought Sensei's love, claims to be stunned when he discovers that Sensei has taken the place of his father: "I was shocked. For was I not my father's flesh?" (50/65). His protestation seems excessive.[42] Contrary to his assertions, he can very well imagine exchanging a biological father for a symbolic one. Clearly, Shizu, who is quite aware of her husband's attachment to Watakushi, has reason to be jealous. She desires her husband's sexual love in addition to his affection. Her demand for children—she raises the issue in front of Watakushi—is a demand for physical proof of her husband's total commitment to her. In short, the intensely intimate relationship between Sensei and Watakushi interferes with Shizu's demand for that commitment.

Shizu's Unwritten Tale

Almost as if *Kokoro* were a popular romance, "the plot thickens" when Watakushi becomes attracted to Shizu. Demonstrating Ken K. Ito's "circularity of the narrative situations,"[43] the Sensei–Shizu–Watakushi triangle begins to replicate the earlier fateful triangle that led to K's suicide. In this new configuration, Watakushi substitutes for K and Sensei is the man impelled down the path to suicide. The moral interaction among the three characters is tested when Watakushi "wifesits" (to protect Shizu against possible burglars) while Sensei is away. Reflecting on an intimate conversation with Shizu about Sensei's attitude toward both of them, Watakushi wonders about his own ambivalent feelings toward women. At the end of Watakushi's extended inquiry into Shizu's difficult life with Sensei, she comes close to disclosing the secret of K's suicide.

Of the novel's four main characters, Shizu is the most difficult to comprehend. Sharalyn Orbaugh views her through the lens of Eve Sedgwick's theories about romantic love as a pretext for male-male intimacy. Alluding to Gayle Rubin's influential essay on "The Traffic in Women," Orbaugh maintains that Shizu is "little more than an item of exchange between [the male characters]."[44] More generally, she believes that it is a feature of Japanese modernism, based on Western models, to represent "male anxiety over 'authentic' genealogy, that is, the search for, or anxiety over, the identity of the father, to the exclusion of women." This means that "many of these narratives concern a genealogical path that is traced from male to male, with absolutely no female 'intervention.'"[45] Orbaugh maintains that this patriarchal "female-excluding genealogy" has its modernist roots in the "male terror of women's reproductive faculties."[46] Finally, she asserts that this alleged terror drives men to seize the prize of a purely male genealogy. In *Kokoro*, the price for this seizure is an anxiety that leads to death. The prize of a male genealogy becomes, quite literally, a joint terminal fiction, as Sensei composes his will and Watakushi his memoirs.

Questioning Shizu's agency (as she does Shizuko's in her essay on Nogi's wife), Orbaugh refers to "Sensei's beautiful but constantly infantilized wife."[47] This characterization of a helpless Shizu derives from the simple fact that there are two male narrators, Watakushi and Sensei, and no self-characterization by Shizu. Nor is there an omniscient narrator to inform readers of Shizu's inmost self. The two men through whose eyes we observe her are focused primarily on psyches other than hers: Sensei's, in the case of Watakushi; and K's, in the case of Sensei. It is, however, imperative to be critical of their representations of her (and of each other). Shizu's own agenda must be recovered from the men's inevitably self-interested characterizations of her.

In order, therefore, to understand Shizu's significance within the two triangles in which she figures, it is important to distinguish between the roles of verbal and physical reproduction. Orbaugh makes an important point about Shizu's silence, referring to the historical model of Shizuko[48] and pointing to their meaningful names (the kanji used for Shizu means "quiet, peaceful, still"). Shizu leaves no record or legacy. She reproduces herself neither by writing nor by bearing a child. Although she is dependent on a man (whether K, Sensei, Watakushi, or some unidentified male other) for physical reproduction, she needed no one to authorize her to tell her version of the story.

The fact that all three male characters in *Kokoro* are, in one way or another, writers makes Shizu's silence especially conspicuous. K leaves a "businesslike" (230/278) suicide note addressed to Sensei; Sensei writes his long testament over a period of ten days; and Watakushi becomes not only the curator and editor[49] of Sensei's testament but also the author of an equally long text that memorializes his relationships with Sensei and with Shizu. Neither K nor Sensei reproduces physically, and one can only speculate about Watakushi's capacity to break this pattern, but these men do make an intense effort to find spiritual heirs through what Ito calls "discursive inheritance."[50] For them, writing becomes a substitute for physical reproduction. In that metaphoric sense Orbaugh is justified in referring to a male genealogy; but male authorship is not simply some Lacanian statement of the realm of "the Father." It can also be what James A. Fujii has called the modernist tendency toward "creative destruction," which in *Kokoro* takes the form of Watakushi's rejecting Sensei's "imperative to remain mute, to reproduce the path of betrayal, self-loathing, and despair" by taking "the narration of *Kokoro* beyond the borders of Sensei's own testament."[51] Referring specifically to Sensei, Ito terms him "a Scheherazade in reverse. Instead of narrating in order to live, he tells his story in order to die."[52] It is not impossible to imagine Watakushi, too, as a Scheherazade in reverse.

Where exactly does Shizu—no Scheherazade of any kind—fit in this pattern? Since Sōseki does not reveal Shizu's thoughts, readers are left to infer them from Watakushi's narrative and Sensei's testament. As Komori Yōichi, the critic who started the *Kokoro ronsō*, acknowledged, readers must read between the lines.[53] The task is made more difficult by the inhibitions of the male narrators, whose obsessive interest in each other obscures their relationships with the ostensible object of their heterosexual affections. The blockage of communication is most obvious in Sensei's final injunction to silence to Watakushi: "So long as my wife is alive, I want you to keep everything I have told you a secret—even after I myself am dead" (248/300). These are literally his last recorded words.

If Sensei means by "secret" his "dark shadow" or his feelings of guilt over his friend K's suicide, then Sensei deceives himself in order to manipulate Watakushi into believing that their relationship is unique and that Shizu is totally excluded from it. In fact, Shizu is well aware of her husband's secret. Not only does she know a great deal, she also wants to share what knowledge she has, even at the risk of breaking her husband's trust. In her first tête-à-tête with Watakushi, she hints at this awareness, although she understandably does not reveal all to the young man who is still a stranger to her: " 'When Sensei was still at the university, he had a very good friend. Just before this friend was due to graduate, he died. He died suddenly.' Then almost in a whisper, she added, 'Actually, his death was not natural.' " Since she herself was the object of both of the men's sincere, simulated, or ambivalent erotic attentions, she must have realized all along that K's "unnatural" death was in all likelihood caused by dramatic developments in the two men's courtship of her. Hinting that she knows more than she is willing to confide, she says, "I can't tell you any more about it. At any rate, it was after this friend's death that Sensei began to change gradually. I don't know why [K] died. I doubt that Sensei does either. On the other hand, when one remembers that the change came after the death, one wonders if Sensei really doesn't know" (41–42/54–55). All that she is conceding here is the general impossibility of knowing for sure why someone took his own life. Her pointing to Sensei's disproportionate grieving and personality change after K's death demonstrates her awareness that the relationship between her rival suitors might have been something more than mere friendship.

Most significantly, Shizu insinuates that the change in Sensei might imply responsibility for, if not complicity in, K's death. That the "friend" who brought about the enormous change in Sensei was K, Shizu's visitor can easily guess, although she confesses that she is not allowed to confirm any such conclusion. At the end of their intimate conversation Shizu appeals to Watakushi to help her understand the fateful alteration in her husband's behavior. She is, moreover, as curious as Watakushi to discover additional information and insights in order to confirm her suspicions. She wants Watakushi to share his knowledge with her as she did hers with him: "But can a man change so because of the death of one friend? I should very much like to know. That is what I want you to tell me" (42/55).

What the historical Shizuko and the fictional Shizu have in common is knowledge of their husbands' suffering and awareness of their inability to alleviate their pain. In Shizu's case, there is guilt in addition to frustration, because she is convinced that she was the reason that the men's courtship (of her) and friendship (with each other) ended so tragically. This conviction accounts for her feelings of responsibility and inadequacy, feelings that persist even when her husband assures her that she is not to blame for his melancholy withdrawal from life. Yet she knows that he must continually bear in mind, not what she *did* but simply what she quite innocently *was*. Sensei assures her that all his troubles are his own, but Shizu is convinced that they are not, and she wants to carry her share of the jointly incurred burden. Although Sensei reveals in his testament that he was irritated by Shizu's laughing at his jealous reaction to her conversations with K, he seems to have kept his annoyance to himself. He never indicates to Shizu that she behaved manipulatively or maliciously during the courtship that preceded K's suicide. It may be that Shizuko is wrong to feel even partly culpable for K's suicide and Sensei's withdrawal, but it is a serious misreading of *Kokoro* to describe Shizu as ignorant and uncomprehending.

Permission

Shizu's Verbal Power

As Nishi Masahiko has noted, permission is an essential element governing relations between sovereign and subjects *(taigi meibun)* and a defining element of junshi.[54] Circumventing the permission required by junshi was not unheard of in traditional practice, but circumvention carried a risk. As we have seen, unless it was clear to all that one's lord granted "tacit understanding" *(mokkei)*, seppuku was "a dog's death" *(inujini)*.[55] From whom was Sensei to receive permission to commit junshi?

In Sōseki's fiction, there is no hierarchy between K and Sensei as there is for junshi proper. K's unanticipated suicide deprives Sensei of any chance to ask K's permission to follow him in death. In the conflict between K and Sensei it seems, at first, that confession might substitute for permission. Confession is a technique that Sensei fails to employ in his difficulties with K but learns subsequently to appreciate. In order to gain peace of mind concerning K's death, Sensei tries, reluctantly and with great difficulty, to confess to Watakushi what he had been unable to confess to K. But his tardiness places him in unwitting competition with Watakushi's father for Watakushi's attention. Sensei's confession, in the form of his testament, can be seen as a plea for permission to die; but permission has already come from the person most entitled to grant it—Shizu.

Contrary to what Orbaugh and others have said about her, Shizu is not completely silent. Even though she does not put her thoughts into writing, she speaks what may be the most powerful word in *Kokoro*. She suggests that junshi might be an appropriate way for Sensei to deal with his sadness about the passing of Emperor Meiji and the era that defined their lives.

Sensei relates this important moment in the final pages of his testament: "Then, at the height of the summer, Emperor Meiji passed away. I felt as though the spirit of the Meiji era had begun with the Emperor and had ended with him. I was overcome with the feeling that I and the others, who had been brought up in that era, were now left behind to live as anachronisms. I told my wife so. She laughed and refused to take me seriously. Then she said a curious thing, albeit in jest: 'Well then, *junshi* is the solution to your problem'" (245/297: de wa junshi de mo shitara yokarō to karakaimashita). Sensei responds in kind to his wife's "joke" (245/297: *jōdan*), but there is no reason to think that she was not as serious, finally, as he was. Continuing to withhold his true motives even in this intimate a moment, Sensei tells Shizu, "'I will commit *junshi* if you like; but in my case, it will be through loyalty to the spirit of the Meiji era.' My remark was meant as a joke; but I did feel that the antiquated word *[junshi]* had come to hold a new meaning for me" (245/297).

It is Shizu, then, who on the occasion of Emperor Meiji's death first speaks openly and articulates thoughts of suicide, and she does so by using a word that resonates with Sensei's need for atonement. By saying *"junshi,"* she demonstrates that she knows Sensei's heart and that he need not have tried to gain the trust of Watakushi in order to hear the word that only she can speak to him. In analogy to Emperor Meiji, who had needed his general and compelled him to live on "as though dead," Shizu had needed Sensei and had prevented him from following K into death. But, unlike Emperor Meiji, Shizu is not about to die in order to enable her husband's payment of his long overdue debt to K. She is, however, willing—with a single word—to release Sensei from his obligation to her of living as though dead. The word *junshi* that she speaks is so powerfully evocative of what Sensei had felt since K's suicide that he can only absorb it in the form of a jest. Jests tend to diguise things too serious for words, and this one not only points to what Sensei should do but signals Shizu's own symbolic death to him. He need no longer stay alive for her sake. In short, when Sensei hears his wife suggest junshi, he responds as if she had given him her permission to die. He does not act immediately, but when Nogi sets the example of junshi, and when Watakushi rejects his appeal to come to his aid, he accepts Shizu's renunciation of her dependence on him and resolves to die with her permission.

Shizu's Unknown Destiny

Once the reader penetrates the screens that the male narrators have set up around her, Shizu can no longer be ignored. It is difficult, after decades of feminist "recuperation" of women's history, for the reader not to speculate about extratextual possibilities. Sōseki has left Shizu's fate open to multiple interpretations that are embedded in his narrative technique of shifting perspectives. There is much more to *Kokoro* than Watakushi's self-centered revelation of Sensei's secret. Sōseki sets the reader to searching for knowledge beyond what Watakushi has discovered. Such a quest is hindered, however, by the multiple viewpoints and conflicting interests of these characters, two of whom (Watakushi and Sensei) control the narration. Atsuko Sakaki has concluded that Watakushi "exerts narrative authority over Sensei" and that "the narratives related by *watakushi* and by Sensei are . . . asymmetrical."[56] Where does this leave Shizu, whose voice is heard only when echoed by the male narrators? In the hands of the reader, whom Sōseki has entrusted with the task of interpretation.

The task is complicated and eased only by Sōseki's interweaving of fictional with historical characters. He has imbricated historical sequence and fictional plot, but a straightforward replication of the Nogi story would have been far less interesting than the novelist's exploration of the uncertainties looming ahead for a younger generation reacting to conflicts of love rather than those of war.

Considering the Nogi palimpsest underlying *Kokoro,* we can imagine that Shizu fully understood what her husband had done, and that she, having long shared his guilt, willingly followed him—and K—in death. In fact, she never mentions any intention to commit suicide, nor does Watakushi report her death. Sōseki tantalizes his readers by leaving them to wonder exactly what Shizu does know about her husband's death. It seems plausible, in light of what she knew or surmised about his melancholy withdrawal from active life, that she understands that he killed himself, but Watakushi does his best to persuade the reader that Shizu has been excluded from Sensei's innermost thoughts. Shizu does not know that her husband has left his testament to Watakushi and instructed him to keep the reason for his suicide a secret. While it is true that Shizu knows neither of Sensei's testament nor of his instructions to Watakushi, she was privy to most of what Sensei tells Watakushi of his past relations with her and K. Watakushi's triumph over Shizu is illusory, and Sensei's instructions to Watakushi are pointless except to constrain him in his future contact with Shizu.

Although we are not told how Shizu responds to Sensei's death, the Jamesian donnée of *Kokoro* would be that Watakushi writes and then publishes the entire story, his own memoirs having been generated by Sensei's testament. This means either that Watakushi has gone against Sensei's injunction or that he has kept the "secret" until Shizu's death.[57] A third possibility is that Watakushi, having written his account and linked it to Sensei's immediately after Sensei's death, then commits suicide to atone for all *his* flaws. Whether or not he wrote with publication in mind, he might in any case have wanted to pay with his life for ignoring Sensei's injunction. If we imagine that Shizu is still alive when Watakushi publishes Sensei's testament, what would she have done after reading not only her husband's thoughts but also Watakushi's interpretation of them? Would she feel betrayed by Sensei for revealing his—or rather their—secret? Would she then emulate Nogi's Shizuko and take her own life? Alternatively, if she lived on in ignorance, as Watakushi has us believe, how did she cope with her husband's death?

Answers to these questions are necessarily speculative. As we have seen, Sensei asked Watakushi specifically not to publish his secret before Shizu's death. If Watakushi himself published the secret, readers are faced with at least three possibilities. One possibility is that Shizu had died before Watakushi published, either from natural causes or by her own hand. But if this was the case, why did Watakushi make no mention of her death? The only justification for such an extraordinary omission would be Watakushi's resolution not to refer to anything that happened after Sensei's death. If Watakushi did not feel rigidly bound in this way, however, did he aspire to highlight his friendship with Sensei while leaving Shizu—his rival for Sensei's affections—in the shadows?[58] A second possiblility is that Watakushi followed Sensei in death immediately after finishing his manuscript, while Shizu was still alive. A third possibility is that Watakushi recorded Sensei's request and then betrayed his trust. If this was the case, then Watakushi edited Sensei's testament and published it along with his own memoirs while Shizu was still alive and able to read the entire story. Following the historic example of Nogi's wife, Shizu may then have committed suicide after reading the last pages of her husband's testament, her "joke" about junshi having now acquired "a new meaning" (245/297) for her as it did for him when he committed suicide.[59] In this conjectured scenario, Sensei and Shizu would both have been inspired by the Nogis' historic precedent. Both would follow K in death, thereby acknowledging their shared culpability.[60] And Watakushi would be left alone to carry the burden of guilt that they had carried before.

However one interprets Shizu's role, it seems clear that both Sensei and Watakushi attempt in their writings to minimize her impact on their relationship. Their protracted efforts to dismiss her—literally by writing her off—testify to her role as an impediment to their male bonding. For Sensei, Shizu stands in the way of his total claim to K. This possessiveness is manifest in his refusal to allow Shizu to visit K's grave again after the one time they went there together. On that occasion, her tender expressions of affection for his deceased friend and rival had greatly disturbed him.[61] Despite all of Sensei's efforts jealously to exclude her from his private cult of memory, however, she is always there as a constant reminder of K's desire to possess her. Although Sensei was able to accept K as a rival for Shizu's love, it was impossible for him to acknowledge Shizu as his rival for K's love. As a powerful player in the game of love, Shizu interferes with the notion of a pure male genealogy. The reaction of Watakushi is to minimize her role and reduce her to a passive object of male sexual desire. Sensei wants to have it both ways: to keep the status quo with Shizu yet to confide in Watakushi.

If Sōseki meant his readers to imagine that Shizu was alive and able to read Watakushi's published account, a number of possibilities compete for attention. Shizu may have been disappointed, if not angered, by the men's portrayals of her as someone too insensitive to understand that Sensei's covert love of K was more intense than his overt love of her. She may have resented Sensei's request that Watakushi keep a secret even when there was none to keep. And what she may have resented most was Sensei's willingness to share with Watakushi the innermost self that he refused to discuss with her. If this was the case, her alternatives were to dwell in disillusionment, a living reminder to Watakushi that publishing Sensei's manuscript was a betrayal of his mentor's trust, or implicitly to reproach all three men by following the historical Shizuko's suicidal example.

Sensei clearly had tried to erect a defensive barrier against his wife's emotional participation in his melancholy, but he could not dispute her knowledge. It is less clear whether Watakushi tried similarly to contain Shizu after Sensei's death. Indeed, his publication of Sensei's testament seems less of a betrayal of Sensei's injunction of silence if we take it to indicate Watakushi's desire to satisfy Shizu's longing to know the full truth behind Sensei's "dark shadow."[62] If this were the case, if Shizu did not already understand the nature of the men's attraction to each other as a cause of their successive suicides, would she have been any more receptive to this truth after reading Sensei's last will and Watakushi's memoirs? Shizu possesses not only a love that is not returned with passion but also an intuitive knowledge that is either unacknowledged, unwanted, or denied. Would it have disturbed the men if she killed herself to dilute the male flow of blood with her own?

CODA

Last Stands in Ancient Rome and Modern Japan

It is easy to condemn General Nogi for his military failures, and it would be even easier to condemn him altogether if he had not ultimately displayed his virtues by an act of self-sacrificial atonement. Yet he was adopted, if reluctantly by some, as a Japanese hero—a *kami*—because, unlike less conflicted military men, he seemed to embody the nation's painful transition from the Meiji era into an increasingly modern world. Nogi had been a divided figure, torn for thirty-five years between wanting to die and having to live. When he was at last free to assert his will to die, he appeared, for all his *bushidō* loyalty, to project a modern sensibility.

Ancient Rome

Transitional moments dramatized by the death of important figures can be found in many cultures, but none sheds more light on the Japanese experience than the traumatic death of the Roman Republic. Nogi's violent death, like that of Marcus Tullius Cicero (106–43 B.C.E.), marked the end of an era.[1] These two men make a strikingly kindred pair despite the fact that they seem at first glance as widely separated culturally as they were spatially and temporally. By coincidence, both men had the same lifespan of sixty-three years. They were both controversial figures, maligned by some and virtually apotheosized by others. Their disputed fame derives from different interpretations of their historical roles. What ties them together most conspicuously—and undeniably—is that they both tortured themselves over vanishing values. For these values, which they themselves occasionally betrayed or abandoned, they died. Aberrations and flights from their own beliefs underline their passionate human struggle. Both men grappled not only with their adversaries but with themselves as they suffered depression and indulged in thoughts of suicide.[2] Their human portraits emerge with dazzling clarity, for in the end they both saved their honor by seeking violent death and thus preserved their integrity. As if she had known them, Emily Dickinson wrote, "I like a look of Agony, / Because I know it's true—."[3]

Inspired by the dramatic changes in their cultures, both Cicero and Nogi had, in their different ways, courted death in order to live their ideals. Although Cicero accomplished amazing feats as an orator, philosopher, and statesman, his love of country and his pride caused him to provoke his death by stubbornly clinging to the ideals of a Roman Republic that was no more. Like the *shishi* of the Bakumatsu period, he learned how to insist and persevere as a *novus homo* who had gained political power through merit rather than inherited status. At the same time, his skill in navigating his way through one of the most tumultuous and sinister periods of the Roman Republic led to his "megalomania" of wanting to "remain at the helm"[4] even beyond the terms of his offices. This determination to cling to power intensified during the civil wars that destroyed the republic. Nogi, by contrast, came from the right kind of samurai family to rise in the world—except that he wanted to be a poet-scholar rather than a warrior. Yet once he accepted the curriculum vitae dictated for him by his father, Nogi became a samurai with a vengeance. The more that radical changes threatened to exterminate samurai culture, the more tenaciously he clung to samurai values.

At times Cicero and Nogi seemed lost, disoriented, uncomprehending.[5] Whether because of tactical errors or hubris resulting from an uncompromising insistence on principles, they went into voluntary or involuntary exile. While lonely Cicero indulged in self-pity, blaming even his closest friend, Titus Pomponius Atticus (110–32 B.C.E.), for his hopeless condition,[6] Nogi quietly farmed the land and studied *bushidō*. However different their behaviors during periods of exile, their return to active political life was characterized by bursts of energy. Christian Habicht has described Cicero as "a man of extremes, in elation as well as dejection."[7] In Nogi's case, one might better define the polar opposites as the sword and the brush, or frenzied military activity alternating with austere meditation. Cicero basked in the adulation he received upon returning from exile. Nogi, in contrast, felt increased pressure to prove himself worthy of the military honors he had received.

On 10 February 46 B.C.E., three years before Cicero's death, Marcus Porcius Cato Uticensis (95–46 B.C.E.) committed suicide because he did not want to owe his life to Julius Caesar (100–44 B.C.E.).[8] For Cicero, Cato became more than a model of principled behavior; he seemed an unreachable star. Habicht goes so far as to surmise that Cicero "had a feeling of inferiority toward Cato."[9] Cato's noble example admonished Cicero not to compromise with traitors but rather to die for the republic's ideals. Why was he still clinging to life when Cato had pointed the way? In Cicero's words, "my troubles are such that I feel guilty in continuing to live." To his alter ego, Atticus, he confessed his shame: "to be alive at all is a disgrace for me."[10]

As noted above, Nogi too held up, like a mirror to his conscience, a famous contemporary who had committed suicide for his ideals. Although Saigō Takamori had taken the rebels' side during the Satsuma Rebellion of 1877, he was turned into a legend by the very Meiji government he had first helped to create and then fought so fiercely. His heroic death underscored the lesson taught by Tamaki Bunnoshin, Nogi's mentor, who had committed seppuku a few months earlier. Nogi was unable to follow these examples because, as an accident of private and historical developments rather than a result of his own free will, he was bound to Emperor Meiji. The comparison makes it clear that Nogi's dilemma was quite distinct. While Cato and Cicero faced a clearly defined enemy, namely those who intended to destroy the Roman Republic and rule as dictators, while Saigō gave his life protesting the Meiji oligarchy's abuse of power, Nogi had no enemy against whom he could win or lose. It was precisely the impotence resulting from owing one's life to supreme authority that Cato tried to preclude with his voluntary death. Paul Plass has commented about Cato's suicide, "if it was a good last move, it was also a terminal one, affording opportunity for self-assertion only of a very unusual kind. . . . [S]uicidal freedom of action is at once vacuous and real, and in the case of Rome, too, questions of whether those who committed suicide were pushed or jumped becomes a genuinely complicated matter when the chief accomplishment of a political career may have been killing oneself."[11]

Clearly, neither Cato nor Nogi would be remembered as cultural icons if it had not been for their dramatic deaths. Although they similarly tried to extricate themselves from thraldom to dictator and emperor, they themselves were unable to reap the benefits of their freedom. Cato's self-assertion allowed him to smile at the absolute certainty of frustrating and infuriating Caesar. This became his greatest legacy to the Romans. Nogi respected the imperial wish that he live at least as long as the emperor did while refusing to extend his loyalty to the emperor's successor: Nogi's junshi denied allegiance to the new Emperor Taishō, the sickly ruler of what Nogi would surely have abhorred as a morally ambiguous era.[12] Having compromised all his life, Nogi finally reclaimed his life by taking it.

Cicero was less uncompromising than Cato and consequently suffered more in his struggle to serve the cause of republican values and avoid dependence on arbitrary power. In the end, however, Cicero too was forced to take a last stand against dictatorship. Realizing that the republic was doomed, he finally gave up his flight from the henchmen of Mark Antony (c. 83–30 B.C.E.). No doubt he would have preferred not to die a violent death, but, when he no longer had a choice, he literally stuck his neck out for the republic. As Habicht observes, "The fact that, for the first time in his career, he risked his life for the cause he judged right, and that he lost it in consequence, atones for former failures. Without his last stand he could hardly have become the standard bearer of republican ideology for centuries to come."[13] On 7 December 43 B.C.E., Cicero was assassinated by the minions of his arch-enemy Mark Antony, but he exposed his throat to be slit, thus annulling his murderers' killing power and asserting his own intent of suicide. His dead body was mutilated, and his severed head and hands displayed on the Roman Forum's orator's platform *(rostra)*.[14]

There are numerous legends about the manner and circumstances of Cato's particularly painful suicide that resonate with Nogi's. Seneca the Younger declares with seeming certainty, "I am sure that the gods looked on with exceeding joy while that hero . . . drove the sword into his sacred breast; while he scattered his vitals, and drew forth by his hand that holiest spirit, too noble to be defiled by the steel. I should like to believe that this is why the wound was not well-aimed and efficacious—it was not enough for the immortal gods to look but once on Cato. His virtue was held in check and called back that it might display itself in a harder rôle; for to seek death needs not so great a soul as to reseek it."[15] The more difficult Cato made his suicide the more impressive his physical strength and spiritual resolve. As Robert J. Goar has noted, "the second blow took more courage than the first—as if to prepare for what was to come."[16] Finally, the sword alone was not enough; it had to be coupled with the courage to die not once but twice. Only then could it bring Cato the freedom that Caesar had denied him.

Plutarch (before 50–after 120 C.E.), the biographer and mythmaker, offers a far more elaborate version of Cato's preparations for suicide and his outwitting of those who had taken his sword into custody because they wanted him to live. Cato shamed his loved ones into retrieving his sword: "Now I am my own master." Plutarch goes on to underline the painful manner of Cato's disembowelment:

> Cato drew his sword from its sheath and stabbed himself below the breast. His thrust, however, was somewhat feeble, owing to the inflammation in his hand, and so he did not at once dispatch himself, but in his death struggle fell from the couch and made a loud noise by overturning a geometrical abacus that stood near. His servants heard the noise and cried out, and his son at once ran in, together with his friends. They saw that he was smeared with blood, and that most of his bowels were protruding, but that he still had his eyes open and was alive; and they were terribly shocked. But the physician went to him and tried to replace his bowels, which remained uninjured, and to sew up the wound. Accordingly, when Cato recovered and became aware of this, he pushed the

physician away, tore his bowels with his hands, rent the wound still more, and so died.[17]

In Plutarch's version, relatives and friends hinder Cato and prevent a speedy disembowelment. Here, then, the feat is not merely to oppose the tyrant Caesar but also to free himself from the most intimate human bonds. In order to free himself from enslavement by Caesar, Cato must first sever his human attachments. In short, he must die twice, or in a variant of Seneca's insight, "reseek" death.

What is remarkable in both accounts of Cato's death is the authors' emphasis on his struggle to carry it out. Physical and mental pain must precede suicide in order to distinguish it from masochistic pleasure. In short, Cato's motivation had to be pure and his resolve unassailable by doubts and hesitation. Ultimate proof of this resolve to die lay in Cato's determined rejection of the last chance to live. He inflicted this test on himself in order to demonstrate that he would indeed remain steadfast. His deep wounds having been dressed by the physician, he ripped them open once again, thus assuring his loved ones that he was serious when he tried to kill himself the first time. Of course, he might have administered the deadly blow to himself in one quick and perfect stab, but he chose not to in order to make it absolutely clear to his witnesses that he was not acting rashly. For the double pain Cato took upon himself in order to demonstrate his mindfulness of others, he was "canonized, even apotheosized," especially by Seneca and Lucan.[18] Cato's virtual deification can be interpreted as an urgent need for solace among those who suffered recurrent reigns of terror during the Roman Empire. The first histories of the empire were written by men—such as Tacitus and Suetonius—who looked back with nostalgia to the age of the republic.

Seppuku, too, requires a "double wound" such as the one that Cato inflicted on himself. Traditionally, the aptly named *kaishakunin* inflicts a second mortal wound only after the suicide himself has cut open his stomach in the prescribed manner. Because the first part of disembowelment requires such tremendous willpower to inflict pain upon oneself and to endure it, the finishing touch is ordinarily left to someone else. More likely than not, the *kaishakunin* is someone trusted to know when the time is right to behead the man committing seppuku, or who will do so only upon receiving a signal from him. Since junshi was officially outlawed, Nogi may not have wanted to ask anyone to be his second; moreover, he might have wanted to "reseek" death himself, by summoning all his dwindling strength and impaling himself on his sword.

In comparison to Cato's anguished act of self-destruction, Cicero's baring his throat to his murderers was a comparatively feeble gesture, an almost feminine invitation to be taken, yet also subversive in its erotic incongruity. It was all the more unnerving for this very reason, since the killer could no longer pretend that his victim was a man worthy of his raw force. Might the exposed throat even have shamed the assassin into admitting the baseness of his mission? No matter, for Cicero had resigned himself to the inevitable and decided to play the game and be a good sport about losing his life, or giving it up, whichever way one may want to look at it. Carlin A. Barton pinpoints Cicero's moment of truth as occurring in the arena, which was "an extraordinarily apt metaphor for civil war." In civil wars, as in gladiatorial games, all killings were suicides and all suicides were also killings. As for Cicero in his litter, the Romans were watching, so to speak, and this time, the thumbs were down for the fighter who wanted to save the republic. Barton concludes that "It is the gladiator rather than the soldier who provides the model for Cicero's noble death." According to this bold analogy, Barton sees Cicero's baring of his throat to his executioner's blade as a "gladiator's gesture of defiant complicity."[19]

Cicero's death aroused far more debate and controversy than Cato's. Sharalyn Orbaugh notes about Nogi's death that "its anachronistic character occasioned tremendous debate about the meaning of the entire corpus of changes that signified modernization during the Meiji period."[20] Some of these debates, discussed in previous chapters, are reminiscent of the declaimers prominent in ancient Roman culture. Lucius Annaeus Seneca (c. 55 B.C.E.–41 C.E.) compiled from memory declaimers of his time, at the request of his sons, one of whom was Seneca (c. 4 B.C.E.–65 C.E.), the Stoic philosopher whose hopeless task it was to mentor the emperor Nero (Lucius Domitius Ahenobarbus, 37–68 C.E.). In ancient Rome as in Japanese culture, control over one's own death was dramatized by the tempting possibilities of supplicating the higher authorities for a pardon or seeking permission to die. The Elder Seneca, in *Suasoriae* 6, wondered whether Cicero should have asked Mark Antony for a pardon or whether he should have emulated Cato (see *Suas.* 6.1–2; 6.10).[21] In order for honor to be preserved in the act of supplication, the favor-granting authority must deserve the supplicant's respect. Thus Pompeius Silo[22] raised the question of the worth of the person who issues the pardon and permission to live: "You should know that it is not expedient for you to live if it is Antony who gives you the permission to live" (*Suas.* 6.4). Cornelius Hispanus thought that, "if Cicero can be made to die, he cannot be made to beg" (*Suas.* 6.7).

The fear of shame inherent in the act of supplication was as important to the ancient Romans as it is in Japanese culture. M. Porcius Latro (d. 4 C.E.), for example, articulated what must have weighed heavily on Cicero: "it is shameful for any Roman, let alone Cicero, to beg for his life. . . . Life will be worthless, harder than death, liberty once lost" (*Suas.* 6.8). But can one simultaneously avoid shame and still assert one's will to live? C. Albucius Silus argued that Cicero should have died of his own volition, "seeing that he had to die even if he did not wish to" (*Suas.* 6.9).

The Roman historian Livy (T. Livius, 59 B.C.E.–17 C.E.) described Cicero's momentous decision of ending his flight from Antony as a form of surrendering his life to the winds of adversity (*venti adversi; Suas.* 6.17). What little choice he still had left he took by offering his neck "without a tremor" (*Suas.* 6.17). The outpouring of grief among the people who saw Cicero's head and hands on the *rostra* was immense. To the famous exposure of the throat, Aufidius Bassus added the telling detail of Cicero drawing "aside the curtain a little" (*Suas.* 6.18), thus calling his killers to task.

Livy's "epitaph" for Cicero applies in uncanny ways to General Nogi as well: "He lived sixty-three years. . . . [W]eighing his virtues against his faults, he was a great and memorable man" (*Suas.* 6.22).

Modern Japan: 1945 and 1970

Since Nogi's death, like Cicero's, signaled the end of an era, his image too became sacred and survived to puzzle, inspire, and haunt his countrymen, never more than during the momentous transitions that followed Japan's defeat in World War II. Among the many millions of Japanese who heard the disembodied radio voice of Emperor Hirohito (1901–1989; r. 1926–1989) on 15 August 1945 announce the end of the Pacific War were some civilians and about three hundred and fifty military men who committed suicide.[23] Motivations were far from uniform.[24] Some of these suicides were by seppuku, but they must be carefully distinguished from junshi. Although the emperor's recorded appeal to "endure the unendurable" might have given the impression that he—or emperorhood itself—had died, Hirohito was still in his prime and, as it turned out, had half his life ahead of him. Clearly, these civilian and military suicides were not following him into death. They did, however, refuse to live on into what they believed to be an age of defeat and shame.

What may have led some to perform self-sacrificial acts, albeit not junshi, was a peculiar phrase in the imperial rescript that left a profound—indeed, the most profound—impression on the people. As John W. Dower has noted, the emperor managed to turn the nation's sacrifice for this war into his own by depicting himself as the nation's "ultimate victim." Hearing him proclaim "my vital organs are torn asunder,"[25] the Japanese could hardly have missed the suggestion of seppuku by a symbolic imperial sword.[26] The emperor's excruciating linguistic gesture seemed to acknowledge the nation's martyrdom for his sake while simultaneously appropriating this martyrdom to himself. His subjects were now called upon to live rather than die for the emperor according to the slogan *ichioku gyokusai*, or the self-destruction of one hundred million. In a sense, they were asked to abjure all they had believed in during the war—and it was the emperor himself who was asking them to perform a leap of faith into an "undiscovered country" even more unknown than the one encountered in 1912. The emperor's public confession and his emotional participation in the nation's trauma allowed most Japanese to opt for life rather than death.

Twenty-five years later, the novelist, playwright, and critic Mishima Yukio (1925–1970) enacted yet another kind of transition. Although Japan was fast rising from the ashes of military defeat, Mishima denied the possibility of meaningful resurrection under an emperor who, at least in the eyes of the international community,[27] had been deprived of his divinity and stripped of his traditional clothes and paraphernalia. Mishima committed seppuku on 25 November 1970, a self-proclaimed martyr for the imperial cause. Among his multiple goals was to restore the authority he believed the emperor had lost.

While it is tempting simply to assert that Mishima's seppuku was actually junshi committed for a secularized and symbolically deceased lord, his motivation and goals were more complicated. Mishima literally invented himself on the movie screen and on the stage as a selfless modern warrior come to rescue the imperial house from the people's corruption by materialism and consumerism. He sought to invent himself in life as well. In his struggle to find his true self he hardened his body through the martial arts and cultivated the samurai spirit as the leader of a "Self-Defense Force" of uniformed, devoted followers. Mark R. Peattie, the authority on Nogi in the West, notes a similar goal in Nogi's sensational death and its reception among the Japanese people, who saw it as "reflect[ing] Nogi's ultimate protest against the luxury and profligacy of contemporary Japan, although it may have been as much an act of atonement for the mistakes of his military career."[28]

Mishima also meant to emulate the heroes of the Bakumatsu era and the Meiji Restoration who gave their lives, sometimes by committing seppuku, not only to protect the nation from foreign invaders and to restore the emperor to power but also to press for social and political reforms. Agreeing that Mishima was motivated by an intense hostility to consumerism and materialism, Marius Jansen insists that his seppuku was inspired by "moral rather than political impulses." Jansen places him in a line of descent from Ōshio Heihachirō (1793–1837), who in his 1837 uprising "would court death to 'save the people,'" and General Nogi, who struggled "against the perversion of warrior purity by selfishness."[29]

In his postmodern reflections on "the process of Japan's transformation into a nation-state of Western-power status" and "the interrelational structure that situates Japan with the West and within Asia," Karatani Kōjin sees the parallel between Nogi's junshi and Mishima's seppuku uncannily reflected in the corresponding reign years of Meiji 45 and Shōwa 45.[30] Although the timing is merely accidental, Karatani hypothesizes that those dramatic deaths appeared as anachronistic suicides in 1912 and 1970 from the perspective of a Western "discursive space."[31] Arguing "that in order for the transformation of discursive space to become clearly fixed in consciousness, some symbolic event must occur," he implies that Nogi's death was such an event. In reference to the case of Mishima, he cites Marx's postulation that "we need tragedy to part cheerfully with the past."[32] Karatani prefers to link the shockingly anachronistic acts of Nogi and Mishima by associating Mishima with the rebels of the 26 February 1935 incident.[33] Mishima himself promoted the latter connection in order "to reenact [in 1970] the Showa Restoration [of 1936]," which Karatani sees as "literally a farce."[34] In short, like Marx on Napoleon and Napoleon III, Karatani sees tragedy in the spirit of Meiji and farce in the spirit of Shōwa that repeated it.[35]

Mishima also falls into the category of Japanese who died as rebels. His public protest can be seen to follow the tradition of the many rebels who committed seppuku, especially in uprisings *(ran)*. He idolized individual figures like Saigō Takamori (1827–1877), the leader of the Satsuma Rebellion, whose aim was to defeat the imperial army in order to protect the emperor from the corruption of his government. He venerated groups such as the League of the Divine Wind (Shinpūren or Jinpūren)[36] and the White Tigers Brigade (Byakkotai), who died for the Aizu domain (Aizu-*han*) in 1868. His novella "Patriotism" ("Yūkoku," 1961)[37] glorifies the officers who died in the unsuccessful coup d'état of 26 February 1936 and singles out one officer who, excluded from participation because of his recent marriage, committed seppuku with his wife in the privacy of his home. He produced, directed, scripted, and starred in *The Rite of Love and Death*, a film based on this novella. The film, premiered in 1965 in Paris, can be regarded as a rehearsal of Mishima's actual seppuku.[38] The motivations for all those rebellions were rooted in unease, frustration, and anger about the usurpation of imperial power; but in no way can it be said that Mishima, in 1970, followed his emperor into death by transforming his desire for seppuku into junshi. Emperor Hirohito had already outlasted many heroes and was to live for another nineteen years. And, if Karatani can be believed, Mishima not only "scorned" the emperor's "counterfeit" existence after Shōwa 20 (1945) but intended his suicide to signify "the killing of the postwar emperor."[39] In short, there are several ways in which Mishima's suicide could be interpreted as junshi, but, finally, his motives seem to have been unrelated to those that impelled Nogi to recover his lost honor by following his lord into death.

Whereas Mishima himself consciously created the circumstances that made him a hero or idol in the eyes of his followers, Nogi struggled to come to terms with the circumstances that defined his path to death. There is significance in the difference between the former having become a popular idol and the latter a *kami.* Their images remain contested. In many ways, the two can hardly be compared. Mishima's life and death directly affected only a relatively small portion of the population. Nogi's successes thrilled and his failures stunned the entire nation. His self-sacrifice, moreover, was amplified by the deaths of his sons and his wife. His stoic attitude toward their violent deaths baffled many who had already made a complete transition to modernity. And it is that same attitude, and the inexpressible pain that underlay it, that allowed those whom he loved the most to be perceived as sacrifices on the altar of the nation. The human toll for Japanese victory in Nogi's battles had been costly, but he was ready to pay the price now registered in Japan's cultural memory. More than that, the emperor's passing and that of his enormously eventful age called for the kind of regeneration that only sacrifice can accomplish.

NOTES

The city of publication of all works in Japanese is Tōkyō unless noted otherwise.

Introduction

1. The date according to the lunar calendar was the twenty-seventh day of the eighth month of Keiō 4.

2. Nogi's seppuku was referred to as *"kappuku"* (an alternate term for seppuku) in *"jūmonji"* style. See the medical examiner's synopsis in Ōhama Tetsuya, *Meiji no gunshin: Nogi Maresuke* (Yūzankaku, 1970), p. 195. For the different physiological effects between the straight-line *(ichimonji)* and the cross-line *(jūmonji)* forms of seppuku, see Chiba Tokuji, *Nihonjin wa naze seppuku suru no ka* (Tōkyōdō, 1994), pp. 30–37.

3. For the suicide report by Iwata Bonpei, complete with last poems and last will, see Ōhama, *Meiji no gunshin,* pp. 187–196.

4. For photographs of Nogi's two sets of attire on 13 September 1912, see Matsushita Yoshio, *Nogi Maresuke* (1960; rev. 4th ed. Yoshikawa kōbunkan, 1997), pp. 208, 210.

5. See Christopher Benfey, *The Great Wave: Gilded Age Misfits, Japanese Eccentrics, and the Opening of Old Japan* (New York: Random House, 2003), p. 287.

6. See Maurice Pinguet, *Voluntary Death in Japan,* trans. Rosemary Morris (Cambridge: Polity Press, 1993), p. 209. Originally published as *La mort volontaire au Japon.* Paris: Éditions Gallimard, 1984.

7. Kenneth G. Henshall, trans., *Literary Life in Tōkyō 1885–1915: Tayama Katai's Memoirs ('Thirty Years in Tōkyō')* (Leiden: E. J. Brill, 1987), p. 250.

8. Stanley Washburn, *Nogi* (London: Andrew Melrose, 1913), p. 124.

9. Richard Barry, "Nogi—Seer, Statesman, and Soldier," *Harper's Weekly,* 28 September 1912, p. 20. Barry began his eulogy with either an error or a falsification, presumably in order to spare readers of *Harper's Weekly* the fact of Nogi's seppuku by turning it into "slitting his throat." Stanley Washburn also was mistaken when he wrote that Nogi "chose to pass the keen edge of his sword across his throat"; Washburn, *Nogi,* p. 2. Washburn's Japanese translator, Meguro Masumi (1881–1963), changed "throat" to *"mune,"* or chest; Meguro Masumi, trans., *Nogi Taishō to Nihonjin* (Kōdansha gakujutsu bunko, 1980), p. 7.

10. George Sansom, *A History of Japan: 1615–1867* (Stanford, Calif.: Stanford University Press, 1963), pp. 53, 92. Sansom compares the practice of junshi to the vendetta, which he considers "more common and less unnatural" (ibid., p. 92).

11. For the "ambivalence" concerning Nogi's death that ran through popular no less than elite culture, see Carol Gluck, *Japan's Modern Myths: Ideology in the Late Meiji Period* (Princeton, N.J.: Princeton University Press, 1985), pp. 221–226.

12. Popular views of the Nogis' junshi are difficult to know. Scholars such as Irokawa Daikichi and George M. Wilson have acknowledged both the need for and the difficulty of discovering the views of ordinary people. Concerning the participation of the common people in the Meiji Restoration, for example, Wilson concedes that it was significant but "substantially unrecorded." George M. Wilson, *Patriots and Redeemers in Japan: Motives in the Meiji Restoration* (Chicago: University of Chicago Press, 1992), p. 66. See also Irokawa Daikichi, *The Culture of the Meiji Period,* translation edited by Marius B. Jansen (Princeton, N.J.: Princeton University Press, 1985); originally published as *Meiji no bunka* (1970).

13. It is customary to refer to Mori Rintarō by his *gō* or nom de plume, Ōgai, which means "beyond the seagulls." For the legend of this *gō,* see Richard John Bowring, *Mori Ōgai and the Modernization of Japanese Culture,* University of Cambridge Oriental Publications No. 28 (Cambridge: Cambridge University Press, 1979), p. 271, n. 9. Similarly, Sōseki is Natsume Kinnosuke's nom de plume, "from the Chinese phrase *sōseki chinryū* (rinsing one's mouth with a stone and resting one's head on a pillow of flowing water), essentially an inversion founded on a mistaken use of the words *stone* and *flowing water*"; see Angela Yiu, *Chaos and Order in the Works of Natsume Sōseki* (Honolulu: University of Hawai'i Press, 1998), p. 11.

14. A discussion of all the writers who wrote about the dramatic junshi of General Nogi and his wife lies beyond the scope of this study.

15. Roy Starrs, "Writing the National Narrative: Changing Attitudes toward Nation-Building among Japanese Writers, 1900–1930," in Sharon A. Minichiello, ed., *Japan's Competing Modernities: Issues in Culture and Democracy 1900–1930* (Honolulu: University of Hawai'i Press, 1998), pp. 208–209.

16. Sharalyn Orbaugh, "General Nogi's Wife: Representations of Women in Narratives of Japanese Modernization," in Xiaobing Tang and Stephen Snyder, eds., *In Pursuit of Contemporary East Asian Culture* (Boulder, Colo.: Westview Press, 1996), pp. 7–31.

Chapter 1. Sacrifice and Self-Sacrifice

1. "Meiji period," in *Kodansha Encyclopedia of Japan,* 9 vols., 1st ed. (Tokyo and New York: Kodansha International, 1983), 5:155.

2. Donald Keene points to the new stipulation that "henceforth there would be only one *nengō* for an entire reign." Keene, *Emperor of Japan: Meiji and His World, 1852–1912* (New York: Columbia University Press, 2002), p. 159.

3. See ibid., p. 725, n. 1.

4. Ibid., p. 706.

5. In her discussion of Susanowo's various treatments for his "sin" *(tsumi)* against Amaterasu, Yoko Williams cites scholars' interpretation of them as punishment, purification, compensation, scapegoating, but not sacrifice; see Williams, Tsumi—*Offence and Retribution in Early Japan* (London and New York: Routledge Curzon, 2003), pp. 133–141. Susanowo's story does not end with his banishment. For vari-

ants of this major episode of his myth and its continuation, see *Nihon shoki* I.37–49. William George Aston, trans., *Nihongi: Chronicles of Japan from the Earliest Times to A.D. 697* (Rutland, Vt., and Tokyo: Charles E. Tuttle, 1972), I: 40–52. Originally published in two volumes by the Japan Society in 1896; reissued in London in 1924.

6. The ancient Maya invented a sophisticated solar calendrical system used throughout Mesoamerica and "added the Long Count to the calendar round system because they took dynastic succession to be the foundation of their society." Calculating time by observing and coordinating the movements of celestial bodies such as the sun, moon, and Venus, they were obsessed with "period ending dates, within a cosmological framework designed to insure the regeneration of life"; Davíd Carrasco, *Religions of Mesoamerica: Cosmovision and Ceremonial Centers* (New York: HarperCollins [HarperSanFrancisco], 1990), p. 116. For a diagram illustrating the "permutation" of the 260-day "Ritual Almanac against the 365-day Solar Year system [creating] the Calendar Round of 18,980 days, or 52 solar years," see John S. Henderson, *The World of the Ancient Maya* (1981; 2nd ed., Ithaca, N.Y., and London: Cornell University Press, 1997), figs. 3–5, p. 53.

7. Eduardo Matos Moctezuma, *The Great Temple of the Aztecs: Treasures of Tenochtitlan,* translated from the Spanish by Doris Heyden (London: Thames and Hudson, 1988), chap. 5, especially pp. 135–145.

8. Johanna Broda, "Templo Mayor as Ritual Space," in Johanna Broda, Davíd Carrasco, and Eduardo Matos Moctezuma, *The Great Temple of Tenochtitlan: Center and Periphery in the Aztec World* (Berkeley: University of California Press, 1987), pp. 63–64.

9. Carrasco, *Religions of Mesoamerica,* p. 88.

10. Doris Heyden, "Dryness before the Rains: Toxcatl and Tezcatlipoca," in Davíd Carrasco, ed., *To Change Place: Aztec Ceremonial Landscapes* (Niwot: University Press of Colorado, 1991), p. 199.

11. Davíd Carrasco, *City of Sacrifice: The Aztec Empire and the Role of Violence in Civilization* (Boston: Beacon Press, 1999), pp. 84, 136.

12. Ibid., p. 128.

13. Heyden, "Dryness before the Rains," pp. 194, 195.

14. The six Nogi Shrines are in Hakodate (Hokkaidō), Nishinasuno (Tochigi), Akasaka (Tōkyō), Fushimi-Momoyama (Kyōto), Chōfu (Shimonoseki), and Zentsūji (Shikoku).

15. The influential journalist, translator, and novelist Kuroiwa Ruikō (Shūroku, 1862–1920) wrote a *waka* on 16 September 1912 "kyō made wa/ sugureshi hito to/ omohishi ni/ hito to umareshi/ kami ni zo arikeru"; quoted from the pamphlet issued by the Nogi Shrine in Chōfu. In Donald Keene's translation: "Should the people worship him as a god? Yes, if he is not worshiped, who should be worshiped? . . . Truly General Nogi was a god." Keene, *Emperor of Japan,* p. 714.

16. Carrasco, *Religions of Mesoamerica,* p. 113.

17. Maya gods and kings performed bloodletting rites to ensure their lineage before and after accession ceremonies, to obtain a vision, to open up a passage to the ancestors, to engage in reciprocal relationships with the gods and, through bloodletting ritual, give birth to them. See Linda Schele, "Bloodletting and the Vision Quest," in

Linda Schele and Mary Ellen Miller (photographs by Justin Kerr), *The Blood of Kings: Dynasty and Ritual in Maya Art* (New York: George Braziller in association with Kimbell Art Museum, Fort Worth, 1986), pp. 175–185.

18. Unless otherwise noted, all translations are my own. Heribert Aigner's definition of suicide is the fruit of an extensive survey of definitions; Aigner, *Der Selbstmord im Mythos: Betrachtungen über die Einstellung der Griechen zum Phänomen Suizid von der homerischen Zeit bis in das ausgehende 5. Jahrhundert v. Chr.* (Graz: Publikation des Instituts für Alte Geschichte und Altertumskunde der Karl-Franzens-Universität Graz, 1982), p. 13.

19. Georges Minois, *History of Suicide: Voluntary Death in Western Culture*, trans. Lydia G. Cochrane (Baltimore and London: Johns Hopkins University Press, 1999), p. 1. Originally published in French as *Histoire du suicide: La société occidentale face à la mort volontaire* (Paris: Librairie Arthème Fayard, 1995).

20. For a comprehensive study of human sacrifice on the occasion of an important person's death, as documented in literature and by archaeological evidence, see Peter Haider, "Gefolgschaftsbestattungen in universalhistorischer Sicht," in Franz Hampl and Ingomar Weiler, eds., *Kritische und vergleichende Studien zur Alten Geschichte und Universalgeschichte*, Innsbrucker Beiträge zur Kulturwissenschaft, vol. 18 (Innsbruck: Institut für Sprachwissenschaft der Universität Innsbruck, 1974), pp. 89–120. The nineteenth-century philosopher Herbert Spencer argued in 1877 that all sacrifice is motivated by fear of the dead and is a way of pleasing or placating them. See Herbert Spencer, "From *The Principles of Sociology*," in Jeffrey Carter, ed., *Understanding Religious Sacrifice: A Reader* (London: Continuum, 2003), p. 42.

21. Jane Ellen Harrison, *Prolegomena to the Study of Greek Religion* (1903; Princeton, N.J.: Princeton University Press, 1991), and Friedrich Schwenn, *Die Menschenopfer bei den Griechen und Römern* (1915; rpt. Giessen: Verlag von Alfred Töpelmann [vormals J. Ricker], 1966).

22. Walter B. Emery, *Archaic Egypt* (Harmondsworth: Penguin, 1961), p. 90.

23. Ibid., p. 135. Although he attributes "the coherence of court and king after death [to] a deep and lasting relationship with the monarch," Henri Frankfort similarly professes uncertainty about the willingness of the human sacrifice: "Kings of the First Dynasty were buried at Abydos in the midst of great squares containing the graves of their suite. It is not necessary to assume that the court was killed at the death of its master, though a few persons actually buried in the king's tomb were no doubt killed to accompany and serve him" (Frankfort, *Kingship and the Gods: A Study of Ancient Near Eastern Religion as the Integration of Society and Nature* [1948; Chicago and London: University of Chicago Press, 1978], pp. 55, 54). More recently, Stephan Seidlmayer has concluded that those buried in the subsidiary tombs of King Horus Aha (Menes) "were in fact killed on the occasion of the royal funeral." Seidlmayer, "The Rise of the State to the Second Dynasty," in Regine Schulz and Matthias Seidel, eds., *Egypt: The World of the Pharaohs* (Cairo: The American University in Cairo Press, 2001), p. 30. Originally published in German as *Ägypten: Die Welt der Pharaonen* (Köln: Könemann, 1998).

24. For the function of *shabtis* as the deceased person's substitute to perform labor in the afterlife, see Rita E. Freed, Yvonne J. Markowitz, and Sue H. D'Auria, eds.,

Pharaohs of the Sun: Akhenaten, Nefertiti, Tutankhamen (Boston: Museum of Fine Arts with Bulfinch Press/ Little, Brown and Company, 1999), pp. 164, 271.

25. See Samuel Johnson, *The History of the Yorubas*, ed. O. Johnson (1921; Lagos, Nigeria: CSS Limited, 2001), pp. 55–57.

26. Wole Soyinka, *Death and the King's Horseman* (New York: Hill and Wang, The Noonday Press, 1987), p. 15. For a discussion of the play and its origins in ritual suicide, see James Booth, "Self-Sacrifice and Human Sacrifice in Soyinka's *Death and the King's Horseman*," in James Gibbs and Bernth Lindfors, eds., *Research on Wole Soyinka* (Trenton, N.J.: Africa World Press, 1993), pp. 127–147.

27. Soyinka, *Death and the King's Horseman*, p. 28.

28. Booth, "Self-Sacrifice and Human Sacrifice," p. 137.

29. Francis R. B. Godolphin, ed., *The Greek Historians: The Complete and Unabridged Historical Works of Herodotus, Thucydides, Xenophon, Arrian*, 2 vols. (New York: Random House, 1942), 1:251. Human sacrifices to the Scythian kings were made from about 600–300 B.C.E. (Herodotus 4.71–72).

30. Bruce Lincoln, *Death, War, and Sacrifice: Studies in Ideology and Practice* (Chicago and London: University of Chicago Press, 1991), p. 195.

31. See Schwenn, *Die Menschenopfer bei den Griechen und Römern*, p. 62.

32. In ancient Rome, the blood shed in gladiatorial games replaced the blood of human sacrifice and was, in either case, dedicated to the lord of the grave; see Schwenn, *Die Menschenopfer bei den Griechen und Römern*, pp. 173–175.

33. *Iliad* 23.175–183. Richmond Lattimore, trans., *The Iliad of Homer* (Chicago: University of Chicago Press, 1951), p. 455.

34. Critics have attributed Achilles' sacrifice of twelve Trojans to his extreme anger, wondering whether this anger sullied the act of sacrifice with the motive of revenge. Similarly, in order to take vengeance on the city of Perusia for having defended Caesar's murderer, Octavian sacrificed three hundred high-ranking Perusians. Friedrich Schwenn claims that the custom of providing companions to the dead allowed the Romans to use a religious practice familiar to them for the purpose of political revenge; see Schwenn, *Die Menschenopfer bei den Griechen und Römern*, p. 173.

35. "Otho's boldness," argues Elizabeth Keitel, was the "two-edged sword by which he seizes power disgracefully and lays it down with distinction." Keitel, "Otho's Exhortations in Tacitus' *Histories*," *Greece & Rome* 34.1 (April 1987): 79.

36. Bruce Lincoln refers to "the case of the *silodouroi* of the Gallic Scotiani, as reported by Caesar (*De Bello Gallico* 3.22) and Athenaeus (*Deipnosophistae* 6.249B). These 600 attendants of the king pledged to live and die with him, sharing his powers, his presence, his dress, and his habits, but also committing suicide on his death should they not fall beside him in battle." Lincoln, *Death, War, and Sacrifice*, pp. 196–197, n. 12.

37. L. F. Janssen, "Some Unexplored Aspects of the *Devotio Deciana*," *Mnemosyne* 4.34 (1981), p. 376, cited in Carlin A. Barton, *The Sorrows of the Ancient Romans: The Gladiator and the Monster* (Princeton, N.J.: Princeton University Press, 1993), p. 44.

38. According to Plutarch (before 50–after 120 C.E.), "There were some, too, who first put their torches to the pyre and then slew themselves, not, so far as could be known, because they were either indebted to the dead for favours, or fearful of punish-

ment at the hands of the victor." *Otho* 17.4, in *Plutarch's Lives*, trans. Bernadotte Perrin, 11 vols., Loeb Classical Library (New York: G. P. Putnam's Sons, 1926), 11:317.

39. Andrew Feldherr, *Spectacle and Society in Livy's* History (Berkeley: University of California Press, 1998), pp. 88, 89.

40. Allen Guttmann, *Sports: The First Five Millennia* (Amherst and Boston: University of Massachusetts Press, 2004), p. 30.

41. Donald G. Kyle, *Spectacles of Death in Ancient Rome* (London and New York: Routledge, 1998), p. 44.

42. Paul Plass, *The Game of Death in Ancient Rome: Arena Sport and Political Suicide* (Madison: University of Wisconsin Press, 1995), p. 24.

43. Haider, "Gefolgschaftsbestattungen in universalhistorischer Sicht," p. 94.

44. See ibid., p. 96.

45. Bitō Masahide, "Junshi," in *Kodansha Encyclopedia of Japan*, 4:84.

46. Mark Edward Lewis, *Sanctioned Violence in Early China* (Albany: State University of New York Press, 1990), pp. 95, 27.

47. Jacques Gernet, *A History of Chinese Civilization*, trans. J. R. Foster and Charles Hartman (Cambridge: Cambridge University Press, 1996), p. 49. Originally published as *Le monde chinois* (Paris: Librairie Armand Colin, 1972).

48. For a photograph of human remains lined up "on the ledges above the coffin chamber," see Plate 20, facing p. 136, in Gina L. Barnes, *The Rise of Civilization in East Asia: The Archaeology of China, Korea and Japan* (1993; London: Thames and Hudson, 1999). See Gernet, *History of Chinese Civilization*, pp. 47, 49.

49. Lewis, *Sanctioned Violence in Early China*, pp. 26–27.

50. Aston adds some examples of human sacrifice to those given in the *Nihon shoki;* see Aston, trans., *Nihongi*, I:179, n. 3.

51. *Nihon shoki* VI.18–19. Aston, trans., *Nihongi*, I:178.

52. Ibid.

53. *Nihon shoki* VI.20. Aston, trans., *Nihongi*, I:180.

54. *Kojiki* 64.10. Donald L. Philippi, trans., *Kojiki* (University of Tokyo Press, 1968), p. 418.

55. *Kojiki* 64.10. Philippi, trans., *Kojiki*, p. 200; see also additional note 22 (pp. 416–418) on "pitö-gaki, literally 'human fence.'"

56. Paul Varley, *Japanese Culture*, 4th ed. (Honolulu: University of Hawai'i Press, 2000), p. 14; see also p. 15.

57. Delmer M. Brown, "The Early Evolution of Historical Consciousness," in Delmer M. Brown, ed., *Cambridge History of Japan: Volume I, Ancient Japan* (Cambridge: Cambridge University Press, 1993), p. 508.

58. Tsunoda Ryūsaku, trans., and L. Carrington Goodrich, ed., *Japan in the Chinese Dynastic Histories: Later Han through Ming Dynasties*, Perkins Asiatic Monographs, No. 2 (South Pasadena, Calif.: P. D. and Ione Perkins, 1951), p. 16.

59. Ibid.

60. See Joan R. Piggot, *The Emergence of Japanese Kingship* (Stanford, Calif.: Stanford University Press, 1997), pp. 28–29. Walter Edwards, "In Pursuit of Himiko: Postwar Archaeology and the Location of Yamatai," *Monumenta Nipponica* 51.1

(Spring 1996): 57, n. 10. For additional examples of voluntary or forced death upon the sovereign's death, see Aston, trans., *Nihongi*, p. 179, n. 3.

61. In tenth-century Russia, the widow of a highly respected man would be buried alive in a well-furnished death chamber. See Haider, "Gefolgschaftsbestattungen in universalhistorischer Sicht," p. 95.

62. See the chart in Gary L. Ebersole, *Ritual Poetry and the Politics of Death in Early Japan* (Princeton, N.J.: Princeton University Press, 1998), p. 130.

63. See ibid., p. 155.

64. See ibid., chap. 3, pp. 123–170.

Chapter 2. The Japanese Custom of Junshi

1. In feudal Europe, hierarchical relationships fostered devotion and loyalty, but "following one's lord into death" by an act of suicidal self-sacrifice ran clearly contrary to Christian doctrine. By contrast, no such religious constraint existed in Japan. Although Shintō—the way of the gods *(kami)*—abhors nothing more than the pollution of death, it consigns to the dead the elevated status of *kami.* If the allegory of Amaterasu's eclipse is any guide to Shintō attitudes toward death, pacification of the dead through ritual laughter and dance is a positive—indeed, almost a cheerful—affair. Shamanesses *(miko)* were employed as mediators to communicate with and control the *kami.* Ordinarily, bloodshed was meticulously avoided in offerings to the *kami.* However, extraordinary threats of pollution required extraordinary offerings, including "human pillars" *(hitobashira)* or human sacrifices *(ikenie)* to stabilize bridges, castles, or other buildings. Buddhism, the religion officially imported in the mid-sixth century, included similar attitudes. No one was condemned for leaving this world, which was seen as fleeting and delusive. To enter nirvana, where the wheel of karma no longer turns, was to be free of all attachments. Warriors in particular were drawn to Zen Buddhism, which used meditation as one of its techniques of gaining enlightenment through detachment by focusing on the abdominal center *(seika tanden)*, a point just below the navel where truth, sincerity, and emotional energy reside and where the sword in seppuku was aimed. Thus, whether it was to join the ancestral *kami* or to achieve Buddhist enlightenment, suicide was no sin *(tsumi).*

2. As junshi evolved, the third of these steps was increasingly questioned: "As long as the motive was pure, *junshi* could be a virtuous act. In time, however, loyalty and obligation came to be seen in terms of exchange of services for favors granted, and duty, too, came to be interpreted as living up to one's social station. Thus, what had been an act of self-effacement became an act of saving face." Bitō Masahide, "Junshi," in *Kodansha Encyclopedia of Japan,* 1st ed. (Tokyo and New York: Kodansha, 1983), 4:85.

3. This Reform Edict (Kaishinshō), promulgated on New Year's Day 646, has in itself been questioned and may contain "latter-day inventions." For a concise account of the tumultuous scholarly debate, see William Wayne Farris, *Sacred Texts and Buried Treasures: Issues in the Historical Archaeology of Ancient Japan* (Honolulu: University of Hawai'i Press, 1998), pp. 203–209. Joan R. Piggot, *The Emergence of Japanese Kingship* (Stanford, Calif.: Stanford University Press, 1997), p. 108.

4. *Kojiki* 64.10. Donald L. Philippi, trans., *Kojiki* (University of Tokyo Press, 1968), p. 417.

5. *Nihon shoki* XXV.31. William George Aston, trans., *Nihongi: Chronicles of Japan from the Earliest Times to A.D. 697* (Rutland, Vt., and Tokyo: Charles E. Tuttle, 1972), II:220.

6. Peter Haider has asserted that in Japan "Gefolgschaftsbestattung" (burial with entourage) was reserved for the emperor and members of the imperial house, with the exception of nobles who claimed similar powers and needs for themselves in the afterlife; Haider apparently did not consider voluntary self-sacrifice for the domainal lord or the head of the household; see Haider, "Gefolgschaftsbestattungen in universalhistorischer Sicht," in Franz Hampl and Ingomar Weiler, eds., *Kritische und vergleichende Studien zur Alten Geschichte und Universalgeschichte,* Innsbrucker Beiträge zur Kulturwissenschaft, vol. 18 (Innsbruck: Institut für Sprachwissenschaft der Universität Innsbruck, 1974), p. 114.

7. A similar case of junshi occurred in 454 C.E., according to *Nihon shoki* XIII.20–21. Imperial Prince Ohokusaka was slandered, and the emperor, believing the allegations, had him slain. The prince's faithful followers felt that this injustice could be corrected only by junshi: "they were all grieved that their lord should die without a crime. . . . 'Alas! Our Lord has died without a crime. Were we three, father and sons, who served him in life, not to follow him in death, we should be no true retainers.' So they cut their throats, and died beside the Imperial corpse. The army, to a man, all wept tears" (Aston, trans., *Nihongi,* I:331).

8. This Himuka Omi, the half-brother of Kurayamada Ishikawa no Maro, is also known by other names, such as "Musashi," "Musa no Omi," or "Shidaru, Kibi no Kasa no Omi"; see Edwin A. Cranston, trans., with commentary and notes, *A Waka Anthology, Volume One: The Gem-Glistening Cup* (Stanford, Calif.: Stanford University Press, 1993), pp. 120, 813, note to poems 184–185; Gary L. Ebersole, *Ritual Poetry and the Politics of Death in Early Japan* (Princeton, N.J.: Princeton University Press, 1998), pp. 224, 226.

9. Nakatomi Kamatari, better known as Fujiwara Kamatari (614–669), "recruited [the] Soga collateral, Soga Yamada Ishikawa Maro . . . to destroy the main line of the Soga *uji,* just as the Soga had done to the Mononobe fifty years earlier." This plot developed into the coup d'état of 645. Piggot, *Emergence of Japanese Kingship,* p. 104.

10. Piggott argues that Naka no Ōe was not made crown prince or "heir-apparent" after the coup of 645 but "senior prince" *(taishi).* Ibid., pp. 108, 105.

11. Naka no Ōe believed the allegations because Himuka had earlier stolen Naka no Ōe's promised bride, the oldest daughter of Soga no Kurayamada, and he was left to marry the second and third daughters. Himuka's triumph was short-lived, however, for these two consorts of Naka no Ōe produced offspring that would yield two future emperors (Mommu and Temmu) and three empresses (Gemmei, Jitō, and Genshō). Himuka had also betrayed Prince Furuhito's ambitions to become emperor to Naka no Ōe. Although Naka no Ōe did not obstruct Furuhito, his elder half-brother declined the throne and withdrew. Nonetheless, conspirators under Himuka brought about "a preemptive attack" on Furuhito, possibly involving Naka no Ōe. According to *Nihongi*

XXV.12, Furuhito died in 645.XI.30 with his children. (One of Furuhito no Ōe's daughters, Yamato-hime, was married to Naka no Ōe when her father was assassinated. She did not follow her father in death, as did her siblings.) Gary L. Ebersole points out that "No offspring are reported from the Tenji–Yamato-hime union, but this may be an attempt by the compilers of the *Nihonshoki* to deny the continuation of the Furuhito no Ōe line or at least any legitimacy in terms of the imperial succession" (*Ritual Poetry and the Politics of Death in Early Japan,* pp. 236–237). Furuhito's "consorts committed suicide by strangling themselves" (*Nihon shoki* XXV.12. Aston, trans., *Nihongi,* II:204; see Ebersole, *Ritual Poetry and the Politics of Death in Early Japan,* p. 226). Thus even this prelude to the Kurayamada junshi involves junshi by family members for a prince crushed in an imperial succession struggle.

12. *Nihon shoki* XXV.42. Aston, trans., *Nihongi* II:232.

13. Hearing that punitive troops were on their way, Koshi was prepared either to meet the emperor's troops or to burn the palace (Oharida *no miya*) that Empress Suiko (554–628; r. 592–628) had built in 603 on Soga land in the Asuka valley.

14. *Nihon shoki* XXV.43. Aston, trans., *Nihongi.* II:233.

15. Ebersole states that Kurayamada strangled himself, "realizing he was in an impossible situation" (*Ritual Poetry and the Politics of Death in Early Japan,* p. 227).

16. The translator of the *Nihongi,* William George Aston (1841–1911), attributed the deadly choice of strangulation "to the objection in China and Japan to the mutilation of the body, [so that] hanging or strangulation is reckoned a less severe punishment than decapitation." *Nihon shoki* XXV.44. Aston, trans., *Nihongi,* II:234, n. 3.

17. See *Nihon shoki* XXV.43; for the term "*junshi,*" see Sakamoto Tanō et al., eds., *Nihon shoki,* 2 vols., Nihon koten bungaku taikei 67 and 68 (Iwanami shoten, 1967), 2:309. Aston, trans., *Nihongi,* II:233–234.

18. Ebersole, *Ritual Poetry and the Politics of Death in Early Japan,* p. 227.

19. Ibid., p. 228. Neither suggesting that Miyatsuko-hime comitted suicide nor ruling it out, Edwin A. Cranston states that she "is reported to have died of grief." He goes on to speculate that, if she was the mother of Prince Takeru, then "it is apparent that Miyatsukohime lived on for at least two years after the tragic events of 649" (Cranston, *Waka Anthology, Volume One,* pp. 120, 122). We cannot know whether the long interval between the violent death of Miyatsuko-hime's family and her own death would make it more or less likely that she followed them in death.

20. For the two *banka* by Kawara no Maro, see *Nihon shoki* XXV.45. Aston, trans., *Nihongi,* II:235; Cranston, *Waka Anthology, Volume One,* pp. 121; Ebersole, *Ritual Poetry and the Politics of Death in Early Japan,* pp. 187–188.

21. Ebersole, *Ritual Poetry and the Politics of Death in Early Japan,* p. 228.

22. Helen Craig McCullough, trans., "*A Tale of Mutsu,*" *Harvard Journal of Asiatic Studies* 25 (1964–1965): 192. For another translation, with commentary, see Paul Varley, *Warriors of Japan as Portrayed in the War Tales* (Honolulu: University of Hawai'i Press, 1994), pp. 30–31. This episode was also depicted in the early-twelfth-century *setsuwa* collection *Konjaku monogatari shū,* vol. 4.

23. Karl F. Friday, *Hired Swords: The Rise of Private Warrior Power in Early Japan* (Stanford, Calif.: Stanford University Press, 1992), p. 119 n.

24. McCullough, trans., "*A Tale of Mutsu,*" p. 192.

25. See Delmer M. Brown and Ichirō Ishida, trans. and study, *The Future and the Past: A Translation and Study of the Gukanshō, an Interpretative History of Japan Written in 1219* (Berkeley: University of California Press, 1979), p. 192. Since Sanetomo was childless, the life-affirming choice of Sanetomo's followers seems appropriate. Taking religious vows as a symbolic form of junshi was frequently practiced by the wives of fallen Taira warriors in the Genpei Wars (1180–1185) and sometimes combined with physical death by drowning, in the preferred Taira form of suicide, less bloody than the preferred seppuku of the Eastern warriors of Minamoto descent and allegiance. In *The Tale of the Heike* (*Heike monogatari*, comp. 1371), the principal consort of Taira no Shigehira (1156–1185) admonishes herself for not following the brave example of Michimori's wife, Kozaishō: "'I ought to have drowned myself after our parting, as Michimori's wife did when he died. . . . My sole reason for staying alive was the hope that you might be spared.'" After her husband's execution, she is free to emulate Kozaishō, though without the suicide: "Then, most touchingly, she became a nun and prayed for Shigehira's welfare in the afterlife" (Helen Craig McCullough, trans., *The Tale of the Heike* [Stanford, Calif.: Stanford University Press, 1988], pp. 398, 400). Kozaishō's suicide by drowning is described in *Heike* 9.19, in ibid., pp. 320–324.

26. The brief episode is cited in Ōkuma Miyoshi, *Seppuku no rekishi* (Yūzankaku, 1973), pp. 7–8. For an English translation, see Michiko Y. Aoki, *Records of Wind and Earth: A Translation of Fudoki with Introduction and Commentaries*, Monograph and Occasional Paper Series, No. 53 (Ann Arbor, Mich.: Association for Asian Studies, 1997), pp. 228–229.

27. See Yamamoto Hirofumi, *Seppuku: Nihonjin no sekinin no torikata* (Kōbunsha, 2003), p. 19.

28. William R. Wilson, trans., *Hōgen monogatari: Tale of the Disorder in Hōgen*, Cornell East Asia Series No. 99 (1971; rpt. Ithaca, N.Y.: East Asia Program, Cornell University, 2001), pp. 106–107.

29. Varley, *Warriors of Japan as Portrayed in the War Tales*, p. 56. Varley notes that, according to another legend, Tametomo did not commit suicide but fled to the Ryūkyū Islands to found a dynasty of kings; ibid., p. 58.

30. Ibid., p. 176.

31. Ibid., pp. 176–177.

32. See Eiko Ikegami, *The Taming of the Samurai: Honorific Individualism and the Making of Modern Japan* (Cambridge, Mass.: Harvard University Press, 1995), p. 109.

33. Helen Craig McCullough, trans., *The Taiheiki: A Chronicle of Medieval Japan* (1959; rpt. Rutland, Vt.: Charles E. Tuttle, 1979), p. 269. Hōjō Nakatoki is identified as "the Rokuhara chieftain of the north," p. 95, n. 4.

34. Ikegami, *Taming of the Samurai*, p. 109.

35. See Yamamoto, *Seppuku*, p. 39; Mishima Geki's junshi is recorded as an "unprecedented case" in *Meitokuki* (compiled c. 1400), cited by Bitō, "Junshi," *Kodansha Encyclopedia of Japan*, 4: 84.

36. Tadayoshi and Hideyasu were the fourth and second sons of the first Tokugawa shōgun, Ieyasu (1542–1616; r. 1603–1605). See Yamamoto, *Seppuku*, p. 39; as Ieyasu's distaste for junshi was well known, his death did not inspire his retainers to follow him.

37. For a statistical chart of Edo-period junshi and *mata junshi*, see Yamamoto, *Seppuku*, p. 42; for an example of *mata junshi*, see ibid., p. 39.

38. An even higher total number of junshi and *mata junshi* is recorded for Nabeshima Shigekata (?–1645). See the statistical chart of Edo-period junshi and *mata junshi* in Yamamoto, *Seppuku*, p. 42.

39. For junshi statistics, see Yamamoto, *Seppuku*, p. 42. For a class analysis of Nabeshima Katsushige's twenty-six retainers, see Yamamoto Hirofumi, *Junshi no kōzō* (Kōbundō, 1994), pp. 125–137.

40. See Ōkuma, *Seppuku no rekishi*, pp. 154–155, 279.

41. Preceding the Tokugawa shōgunate's prohibition of junshi in 1663, Mitsushige had in 1661 prohibited junshi in the Nabeshima fief (Saga *han*) because the custom had become rampant and thirty-six of his uncle's retainers were planning to commit junshi. See Ikegami, *The Taming of the Samurai*, p. 283.

42. Ikegami, *The Taming of the Samurai*, p. 281.

43. Ironically, the early Tokugawa thinker whom Nogi seems to have revered most was the unconventional and innovative Confucian scholar Yamaga Sokō (1622–1685). Sokō developed a samurai ethic that held duty and honor above one's own life but that "rejected the moral legitimacy of *junshi* . . . , considering it the questionable result of homosexual liaisons between masters and vassals." Ikegami, *The Taming of the Samurai*, p. 310.

44. See Yamamoto, *Seppuku*, pp. 40–41.

45. See Thomas Cleary, trans., *Code of the Samurai: A Modern Translation of the* Bushido Shoshinsu [sic] (Boston, Rutland, Vt., and Tokyo: Tuttle Publishing, 1999). Daidōji Yūzan regrets that the ban on junshi left warriors eager to perform outstanding service in return for favors without an outlet for the love of their lord; see Cleary, trans., *Code of the Samurai*, p. 90.

46. The brief document (article 159) banning junshi can be found in Ishii Ryōsuke, ed., *Tokugawa kinreikō*, 11 vols. (Sōbunsha, 1959), 1: 65.

47. The 1615 *Buke shohatto* consisted of 13 articles; it was revised and expanded in 1631; 1635 (19 articles); 1683; 1710 (minor changes).

48. See Ōkuma, *Seppuku no rekishi*, pp. 158–159.

49. Ikegami, *The Taming of the Samurai*, p. 220. See also Maurice Pinguet, *Voluntary Death in Japan*, trans. Rosemary Morris (1984; rpt. Cambridge: Polity Press, 1993), pp. 140–141. Originally published as *La mort volontaire au Japon* (Paris: Éditions Gallimard, 1984).

50. The case of the forty-seven *rōnin* lies beyond the scope of my study, which focuses on junshi, not vendettas and seppuku as a form of punishment. Bitō Masahide states that some Akō *rōnin* had proposed junshi *(oibara)* at the Asano family temple if surrender of their lord's castle could not be avoided. All their various options—holding the castle *(rōjō)*, junshi, restoring the Asano house, assassinating Kira—had "the single purpose of restoring their blemished honor"; Bitō, "The Akō Incident, 1701–1703," trans. Henry D. Smith II, *Monumenta Nipponica* 58.2 (Summer 2003): 157, 162. In popular opinion, "since they had acted in full awarness of their inevitable punishment, their deaths were regarded as a form of *junshi*." Bitō, "Junshi," in *Kodansha Encyclopedia of Japan*, 4:85.

51. Yamamoto, *Junshi no kōzō*, p. 39.

52. The samurai wore two swords *(daishō)*, the *katana* and the *wakizashi*. For seppuku, the guardless dagger *(aikuchi)* is traditionally used.

Chapter 3. Nogi's Life Sentences

1. Ōhama Tetsuya, *Meiji no gunshin: Nogi Maresuke* (Yūzankaku, 1970), pp. 10–11.

2. Rank was hereditary and had become frozen around the beginning of the Tokugawa period. See Albert M. Craig, *Chōshū in the Meiji Restoration* (Cambridge, Mass.: Harvard University Press, 1961), p. 107.

3. In Chōshū, there were "seventeen ranks of *shi* and twenty-three of *sotsu*." *Sotsu* (soldiers) were samurai below the class of *shi*. Craig, *Chōshū in the Meiji Restoration*, p. 101.

4. According to Albert M. Craig, there were 1,378 members in the *ōgumi* group, whose incomes ranged from 40 to 250 *koku*; however, only "569 of the group had incomes over 100 *koku*." Craig, *Chōshū in the Meiji Restoration*, pp. 101–102.

5. Ōhama, *Meiji no gunshin*, p. 9.

6. For the variant spelling of the name, see Ōhama, *Meiji no gunshin*, genealogical chart, p. 11; Yoshikawa Torajirō, "Shōnen jidai no Nogi Maresuke," p. 56; in Kuwahara Takeshi and Sugahara Kazutora, eds., *Nogi Maresuke no sekai* (Shinjinbutsu ōraisha, 1992).

7. Ōhama, *Meiji no gunshin*, p. 10, n. 2.

8. Matsushita Yoshio, *Nogi Maresuke*, Jinbutsu sōsho series (1960; rev. 4th ed., Yoshikawa kōbunkan, 1997), p. 41; Yoshikawa, "Shōnen jidai no Nogi Maresuke," p. 56.

9. For details on Nogi's given names, see Ōhama, *Meiji no gunshin*, pp. 8–9.

10. Robert Jay Lifton, Shūichi Katō, and Michael R. Reich, *Six Lives Six Deaths: Portraits from Modern Japan* (New Haven, Conn.: Yale University Press, 1979), p. 38.

11. Denis Warner and Peggy Warner, *The Tide at Sunrise: A History of the Russo-Japanese War, 1904–1905* (New York: Charterhouse, 1974), p. 49.

12. Ōhama, *Meiji no gunshin*, p. 12 (my emphasis).

13. See ibid.

14. In his Nogi genealogy, Matsushita registers only one older brother, Gentarō; see Matsushita, *Nogi Maresuke*, p. 219. In "Shōnen jidai no Nogi Maresuke," Yoshikawa Torajirō notes that Maretsugu lost a son to his first wife, Hideko, presumably when he divorced her; see Yoshikawa, "Shōnen jidai no Nogi Maresuke," p. 56. Ōhama Tetsuya's chronological table lists Nogi as being born on the eleventh day of the eleventh month of Kaei 2 (25 December 1849) as the third child of Nogi Jurō Maretsugu and his wife, Hisako; Ōhama, *Meiji no gunshin*, pp. 8, 296.

15. Nogi Maretsugu instructed his son, from age seven to fourteen, in *bushidō* military and literary skills—from military history, etiquette, horsemanship, archery, and swordsmanship to penmanship, Chinese classics, and poetry. The son was rather averse to the military aspects of his *bushidō* training and much preferred to immerse himself in the literary skills. For a detailed list of Nogi's teachers and their areas of expertise in samurai arts *(bugei)*, see Ōhama, *Meiji no gunshin*, p. 12.

16. Matsushita, *Nogi Maresuke,* p. 7. Ōhama records the Nogi family's move to Toyoura in the old province of Nagato (which Sasaki Shirō Takatsuna had governed after the Genpei War) in November 1858; Ōhama, *Meiji no gunshin,* p. 296.

17. See Japan National Tourist Organization, ed., *The New Official Guide: Japan* (Tokyo: Japan Travel Bureau, 1975), p. 784.

18. The Battle of Ishibashiyama on 1180.VIII.23 is merely hinted at in the *Heike monogatari* 5.10, after Retired Emperor Go-Shirakawa responded to Mongaku's pleas to recall Yoritomo from exile in Izu and authorize him to defeat the Taira: "People say that Yoritomo put the edict in a brocade bag and wore it around his neck, even during the battle of Ishibashiyama"; Helen Craig McCullough, trans., *The Tale of the Heike* (Stanford, Calif.: Stanford University Press, 1988), p. 184.

19. For Nogi's veneration of his ancestors, and of Sasaki Shirō Takatsuna in particular, see Togawa Yukio, *Ningen Nogi Maresuke* (Kōjinsha, 1988), pp. 11–16; genealogical chart, p. 16. Nogi was president of Gakushūin from 1907 to 1912; see Takie Sugiyama Lebra, *Above the Clouds: Status Culture of the Modern Japanese Nobility* (Berkeley: University of California Press, 1993), p. 267. He was able to influence the new generation, including the future emperor Hirohito (1901–1989; r. 1926–1989); see Herbert P. Bix, *Hirohito and the Making of Modern Japan* (New York: HarperCollins, 2000). Bix points out that Nogi "refused to pamper the little princes" (p. 36) under his tutelage. Yet even Nogi's "spartan curriculum" (p. 37) may not have prepared the eleven-year-old Hirohito for his mentor's junshi. On 10 September 1912, Nogi paid his imperial charge a last visit and gave him two books to study by *kogaku* Confucianist Yamaga Sokō (1622–1685) and Miyake Kanran (1674–1718), a Confucian scholar of the early Mito school (see pp. 41–42).

20. McCullough, trans., *The Tale of the Heike,* p. 284 (my emphasis).

21. Paul Varley, *Warriors of Japan as Portrayed in the War Tales* (Honolulu: University of Hawai'i Press, 1994), p. 94.

22. McCullough, trans., *The Tale of the Heike,* p. 285.

23. Ibid., p. 286.

24. When Kagesue tried to trick Takatsuna, he ended up helping him by losing his own momentum of crossing the river. Kagesue was cunning in a premeditative way, as his father Kagetoki (?–1200) would turn out to be in his Reverse-Oars debate with Yoshitsune (*Heike* 11.1), which showed that neither father nor son was ready to risk all.

25. McCullough, trans., *The Tale of the Heike,* p. 287.

26. Yoritomo's close relations with "the powerful Sasaki family in Ōmi Province" ran into trouble on 1191.III.29, because of a dispute over taxes with the Enryakuji monks. Yoritomo thought it prudent to pacify Enryakuji even at the expense of some of his most favored retainers, but then seized the first opportunity to reinstate the Sasaki family in 1193.X. Mikael S. Adolphson, *The Gates of Power: Monks, Courtiers, and Warriors in Premodern Japan* (Honolulu: University of Hawai'i Press, 2000), p. 176; see also pp. 177–178.

27. Ōhama, *Meiji no gunshin,* p. 8. Matsushita, however, lists Genzaburō, *Nogi Maresuke,* p. 6. At that time, Nogi was also known as Yoritoki, a name that resounds with those of leading Minamoto warriors. Ōhama, *Meiji no gunshin,* p. 8.

28. See Thomas M. Huber, *The Revolutionary Origins of Modern Japan* (Stanford, Calif.: Stanford University Press, 1981), pp. 120, 123. However, the Kiheitai and its spinoff, the *shotai*, soon irritated the wealthiest, conservative Senpōtai in Hagi; see ibid., p. 124. Huber notes that Shōin himself had, in the summer of 1858, pioneered "using commoners as soldiers" and "drilling commoners in the use of the rifle"; ibid., p. 76.

29. Satsuma is in the western part of modern Kagoshima Prefecture, and Aizu in the western part of modern Fukushima Prefecture.

30. Huber, *Revolutionary Origins*, p. 133.

31. Tamaki Bunnoshin was also known as Masakane.

32. Cited in Ōhama, *Meiji no gunshin*, p. 14. For illumination on the emotional content of this appellation, as in Bashō-ō, I thank Earl Miner and Hiroaki Sato.

33. The translators of Kido Takayoshi's diary refer to Tamaki Bunnoshin as "a white-haired old fanatic." Sidney Devere Brown and Akiko Hirota, trans., *The Diary of Kido Takayoshi*, 3 vols. (University of Tokyo Press, 1986), III:389, n. 10; concerning Tamaki Bunnoshin's suicide, see III:392.

34. Huber, *Revolutionary Origins*, p. 7.

35. Ibid., p. 11.

36. Tsunoda Ryusaku, Wm. Theodore de Bary, and Donald Keene, eds., *Sources of Japanese Tradition* (New York: Columbia University Press, 1958; 2 vols. 1964), 1:386.

37. Ibid., 1:388.

38. Huber, *Revolutionary Origins*, p. 36.

39. Ibid., p. 167.

40. Craig, *Chōshū in the Meiji Restoration*, p. 155.

41. For a vivid account and analysis of Ii's assassination by eighteen Mito swordsmen on the snowy morning of 24 March 1860, see George M. Wilson, "Murder at the Shogun's Gate: The Sakuradamongai Incident in Meiji Restoration History," unpublished manuscript, 1999.

42. See Ōhama, *Meiji no gunshin*, p. 16.

43. Huber, *Revolutionary Origins*, p. 24.

44. Ibid., p. 25.

45. Lifton et al., *Six Lives Six Deaths*, p. 39.

46. The incident, also known as the Hamaguri Gate Incident (Hamaguri *gomon no hen*), occurred on 20 August 1864.

47. The Shimonoseki bombardment *(shikoku kantai* Shimonoseki *hōgeki jiken)* occurred on 5–8 September 1864 and is also known as the Bakan War (Bakan *sensō*).

48. Around the same time, 352 Mito rebels were beheaded for their subversive anti-*bakufu* move to drive foreigners out of Yokohama. The atmosphere was explosive.

49. See Huber, *Revolutionary Origins*, p. 167.

50. See ibid., pp. 169, 170.

51. Mark R. Peattie writes that Nogi was then "at Kokura, in a unit of the Hōkokutai (one of the loyalist patriotic corps) commanded by Yamagata Aritomo." Peattie, "The Last Samurai: The Military Career of Nogi Maresuke," *Princeton Papers in East Asian Studies* 1 (1972): 90.

52. Lifton et al., *Six Lives Six Deaths*, p. 41. For the written pledge (*meiyakujō*), see Ōhama, *Meiji no gunshin*, p. 18.

53. Huber, *Revolutionary Origins*, p. 197; See Ōhama, *Meiji no gunshin*, p. 299. The fighting in Oda occurred in the first lunar month of 1865.

54. See Huber, *Revolutionary Origins*, p. 170.

55. Ibid., p. 181.

56. Matsushita lists only Bunzō, *Nogi Maresuke*, p. 6; Ōhama lists both Yoritoki and Bunzō; *Meiji no gunshin*, p. 8. For the date of June 1866 as the name change to Bunzō, see http://www007.upp.so-net.ne.jp/togo/human/no/maresuke.html (accessed 21 January 2003).

57. See Lifton et al., *Six Lives Six Deaths*, p. 42.

58. Ōhama, *Meiji no gunshin*, pp. 8, 302.

59. Lifton et al., *Six Lives Six Deaths*, p. 43.

60. The information on the various laws abolishing samurai status is derived from John M. Rogers, "Divine Destruction: The Shinpūren Rebellion of 1876," in Helen Hardacre, with Adam L. Kern, eds., *New Directions in the Study of Meiji Japan*, Brill's Japanese Studies Library, vol. 6 (Leiden, New York, and Köln: Brill, 1997), pp. 416–417.

61. Huber, *Revolutionary Origins*, p. 222. For even more radical income devaluations among *shizoku* in Kumamoto, see Rogers, "Divine Destruction," p. 416.

62. See Peattie, "The Last Samurai," p. 91.

63. Ibid., p. 93.

64. See Ōhama, *Meiji no gunshin*, p. 29.

65. Peattie, "The Last Samurai," p. 92.

66. Lifton et al., *Six Lives Six Deaths*, p. 44.

67. This was just after the Jinpūren or Shinpūren Rebellion had been quelled on 24 October and another rebellion had broken out at Akizuki on 27 October.

68. See Ōhama, *Meiji no gunshin*, p. 45.

69. Peattie, "The Last Samurai," p. 93. Peattie, referring to Ōhama (see below), interprets Tamaki's seppuku as atonement "for the treason of his adopted son." This statement must be understood from the viewpoint of the imperial victors, meaning that Tamaki was on the side of his adopted son and ended his own life as a result of the failed rebellion: "Tamaki, when he realized that the cause had failed, committed seppuku"; Lifton et al., *Six Lives Six Deaths*, p. 45. Tamaki's seppuku means that, while he supported his adopted son Masayoshi's rebellion, he wanted to take responsibility for its failure; see Craig, *Chōshū in the Meiji Restoration*, p. 265, n. 15: "having learned that certain students of his had participated in the revolt of Maebara, he committed suicide." Donald Calman furthermore speculates that "Bunnosuke himself was involved [in the rebellion], or at least that he had inspired Masayoshi's participation"; Calman, *The Nature and Origins of Japanese Imperialism: A Reinterpretation of the Great Crisis of 1873* (London and New York: Routledge, 1992), p. 189. Ōhama notes that Nogi's diary is silent on this important event, see Ōhama, *Meiji no gunshin*, pp. 44–45.

70. Calman, *Nature and Origins of Japanese Imperialism*, p. 189.

71. See Peattie, "The Last Samurai," p. 93.

72. Ibid., p. 93, cited from Ōhama, *Meiji no gunshin*, p. 49.

73. Peattie, "The Last Samurai," p. 93.

74. The concept of "liminal ritual" and "liminality" gained currency through Arnold van Gennep's *The Rites of Passage*, trans. Monika B. Vizedom and Gabrielle L. Caffee (Chicago: University of Chicago Press, 1960), and Victor Turner's works. Turner defines the liminal as "that which is neither this nor that, and yet is both" in *Forest of Symbols: Aspects of Ndembu Ritual* (1967; rpt. Ithaca, N.Y.: Cornell University Press, 1981), p. 99.

75. See Robert G. Hamerton-Kelly, ed., *Violent Origins: Walter Burkert, René Girard, and Jonathan Z. Smith on Ritual Killing and Cultural Formation*, with an introduction by Burton Mack and a commentary by Renato Rosaldo (Stanford, Calif.: Stanford University Press, 1987).

76. See Warner and Warner, *The Tide at Sunrise*, p. 50.

77. James H. Buck, trans., *The True Story of* THE SIEGE OF KUMAMOTO CASTLE: *Kumamoto Rojo no Jikkyo by Takehiko Ideishi* (New York: Vantage Press, 1976), p. 35. For accounts of the loss of the flag and its aftermath, see also Okada Mikihiko, *Nogi Maresuke: kōki naru Meiji* (Tentensha, 2001), pp. 32–37; Matsushita, *Nogi Maresuke*, pp. 26–37.

78. One might argue that the loss of the flag stands in no realistic relation to the sacrifice of a single life for a lost flag (and even its bearer, Lieutenant Kawarabayashi Yūta). For a detailed account of Kawarabayashi's loss, see Peattie, "The Last Samurai," pp. 94–95.

79. In retrospect, it is ironic that it was the Western-oriented Satsuma daimyō Shimazu Nariakira (1809–1858) who had petitioned the shōgunal government to institute the Rising Sun flag *(hinomaru)* in order to distinguish Japanese ships from those of foreigners; see Takashi Fujitani, *Splendid Monarchy: Power and Pageantry in Modern Japan* (Berkeley: University of California Press, 1996), p. 49. The irony lies in the fact that Nariakira was the lord of Saigō Takamori, the leader of the Satsuma Rebellion against the Meiji oligarchy (headed by the emperor), to whom Nogi lost the imperial colors.

80. Peattie, "The Last Samurai," p. 114, n. 33.

81. Ibid., pp. 94 and 114, n. 32. Nogi was mortified to discover later that the lost regimental banner had been found by one of the rebels (who was killed and whose widow kept the flag as a "family treasure" until she finally surrendered it to the authorities). Nogi's regiment did not receive a new flag until 15 September 1878; see Rikugunshō, ed., *Meiji gunji shi: Meiji Tennō go-denki shiryō* (Hara shobō 1966), p. 304; cited in Peattie, "The Last Samurai," p. 115, n. 38.

82. Lifton et al., *Six Lives Six Deaths*, p. 45; Warner and Warner, *The Tide at Sunrise*, p. 50: "Weeping, he agreed to confess his guilt and ask for punishment."

83. Nogi wanted to recover the flag at the risk of his life but was "physically restrained" by his men; Lifton et al., *Six Lives Six Deaths*, p. 45.

84. Ibid.

85. The besieged Kumamoto Castle was defended for about fifty days by Major General Tani Tateki (also: Kanjō; 1837–1911) until relief arrived.

86. See Fujitani, *Splendid Monarchy*, p. 55.

87. There were, however, relatively brief phases of imperial visibility, such as during the times of prominent senior "retired" emperors (1086–1156), the charismatic

figures of Retired Emperor Goshirakawa (1127–1192; r. 1155–1158), and the Kemmu Restoration (1333–1336) of Emperor Godaigo (1288–1339; r. 1318–1339).

88. Yanai Nazaemon, cited from Fukushima-ken Kyōikukai, ed., *Meiji tennō gojunkōroku* (Fukushima: Fukushima-shi, 1936), p. 110, in Fujitani, *Splendid Monarchy*, p. 51.

89. See Fujitani, *Splendid Monarchy*, "The Emperor's Two Bodies," pp. 155–170.

90. See ibid., p. 227.

91. See Matsushita, *Nogi Maresuke*, pp. 30–31.

92. See Carol Gluck, *Japan's Modern Myths: Ideology in the Late Meiji Period* (Princeton, N.J.: Princeton University Press, 1985), p. 75. In addition, the emperor would make 102 imperial excursions *(gyōkō)* in his reign; see ibid., p. 74; for Emperor Meiji's touring of the country *(jungyō* or *junkō)*, see also Emiko Ohnuki-Tierney, *Kamikaze, Cherry Blossoms, and Nationalisms: The Militarization of Aesthetics in Japanese History* (Chicago and London: University of Chicago Press, 2002), pp. 78–79.

93. See Mark Jolly, "Nogi's Last Lesson" (Senior Honors thesis, University of Massachusetts at Amherst, Department of Asian Languages and Literatures, 2000), p. 65. Translated from Togawa Yukio, "Meiji no bujin," in Tsubota Itsuo, ed., *Meiji no itsuzai*. Jinbutsu tanbō, Nihon no rekishi 18 (Akatsuki kyōiku tosho, 1975), pp. 124–134; p. 129: According to Togawa, Emperor Meiji admonished Nogi three times to live, for the sake of the nation and the people: "Meiji tennō ga saisan, Nogi ni 'iki yo' to satosareta no wa, ikite kokka ya kokumin ni tsukuse to iu imi de atta."

94. Warner and Warner, *The Tide at Sunrise*, p. 50.

95. Lifton et al., *Six Lives Six Deaths*, p. 46. Cited in Ōhama, *Meiji no gunshin*, p. 57. *Kundoku* by Kyoko Selden. According to Fujikawa Teruko (personal communication), Nogi's line echoes the most famous aphorism of the Heart Sūtra or *Hannya shingyō*, "shiki soku ze kū, kū soku ze shiki" (Form is no other than Emptiness, Emptiness is no other than Form).

96. Peattie, "The Last Samurai," p. 93, cited from Ōhama, *Meiji no gunshin*, p. 49.

97. See Lifton et al., *Six Lives Six Deaths*, p. 46.

98. Richard Michael Connaughton, *The War of the Rising Sun and Tumbling Bear: A Military History of the Russo-Japanese War 1904–5* (London: Routledge, 1988), pp. 168–169.

99. See Ōhama, *Meiji no gunshin*, p. 71. It is remarkable that, even during his relatively short exposure to a radically different culture, "Noghi" struggled to keep a diary in German, mainly noting the weather—"Schönes Wetter." "Regnet *[sic]*." "Wolkig."—or his visits with friends and officials but persisting in his efforts. Nogi jinja shamusho, ed., *Nogi Maresuke zenshū*, 4 vols. (Kokusho kankōkai, 1994), 2:437–608; reverse pagination for Nogi's handwritten diary in German, pp. 1–171. Lifton, Katō, and Reich apparently did not have access to this diary, as they assessed Nogi's stay in Germany negatively: "During the entire year abroad, Nogi never described German landscapes, towns, food, or people. Alienated by German society, he was not interested in the environment, the culture, or the people, with whom he had almost no serious communication." Lifton et al., *Six Lives Six Deaths*, p. 48.

100. See Lifton et al., *Six Lives Six Deaths*, p. 49. Minamoto Ryōen has pointed to the incompatibility of the two men's characters, grounded in their different upbring-

ings; see Minamoto, "Nogi Taishō no jisatsu to sono seishin shiteki haikei," *Kokoro* 16 (December 1963): 13.

101. See Matsushita, *Nogi Maresuke,* p. 65.

102. Peattie, "The Last Samurai," p. 97.

103. In his 1994 study, *Japan's First Modern War,* social historian Stewart Lone laments the relative paucity of research both in Japan and in the West on this short but consequential war for Asia and the Western world. According to Lone, Japanese critics have presented the Sino-Japanese war as "a war of aggression conducted by the Tennosei (Emperor system)," thereby protesting the "official" view of it as a war "to liberate Korea [from Chinese influence] and defend Japan." Lone rejects as reductionist the Marxist interpretation that Japan was seeking "to seize the Korean market." See Stewart Lone, *Japan's First Modern War: Army and Society in the Conflict with China, 1894–95* (New York: St. Martin's Press, 1994), pp. 1–3.

104. Military historian S. C. M. Paine has shed additional light on this war from the perspectives of directly involved Asian nations and indirectly involved Western nations. See Paine, *The Sino-Japanese War of 1894–1895: Perceptions, Power, and Primacy* (Cambridge: Cambridge University Press, 2003), pp. 92, 99–100, 103–106.

105. For the Imperial Rescript in English translation, see F. Warrington Eastlake and Yamada Yoshiaki, *Heroic Japan: A History of the War Between China and Japan* (London: Sampson, Low, Marston and Company, 1897; rpt. Washington, D.C.: University Publications of America, 1979), pp. I–II.

106. See Inoue Haruki, *Ryojun gyakusatsu jiken* (Chikuma shobō, 1995), p. 301.

107. See Eastlake and Yamada, *Heroic Japan,* p. 152. The fortress of Port Arthur faces that of Weihaiwei.

108. Paine, *Sino-Japanese War of 1894–1895,* p. 204.

109. Lone, *Japan's First Modern War,* p. 154; Lone warns that these figures might be inflated; see ibid., pp. 207–208, n. 28.

110. Peattie, "The Last Samurai," p. 98.

111. There were, however, rumors that the Chinese defenses were in shambles. Lieutenant-General Yamaji Motoharu (1842–1897) had boastfully predicted a quick victory. See Paine, *Sino-Japanese War of 1894–1895,* pp. 207–209.

112. See Ernst L. Presseisen, *Before Aggression: Europeans Prepare the Japanese Army* (Tucson: University of Arizona Press, 1965), p. 142: "The battle for Port Arthur showed . . . Meckel's influence. The capture of the city was accomplished in his best textbook style."

113. Meckel's pupil, Erich Ludendorff, correctly predicted that Japan, despite its relative small number of forces—only 26,000 and 13,000 reserves to capture Port Arthur—would win the war, but the Kaiser, though not the German chief of staff, remained unconvinced. See Presseisen, *Before Aggression,* pp. 140–141.

114. Lone, *Japan's First Modern War,* p. 157. Lone notes the few exceptions; ibid.

115. See the reports by foreign war correspondents Thomas Cowan (London *Times*), James Creelman (New York *World*), and Frederick Villiers (London *Standard*). See also Inoue, *Ryojun gyakusatsu jiken,* p. 86. In addition, James Allan gives a highly emotional participant-observer account of the massacre in his *Under the Dragon Flag: My Experiences in the Chino-Japanese War* (London: William Heinemann, 1898; rpt.

Wilmington, Del.: Scholarly Resources, Inc., 1973), pp. 76–100. Lone considers Allan's "explanation of his experiences at Port Arthur [as] highly suspicious." Lone, *Japan's First Modern War,* p. 208, n. 34.

116. Despite his personal involvement in the gruesome situation, James Allan managed to weigh the horrors committed on both sides: "This is war! Away, in the splendid pavilion of the vanquished, the conquering marshal, surrounded by his generals and officers, was installed in triumph, secure of his country's applause and his emperor's favour; but here, amid these desolated homes, these mutilated heaps of death, was the night side, the shadow, of their glory. And this was but the first day of four! It must be admitted that the Chinese drew it upon themselves, that everywhere else the Japanese behaved with admirable clemency and moderation . . ."; *Under the Dragon Flag,* p. 89. For Allan's description of Chinese atrocities preceding the Japanese assault on Port Arthur, see ibid., pp. 66–68.

117. See Paine, *Sino-Japanese War of 1894–1895,* pp. 210–211 and n. 67.

118. Inoue, in the first detailed study on the massacre at Port Arthur, points out that Nogi was bound to follow orders through the chain of command, from General Ōyama via the commander of the First Division of the Second Army, Lieutenant-General Yamaji Motoharu (1842–1897); see Inoue, *Ryojun gyakusatsu jiken,* pp. 115–116; 152. The massacre left an ineradicable stain on the Japanese army that had built a reputation for self-discipline and for taking a high moral ground. For examples of this perception in newspapers and for Marshal Ōyama's admonition to treat the enemy fairly, see Paine, *Sino-Japanese War of 1894–1895,* pp. 209–210.

119. Sources differ concerning the length of the massacre. Paine cites *The Japan Weekly Mail* (Yokohama) of 22 December 1894 and the *New York Times* of 18 December 1894, according to which the massacre was still going on when Thomas Cowan left the scene on 26 November. See Paine, *Sino-Japanese War of 1894–1895,* p. 212 and n. 76.

120. Although estimates of the massacred dead can hardly be expected to be accurate, James Creelman's figure of 60,000 is implausible. According to Paine, Creelman's sensationalistic tendencies cast doubt on his credibility: "The handsome Creelman was known to be willing to do just about anything for a scoop": Paine, *Sino-Japanese War of 1894–1895,* p. 210. Lone concludes, "That the entire city population was not massacred . . . is suggested by the speed with which Port Arthur's streets again filled after the Japanese occupation." Lone, *Japan's First Modern War,* p. 157.

121. See Lone, *Japan's First Modern War,* pp. 155–159.

122. See ibid., pp. 160–161. Donald Keene vividly describes the Japanese government's efforts—including bribes to foreign news agencies—to control the damage wrought by the gruesome reports by foreign correspondents; see Donald Keene, *Emperor of Japan: Meiji and His World, 1852–1912* (New York: Columbia University Press, 2002), pp. 492–495.

123. Paine, *Sino-Japanese War of 1894–1895,* p. 212. Paine refers to Ariga Nagao's book, *La Guerre Sino-Japonaise au point de vue du droit international* (Paris: A. Pedone, 1896), pp. 6, 85–86.

124. This figure is cited from the *Tōkyō Asahi Shinbun* (1 December 1894) by Inoue, *Ryojun gyakusatsu jiken,* p. 289.

125. See Inoue, *Ryojun gyakusatsu jiken*, p. 173.

126. Kamei selected three hundred of his photographs for his presentation to the emperor. After returning home from the front, he made some changes in his diary. The information on Kamei Koreaki is drawn from Inoue, *Ryojun gyakusatsu jiken*, pp. 118–119. For an edition of his diary with photographs, see Kamei Koreaki, *Nisshin sensō jūgun shashinchō* (Hakushobō, 1992).

127. See Shimana Masao, *Nogi 'shinwa' to Nis-Shin/ Nichi-Ro* (Ronsōsha, 2001), pp. 161–162.

128. Judging from his German diary, Ōgai did not seem to have the kind of fondness for Kamei that he had for Nogi; see especially the entries for 21 April and 3 November 1887 (in the latter, Kamei teases Ōgai about his modest uniform, but Nogi comes to his rescue, and Ōgai has a laugh at Kamei's expense). Heike Schöche, ed. and trans., *Mori Ōgai: Deutschlandtagebuch 1884–1888* (Tübingen: konkursbuchverlag, 1992), pp. 188, 190; 225–226. For the Kamei–Ōgai relationship, see also Yanagita Izumi, "Hakushaku Kamei Koreaki no bijutsu kenkyū oyobi bijutsuron," in Kamei, *Nisshin sensō jūgun shashinchō*, pp. 319–320.

129. See Inoue, *Ryojun gyakusatsu jiken*, p. 120.

130. See Wada Masao, ed., *Nogi Maresuke nikki* (Kin'ensha, 1970), pp. 532–534. Two additional entries, for 4 and 5 October 1896, are given in Nogi jinja shamusho, ed., *Nogi Maresuke zenshū*, 2:191–193.

131. Inoue Haruki adds to this unseemly picture a foreign war correspondent who joined the exuberant melee by galloping around the gleeful crowd. Inoue, *Ryojun gyakusatsu jiken*, p. 193.

132. For details on the parade and other celebratory events, see Fujitani, *Splendid Monarchy*, p. 125.

133. Peattie, "The Last Samurai," pp. 98–99.

134. See Paine, *Sino-Japanese War of 1894–1895*, p. 229. Paine comments, "By committing suicide, he chose a noble death and in doing so wiped away the stain of defeat and became a tragic war hero in Japan as well as in China." Ibid., p. 230.

135. Keene, *Emperor of Japan*, p. 501.

136. See Calman, *The Nature and Origins of Japanese Imperialism*, p. 20. Calman cites Basil H. Chamberlain, *Things Japanese* (London: John Murray, 1905), p. 220.

137. Graf E. zu Reventlow commented on the ease with which the Russians had snatched away Port Arthur from the Japanese with the stroke of a pen after the Sino-Japanese War. He predicted that the Japanese, having fought even harder to reclaim the fortress from the Russians, would not put up with another such stroke of a pen against them. See Graf E. zu Reventlow, *Der Russisch-Japanische Krieg: Nebst einer Beschreibung von Japan, Korea, Russisch-Asien u. einer Geschichte dieser Länder, von Dr. H. Döring*, 3 vols. (Berlin-Schöneberg: Internationaler Welt-Verlag, 1906), 2:470.

138. See Peattie, "The Last Samurai," p. 99. Peattie translates *hakushaku* as "baron."

139. See Lebra, *Above the Clouds*, p. 28. *Kazoku* ranks were formally created by imperial ordinance in 1884.

140. The emperor could rely on Nogi not to manipulate him for personal gain. In recognition of Nogi's devotion, he composed a poem as he journeyed, in November

1902, past Tabaruzaka, where the young officer had fought in 1877. He had his imperial *tanka* delivered to the "aging pine" who replied with a *tanka* on the color of the autumn leaves and the blood of his fallen comrades. For this poetry exchange, see Keene, *Emperor of Japan*, p. 582.

141. Stewart Lone has suggested that Katsura resigned his governorship of Taiwan in October 1896 because he had been "needlessly humiliated" in the intrigues of "the army minister affair." See Lone, *Army, Empire and Politics in Meiji Japan: The Three Careers of General Katsura Tarō* (London: Macmillan Press, 2000), pp. 50–51.

142. Ibid., p. 51; Peattie, "The Last Samurai," p. 99.

143. Peattie, "The Last Samurai," p. 100. Peattie cites from Nogi's instructions of 2 December 1896, in Shukuri Shigeichi, *Nogi Maresuke* (Taikyōsha, 1929), p. 399.

144. Peattie, "The Last Samurai," p. 100; quoting Ōhama, *Meiji no gunshin*, p. 81.

145. Nogi was replaced by Kodama Gentarō (1852–1906), the same person who would also replace him in the final moments in the battle for 203-Meter Hill at Port Arthur in 1904.

146. The details about the Kagawa episode are given in Peattie, "The Last Samurai," pp. 100–101.

147. Peattie, "The Last Samurai," p. 101. Peattie quotes Nogi's views on a military officer's responsibility not lying outside himself from Ōhama, *Meiji no gunshin*, p. 72: "kōtō bukantō no sekinin ni hoka narazaru nari."

148. Peattie, "The Last Samurai," p. 101. Zentsūji refers to the town famous for its temple of the same name, founded in 813 by Kūkai, posthumously known as Kōbō daishi (774–835). The town also maintains the military headquarters and one of several Nogi shrines.

149. Peattie, "The Last Samurai," p. 97.

150. Lifton et al., *Six Lives Six Deaths*, p. 51.

151. For Nogi's poem in response to Katsusuke's death, see the printed and calligraphic texts in Matsushita, *Nogi Maresuke*, pp. 141–142; for a translation, see Warner and Warner, *The Tide at Sunrise*, p. 302.

152. Warner and Warner, *The Tide at Sunrise*, p. 300.

153. Tadayoshi Sakurai, *Human Bullets: A Soldier's Story of Port Arthur*, with an introduction by Count Shigenobu Okuma, trans. Matsujiro Honda, ed. Alice Mabel Bacon (Boston and New York: Houghton, Mifflin and Company, 1907), p. 215. Originally published in Japanese as *Nikudan: Ryojun jisseki*, 1906. Sakurai's book was an international bestseller.

154. See Stanley Washburn, *Nogi* (London: Andrew Melrose, 1913), pp. 83–84. For the Japanese version, see Meguro Masumi, trans., *Nogi Taishō to Nihonjin* (Kōdansha gakujutsu bunko, 1980), pp. 64–65.

155. Roger F. Hackett, *Yamagata Aritomo in the Rise of Modern Japan, 1838–1922* (Cambridge, Mass.: Harvard University Press, 1971), p. 227.

156. Hackett, *Yamagata Aritomo*, p. 227. Hackett translated Yamagata's poem from Tokutomi Iichirō, ed., *Kōshaku Yamagata Aritomo den*, 3 vols. (Yamagata Aritomo-kō kinen jigyōkai, 1933), 3:656.

157. I have adapted the episode from Reventlow, *Der Russisch-Japanische Krieg*, 2:430–431.

158. For details on Nogi's removal from command at Port Arthur, see Peattie, "The Last Samurai," p. 118, n. 92. There had been calls for Nogi's replacement since his costly August assault on Port Arthur, and even for his suicide to atone for his lack of success; see Reventlow, *Der Russisch-Japanische Krieg,* 2:404.

159. Warner and Warner, *The Tide at Sunrise,* p. 434.

160. Lifton et al. assert that Kodama "assumed de facto control" from Nogi on 30 November, and that Nogi Yasusuke died the next day in an assault on 203-Meter Hill; *Six Lives Six Deaths,* p. 52; see also Matsushita, *Nogi Maresuke,* p. 176. In that case, neither son died directly under Nogi's command. According to Ōhama, however, Yasusuke died on 30 November; see *Meiji no gunshin,* p. 309.

161. Tomoko Aoyama deplores the fact that critics "have either ignored this text or attacked its alleged weaknesses." She argues that Ōgai's *Uta nikki* stands in the literary tradition of the eighth-century poetry collection *Man'yōshū* and travel diaries and should not be classified as twentieth-century war literature in the European sense. Aoyama, "Japanese Literary Responses to the Russo-Japanese War," in David Wells and Sandra Wilson, eds., *The Russo-Japanese War in Cultural Perspective, 1904–05* (London; New York: Macmillan; St. Martin's Press, 1999), p. 62; see also pp. 61–65.

162. All quotations of Hiroaki Sato's translation are from "General Nogi," in J. Thomas Rimer, ed., *Not a Song Like Any Other: An Anthology of Writings by Mori Ōgai* (Honolulu: University of Hawai'i Press, 2004), pp. 295–296.

163. The hill is so named because it is 203 meters above sea level.

164. The winter star informs only friends.

165. Warner and Warner, *The Tide at Sunrise,* p. 434.

166. See Reginald Hargreaves, *Red Sun Rising: The Siege of Port Arthur* (Philadelphia and New York: J. B. Lippincott, 1962), p. 84.

167. Although Stoessel was given a hero's welcome upon his return to Russia, he was court-martialed in 1907 for having surrendered despite sufficient supplies and senior officers' willingness to fight on. His death sentence was commuted to a prison term, which in turn was cut short by the czar's pardon in 1909.

168. Sebastian Dobson, "Reflections of Conflict: Japanese Photographers and the Russo-Japanese War," in Frederic A. Sharf, Anne Nishimura Morse, and Sebastian Dobson, *A Much Recorded War: The Russo-Japanese War in History and Imagery,* exh. cat. (Boston: Museum of Fine Arts, 2005), p. 52.

169. Warner and Warner, *The Tide at Sunrise,* p. 447.

170. For Nogi's speech to the cenotaph of the departed under his command, see Wada, ed., *Nogi Maresuke nikki,* p. 850. For a rendering in English, see David H. James, *The Rise and Fall of the Japanese Empire* (London: George Allen and Unwin, 1951), p. 107.

171. Among Nogi's poems, his *kanshi* on 203-Meter Hill, which he addressed as "Nireisan," or a tumulus for his brave men's spirits, is a chilling expression of his guilt; see Wada, ed., *Nogi Maresuke nikki,* p. 939.

172. Warner and Warner, *The Tide at Sunrise,* p. 448.

173. For a vivid account of this almost legendary episode, see Ruth Benedict, *The Chrysanthemum and the Sword: Patterns of Japanese Culture* (1946; rpt. New York: World Publishing, 1967), pp. 307–308.

174. Fujitani, *Splendid Monarchy*, p. 127.

175. Keene, *Emperor of Japan*, p. 619.

176. See Richard John Bowring, *Mori Ōgai and the Modernization of Japanese Culture* (Cambridge: Cambridge University Press, 1979), p. 121.

177. See Toku Baelz, ed., *Awakening Japan: The Diary of a German Doctor: Erwin Baelz* (1932; rpt. Bloomington: Indiana University Press, 1974), pp. 335–336. Originally published in German: Erwin Baelz, *Das Leben eines deutschen Arztes im erwachenden Japan* (Stuttgart: J. Engelhorns Nachf., 1931). This diary entry is dated 11 January 1905. For Kaiser Wilhelm's correspondence with Emperor Mutsuhito and General Nogi and their Russian counterparts, see Reventlow, *Der Russisch-Japanische Krieg*, 2:468–470. For an account of Nogi's Spartan appearance and his humble reception of Prinz Karl von Hohenzollern's congratulations on behalf of the German emperor, see Bronsart v. Schellendorff, *Sechs Monate beim Japanischen Feldheer* (Berlin: Ernst Siegfried Mittler und Sohn, 1906), pp. 161–163.

178. For a list of honors and awards, see Peattie, "The Last Samurai," p. 107.

179. See ibid., p. 97; p. 116, n. 47.

180. See Keene, *Emperor of Japan*, p. 720.

181. For a powerful description of this scene, see Shiba Ryōtarō, *Junshi* (1978; Bungei shunjū, 1999), pp. 125–127.

182. The term used was "kappuku," the equivalent of "seppuku."

183. Keene, *Emperor of Japan*, pp. 712–713; translated from Minamoto, "Nogi taishō no jisatsu to sono seishinteki haikei," p.15. For Nogi's report and supplication for death and the emperor's reply, see also Matsushita, *Nogi Maresuke*, pp. 186–187. The intimate exchange between Nogi and the emperor was witnessed by Duke Tokudaiji, General Okami, and two or three others. It was only after Nogi's death that General Okami divulged the content of the overheard conversation; see Minamoto, "Nogi taishō no jisatsu to sono seishinteki haikei," p. 15. Nogi's brief diary entry indicates only the importance of the audience with the emperor; see Wada, ed., *Nogi Maresuke nikki*, p. 731.

184. Lifton et al., *Six Lives Six Deaths*, p. 57.

185. Keene, *Emperor of Japan*, p. 646. For the *kanshi*, see Wada, ed., *Nogi Maresuke nikki*, p. 943; Matsushita, *Nogi Maresuke*, p. 188.

186. Properly speaking, Nogi had wanted to die and requested "appropriate" punishment for his loss of the imperial colors. Although General Yamagata had advocated "extreme" punishment, Major General Nozu merely issued a "reprimand." Thus "Nogi was pardoned because of his battlefield successes and was never punished." Lifton et al., *Six Lives Six Deaths*, p. 45.

187. Cited from Gaimushō, ed., *Komura Gaikōshi*, 2 vols. (Kuretani shoten, 1953), 2:489, in Shumpei Okamoto, *The Japanese Oligarchy and the Russo-Japanese War* (New York: Columbia University Press, 1970), p. 28.

188. Reinhard Zöllner reports such a "revealing" error in "The Sun Also Rises: Go-Daigo in Revolt," his review of *Kenmu: Go-Daigo's Revolution*, by Andrew Edmund Goble (Cambridge, Mass.: Harvard University Press, 1996), *Monumenta Nipponica* 53.4 (Winter 1998): 517. On 19 September 1912, the *Tōkyō nichinichi shinbun* portrayed Nogi as the ideal heir to Kusunoki Masashige. See Keene, *Emperor of Japan*, p. 714.

189. Among his greatest admirers were the League of the Divine Wind and, later, Mishima Yukio (1925–1970).

190. Morris describes the artistically inept Saigō thus: "He has no neck; the bomb that is his head rests squarely on a chest as solid as a launching pad"; Ivan Morris, *The Nobility of Failure: Tragic Heroes in the History of Japan* (New York: Holt, Rinehart and Winston, 1975), p. 217. Morris draws interesting parallels between Kusunoki Masashige, Ōshio Heihachirō, and Saigō Takamori, but he rarely mentions Nogi, except in footnotes. Was there a limit to the degree of failure that Morris was able to subsume under the high moral ground of nobility and sympathy for the loser *(hōganbiiki)?*

191. Morris, *Nobility of Failure,* p. 421, chap. 9, n. 46.

192. See Gregory M. Pflugfelder, *Cartographies of Desire: Male-Male Sexuality in Japanese Discourse, 1600–1950* (Berkeley: University of California Press, 1999), pp. 208–211.

193. For the account of Ōshio's and Saigō's near-drowning experiences, see Morris, *Nobility of Failure,* pp. 190–191 and 234–235.

194. Morris established a compelling parallel between Ōshio's revelatory experience of nearly drowning in Lake Biwa (not long after his retirement at age thirty-seven) and Saigō's failed attempt; see *Nobility of Failure,* pp. 190–191.

195. For a detailed evocation of Saigō's last moments and a critique of apotheosizing Saigō, see Charles L. Yates, *Saigō Takamori: The Man behind the Myth* (London and New York: Kegan Paul International, 1995), pp. 167–168. See also Morris, *Nobility of Failure,* pp. 267–268. Keene, *Emperor of Japan,* p. 284.

196. See Morris, *Nobility of Failure,* pp. 253–257.

197. For Saigō's relationship with Ōkubo, see ibid., pp. 270–272.

Chapter 4. The Sword and the Brush

1. See Takashi Fujitani, *Splendid Monarchy: Power and Pageantry in Modern Japan* (Berkeley: University of California Press, 1996), p. 149.

2. See Toshiaki Kawahara, *Hirohito and His Times: A Japanese Perspective* (Tokyo and New York: Kodansha International, 1990), pp. 20–21. Dallas Finn estimates an "audience of over 100,000"; Finn, *Meiji Revisited: The Sites of Victorian Japan* (New York: Weatherhill, 1995), p. 244.

3. Donald Keene, *Emperor of Japan: Meiji and His World, 1852–1912* (New York: Columbia University Press, 2002), p. 712.

4. See Mark R. Peattie, "The Last Samurai: The Military Career of Nogi Maresuke," *Princeton Papers in East Asian Studies* 1 (1972): 108.

5. Cited in Richard John Bowring, *Mori Ōgai and the Modernization of Japanese Culture* (Cambridge: Cambridge University Press, 1979), p. 199.

6. Robert Jay Lifton, Shūichi Katō, and Michael R. Reich, *Six Lives Six Deaths: Portraits from Modern Japan* (New Haven, Conn.: Yale University Press, 1979), p. 33.

7. Carol Gluck, *Japan's Modern Myths: Ideology in the Late Meiji Period* (Princeton, N.J.: Princeton University Press, 1985), p. 221.

8. Lifton et al., *Six Lives Six Deaths,* p. 33. Richard Bowring, citing Mori Ōgai's diary, and Edward Seidensticker assumed that the cortege left at 8 p.m. and arrived at the funeral pavilion in the Aoyama Parade Grounds as late as 11 p.m. See Bowring,

Mori Ōgai and the Modernization of Japanese Culture, p. 199; Edward Seidensticker, *Low City, High City: Tokyo from Edo to the Earthquake* (New York: Alred A. Knopf, 1983), p. 254. According to Donald Keene, the emperor's coffin "left the *arakinomiya* and was placed aboard the hearse at seven in the evening. . . . At eight . . . the solemn procession began to move slowly from the court entrance." Keene, *Emperor of Japan*, p. 710.

9. For the precise timing of Emperor Meiji's death, down to the second, see Kawahara, *Hirohito and His Times*, p. 20.

10. For a chronology and diagnosis of Emperor Meiji's illness, see ibid., pp. 18–19.

11. Fujitani, *Splendid Monarchy*, p. 146. Fujitani relies on the medical bulletins collected in *Meiji tennō gotaisōgō*, a special issue of *Fūzoku gahō*, no. 438 (October 1912), p. 37.

12. See Fujitani, *Splendid Monarchy*, p. 146.

13. Also *akari, agari, araki no miya*, or *hinkyū*, the palace of temporary interment. See my discussion, p. 19.

14. For a table on "The Chronology of Double Burial," see Gary L. Ebersole, *Ritual Poetry and the Politics of Death in Early Japan* (Princeton, N.J.: Princeton University Press, 1989), p. 130.

15. Fujitani, *Splendid Monarchy*, p. 149.

16. For Nogi's testament, see the facsimile foldout in Nogi jinja shamusho, ed., *Nogi Maresuke zenshū: ge* (Kokusho kankōkai, 1994), between pp. 550 and 551; for a modernized typed text version, see Okada Mikihiko, *Nogi Maresuke: kōki naru Meiji* (Tentensha, 2001), pp. 269–271; http://www2a.biglobe.ne.jp/~kimura/nogi.htm; for English translations, see Lifton et al., "Complete Testament of Nogi Maresuke," in *Six Lives Six Deaths*, pp. 31–32; *New York Times*, 13 October 1912.

17. My summary of these ten articles is: (1) the reasons for committing suicide; (2) the loss of his two sons and his wish not to adopt an heir; (3) the distribution of property; (4) the distribution of military articles by (Navy Officer) Tsukuda in agreement with Shizuko; (5) the donation of gifts from the emperor and the imperial family to the Gakushūin (entrusted to Messrs. Matsui and Igaya); (6) the donation of books to the Gakushūin and to the Chōfu Library; (7) the preservation of the writings by Nogi's male forebears (entrusted to either Marquis Sasaki or the Sasaki Shrine); (8) the donation of samurai weapons (received from Lord Mōri of Chōshū) to the Army Exhibition Hall; (9) the bequeathal of the Ishibayashi house to brother Shūsaku and the Nakano house to wife, Shizuko; (10) the donation of Nogi's body (except hair and [false] teeth) to a medical school, and the requirement that his nephew Masayuki be in military uniform when wearing the gold watch Nogi had received from the emperor.

18. My translation of Nogi's testament, article 1; Okada, *Nogi Maresuke*, p. 269.

19. In his description of the graveyard at Daishō-in in Hagi, Donald Keene notes the tombs of the first Mōri daimyō's seven retainers who committed junshi and the retainer of one of these who committed mata junshi. Keene, "Hagi," in *Travels in Japan* (Gakueisha, 1981), p. 100.

20. My translation of Nogi's testament, article 10, middle section; Okada, *Nogi Maresuke*, p. 270.

21. Matsushita Yoshio, *Nogi Maresuke* (Kogawa kōbunkan, 1960), pp. 214, 216.

22. For statistics on adoption, see Takie Sugiyama Lebra, *Above the Clouds:*

Status Culture of the Modern Japanese Nobility (Berkeley: University of California Press, 1993), p. 113 (Table 7) and p. 120 (Table 8).

23. Nogi struggled with the idea of ancestor worship as conceived in 1897 by Hozumi Yatsuka (1860–1912) and as required by the Civil Code of 1898, Article 987: "Ownership of the genealogical record, articles of worship, and tombs is a special right pertaining to succession to a house." For Hozumi's ideas about ancestor worship as key to the relationship between state and household, see Richard H. Minear, *Japanese Tradition and Western Law: Emperor, State, and Law in the Thought of Hozumi Yatsuka* (Cambridge, Mass.: Harvard University Press, 1970), pp. 71–76. William J. Sebald, trans., *The Civil Code of Japan* (Kobe: J. J. Thompson, 1934), p. 232; cited from Robert J. Smith, *Ancestor Worship in Contemporary Japan* (Stanford, Calif.: Stanford University Press, 1974), p. 33.

24. Lifton et al., *Six Lives Six Deaths*, p. 59.

25. See Idota Hirofumi, *Nogi Maresuke junshi—igo: hakushaku kasaikō o megutte* (Shinjinbutsu ōraisha, 1989), p. 117. For the pronunciation of Mōri's first name, see ibid., p. 135.

26. See Matsushita, *Nogi Maresuke*, p. 224, and Ōhama Tetsuya, *Meiji no gunshin: Nogi Maresuke* (Yūzankaku, 1970), p. 197.

27. See Matsushita, *Nogi Maresuke*, pp. 219, 224. Referring to Ōhama, *Meiji no gunshin*, pp. 197–201, Peattie notes that "after a number of years of controversy the second Count Nogi gave up his title in 1920"; Peattie, "The Last Samurai," 1:120, n. 123.

28. See René Girard, *Violence and the Sacred*, trans. Patrick Gregory (Baltimore and London: Johns Hopkins University Press, 1977); originally published in French as *La violence et le sacré* (Paris: Éditions Bernard Grasset, 1972).

29. In China, there was the practice of *ling chi*, "the thousand cuts," a most severe form of punishment dating back to the Five Dynasties (907–960) and last seen on 10 April 1905, when a Frenchman named Carpeaux visited Beijing and took the only known photograph of the practice; see Wang Ping, *Aching for Beauty: Footbinding in China* (Minneapolis: University of Minnesota Press, 2000; rpt. New York: Anchor Books, 2002), p. 140 and p. 141, fig. 11. Although this Chinese practice of dismemberment was not voluntary, it served the same purpose as Nogi's junshi and his wish for posthumous dismemberment. Wang Ping interprets *ling chi* as "the moment when the body of a man, through the most violent, most painful fetishization, became connected with sovereignty" (ibid., p. 141).

30. See Richard Barry, "The Suicide of a True Shintoist: Richard Barry Defends His Belief that Nogi Wished to Die for His Ideals," *New York Times*, 19 September 1912, p. 10.

31. See Oscar Ratti and Adele Westbrook, *Secrets of the Samurai: A Survey of the Martial Arts of Feudal Japan* (Rutland, Vt.: Charles E. Tuttle, 1973), p. 116.

32. Peattie, "The Last Samurai," 1:88.

33. Ivan Morris, *The Nobility of Failure: Tragic Heroes in the History of Japan* (New York: Holt, Rinehart and Winston, 1975), p. 403, chap. 8, n. 6. See also p. 469, "junshi": "not to be outdone, [Nogi's] wife, Shizuko, also killed herself."

34. Lifton et al., *Six Lives Six Deaths*, p. 34, n. 3.

35. Keene, *Emperor of Japan*, p. 712.

36. Gluck, *Japan's Modern Myths*, p. 225. The eulogist Gluck refers to is Inoue Tetsujirō, whose article she cites: "Shisō no keitōjō yori mitaru Nogi Taishō," *Jinkaku to shūyō* (Kōbundō, 1915), p. 342.

37. Gluck, *Japan's Modern Myths*, p. 224.

38. See Maurice Pinguet, *Voluntary Death in Japan*, trans. Rosemary Morris (Cambridge: Polity Press, 1993), pp. 208–209. Originally published as *La mort volontaire au Japon* (Paris: Gallimard, 1984).

39. Kawahara, *Hirohito and His Times*, pp. 20, 21.

40. See Peattie, "The Last Samurai," 1:95.

41. For the history of the impoverished but well-situated Yuji family, see Togawa Yukio, *Ningen Nogi Maresuke* (Kōjinsha, 1988), pp. 86–88. Togawa identifies Shizuko as the seventh daughter of Yuji Sadayuki (see ibid., p. 87). Ōhama identifies her as Sadayuki's fourth daughter, before marriage known as Shizuko (spelled with the kanji for "determination-harbor-female name suffix"); Ōhama, *Meiji no gunshin*, p. 62.

42. Lifton et al., *Six Lives Six Deaths*, p. 46. Cited in Ōhama, *Meiji no gunshin*, p. 57.

43. Interestingly, Nogi passed on to his sons Katsusuke and Yasusuke the second kanji, "-suke," of his given name Maresuke (having taken over, in turn, the first component "Mare" from his father Maretsugu).

44. Richard Michael Connaughton, *The War of the Rising Sun and Tumbling Bear: A Military History of the Russo-Japanese War 1904–5* (London: Routledge, 1988), p. 168.

45. Denis Warner and Peggy Warner, *The Tide at Sunrise: A History of the Russo-Japanese War, 1904–1905* (New York: Charterhouse, 1974), p. 300.

46. Ibid., p. 301.

47. I am indebted for these details to Lifton et al., *Six Lives Six Deaths*, pp. 47, 49, 51.

48. For the document and its history, see Suenaga Katsusuke, "Nogi Taishō fujin no 'Haha no oshie,'" *Bungei shunjū* 40.4 (April 1962), pp. 204–210. For a discussion of the document by Shibusawa Hideo, Enchi Fumiko, and Yoshida Sei'ichi, see "Onna daigaku no saininshiki: 'Haha no oshie' o yonde," *Bungei shunjū* 40.4 (April 1962), pp. 211–215.

49. Sharalyn Orbaugh, "General Nogi's Wife: Representations of Women in Narratives of Japanese Modernization," in Xiaobing Tang and Stephen Snyder, eds., *In Pursuit of Contemporary East Asian Culture* (Boulder, Colo.: Westview Press, 1996), p. 19.

50. Ibid., p. 12.

51. Pliny *Ep.* 3.16.6; Mart. 1.13; cf. Dio 60.16.6; Plut. *Brut.* 13.3–6. Paul Plass considers Arria's celebrated "gesture [to be] encouragement rather than threat." Plass, *The Game of Death in Ancient Rome: Arena Sport and Political Suicide* (Madison: University of Wisconsin Press, 1995), p. 112.

52. See Ryunosuke Akutagawa, "The General," trans. W. H. H. Norman, in *Hell Screen ("Jigoku Hen") and Other Stories by Ryunosuke Akutagawa* (printed in Occupied Japan; The Hokuseido Press, 1948), p. 166. Akutagawa Ryūnosuke, "Shōgun," in *Akutagawa Ryūnosuke shū*, ed., Nakamura Shin'ichirō, Nihon bungaku zenshū 22 (Shinchōsha, 1959), p. 354.

53. See Pinguet, *Voluntary Death in Japan*, pp. 208–209.

54. It is interesting that Mishima, as actor in his film *The Rite of Love and Death,* chose to use the military hat of Lieutenant Takeyama to conceal his eyes.

55. Several photographs were taken, including one with Nogi holding the hat in his hand next to his right thigh. See Kuwahara Takeshi and Sugahara Kazutora, eds., *Nogi Maresuke no sekai* (Shinjinbutsu ōraisha, 1992), dust jacket (front).

56. Roland Barthes, *Empire of Signs,* trans. Richard Howard (New York: Hill and Wang, 1982), pp. 91–94. Originally published in French as *L'empire des signes* (Genève: Éditions d'Art Albert Skira S.A., 1970). Barthes identifies the photographs of the Nogis as having been "taken the day before their suicide in September 1912. From *Japon illustré*"; ibid., p. x.

57. Orbaugh, "General Nogi's Wife," pp. 19, 20.

58. Barthes, *Empire of Signs,* p. 94.

59. Ibid., pp. 91, 94.

60. See Nakanishi Susumu, *Jisei no kotoba* (Chūō kōron shinsha, 1986), p. v.

61. For a reproduction of the Nogis' *jisei,* see *Nogi Maresuke zenshū* (1994), vol. 3 (ge), pp. 549–550; Matsushita, *Nogi Maresuke,* facing "Preface," p. 1 (Nogi's second poem) and p. 211 (Nogi's first poem and his wife Shizuko's poem).

62. Trans. Orbaugh (with Joshua Mostow), "General Nogi's Wife," p. 11.

63. Ibid.

64. Ibid., p. 22. The somewhat puzzling translation in Lifton et al., *Six Lives Six Deaths,* p. 31, reads: "Departing there is no day of return,/ Hearing the ceremonial promenade there is no meeting."

65. Orbaugh, "General Nogi's Wife," pp. 22, 23.

66. Ibid., p. 23.

67. Nakanishi Susumu regards Nogi Shizuko's *jisei* as superior to her husband's, and her composure as a sign of her independent decision to die. See Nakanishi, *Jisei no kotoba,* p. 66.

68. James Edward Ketelaar, *Of Heretics and Martyrs in Meiji Japan: Buddhism and Its Persecution* (Princeton, N.J.: Princeton University Press, 1990), p. 50.

69. Ibid., p. 44.

70. For this term, see Eric Hobsbawm and Terence Ranger, eds., *The Invention of Tradition* (Cambridge: Cambridge University Press, 1983).

71. See Fujitani, *Splendid Monarchy,* p. 152. Emperor Kōmei was the last emperor to be buried with Buddhist funeral rites, and his chief consort was laid to rest in the emperor's mausoleum at the imperial family's ancestral Buddhist temple, Sennyūji, in southeastern Kyōto; see Ketelaar, *Of Heretics and Martyrs in Meiji Japan,* p. 44.

72. Shintō funerals were not uncommon; see Elizabeth Kenney, "Shinto Funerals in the Edo Period," *Japanese Journal of Religious Studies* 27.3–4 (Fall 2000): 239–271. See also Edmund T. Gilday, "Bodies of Evidence: Imperial Funeral Rites and the Meiji Restoration," *Japanese Journal of Religious Studies* 27.3–4 (Fall 2000): 273–296.

73. For details on this debate, see Ketelaar, *Of Heretics and Martyrs in Meiji Japan,* p. 45.

74. See Matsushita, *Nogi Maresuke,* p. 204.

75. I am indebted to my student Mark E. Jolly for locating, translating, and interpreting this source as part of his Senior Honors thesis, "Nogi's Last Lesson" (University

of Massachusetts at Amherst, Department of Asian Languages and Literatures, 2000), pp. 62–66. Togawa Yukio, "Meiji no bujin," in Tsubota Itsuo, ed., *Meiji no itsuzai*, Jinbutsu tanbō, Nihon no rekishi 18 (Akatsuki kyōiku tosho, 1975), pp. 124–134.

76. For a detailed description of the imperial body's railway journey to the old capital and of the Fushimi-Momoyama mausoleum, see Dallas Finn, *Meiji Revisited: The Sites of Victorian Japan* (New York: Weatherhill, 1995), pp. 245–246 and fig. 86 (Emperor Meiji's mausoleum).

77. Japan National Tourist Organization, ed., *The New Official Guide: Japan* (Tokyo: Japan Travel Bureau, 1975), p. 675. The Nogi Jinja also houses his personal effects, including his false teeth, and several sets of statues and paintings of both Maresuke and Shizuko.

Chapter 5. Mori Ōgai's Junshi Stories

1. See Ōgai's diary entries for 13, 15, and 18 September 1912. Cited by Matsui Toshihiko, *Gun'i Mori Ōgai: tōsuiken to bungaku* (Ōfūsha, 1989), p. 13.

2. For a brief history of the relationship between Nogi and Ōgai, see Matsushima Ei'ichi, "Ōgai to Nogi Taishō," *Kokubungaku kaishaku to kanshō* 49:2 (1984): 180–185. Curiously, the men first met on 18 April 1887, during their study abroad in Berlin, Germany. In his entry for that day, Ōgai characterizes Major General Nogi as "a tall, prominent, reticent man" *(chōshin kyotō chinmokukaku no hito nari);* Mori Ōgai, *Doitsu nikki, Kokura nikki,* in *Mori Ōgai zenshū* (Chikuma shobō, 1996), 13:160. For other entries on Nogi, see 31 May, 12 June, 4 September, 10 and 23 October, 3 November, and 28 December 1887.

3. It is unclear whether Mori Oto was born in 1889 or 1890 and whether he was Ōgai's son; see Yoshiyuki Nakai, "The Young Mori Ōgai (1862–1892)" (Ph.D. diss., Harvard University, 1974), pp. 222–224.

4. Ibid., p. 129.

5. For a brilliant study of the role of writing during periods of political and cultural transition, see Jan Assmann, *Das kulturelle Gedächtnis: Schrift, Erinnerung und politische Identität in frühen Hochkulturen* (München: C. H. Beck, 1997).

6. Alan Wolfe, *Suicidal Narrative in Modern Japan: The Case of Dazai Osamu* (Princeton, N.J.: Princeton University Press, 1990), p. 33. Wolfe focuses his literary analysis on Mori Ōgai's "The Incident at Sakai" (1914); see ibid., pp. 33–34. While Stephen Snyder does not mention the impact of Nogi's death on *Gan* as the end point in Ōgai's original fiction, Dennis C. Washburn, although reluctant to attribute Ōgai's new direction toward historical fiction to Nogi's junshi, does not deny its importance. See Stephen Snyder's article "Ōgai and the Problem of Fiction: *Gan* and Its Antecedents," *Monumenta Nippponica* 49.3 (Autumn 1994), pp. 353–373, which focuses on the literary reasons why *Gan* is an end point in Ōgai's writing of one type but not on the reasons for its discontinuance; and Dennis C. Washburn, *The Dilemma of the Modern in Japanese Fiction* (New Haven, Conn., and London: Yale University Press, 1995), p. 189: "it would be misleading to claim [since Ōgai had long prepared the materials for the story about Okitsu Yagoemon] that Nogi's death by itself moved Ōgai toward an interest in historical subjects." Richard John Bowring wonders whether Ōgai was "running away from reality when he turned to history" but argues that his new "concen-

tration on historical subjects can be in large part attributed to this one event [of Nogi's junshi], although . . . other factors were leading him in the same direction." Bowring, *Mori Ōgai and the Modernization of Japanese Culture* (Cambridge: Cambridge University Press, 1979), p. 194.

7. Translated as *The Wild Geese*, 1959; *The Wild Goose*, 1995. The last three chapters of *Gan* were added in 1915 (although they were written considerably earlier); see Snyder, "Ōgai and the Problem of Fiction," p. 355, n. 8.

8. Yagoemon's birth year is 1595 in the second version of the story (see 54; 2:6). Unless otherwise noted, Ōgai page references are to Dilworth and Rimer, eds., *The Historical Fiction of Mori Ōgai* (rpt. 1991) and *Ōgai rekishi bungaku shū.*

9. According to Bowring, Ōgai did not realize his error until after the publication of the first version: "In the revised version of the work he felt obliged to change both the reason for the testament and the ending accordingly." Bowring, *Mori Ōgai and the Modernization of Japanese Culture*, p. 201.

10. The Higo domain was assessed at 540,000 *koku.* For the domains' "putative yield" or *kokudaka* statistics of 1690, see Conrad Totman, *Early Modern Japan* (Berkeley: University of California Press, 1993), p. 119 and n. 10.

11. Eiko Ikegami, *The Taming of the Samurai: Honorific Individualism and the Making of Modern Japan* (Cambridge, Mass., and London: Harvard University Press, 1995), p. 218.

12. Ikegami, *Taming of the Samurai*, p. 142.

13. Fujita Satoru cites a scholar of Date Masamune (1567–1636) who pointed out in 1995 that, according to Masamune's letters, *shibafune* is taken from the warrior Noh *Kanehira;* Fujita, "Kaidai," in *Ōgai rekishi bungaku shū*, 2:446. The ferryboat, laden with brushwood, will not take any human unless he feels a burning longing to cross the symbolic river to the other world. The *shite* in *Kanehira* speaks these heavily tinged Buddhist lines: "With the wordly chore's/ Bitterness burdened, the brushwood boat/ Ere the wood is kindled/ Burns to be rowed (Yo no waza no/ Uki no mi ni tsumu shiba-bune ya/ Takanu saki yori/ Kogaruran)." See Chifumi Shimazaki, *Warrior Ghost Plays from the Japanese Noh Theater: Parallel Translations with Running Commentary*, Cornell East Asia Series 60 (Ithaca, N.Y.: Cornell University East Asia Program, 1993), pp. 142–143.

14. See Kumakura Isao, "Kan'ei Culture and *Chanoyu*," trans. Paul Varley, in Paul Varley and Kumakura Isao, eds., *Tea in Japan: Essays on the History of* Chanoyu (Honolulu: University of Hawai'i Press, 1989), pp. 138–139.

15. Hosokawa Tadatoshi's oldest son is known by a number of names. The proper reading for Mitsuhisa is Mitsunao; see Fujita, *Ōgai rekishi bungaku shū*, 2:366; 2:27, n. 7.

16. His infant name *(yōmyō)* was Rokumaru.

17. Bowring, *Mori Ōgai and the Modernization of Japanese Culture*, p. 201.

18. Bernard Faure, *Visions of Power: Imagining Medieval Japanese Buddhism*, trans. from the French by Phyllis Brooks (Princeton, N.J.: Princeton University Press, 1996), p. 148. Faure goes on to say, "It is not simply, as it has often been presented, a final act of defiance on the part of a preeminently individualistic thinker. The deceased was apparently considered to be a collective property, a fact evidenced by the auctioning of the dead man's possessions to cover the growing costs of funerals" (ibid.).

19. The new emperor, posthumously known as Emperor Taishō, would impress himself upon the Japanese public in his own sadly pathetic way, since, "figuratively speaking, there was no one to replace him [the late Emperor Meiji]." Stephen Dodd's comment on the passing of Emperor Meiji seems to echo Murasaki Shikibu's lament on the passing of the unsurpassed hero of her *Genji monogatari:* "The shining Genji was dead, and there was no one quite like him"; Edward G. Seidensticker, trans., *The Tale of Genji,* 2 vols. (New York: Alfred A. Knopf, 1976), p. 735. Dodd relates an episode that illustrates the absurdity of succeeding an emperor of Mutsuhito's stature: "Rumors that after reading an imperial rescript, the new emperor of the Taishō period would roll it into a 'telescope' to peer at his surrounding audience." Stephen Dodd, "Different Feelings: The Intellectual Shift between Meiji and Taishō," in Amy Vladeck Heinrich, ed., *Currents in Japanese Culture: Translations and Transformations,* pp. 265–266 (New York: Columbia University Press, 1997).

20. Ōgai finished "Sahashi Jingorō" on 9 March 1913, after "Okitsu Yagoemon" (first version) and "Abe ichizoku." Fujita Satoru marvels at the short time span it took Ōgai to absorb the three-volume *Tsūkō ichiran,* published on 28 February 1913, by the time he completed "Sahashi Jingorō." See Fujita Satoru, "Kaidai," in *Ōgai rekishi bungaku shū,* 2:454.

21. For the textual history of "Sahashi Jingorō," see Fujita, "Kaidai," in *Ōgai rekishi bungaku shū,* 2:451. For a meticulous discussion of the source materials for "Sahashi Jingorō," see Ogata Tsutomu, *Mori Ōgai no rekishi shōsetsu: shiryō to hōhō* (Chikuma shobō, 1979), chapter "Sahashi Jingorō: ji," pp. 115–133. Originally published as "'Sahashi Jingorō' no tenkyo to hōhō," in *Bungaku* 32 (October 1964).

22. See Seita Fumitake, "Mori Ōgai no rekishi shōsetsu ni okeru ningenzō no keisei: 'matsu' 'taeru' to iu keiki o chūshin ni," in Nihon bungaku kenkyū shiryō kankōkai, ed., *Mori Ōgai II,* Nihon bungaku kenkyū shiryō sōsho, 100 vols. (Yūseidō, 1979; 4th rpt. 1991), 46:194–195. Seita believes that Ōgai may have chosen his original title out of nostalgia for things past and lost; see ibid. On the timing and circumstances of the title change, see also Bowring, *Mori Ōgai and the Modernization of Japanese Culture,* pp. 208 and 281, n. 8.

23. The general consensus is that Ōgai himself wrote the advertising announcement *(kōkokubun)* for *Iji,* but Yamazaki Kazuhide has raised some doubts; see Katsukura Toshikazu, "Mori Ōgai 'Sahashi Jingorō' shiron: ekken no ba no kōzu to Nikkan heigō mondai ni tsuite," *Fukushima Daigaku kyōiku gakubu ronshū,* 63 (December 1997): 71, n. 2.

24. Bowring, *Mori Ōgai and the Modernization of Japanese Culture,* p. 205.

25. Fujita Satoru notes that the heron scene is Ōgai's invention; see Fujita Satoru, "Kaidai," in *Ōgai rekishi bungaku shū,* 2:453.

26. Ōgai uses the kanji for *kizu* that means "flaw, blemish, defect, disfigurement, bruise" rather than the one that means "wound, injury, cut, scar." The choice of kanji seems to point to Jingorō's excellent martial skills, in that he manages to knock out Hachiya with such a clean blow that there seems to be no "disfigurement." J. Thomas Rimer's translation, "No sign of any *wound* could be found on his body" (my emphasis), underlines the supernatural power with which Hachiya's life had been taken—like the heron's the day before. All fingers point to Jingorō, who has disappeared. Rimer, trans.,

"Sahashi Jingorō," in David Dilworth and J. Thomas Rimer, eds., *The Historical Fiction of Mori Ōgai* (1977; rpt. Honolulu: University of Hawai'i Press, 1991), p. 250.

27. According to Fujita Satoru's biographical character entry, the "cousin" Sahashi Gendayū died in 1653, at the age of sixty-one; see Fujita Satoru, "Kaidai," in *Ōgai rekishi bungaku shū,* 2:92; 347. As has been noted, this cannot be the cousin whom Ōgai names as the one who negotiated with Ieyasu the terms of Jingorō's first return not long after Hachiya's first death anniversary in about 1578.

28. See Katsukura, "Mori Ōgai 'Sahashi Jingorō' shiron," pp. 80–79 (reverse pagination).

29. Eric Wesley Johnson, "Mori Ōgai: The Fiction from 1909 to Early 1914" (Ph.D. diss., University of Chicago, 1973), p. 268.

30. Katsukura has noted that Ieyasu's terms contain the threat of a death penalty in case of Jingorō's failure. Katsukura, "Mori Ōgai 'Sahashi Jingorō' shiron," pp. 80–79 (reverse pagination).

31. See Ogata, *Mori Ōgai no rekishi shōsetsu,* p. 130.

32. See ibid.

33. Ōgai uses the term *wakashu* (2:94, 95) to suggest that Jingorō had assumed the role as Amari's boy lover.

34. The incident, involving Nobuyasu's mother (Tsukiyama-dono), is known as the Tsukiyama Incident (Tsukiyama-dono jiken). Katsukura Toshikazu points to Jingorō's perception of Ieyasu's moral hypocrisy when he orders his son and wife to die; see Katsukura, "Mori Ōgai 'Sahashi Jingorō' shiron," p. 76.

35. Bowring, *Mori Ōgai and the Modernization of Japanese Culture,* p. 207.

36. Ogata, *Mori Ōgai no rekishi shōsetsu,* p. 132. Ogata makes a rough comparison between Sahashi Jingorō and Takenouchi Kazuma (1623–1643) in "Abe ichizoku," men who act on impulse upon being rebuffed by their lords.

37. See ibid., p. 133. On the grounds that there is no historical evidence of rebellion *(hangyaku)* or resistance *(hankō),* Katsukura objects to critics who follow Ogata's view that Jingorō rebels against the feudal structure by turning his back on Japan; Katsukura, "Mori Ōgai 'Sahashi Jingorō' shiron," pp. 80–79 (reverse pagination).

38. See Katsukura, "Mori Ōgai 'Sahashi Jingorō' shiron," p. 76.

39. My translation of "Rekishi sono mama to rekishibanare." For an English translation of the essay by Darcy Murray, see Dilworth and Rimer, eds., *Historical Fiction of Mori Ōgai,* pp. 179–184.

40. Stephen Turnbull, *Samurai Invasion: Japan's Korean War 1592–1598* (London: Cassell, 2002), p. 235. The information on the Korean embassies is derived from Turnbull's account; ibid., pp. 235–236. Turnbull mistakenly gives the year 1608 for the Korean embassy and Sō Yoshitoshi's name as Yoshitomo.

41. Ieyasu's son repatriated 1,340 Koreans. Ieyasu's fear of being outwitted from abroad is not unfounded even if it was Yoshitoshi rather than Jingorō who secretly took a profit from the embassy (although one need not rule out Jingorō's profit taking).

42. Ieyasu's fear of exposing his anxiety prevents him from confronting the Korean official and asking him if he is indeed Jingorō. This encounter, like the previous ones (mediated by Jingorō's cousin and Ieyasu's chief retainer), is hypothetical. The "Korean" official is a character invented by Ōgai (see 2:87, n. 7).

43. Karatani Kōjin, *Origins of Modern Japanese Literature,* translation edited by Brett de Bary (Durham, N.C., and London: Duke University Press, 1993), p. 152.

44. Karasumaru Mitsuhiro is also famous for having solved the *Mu kōan,* "Does a dog have Buddha nature?" and for writing a poem about his *satori* for the Zen monk Isshi Bunshu (1608–1646), who had given him instructions. See Stephen Addiss, *The Art of Zen: Paintings and Calligraphy by Japanese Monks, 1600–1925* (New York: Harry N. Abrams, 1989), pp. 37, 39.

45. The Hosokawa also took the head of the rebel's charismatic young leader, Amakusa Shirō, whose real name was Masuda Tokisada (1621–1638).

46. Marcel Mauss, *The Gift: Forms and Functions of Exchange in Archaic Societies,* trans. Ian Cunnison (New York: W. W. Norton, 1967), p. 41. Mauss's *Essai sur le don: Forme archaïque de l'échange* was first published in 1925.

47. We hear of no personal feelings as he is wounded in the Shimabara Rebellion (except that he may implicitly have envied his brother's glorious death, just as Nogi envied his brother's and mentor's deaths in the Hagi uprising).

48. See *Mori Ōgai zenshū* (1971; Chikuma shobō, 1995), 4:227, n. 7. Fujita Satoru's note explains *saizō no daion* as the obligation incurred upon being granted life when one expected to die; *Ōgai rekishi bungaku shū,* 2:13, n. 8.

49. Yagoemon's year of death is given alternately as 1648 and 1660.

50. The Kōtōin was established in 1601 by Hosokawa Tadaoki, who had, just the year before, ordered the execution of his Christian wife, Gracia (1578–1600), to avoid her capture by the enemy. Tadaoki studied Zen under the young Seigan. Since he was twenty-five years older than Seigan, and Seigan was ten years older than Yagoemon, it is possible to see Seigan as a pivotal link between lord and subject, and perhaps as a repository of both men's displaced affection. For Seigan Sōi's career as a Zen abbot and calligrapher, see Addiss, *The Art of Zen,* pp. 40–41; plate 17.

51. Allen Guttmann and Lee Thompson, *Japanese Sports: A History* (Honolulu: University of Hawai'i Press, 2001), p. 108.

52. Ibid., p. 50.

53. See ibid., p. 52. It is interesting to note that the then ruler of Satsuma Province was Shimazu Hisamitsu (1817–1887), the successor of Saigō Takamori's lord Shimazu Nariakira (1809–1858).

54. The first version is marked as "first manuscript/ draft" *(shokō).*

55. Bowring, *Mori Ōgai and the Modernization of Japanese Culture,* p. 205.

56. There are several translations (listed in alphabetical order): David Dilworth, trans., "Abe ichizoku," pp. 59–99, in Dilworth and Rimer, eds., *Historical Fiction of Mori Ōgai;* Hiroaki Sato, trans., "The Abe Family," in Hiroaki Sato, *Legends of the Samurai* (Woodstock, N.Y.: The Overlook Press, 1995), pp. 341–379; Tomoko Yamamoto, trans., with corrections by Veronica M. Jeffers, *The Abe Family, by Mori Ōgai* (Tokyo: Personal Publishing Service of Asahi Shimbun, 1990).

57. Dates given in my analysis of "Abe ichizoku" refer to the year in the Western calendar, followed by the month and day according to the lunar calendar.

58. The correct reading of the name bestowed in 1642 on Tadatoshi's oldest son is Mitsunao; see Fujita, *Ōgai rekishi bungaku shū,* 2:27, n. 7.

59. The phrase "the brush and sword in accord" *(bunbu no itchi)* apparently was

in need of reinvigoration in the eighteenth century; see Robert T. Singer, with contributions by Herman Ooms et al., *Edo: Art in Japan 1615–1868*, exh. cat., National Gallery of Art, Washington, D.C. (New Haven, Conn.: Yale University Press, 1998), p. 132.

60. Unless otherwise noted, the translation cited is that by Sato, *Legends of the Samurai.*

61. Ōgai's spelling for *shide no yama,* or "mountain of departure for death," is unusual in that the usual kanji for "departure" is replaced by "heaven."

62. Sato translates *fuji* (S: 347) as "Incomparable" and explains in a footnote that this set of kanji is an alternate reading for Mount Fuji. David Dilworth translates *fuji* as "All is One"; see Dilworth, trans., "The Abe Family," in Dilworth and Rimer, eds., *Historical Fiction of Mori Ōgai,* p. 71. Tomoko Yamamoto does not attempt a translation of the two characters; see Yamamoto, trans., *The Abe Family,* p. 12.

63. Donald Keene, trans., *Major Plays of Chikamatsu* (New York: Columbia University Press, 1961), pp. 49–50.

64. Ikegami, *Taming of the Samurai,* p. 219.

65. Naitō Saheiji was, in reality, Chōjūrō's younger cousin; Fujita, *Ōgai rekishi bungaku shū,* 2:37, n. 1.

66. Expectations of family reward for junshi would take a turn for the macabre when, after the Tokugawa shōgunate's ban on junshi in 1663, families were punished, sometimes by decimating or extinguishing the family line. See Ikegami, *Taming of the Samurai,* pp. 219–220.

67. Marvin Marcus, "Mori Ōgai and the Biographical Quest," *Harvard Journal of Asiatic Studies* 51.1 (June 1991): 237.

68. Marvin Marcus, *Paragons of the Ordinary: The Biographical Literature of Mori Ōgai* (Honolulu: University of Hawai'i Press, 1993), pp. 72, 73.

69. Carlin A. Barton, *Roman Honor: The Fire in the Bones* (Berkeley: University of California Press, 2001), p. 13.

70. Delayed by the elders, Gosuke was the last of the eighteen retainers to commit junshi with Tadatoshi's permission.

71. Ikegami has noted that "*Junshi* was sometimes related to the homosexual association of the master and vassal"; Ikegami, *Taming of the Samurai,* p. 219.

72. Translators do not agree on the manner of execution. Sato and Yamamoto translate *shibarikubi* (4:270) as death by hanging (S: 366; Yamamoto, 54), while Dilworth (p. 87) translates the term *shibarikubi* as used during *sengoku jidai* (according to one of the two definitions given in the *Kōjien*): Gonbē was "decapitated while kneeling with his hands tied behind his back . . . he was beheaded in broad daylight as if he were some common thief." For the historical date of Priest Ten'yū's departure from Kumamoto and for the manner of Gonbē's execution, see Fujita, *Ōgai rekishi bungaku shū,* 2:61, nn. 4 and 6.

Chapter 6. Mori Ōgai's "Sakai jiken"

1. *New York Times,* 4 June 1868, in Kokusai nyūsu jiten shuppan iinkai, ed., *Gaikoku shinbun ni miru Nihon 1852–1873,* vol. 1, pt. 2 (Mainichi Communications, 1989), p. 477. See also *New York Times,* 18 May 1868, in ibid., p. 472. Fears of assassi-

nation in the legation in Edo were running so high that some foreigners committed suicide; see Lord Redesdale (Algernon Bertram Freeman-Mitford), *Memories*, 2 vols. (1915; rpt. New York: E. P. Dutton, n.d.), 1:389.

2. The historical facts of the event were—and will probably remain—unclear. Historians eventually agreed that eleven French sailors were killed by Tosa men who were on duty in Sakai. Beyond that, there is little agreement about what happened and no consensus about the moral significance of the facts. From the perspective of most foreigners, the Sakai Incident was entirely the fault of the Japanese, who had trapped and threatened French sailors innocently seeking some onshore entertainment. John R. Black, for example, blamed the Sakai Incident entirely on the Japanese: "How shall I describe the feelings of indignant horror with which foreigners of all nationalities were filled on hearing of this treacherous, cold blooded, and cruel assault upon unarmed, unsuspicious men, who had a few moments before been showing their good-feeling by sharing their bread with Japanese children." Black, *Young Japan: Yokohama and Yedo 1858–79*, with an introduction by Grace Fox, Oxford in Asia Historical Reprints, 2 vols. (1883; rpt. Tokyo: Oxford University Press, 1968), 2:167–168.

From the perspective of many Japanese, in contrast, the behavior of the French had been highly provocative and disrespectful. Marius B. Jansen described the grappling of the Japanese with "self-confident outsiders" almost as if he were applying Sir Francis Hall's observations to the Sakai Incident: "On the one hand commoners' discovery that the samurai, for all their vaunted bravery and courage, seemed helpless to do anything about this [strutting about], had to speed the realization that Japan's social structure no longer made much sense. For sworded samurai and *rōnin*, on the other hand, such unconscionable behavior must have been an infuriating reminder of inferiority. Add liquor to such rage, and another careless foreigner was likely to be in danger of his life"; Jansen, *The Making of Modern Japan* (Cambridge: The Belknap Press of Harvard University Press, 2000), p. 317. Nakayama Gishū (1900–1969) was critical of the Tosa soldiers for having shot at French sailors who were fleeing from the scene of the altercation. He also noted that the French sailors fled without resisting, as is clear from the types of wounds found on their dead bodies; see Nakayama, "Tosa hei no yūkan na hanashi," in *Nakayama Gishū*, Nihon no bungaku 61 (Chūō kōronsha, 1967), pp. 479, 485. Originally published in 1965.

3. The High Treason or Kōtoku Incident (Taigyaku *jiken*; Kōtoku *jiken*) of 1911 has also been mentioned as a source of inspiration for Ōgai's "Sakai jiken;" see, e.g., Ogata Tsutomu, *Mori Ōgai no rekishi shōsetsu: shiryō to hōhō* (Chikuma shobō, 1979), p. 205; Ōoka Shōhei, "'Sakai jiken' no kōzu: Mori Ōgai ni okeru kirimori to netsuzō," in Ōoka Shōhei, *Bungaku ni okeru kyo to jitsu* (1975; rpt. Kōdansha, 1976), p. 49. However, this incident may be better reflected in Ōgai's "Ōshio Heihachirō," a story that expresses resistance to the authorities' censorship and other forms of thought control. Immersing himself in the life of Ōshio Heihachirō, in turn, may have prompted Ōgai to move to a different but related topic treated in a source already in his possession and to write "Sakai jiken." For the source, see Sasaki Kōzō, *Senshū: Sakai rekkyo shimatsu* (1893); reprinted in Tosa shidankai, ed., *Senshū: Sakai do hanshi rekkyo jikki: Myōkokuji no seppuku*, Tosa shidan fukkoku sōsho 3 (Kōchi: Tosa Shidankai, 1979).

4. The term *junshi shōsetsu* is used for Ōgai's "Okitsu Yagoemon no isho," "Abe ichizoku," and the heterodox "Sahashi Jingorō." See Fukumoto Akira, "*Iji:* bihō no 'seiri' ni koraeeru fukashigi na shōhakusei," in *Mori Ōgai,* Issatsu no kōza, Nihon no kindai bungaku (Yūseidō, 1984), 6:113–126.

5. For the textual history and reception of "Sakai jiken," see Fujita Satoru, "Kaidai," in *Ōgai rekishi bungaku shū* (Iwanami shoten, 2000), 2:461–465.

6. I have consulted Sasaki, *Senshū,* reprinted in Tosa shidankai, ed., *Senshū.*

7. Sasaki's death date is unknown according to Yamamoto Takeshi, "'Rekkyo jikki' no jisshō shugi ni tsuite," in Sasaki, *Senshū,* reprinted in Tosa shidankai, ed., *Senshū* (1979), p. 2.

8. See Ōoka, "'Sakai jiken' no kōzu," p. 11.

9. Ōgai was less meticulous in finding the best historical sources on the Sakai Incident than he had been in his previous historical novellas, "Abe ichizoku" (January 1913) and "Ōshio Heihachirō" (January 1914); see Ogata, *Mori Ōgai no rekishi shōsetsu,* pp. 204–205. For an extensive discussion of historical sources concerning the Sakai Incident, see Ōoka Shōhei, *Sakai-kō jōi shimatsu* (Chūō Kōronsha, 1989). Originally published in *Chūō kōron bungei tokushū* (Winter 1984–Winter 1988). Page numbers refer to the reprint.

10. H. S. Versnel, "Destruction, *devotio,* and Despair in a Situation of Anomy: The Mourning for Germanicus in Triple Perspective," in Giulia Piccaluga, ed., *Perennitas: Studi in Onore di Angelo Brelich* (Rome: Ateneo, 1980), p. 554.

11. Mori Ōgai, "Ōshio Heihachirō," in *Ōgai rekishi bungaku shū* (Iwanami shoten, 2000), 2:238. For translations of this passage, see Richard John Bowring, *Mori Ōgai and the Modernization of Japanese Culture* (Cambridge: Cambridge University Press, 1979), p. 213; Marvin Marcus, *Paragons of the Ordinary: The Biographical Literature of Mori Ōgai* (Honolulu: University of Hawai'i Press, 1993), pp. 138–139; Shion Kono, "Self-Commentary in Mori Ōgai's Historical Fiction and the Rhetoric of Annotation in Modern Japan," forthcoming in the *Journal of Japanese Studies* (Summer 2006).

12. See Ōgai's famous essay "Rekishi sono mama to rekishibanare" (January 1915). Unless otherwise noted, all translations in the chapter on "Sakai jiken" are my own. Through his implicit juxtaposition of past and present events, Ōgai engaged the reader in asking critical questions about the continuity and discontinuity of Japanese values. As Dennis C. Washburn interprets Ōgai's efforts to arrive at a theory of historical narratives, "Although constrained by the demand that they record events as they are or were, historical narratives must always suggest the contingency of events, the possibility of different outcomes, not merely to create aesthetic interest but to create space for the interpretation of events." Washburn, *The Dilemma of the Modern in Japanese Fiction* (New Haven, Conn.: Yale University Press, 1995), p. 192.

13. Jan Assmann, *Das kulturelle Gedächtnis: Schrift, Erinnerung und politische Identität in frühen Hochkulturen* (München: C. H. Beck, 1997), pp. 33, 34. My translation.

14. Describing the narrative technique of Ishikawa Jun (1899–1987), William Jefferson Tyler adopted Ishikawa's phrase *awasekakō,* or "writing on simultaneously," in "The Art and Act of Reflexivity in *The Bodhisattva,*" in Tyler, trans., *The Bodhisattva or Samantabhadra: A Novel by Ishikawa Jun* (New York: Columbia University Press, 1990), p. 152.

15. Alan Wolfe, *Suicidal Narrative in Modern Japan: The Case of Dazai Osamu* (Princeton, N.J.: Princeton University Press, 1990), p. 33.

16. By the lunar calendar, as used in Ōgai's story, the Sakai Incident occurred in Keiō 4.II.15.

17. For a full account, see Reinier H. Hesselink, "The Assassination of Henry Heusken," *Monumenta Nipponica* 49.3 (Autumn 1994): 331–351.

18. For a contemporary account, see F. G. Notehelfer, ed., *Japan through American Eyes: The Journal of Francis Hall, Kanagawa and Yokohama, 1859–1866* (Princeton, N.J.: Princeton University Press, 1992), pp. 447–451, 454, 468, 469, 470, 516.

19. In the Richardson Affair, the British demanded £100,000 from the Tokugawa shōgunate and £25,000 from Satsuma, making a total of 440,000 silver dollars. For details, see Conrad Totman, *The Collapse of the Tokugawa Bakufu, 1862–1868* (Honolulu: University of Hawai'i Press, 1980), pp. 14–15; 68–73. See also Jansen, *The Making of Modern Japan*, pp. 314–315.

20. For the complex negotiations leading up to and following the Satsuei War, see Mitsuru Hashimoto, "Collision at Namamugi," trans. Betsey Scheiner, *Representations* 18 (Spring 1987): 84–87.

21. Gordon Daniels, "The British Role in the Meiji Restoration: A Re-Interpretive Note," *Modern Asian Studies* 2.4 (1968): 310.

22. Max von Brandt was attaché, or *dairi kōshi* (1867–1868), and minister plenipotentiary, or *zenken kōshi* (1872–1875), to Japan.

23. Max von Brandt, *Dreiunddreissig Jahre in Ost-Asien: Erinnerungen eines deutschen Diplomaten*, 3 vols. (Leipzig: Georg Wigand, 1901), 2:189. My translation. See 2:204–207 for a description of the incident itself.

24. Grace Fox, *Britain and Japan, 1858–1883* (Oxford: Clarendon Press, 1969), p. 221.

25. After all, von Brandt argued, the Japanese were aiming so high that only two people were wounded by their initial volleys. See von Brandt, *Dreiunddreissig Jahre in Ost-Asien*, 2:185–186.

26. Among these treaties were the Harris Treaty of 29 July 1858 and the Treaty of Edo, signed on 26 August 1858. After the Meiji Restoration, revising the so-called Unequal Treaties became the ambition of the Japanese government.

27. Fox, *Britain and Japan*, p. 223.

28. Sir Ernest Satow, *A Diplomat in Japan* (1921; rpt. New York: ICG Muse, 2000), pp. 322–323; 324. Sir Harry Parkes, an advocate for clemency in the Bizen Affair, emphasized that the Japanese had shared the judgment of capital punishment: "The offender had been sentenced to death, not upon the demand of the foreign Representatives only, but because, as stated by the Japanese authorities in communication with the Representatives, he had incurred that penalty according to Japanese law." Hugh Cortazzi, ed., *Mitford's Japan: The Memoirs and Recollections, 1866–1906, of Algernon Bertram Mitford, the first Lord Redesdale* (London: Athlone Press, 1985), p. 82.

29. The new government may have changed its mind about condemning Hiki to death not because it wanted to comply with the foreigners' wishes but because of Hiki's political importance. Hiki, the second son of Ikeda Izumo and adopted into the Hiki family, was quite wealthy, with an income of 16,000 *koku*. More important, the

new government might have wanted to cultivate this man because of the loyalist passion he had displayed in 1867 in the form of a proposal to the highest *bakufu* council *(rōjū)* to abolish the tyranny of the *bakufu* and restore imperial power. Although Hiki had to suffer temporary confinement at the time of his retainer Taki's *kappuku,* he later had the honor of serving in the *han*'s Ikeda contingent with Emperor Meiji's eastern expedition (Meiji Tennō *tōsei*). For data on Hiki, see Miyazaki Tomihachi and Yasuoka Akio, eds., *Bakumatsu ishin jinmei jiten* (Shinjinbutsu ōraisha, 1994), p. 800.

30. Satow, *A Diplomat in Japan,* p. 327. According to Mitford, this officer was "Taki Zensaburo," Cortazzi, ed., *Mitford's Japan,* pp. 80, 84.

31. See von Brandt, *Dreiunddreissig Jahre,* 2:185–186; 193.

32. See Satow, *A Diplomat in Japan,* pp. 337, 340. Donald Keene notes that "Purists in Japan prefer *kappuku.* But regardless of name, the act consisted of drawing a dagger deeply across the abdomen to reveal that the intestines were free of impurity." Keene, *Emperor of Japan: Meiji and His World, 1852–1912* (New York: Columbia University Press, 2002), p. 750, n. 17.

33. It would take two more incidents, the Sakai Incident of 8 March and the assault on Parkes of 23 March, for foreigners to realize that punishment by seppuku was more honorable than punitive and that it created martyrs. On 28 March, the imperial government posted an edict that promised to deter attacks on foreigners by stripping convicted criminals of samurai status, and hence the right to receive punishment by seppuku. Mitford, who had been entrusted to demand such an edict, tries to bring home to readers of his 1915 *Memoirs* the monumental change for the Japanese warrior class: "Only think of what [execution like common criminals] must mean to these proud and chivalrous heirs of the centuries! The privilege of self-immolation was one of the dearest and most precious rights of the very class which had brought about the revolution, the class, indeed, to which the members of the Government themselves belonged"; Redesdale, *Memories,* p. 465. See also the continuing debate on the edict, in ibid., pp. 492–494.

34. Cortazzi, ed., *Mitford's Japan,* p. 87.

35. Foreigners seem to have suspected substitutions since the days of Francis Hall; see Notehelfer, ed., *Japan through American Eyes,* p. 451: "It has been stated that a man has been delivered up to the government who was one of the assailants in the recent affray upon the Tokaido, that he is in fact the one who slew Richardson. But who knows that this is the man, or some poor coolie or malefactor, who is made to represent him."

36. According to Saigō Takamori, "Hiki Tatéwaki, the *karō* who was riding in the palanquin, could not be regarded as free from blame, and that he would be imprisoned in the charge of three clans. The officer who had been riding on horseback would be executed [i.e., Taki]." Satow, *A Diplomat in Japan,* p. 334.

37. Maurice Pinguet refers to Taki's seppuku as *tsumebara,* or "forced" seppuku with ritual self-control, the highest form of self-punishment under the Tokugawa penal code for samurai. See Pinguet, *Voluntary Death in Japan,* trans. Rosemary Morris (1984; rpt. Cambridge: Polity Press, 1993), pp. 130, 136, 144, 150–152.

38. See von Brandt, *Dreiunddreissig Jahre,* 2:194.

39. See ibid., 2:194–198.

40. Cortazzi, ed., *Mitford's Japan*, p. 82.

41. Ibid., pp. 88–89.

42. The report was countersigned by Satow. Although Parkes was personally inclined toward clemency and the commutation of Taki's sentence, precisely because "the life of no foreigner had been lost," he was in the minority; see Cortazzi, ed., *Mitford's Japan*, p. 83. Parkes became "so convinced of Imperial goodwill that he regarded the execution of the Bizen officers *[sic]* as an unnecessary punishment." Daniels, "The British Role in the Meiji Restoration," p. 310.

43. Satow, *A Diplomat in Japan*, p. 342; for a direct quotation of Taki's words, see Cortazzi, ed., *Mitford's Japan*, p. 86.

44. See Nakayama, "Tosa hei no yūkan na hanashi," p. 477.

45. See V. Dixon Morris, "The City of Sakai and Urban Autonomy," pp. 23–54, in George Elison and Bardwell L. Smith, eds., *Warlords, Artists, and Commoners: Japan in the Sixteenth Century* (Honolulu: University of Hawai i Press, 1981).

46. Cited in Michael Cooper, ed., *They Came to Japan: An Anthology of European Reports on Japan, 1543–1640* (Berkeley: University of California Press, 1965), p. 329.

47. The last shōgun was the seventh son of Tokugawa Nariaki (1800–1860), lord of Mito. Yoshinobu was adopted into the Hitotsubashi family and was also known as Hitotsubashi Keiki.

48. For "Sakai jiken," page references are to volume 2 of Mori Ōgai, *Ōgai rekishi bungaku shū* (Iwanami shoten, 2000).

49. The port of Hyōgo and the city of Ōsaka were opened to foreigners on New Year's Day of 1868. Article 3 of "Regulations for the trade and residence of foreigners at Osaka" specified, "The town of Sakai is outside the limits, but foreigners will be at liberty to visit it"; Document No. 1, Enclosure No. 1, R. B. Van Valkenburgh to William H. Seward, 2 January 1868, in *Papers Relating to Foreign Affairs 1868*, Third Session of the Fortieth Congress, 1868, Part I (1869; rpt. New York: Kraus Reprint, 1965), p. 611. Although the port of Sakai was still closed, the Foreign Office had instructed the garrison in Sakai not to obstruct surveying troops dispatched by foreigners. See Ishii Takashi, *Meiji ishin no kokusaiteki kankyō* (Yoshikawa kōbunkan, 1966), p. 800, and Document No. 25, R. B. Van Valkenburgh to William H. Seward, 11 March 1868, in *Papers*, pp. 698–699.

50. Originally from a small fief at Kakegawa in Tōtōmi Province, Yamanouchi Kazutoyo (1546–1605; Tosa daimyō 1600–1605) was richly rewarded for his part in the struggle for power between Toyotomi Hideyoshi (1536/37–1598) and Tokugawa Ieyasu. Although he did not fight in the decisive battle of Sekigahara (1600), Kazutoyo's shift of allegiance to Ieyasu brought him the Tosa domain. For this great gift, which included the assignment to the Yamanouchi of the Tosa *gōshi*, or "country samurai" who were originally the vassals of the previous Tosa daimyō family of Chōsokabe, the Yamanouchi remained deeply indebted to the Tokugawa *bakufu*. For a history of *gōshi* and the creation of this rank in 1613, see Marius B. Jansen, *Sakamoto Ryōma and the Meiji Restoration* (1961; rpt. Princeton, N.J.: Princeton University Press, 1994), pp. 26–32.

51. Takechi Zuizan was also known as Hanpeita.

52. Jansen, *Sakamoto Ryōma*, pp. 108–109; cited from the Tosa Loyalist Party's

manifesto in volume 1 of Nihon shiseki kyōkai, ed., *Takechi Zuizan kankei monjo*, 2 vols. (1916; rpt. Tōkyō Daigaku shuppankai, 1972), 1:36–53.

53. See Jansen, *Sakamoto Ryōma*, pp. 118–120.

54. See Jansen, ibid., pp. 148–151.

55. Even after his retirement—forced by his tyrannical opponent Ii Naosuke (1815–1860) in 1859—Yōdō, rather than his son and successor, had remained in charge of Tosa. To the bitter end, Yōdō continued to advise the dying Tokugawa regime on how to survive, not by continuing its old policies, but by carrying out political and military reforms.

56. For a description of the *Icarus* Affair, see Jansen, *Sakamoto Ryōma*, pp. 304–11. Satow, *A Diplomat in Japan*, p. 266: "Old Yōdō said that he had received a letter from a friend advising him to try to compromise the matter, as the English were greatly incensed at the murder of their men, but he would do nothing of the kind. If his people were guilty he would punish them; he could do no more; but if they were innocent he would declare their innocence through thick and thin." The charges against Tosa were withdrawn on 4 October 1867. A year later a Fukuoka man was found to have committed the crime and then suicide. See Jansen, *Sakamoto Ryōma*, pp. 307–308 and n. 73.

57. In the end, however, Yōdō would in turn be persuaded by moderate Tosa restorationists like Sakamoto Ryōma (1835–1867) and Gotō Shōjirō (1838–1897) to avoid a clash with loyalist rebels from Chōshū and Satsuma and to join their coup d'état to abolish the shōgunate. It was during this demoralizing time in Yōdō's otherwise prominent political career that he was confronted with the Sakai Incident.

58. Not only that, Yōdō had provoked the emperor's coming out of hiding, so to speak, when at the Kogosho Conference (Kogosho *kaigi*) of 3 January 1868 he "accused Iwakura [Tomomi (1825–1883)] and others of 'stealing the emperor,' no less." John Breen, "The Imperial Oath of April 1868: Ritual, Politics, and Power in the Restoration," *Monumenta Nipponica* 51.4 (Winter 1996): 417.

59. Cortazzi, ed., *Mitford's Japan*, p. 97; see also pp. 96, 100.

60. Ibid., p. 98. Dr. William Willis (1837–1894) was present to cure Yōdō's bout with a severe illness. See also Hugh Cortazzi, "The Pestilently Active Minister: Dr. Willis's Comments on Sir Harry Parkes," *Monumenta Nipponica* 39.2 (1984): 156.

61. Cortazzi, ed., *Mitford's Japan*, p. 103. After the fall of the shōgunate, Yōdō was willing to embrace the emperor as his new lord. The last shōgun, Yoshinobu, himself expressed his adaptability when, at the breaking point, he told a concerned Roches that "No matter what the situation, it is impossible for me to challenge the Tennō. . . . [e]ven if I die I cannot oppose the throne"; Akiyama Kenzō, *The History of Nippon*, trans. Toshirō Shimanouchi (Kokusai Bunka Shinkokai, 1941), p. 248. After his banishment and his retirement in October 1869, Yoshinobu was in the 1890s "restored to honor" by the emperor. Not surprisingly, he himself, "in his memoirs (1915) and in an authorized biography (1918), became a loyalist." Marius B. Jansen, ed., *The Emergence of Meiji Japan* (Cambridge: Cambridge University Press, 1995), pp. 195, 197.

62. When ordered to return on 12 March, Mitford gave Yōdō's message of apology to the French minister; see Ōoka, *Sakai-kō*, p. 229.

63. Satow, *A Diplomat in Japan*, p. 348.

64. Mitford describes M. Roches as "a handsome swashbuckler, who had been an interpreter in the French army in Algeria. He was far more a picturesque Spahti than a diplomatist"; Cortazzi, ed., *Mitford's Japan*, p. 22. Medzini explains that Roches "was not accustomed to multinational action." Fellow diplomats criticized his policies in Japan as *"politique personnelle"*; Meron Medzini, *French Policy in Japan during the Closing Years of the Tokugawa Regime*, Harvard East Asian Monographs 41 (Cambridge, Mass.: Harvard University Press, 1971), pp. 72, 74, 227, n. 1. More recently, Roches received the sophisticated scrutiny of Jean-Pierre Lehmann, who views the flamboyant diplomat's difficulties with Sir Harry Parkes and other foreign delegates residing in Japan within the context of his earlier missions to Algeria, Tangiers, Trieste, Tripoli, and Tunis. Lehmann emphasizes Roches' ability to form intimate ties not only with Arab leaders but with the shōgun Yoshinobu (or Keiki), whose officials came to him "when the internal political situation was getting worse"; Lehmann, "Léon Roches—Diplomat Extraordinary in the Bakumatsu Era: An Assessment of His Personality and Policy," *Modern Asian Studies* 14.2 (1980): 287. As before to the Arabs, Roches felt an uncanny affinity to the Japanese; see ibid., p. 290. Although he could see that the shōgunate was doomed, he stood by Yoshinobu, believing that "the alternative to the shogunate was xenophobic, feudal anarchy," as expressed in the Bizen Affair and the Sakai Incident; ibid., pp. 303; 303, n. 98. Lehmann assesses Roches' economic and military legacy as positive, but concedes that "as a diplomat there can be no doubt that Roches was a complete failure in Japan; he had totally misjudged the situation." Ibid., p. 305.

65. Léon Roches' five demands are enclosed, in English, in Document No. 35, R. B. Van Valkenburgh to William H. Seward, 8 April 1868, in *Papers*, p. 711. See also Medzini, *French Policy*, p. 168. For a French rendering in *Le Moniteur Universel*, 18 May 1868, see Kokusai nyūsu jiten shuppan iinkai, ed., *Gaikoku*, vol. 1, pt. 2, p. 472. According to the official view, the Japanese were "pleased with the moderation with which the French Minister was treating the affair"; Satow, *A Diplomat in Japan*, p. 349. In his letter to his wife of 19 March 1868, Parkes credits himself with making "reasonable" Roches' demands with "some reductions, made I think at my instance." Stanley Lane-Poole and Frederick Victor Dickins, *The Life of Sir Harry Parkes*, 2 vols. (1894; rpt. Wilmington, Del.: Scholarly Resources, 1973), 2:83. See also Kunaichō, ed., *Meiji tennō ki*, 13 vols. (Yoshikawa kōbunkan, 1968–1975), 1:630.

66. See Ōoka, "'Sakai jiken' no kōzu," pp. 26–27.

67. Medzini, *French Policy*, p. 168.

68. Mark David Ericson, "The Tokugawa *Bakufu* and Léon Roches" (Ph.D. diss., University of Hawai'i, 1978), p. 319. Ericson relies on Japanese scholarship that stresses "the moderate and subdued response of Roches to the Sakai massacre." Ibid., p. 329, n. 123.

69. *Documents Diplomatiques 1869*, No. XI (Janvier 1869) (Paris: Imprimerie Impériale, 1869), p. 213; my translation. In reality, Roches' subordinates had encountered serious resistance and chosen retreat over defeat: "The commanding officer of the Dupleix immediately sent armed boats toward the shore, but finding the forts were manned and every preparation had been made to resist an attack, prudently retired to

his ship"; Document No. 25, R. B. Van Valkenburgh to William H. Seward, 11 March 1868, in *Papers*, p. 699. According to Ōgai, Censor General Sugi, perplexed by the incident, ordered the Tosa men to fortify Sakai, with volunteers from the recently defeated *bakufu* forces (see "Sakai jiken," 2:272).

70. See Ericson, "The Tokugawa *Bakufu*," p. 318. See also Document No. 13, R. B. Van Valkenburgh to William H. Seward, 28 February 1868, in *Papers*, pp. 677–678; enclosure: memorandum of neutrality, signed on 28 February1868 by the foreign delegates (and a representative of Roches), p. 678.

71. See Satow, *A Diplomat in Japan*, p. 350.

72. Cortazzi, ed., *Mitford's Japan*, p. 99; see also Satow, *A Diplomat in Japan*, p. 351.

73. Although Ōgai erroneously thought, on the basis of his source, that the French had originally demanded the execution of twenty men, it was the Japanese themselves who seem to have arrived at this number. The French had merely demanded that the officers and those guilty of killing the eleven sailors be executed. Unable or unwilling to specify a number, the French absolved themselves of investigating and left the burden of establishing guilt to the Japanese authorities. Although the specific numbers emerging from the Japanese side were arbitrary, their incremental reduction is significant, as the planned executions were transformed into a series of self-sacrifices. For the list of French demands, see the note by Léon Roches to the imperial government, 12 March 1868, in *Papers*, p. 711; see also Medzini, *French Policy*, p. 168; and Parkes, in a letter to his wife of 19 March 1868, Lane-Poole and Dickins, *The Life of Sir Harry Parkes*, 2:83: Roches "demanded (1) the execution of the men concerned in the massacre, leaving it to the Japanese to determine the number—reserving however a limit beyond which he would not have been contented." See also Ōgai, "Sakai jiken," 2:275, n. 8.

74. Kokusai nyūsu jiten shuppan iinkai, ed., *Gaikoku*, vol. 1, pt. 2, p. 472. My translation.

75. Cortazzi, ed., *Mitford's Japan*, p. 104.

76. Ibid.

77. Von Brandt, *Dreiunddreissig Jahre*, 2:208. My translation.

78. See Satow, *A Diplomat in Japan*, p. 351, n. *.

79. Ibid., p. 344.

80. Satow chose to overlook the facts that more than twenty men had professed their implication in the slaughter of the eleven French sailors and that the number "twenty"—for the Tosa men—had been set arbitrarily by the French minister, at least according to his understanding; see ibid., p. 350.

81. Criticized by a Christian journalist for attending Taki's seppuku, Satow revealed how greatly impressed he was by Taki's dignity and courage. "As for being ashamed of having been present at a *harakiri* on the ground that it was a disgusting exhibition, I was proud to feel that I had not shrunk from witnessing a punishment which I did my best to bring about. It was no disgusting exhibition, but a most decent and decorous ceremony, and far more respectable than what our own countrymen were in the habit of producing for the entertainment of the public in the front of Newgate prison." Ibid., pp. 343–344.

82. It is important to note, though, that von Brandt and Parkes understood du

Petit Thouars' abrupt leave not as a termination but as a postponement of the executions; see von Brandt, *Dreiunddreissig Jahre,* 2:208. According to Sir Harry Parkes, "the French officers applied for the reprieve of the remaining nine and the executions were stayed." Letter to his wife of 19 March 1868, in Lane-Poole and Dickins, *The Life of Sir Harry Parkes,* 2:84.

83. Bergasse de *[sic]* Petit Thouars, letter presumably to the commander of the *Vénus,* 16 March 1868, in *Papers,* p. 713.

84. Bergasse de *[sic]* Petit Thouars, letter presumably to the commander of the *Vénus,* 16 March 1868, in *Papers,* p. 713.

85. Parkes, letter to his wife of 24 March 1868, cited in Lane-Poole and Dickins, *The Life of Sir Harry Parkes,* 2:88. Parkes wrote about having escaped an assassination attempt, on 23 March, en route to an audience with the emperor. The audience with the emperor was postponed to 26 March, and Parkes and Mitford were the first foreigners not only to hear but to see the emperor. See Redesdale, *Memories,* pp. 456–461.

86. Shimazaki Tōson, *Before the Dawn,* trans. William E. Naff (Honolulu: University of Hawai'i Press, 1987), p. 421. The list of writers who have touched upon the Sakai Incident extends to the present. See, for example, Nakazawa Shōji, *Ozannen-san,* 2 vols. (Orijin shobō, 1977). For a list of authors who have used the Sakai Incident, see Okabayashi Kiyomi, " 'Rekkyo jikki' to 'Sakai jiken,' " in Tosa shidankai, ed., *Senshū: Sakai do hanshi rekkyo jikki: Myōkokuji no seppuku,* pp. 29–30. Tosa shidan fukkoku sōsho 3 (Kōchi: Tosa shidankai, 1979).

87. Steve Rabson has suggested that the two authors had clashed over authenticity of narration. Ōgai "overreacted" in his coauthored review of Tōson's "Utatane" (November 1897; Restless sleep) to elements of the fantastic in "a story that dwells on the suffering caused by armed conflict [the Sino-Japanese War] and portrays military men and their missions in this context." Steve Rabson, "Shimazaki Tōson on War," *Monumenta Nipponica* 46.4 (Winter 1991): 457.

88. Ōgai's count of thirteen dead French sailors (p. 271) is based on his source, Sasaki, *Senshū,* p. 8. Ōoka Shōhei attributes the error to misreading one Frenchman's name as three; Ōoka, " 'Sakai jiken' no kōzu," p. 19. Richard Bowring also notes that thirteen foreigners were shot; Bowring, *Mori Ōgai,* p. 214. David Dilworth mistranslates "sixteen dead" for Ōgai's thirteen (Dilworth and Rimer, eds., *The Historical Fiction,* p. 133), and Alan Wolfe reports "the eventual deaths of sixteen French soldiers" (Wolfe, *Suicidal Narrative,* p. 33). For the count of eleven Frenchmen who died in the altercation, see Keene, *Emperor of Japan,* p. 132; Satow, *A Diplomat in Japan,* p. 349; Medzini, *French Policy,* p. 168. In reference to Roches' letters of 11 and 15 March 1868 to Marquis de Moustier, Jean-Pierre Lehmann notes that "fifteen French sailors were massacred." Lehmann, "Léon Roches," p. 303, n. 98.

89. The only source for the flag episode known to me is Sasaki, *Senshū,* p. 7. There is no mention of flag theft in Max von Brandt's detailed account of the Sakai Incident; see von Brandt, *Dreiunddreissig Jahre,* 2:205–207. On 8 March 1868, Bergasse du Petit Thouars reported on the details of the Tosa men's assault on the French without mentioning flags, nor did he mention them in his follow-up report on 10 March 1868. Léon Roches was equally unaware of his men's violation of the Japanese flag in his report to Count de la Tour on 10 March; ironically, he wondered whether "the French

flag" had provoked the Tosa men and went on to appeal to the Minister of the King of Italy to help "shield all flags and all foreigners from similar indignities [such as the Sakai outrage]." R. B. Van Valkenburgh does not mention the Japanese flag in his account of 11 March to William H. Seward, Secretary of State, Washington, D.C. Provided that there was no cover-up of the flag incident, one has to assume that the foreign delegates never learned about it from the French soldiers, who were either killed or wounded or simply unaware that one of them had taken the Japanese flag. Not surprisingly, they also did not hear about it from the Japanese, who would not have wanted to divulge the incident, partly because they were ashamed to have lost the flag and also because Umekichi had triggered the deadly shooting spree with his violent retrieval of the flag. As du Petit Thouars indicated on 8 March, "the men firing at the crew of the launch have not furnished the shadow of a pretext to the abominable crime of which they have been the victims." For the reports cited above, see *Papers*, pp. 701–702; 703–704; 700–701; 699; 702.

90. The seed for a new system of allegiance of the common soldier to his emperor was planted, and Richard John Bowring has pointed out that "it is this shift which will enable General Nogi to die with his Emperor over forty years later"; Bowring, *Mori Ōgai*, p. 215. Were the Tosa men emulating Takechi Zuizan (1829–1865), the leader of Tosa's *sonnō jōi* faction? Known as "*Tennōzuki*, 'Emperor lover,'" Takechi was forced to commit seppuku in 1865; Jansen, *Sakamoto Ryōma*, pp. 149, 87. See also Albert M. Craig, *Chōshū in the Meiji Restoration*, Harvard Historical Monographs 47 (Cambridge, Mass.: Harvard University Press, 1961), pp. 154; 193–194.

91. The *Icarus* Affair occurred on 5 August 1867.

92. From his list of names, Ōgai seems to have omitted Kakiuchi Tokutarō (1848–?), one of the twenty-nine, because he conflated Doi's family name and Kakiuchi's first name by mistake (see "Sakai jiken," 2:276 and 2:277, n. 6).

93. Ōgai refers to forty-one men who denied involvement in the shooting of the French. This leaves three men unaccounted for.

94. Yōdō's order is delivered by the *han* elder *(karō)* Fukao Kanae (1827–1890) (2:275), not, as in Dilworth's translation, by Nagao Tarobē (Dilworth and Rimer, eds., *The Historical Fiction*, p. 136).

95. Ōgai's text here refers to twenty common soldiers *(heisotsu);* this is later adjusted to include the two officers and their lieutenants. See Ōgai, "Sakai jiken," 2:275 and n. 8.

96. Since Yōdō cannot be certain at this moment that Date will be able to negotiate seppuku for the men with Roches, he can only encourage them to die honorably. The provocative term Yōdō's representative Fukao uses is "criminal" or "murderer" *(geshunin)*, which, for ordinary people, implied punishment by beheading. See ibid., 2:278 and n. 2.

97. In his handling of the Sakai Incident, Yōdō anticipates Emperor Meiji, who declared, on 5 April 1868, the "inseparable quality of politics and ritual" *(saisei itchi no gofukoku)* and decreed, following the legendary Emperor Jimmu, that his subjects "perform sacrifice to the Heavenly Deities, and therewith develop filial duty"; Breen, "The Imperial Oath of April 1868," p. 417. Breen highlights the aspect of sacrifice as legitimization of imperial rule, in reference to the *Nihongi;* see W. G. Aston, trans.,

Nihongi: Chronicles of Japan from the Earliest Times to A.D. 697 (1896; rpt. Rutland, Vt., and Tokyo: Charles E. Tuttle, 1972), p. 134.

98. Nathan Rosenstein, "Sorting out the Lot in Republican Rome," *American Journal of Philology* 116.1 (1995): 44, n. 7; 69, n. 81.

99. According to Satow, Date Munenari reported to Sir Harry Parkes concerning his negotiations with Roches, "Two officers and eighteen rank and file were to perform *harakiri* at Sakai at 2 p.m."; Satow, *A Diplomat in Japan*, p. 351. Ōoka notes that Date needed the names of twenty men quickly—by lot—so that he could solicit Roches' consent to twenty Tosa men's *kappuku* with Japanese *kaishakunin* in return for the imperial court's granting of his five demands. News from Date about his successful negotiation did not arrive until midnight of 15 March. See Ōoka, *Sakai-kō*, pp. 236–238.

100. For the terminology of positive and negative charges contained within the sacrificial victim, see Carlin A. Barton, "The Emotional Economy of Sacrifice and Execution in Ancient Rome," *Historical Reflections/ Réflexions Historiques* 29.2 (Summer 2003): 350–351.

101. Ōgai seems to have thought that the French set the number of men to die. For the argument that it had been left to the Japanese to determine the number, see n. 73.

102. Dario Sabbatucci, "Ordeal," trans. Miriam Friedman, in Mircea Eliade, ed., *Encyclopedia of Religion*, 16 vols. (New York: Macmillan, 1987), 11:92.

103. See Ōgai, "Sakai jiken," 2:279, n. 3. See also Ōoka, *Sakai-kō*, pp. 227–228.

104. See James Edward Ketelaar, *Of Heretics and Martyrs in Meiji Japan: Buddhism and Its Persecution* (Princeton, N.J.: Princeton University Press, 1990), pp. 7, 87ff. Divine Imperial rule began with the legendary Emperor Jimmu's founding of the nation.

105. *Kodansha Encyclopedia of Japan*, 9 vols., 1st ed. (Tokyo and New York: Kodansha International, 1983), 6:101 ("omikuji").

106. Those who rejected their "luck" did so because their willingness for sacrifice remained in principle only and was not allowed to flower into action. In their view, the principle of devotion to a cause may have been religiously sanctioned, but when not acted upon, came into conflict with the principle of honor. Even the least educated among them would have heard of the unity of knowledge and action promoted by sixteenth-century Chinese neo-Confucianist Wang Yangming (J. Ō Yōmei, 1472–1528) and his followers in Japan, including the groundbreaking leaders of the Meiji Restoration.

107. For the first usage of *junnan*, in 1872, see Nihon Kokugo Daijiten Dainihan Henshū Iinkai, ed., *Nihon kokugo daijiten*, 14 vols. (Shōgakukan, 2002), 6:1483.

108. On New Year's Day of 1878, Nogi Maresuke summed up the previous year's traumatic events in the last line of a *zekku*, most notably his loss of the imperial banner in the Satsuma Rebellion: *waga mi wa sunawachi kore shi shite tami o amasu*; Ōhama Tetsuya, *Meiji no gunshin: Nogi Maresuke* (Yūzankaku, 1970), p. 57; Wada Masao, ed., *Nogi Maresuke nikki* (Kin'ensha, 1970), p. 184. A more literal translation than "living as though dead" is "My body is nothing but a subject spared death."

109. Paul Varley, *Warriors of Japan as Portrayed in the War Tales* (Honolulu: University of Hawai'i Press, 1994), p. 38.

110. The term *kenshin* was first used in 1900. *Nihon kokugo daijiten*, 5:69 (Ōgai's "Saigo no ikku" [1915] is listed).

111. Seppuku was a traditional privilege of the samurai class that would, only three years later, be denied. Furthermore, the "Revised Laws of 1873 *(Kaitei ritsurei)* abolished *jisai* as the *shizoku*'s legal prerogative, forcing the *shizoku* to surrender an important right, the right to determine the manner and timing of their death in cases of criminal conviction"; John M. Rogers, "Divine Destruction: The Shinpūren Rebellion of 1876," in Helen Hardacre with Adam L. Kern, eds., *New Directions in the Study of Meiji Japan* (Leiden: Brill, 1997), p. 419. For a case of speedy justice for Japanese would-be assassins of foreigners in 1871, see Keene, *Emperor of Japan*, p. 767, n. 34.

112. No one has better formulated the universal applicability of this pattern than Victor Turner: "when a major public dramatic process gets under way, people, whether consciously, preconsciously, or unconsciously, take on roles which carry with them, if not precisely recorded scripts, deeply engraved tendencies to act and speak in suprapersonal or 'representative' ways appropriate to the role taken, and to prepare the way for a certain climax that appropriates to the nature of the climax given in a certain central myth of the death or victory of a hero or heroes . . . in which they have been deeply indoctrinated or 'socialized' or 'enculturated' in the vulnerable and impressionable years of infancy, childhood, and latency." Turner, "Hidalgo: History as Social Drama [1970]," in Turner, *Dramas, Fields, and Metaphors: Symbolic Action in Human Society* (Ithaca, N.Y., and London: Cornell University Press, 1974), p. 123.

113. Wolfe, *Suicidal Narrative*, p. 34.

114. Thomas M. Huber, *The Revolutionary Origins of Modern Japan* (Stanford, Calif.: Stanford University Press, 1981), p. 3.

115. Ibid., p. 226.

116. See George M. Wilson, *Patriots and Redeemers in Japan: Motives in the Meiji Restoration* (Chicago: University of Chicago Press, 1992). The frenzied mass movement known as *ee ja nai ka* or "what the hell" lasted from fall 1867 to spring 1868; see Wilson, *Patriots and Redeemers*, p. 100.

117. The first order was issued by Fukao Kanae (1827–1890) on behalf of Lord Yōdō (for twenty men to sacrifice themselves willingly) and by Kominami on behalf of Lord Toyonori (for nine men to be eliminated by lot from sacrifice).

118. For Roches' consent, see Ōoka, *Sakai-kō*, pp. 236–238. In his report, Roches does not acknowledge his consent; le Ministre de France au Japon [Léon Roches] au Ministre des affaires étrangères, 19 March 1868, *Documents Diplomatiques 1869*, p. 215.

119. Unaware of Date's arrangement with Roches, critics disagree on who issued permission for seppuku in Ōgai's story. In his translation, David Dilworth points to Lord Toyonori (Dilworth and Rimer, eds., *The Historical Fiction*, p. 139). Ōoka Shōhei argues that the instructions were Yōdō's (Ōoka, "'Sakai jiken' no kōzu," p. 33). Nakayama Gishū maintains that, through tawdry, soothing words, the cunning Yōdō and Kominami deceived the sixteen men into meekly accepting their fate of voluntary death, inspired by honor (Nakayama, "Tosa hei," p. 481).

120. See Ōgai, "Sakai jiken," 2:284 and n. 5.

121. It is ironic that Kominami, who was first stripped of rank and family name by Yōdō for joining Takechi's loyalist cause in 1862 and then restored to honor in 1867 as great inspector *(ōmetsuke)*, is now in a position vicariously to confirm his loy-

alist beliefs. For Kominami's involvement in Takechi's movement, see Jansen, *Sakamoto Ryōma,* p. 121.

122. See ibid., pp. 149, 151.

123. For the rites of dressing up the victim in sacrifice, see Henri Hubert and Marcel Mauss, *Sacrifice: Its Nature and Function,* trans. W. D. Hall (Chicago: University of Chicago Press, 1969), pp. 29–30 (originally published as "Essai sur la nature et la fonction du sacrifice," *L'Année sociologique,* 1898): "These adornments imparted to [the sacrificial victim] a religious character"; ibid., p. 29. For the importance of the "proper ritual form" and "formal etiquette" of seppuku, which "not only signified the honor of the accused individual but embodied the authority of the state as well," see Eiko Ikegami, *The Taming of the Samurai: Honorific Individualism and the Making of Modern Japan* (Cambridge, Mass., and London: Harvard University Press, 1995), pp. 254, 255.

124. David Dilworth mistakenly gives Minoura's name as Shinoura throughout his translation of "Sakai jiken," see Dilworth and Rimer, eds., *The Historical Fiction.*

125. Minoura's *kanshi* is prominently positioned on the inside of Sasaki Kōzō's book cover; for the *kanshi* in context, see Sasaki, *Senshū,* pp. 46–47; 57. For extensive discussion of this and other farewell poems *(jisei),* see Ōoka, *Sakai-kō,* pp. 267–274.

126. Ōgai's narrator comments on Minoura's *kanshi,* emphasizing the commander's outdated adherence to the antiforeign stance of *jōi.* Ironically, Minoura expresses this antiforeign stance through poetry in foreign script, which is subject to many prosodic rules but open to a variety of Japanese readings *(yomikudashi* or *kundoku).* In his brief history of *kanshi,* Burton Watson notes that "[i]n a time when strict seclusionist policies were in force the *kanshi* represented a kind of defiant gesture in the direction of internationalism." Burton Watson, trans., *Kanshi: The Poetry of Ishikawa Jōzan and Other Edo-Period Poets* (Berkeley, Calif.: North Point Press, 1990), p. xiii.

127. Fujita notes that in his youth Minoura served as Yōdō's tutor (and that the commander of the Eighth Tosa Infantry Division, Nishimura Saheiji [1845–1868], was Yōdō's page); *Ōgai rekishi bungaku shū* 2:372, 360; see also Ōoka, *Sakai-kō,* p. 230. If it is true that the sixteen-year-old Minoura tutored his lord, a retired daimyō twice his age (rather than Yōdō's fourteen-year-old son Toyonori, nominal Lord of Tosa since 1859), then Minoura recalls the genius of Yoshida Shōin (1830–1859), who at age ten lectured his lord, Mōri Takachika (1819–1871), on military strategy. Ōgai also presents Minoura as having "tutored Lord Yōdō" *(Yōdō-kō no jidoku ni nari)* (2:290) in 1860. Subsequently Minoura was in attendance on Lord Yōdō for seven or eight years.

128. See Ōoka, "'Sakai jiken' no kōzu," pp. 38–39.

129. Curiously, Ōgai does not make use of the Japanese *waka* that are also given in his source. (This seems especially odd because two of the *waka* use the term *kōkoku.*) Satow cites prose translations of the "Patriotic death poems by the men who suffered the extreme penalty [and which] were afterwards circulated among the people"; Satow, *A Diplomat in Japan,* p. 351; for the poems, see ibid., pp. 351–352. See also Sasaki, *Senshū,* pp. 57–60. Ōoka Shōhei has pointed out Satow's omission of the poems by Minoura and Ikegami Yasakichi (1831–1868); see Ōoka, *Sakai-kō,* p. 269.

130. The famous topos of poetry and the bell occurs in T'ang poetry and in the Noh *Miidera,* for example. See Karen Brazell, ed., *Traditional Japanese Theater: An Anthology of Plays* (New York: Columbia University Press, 1998), pp. 170–175.

131. For the definitions of *devotio, votum,* and *consecratio,* see H. S. Versnel, "Two Types of Roman *Devotio,*" *Mnemosyne* 29 (1976): 367–369.

132. I am following the times suggested in Ōgai, "Sakai jiken," 2:294, 296.

133. Nakayama Gishū explains the seconds' difficulties by pointing to their inexperience and their close relationship with the men they must kill as inhibiting factors. See Nakayama, "Tosa hei," p. 482.

134. Seneca the Younger, forced to commit suicide in 65 C.E., remarked in *De providentia* II.12 about Cato's struggle to commit suicide, "to seek death needs not so great a soul as to reseek it." *Seneca: Moral Essays,* trans. John W. Basore, 3 vols. (1928; rpt. Cambridge, Mass.: Harvard University Press, 1963), 1:13.

135. Bergasse du Petit Thouars reported a sudden change of place to his superiors on 16 March 1868: "contrary to the agreement, the Japanese had notified the lieutenant in command of the forces landed that the execution would not take place on the wharf, but in a temple at some distance from the landing-place"; Document No. 35, R. B. Van Valkenburgh to William H. Seward, 8 April 1868, *Papers,* p. 713. The change helped to dissociate the Tosa men's purpose at Myōkokuji from the crime they were accused of having committed on the wharf at Sakai.

136. Satow clearly realized that the judicial system needed to be improved to solve international conflicts. He suggested "the establishment of mixed courts for trying cases between foreigners and Japanese, instead of deciding them according to the laws of the defendant's nationality." Satow, *A Diplomat in Japan,* p. 335.

137. Another attack on foreigners occurred only a few days later, on 23 March 1868, en route to an audience with the emperor; it was described by two of the assaulted men, Sir Harry Parkes (in a letter to his wife of 24 March) and Algernon B. Mitford (in a letter published in the London *Times* of 20 May 1868); cited in Lane-Poole and Dickins, *The Life of Sir Harry Parkes,* 2:87–89; 89–95.

138. Wolfe, *Suicidal Narrative,* p. 34.

139. For details on Watsuji Tetsurō's (1889–1960) concept of *kenshin,* see Varley, *Warriors of Japan,* pp. 32–33, 37, 59, 179.

140. Cortazzi, ed., *Mitford's Japan,* p. 104. See also von Brandt, *Dreiunddreissig Jahre,* 2:208. Satow does not mention any curses but instead gives the Tosa men's death poems, written before their seppuku. Satow, *A Diplomat in Japan,* pp. 351–352, n. *.

141. For even more viciously antiforeign language, see Sasaki, *Senshū,* p. 47.

142. Anthony F. C. Wallace, with the assistance of Sheila C. Steen, *The Death and Rebirth of the Seneca* (New York: Alfred A. Knopf, 1970), pp. 103, 105.

143. H. S. Versnel has argued that a lawless, anomic state can trigger self-destruction; see Versnel, "Destruction, *devotio,* and Despair in a Situation of Anomy," p. 573, n. 157.

144. Barton, "Emotional Economy," p. 344.

145. In contrast to the disrupted seppuku of the Tosa men, the ritual procedure in the Bizen Affair went smoothly, although it was, beneath the surface, equally subversive. Taki performed his *kappuku* in the prescribed manner without uttering a single curse. Mitford, an eyewitness, quotes Taki's words: "'I and I alone unwarrantably gave the order to fire on the foreigners at Kobe, and again as they tried to escape, on

the 11th of last month (4 February). For this crime I disembowel myself, and I beg you who are present to do me the honour of witnessing the act' " (Cortazzi, ed., *Mitford's Japan*, p. 86). The foreigners were impressed, but failed to see that Taki, while acknowledging his "crime," was dying for—and on behalf of—his lord (Hiki).

146. Ideally, the witness of *devotio* would perceive the curse as an appeal for justice; see Barton, "Emotional Economy," p. 344, n. 11, citing H. S. Versnel, "Beyond Cursing: The Appeal to Justice in Judicial Prayers," in Christopher A. Faraone and Dirk Obbink, eds., *Magika Hiera: Ancient Greek Magic and Religion* (New York and Oxford: Oxford University Press, 1991), pp. 60–106.

147. For this pattern, see Hubert and Mauss, *Sacrifice*, pp. 39–40: "the most perfect way of effecting communication was to hand over to the sacrifier a portion of the victim, which he consumed."

148. Hubert and Mauss, *Sacrifice*, p. 28. Hubert and Mauss define "sacrifier" thus: *"We give the name 'sacrifier' to the subject to whom the benefits of sacrifice . . . accrue, or who undergoes its effects."* Ibid., p. 10 (original emphasis).

149. See Bergasse de *[sic]* Petit Thouars, letter of 16 March 1868, presumably to the commander of the *Vénus*, in *Papers*, p. 713. Quoted above; see p. 133.

150. Hubert and Mauss, *Sacrifice*, p. 62.

151. See Sasaki, *Senshū*, p. 52.

152. Satow, *A Diplomat in Japan*, p. 351, n. *.

153. For this comparison, see Sasaki, *Senshū*, p. 70.

154. See Ōoka, " 'Sakai jiken' no kōzu," pp. 46–47. See Sasaki, *Senshū*, pp. 69–70.

155. See Ogata, *Mori Ōgai*, p. 209.

156. David Dilworth attributes the verdict of exile to Lord Toyonori (Dilworth and Rimer, eds., *The Historical Fiction*, p. 150), but the original is nonspecific; by attaching the honorific *go/mi* to the term *shobun* (5:124) for "punishment" or "disposal," the text merely points to a higher authority than the censor.

157. Roches asked Date to halt the punishment of the remaining nine men and sent a petition to the emperor to spare their lives on 17 March; see Ōgai, "Sakai jiken," 2:301, n. 2. Was it in hope of creating some emotional distance from the seppuku at Myōkokuji that the men were kept in limbo about the commutation of their sentence? The historical facts reveal that they could have been told as early as 23 March, when the new government had informed Toyonori of the commutation of their sentence to exile.

158. Elizabeth Wilson (Mitchell), "Reading Ōgai's 'Sakai jiken': An Exercise in Disclosing Meanings," unpublished paper (University of Michigan, Department of Asian Languages and Cultures, 11 September 1989), pp. 13, 14.

159. Yoshiyuki Nakai notes that a "break in the Mori family line occurred in 1842, twenty years before Ōgai's birth, when, for some unknown reason, the eleventh generation, Mori Shūan, was banished from the domain by the daimyo." One Sasada Tsunakiyo continued the Mori house as Mori Hakusen, Ōgai's grandfather; Yoshiyuki Nakai, "The Young Mori Ōgai (1862–1892)" (Ph.D. diss., Harvard University, 1974), p. 2. The themes of banishment and the continuation of the family line also loom large in Ōgai's "Sanshō Dayū" (January 1915; Sanshō the Steward).

160. Matsushima Ei'ichi has cast doubt on scholars' emphasis on the demotion that Ōgai's appointment supposedly entailed. According to Ōgai's *Kokura nikki*, Ōgai

probably associated this disillusioning appointment with traditional bureaucratic practices of the past, but persevered and was transferred in 1902 to the first division in Tōkyō. Matsushima sees Ōgai's Kokura experience as representative of Meiji-era vicissitudes. Matsushima Ei'ichi, "Ōgai to Nogi Taishō," *Kokubungaku kaishaku to kanshō,* 49.2 (January 1984): 181.

161. Helen M. Hopper has highlighted Ōgai's critical role in Japanese society for the years 1909–1912, referring back to the 1890s: "In the late 1890s Ōgai had focused his power as editor of the Japanese Medical Journal on attacking leaders of the medical profession, including his superiors in the army, for their incompetence. The controversy which ensued was violent and finally Ōgai was transferred, banished in fact, from Tokyo to a small outpost in Kokura, Kyushu." Hopper, "Mori Ōgai's Response to Suppression of Intellectual Freedom, 1909–12," *Monumenta Nipponica* 29.4 (Winter 1974): 391.

162. J. Thomas Rimer, *Mori Ōgai* (Boston: Twayne Publishers, 1975), p. 28.

163. Eric Wesley Johnson describes the parting scene: "Ōgai's son Oto, his mother Mineko, and his two younger brothers went to the station to see him off. Ōgai was already aboard the train when an unexpected latecomer walked through the platform gate and came up to his window. It was General Nogi"; Johnson, "Mori Ōgai: The Fiction from 1909 to Early 1914" (Ph.D. diss., University of Chicago, 1973), p. 16. See also Bowring, *Mori Ōgai,* p. 121. It is interesting that during Ōgai's time in Kokura Nogi spent about three "happy" years as head of the Eleventh Division at Zentsūji in Kagawa Prefecture, Shikoku. See Mark R. Peattie, "The Last Samurai: The Military Career of Nogi Maresuke," *Princeton Papers in East Asian Studies* 1 (1972): 100.

164. Hubert and Mauss, *Sacrifice,* pp. 30–33.

165. See Karl Meuli, *Der Griechische Agon: Kampf und Kampfspiel im Totenbrauch, Totentanz, Totenklage und Totenlob* (Köln: Sporthochschule Köln, 1968), p. 23. This work was published posthumously. It was originally submitted as a Habilitationschrift, Universität Basel, in 1926. The 1968 publication includes notes Meuli added after 1926.

166. Ivan Morris, *The World of the Shining Prince: Court Life in Ancient Japan* (1964; rpt. Harmondsworth: Penguin, 1979), p. 68.

167. Another term for "exile" is *sasurau hito,* or "wandering, roaming, or drifting person."

168. I have adopted Carlin A. Barton's terminology of positive and negative charges contained within the sacrificial victim. Barton, "Emotional Economy," pp. 350–351.

169. The exiles' potential return and reintegration into society must linger in the consciousness and conscience of the public until their recall can administer the shock necessary to revive the cultural memory. As Jan Assmann has shown, cultural survival of a catastrophic present requires remembrance of the historic past. See Assmann, *Das kulturelle Gedächtnis,* p. 297.

170. Okabayashi Kiyomi, who argues that Ōgai followed Sasaki Kōzō's source so closely as to adopt its mistakes, uses the example of Ōgai giving Kawatani's date of death as 1868.IX.4 rather than the date of 1868.IX.5 (20 October 1868) that appears on his gravestone. Okabayashi, "'Rekkyo jikki' to 'Sakai jiken,'" p. 32.

171. Johnson, "Mori Ōgai," p. 370.

172. Ibid., pp. 356, 370.

173. See Document No. 52, R. B. Van Valkenburgh to William H. Seward, 26 May 1868, and Document No. 56, William H. Seward to R. B. Van Valkenburgh, 15 July 1868, in *Papers*, pp. 743–744; 779.

174. Von Brandt, *Dreiunddreissig Jahre*, 2:208–209. My translation.

175. See Ōoka, "'Sakai jiken' no kōzu," p. 50.

176. Loose foldout "Resshi kappuku chūkonhi kensetsu shuisho," in Ogawa Masa'ichi, ed., *Rekkyo: Meiji ishin Senshū Sakai Tosa-hanshi kappuku jiken jikki* (Ōsaka: Resshi Kappuku Chūkonhi Kensetsukai, 1929), n p. The plan shows a monument that is 32 *shaku* at the base and 34 *shaku* tall, topped by an eagle with an 8-*shaku* wingspan. One *shaku* is approxiately 30 cm.

177. Doi was among the nine, not the eleven, but he stands out among the twenty for having inspired his comrades to request honorable death by seppuku.

178. The illustrations precede p. 1 of Ogawa, ed., *Rekkyo.*

179. Le Ministre de France au Japon [Léon Roches] au Ministre des affaires étrangères, 19 March 1868, *Documents Diplomatique 1869*, pp. 214–216. Roches' successor, M. Outrey, confirmed the payment of the indemnities; see ibid., p. 217.

180. Document No. 25, Bergasse du Petit Thouars to the captain commanding ad interim the squadron in the China Seas, 10 March 1868, in *Papers*, pp. 703–704.

Chapter 7. Natsume Sōseki's *Kokoro*

1. Ōgai translated into Japanese Kleist's "Das Erdbeben in Chili" ("Jishin," March 1890) and "Die Verlobung in St. Domingo" ("Aku innen," April–July 1890); see Richard John Bowring, *Mori Ōgai and the Modernization of Japanese Culture* (Cambridge: Cambridge University Press, 1979), p. 263.

2. See James A. Fujii, *Complicit Fictions: The Subject in the Modern Japanese Prose Narrative* (Berkeley: University of California Press, 1993), pp. 127–128: "Another clear sign confirming this work's canonical status is the secure place it occupies on the list of required reading and study in the Japanese general education curriculum, though it should be noted that only the third, or last, part of *Kokoro* is excerpted for reading."

3. Isamu Fukuchi, "*Kokoro* and 'the Spirit of Meiji,'" *Monumenta Nipponica* 48.4 (Winter 1993): 469–488.

4. Unless otherwise noted (as here), all translations of *Kokoro* are by Edwin McClellan. Page numbers refer to this English translation and the Japanese original, respectively; Natsume Sōseki, *Kokoro*, trans. Edwin McClellan (Washington, D.C.: Regnery Gateway, 1957); Natsume Kinnosuke, *Sōseki zenshū*, 28 vols. (1994; rpt. Iwanami shoten, 2002), vol. 9: *Kokoro: Sensei no isho*

5. Fukuchi, "*Kokoro* and 'the Spirit of Meiji,'" p. 483. For Fukuchi's comments on Etō Jun, see ibid., pp. 480, 482.

6. Jay Rubin, "Sōseki on Individualism: *Watakushi no Kojinshugi*," *Monumenta Nipponica* 34.1 (1979): 22–23. Rubin quotes from Sōseki, *Kokoro*, trans. McClellan, p. 30.

7. Karatani Kōjin provides some basis for his hypothesis of Sōseki's increasing aversion to Meiji politics in his chapter on "The Discovery of Landscape," in *Origins of*

Modern Japanese Literature, translation edited by Brett de Bary (Durham, N.C., and London: Duke University Press, 1993).

8. Kojin Karatani, "The Discursive Space in Modern Japan," trans. Seiji M. Lippit, in *Japan in the World,* special issue of *Boundary 2,* ed. Masao Miyoshi and H. D. Harootunian, 18.3 (Fall 1991): 191, 213.

9. Ibid., p. 213. Karatani moves seamlessly from interpreting Sensei to interpreting Sōseki's ideas about the Meiji era and Nogi's death, thereby suggesting an understanding of *Kokoro* that is based on the identification of author and main protagonist. Yet while one is the product of the other, it is difficult to know to what extent the protagonist reflects the views of the author. Do the motivations that Karatani attributes to Sōseki fit Sensei?

10. Rubin, "Sōseki on Individualism," p. 22.

11. Komori Yōichi began the debates in 1985. They eventually involved novelists, playwrights, and critics such as Ōoka Shōhei, Hata Kōhei, Miyoshi Yukio, Ōkawa Kōichi, and Tanaka Minoru. Atsuko Sakaki's detailed discussion of these debates does not reveal any interest on the part of the discussants in the roles of either Nogi Maresuke or Shizuko. The *Kokoro ronsō* focuses on Watakushi and his possible relations with Shizu; see Atsuko Sakaki, *Recontextualizing Texts: Narrative Performance in Modern Japanese Fiction* (Cambridge, Mass., and London: Harvard University Asia Center, 1999), pp. 31–53. As Angela Yiu has pointed out, the debate started by Komori and others evolved into the "Sōseki boom" of the 1990s that "produced over two hundred critical articles, over two-fifths of the 450 articles on *Kokoro* since its publication"; Yiu, *Chaos and Order in the Works of Natsume Sōseki* (Honolulu: University of Hawai'i Press, 1998), p. 9. Yiu relies on data published in "*Kokoro* ronsō ikō," *Sōseki kenkyū* 6 (1996): 156–195. The debates concentrate largely on temporal relationships between the novel's two narrations (Watakushi's and Sensei's); see Sakaki, *Recontextualizing Texts,* p. 33.

An excellent example of this concentration is Ken K. Ito's sophisticated essay, "Writing Time in Sōseki's *Kokoro.*" Ito offers a useful "narratological" distinction between story and discourse, defining the former as "content" and the latter as "all the elements of language and narration that are employed to tell the story"; Ito, "Writing Time in Sōseki's *Kokoro,*" in Dennis Washburn and Alan Tansman, eds., *Studies in Modern Japanese Literature: Essays and Translations in Honor of Edwin McClellan* (Ann Arbor: University of Michigan, Center for Japanese Studies, 1997), p. 4. Ito adopted the terms "story" and "discourse" from Seymour Chatman, *Story and Discourse: Narrative Structure in Fiction and Film* (Ithaca, N.Y.: Cornell University Press, 1978). His short summary of *Kokoro*'s "story" does not, however, mention Nogi's junshi, and his fine analysis of the novel's "discourse" refers to it only in order to reconstruct the sequence and the chronology of events. History is not treated as a separate category in its own right, nor is it linked to the fictional plane; Ito, "Writing Time in Sōseki's *Kokoro,*" pp. 4–7. In his synopsis of *Kokoro,* James A. Fujii also does not refer to historical events; see Fujii, *Complicit Fictions,* pp. 137–138. William Jefferson Tyler integrates the deaths of Emperor Meiji and General Nogi into his concise synopsis of *Kokoro*'s plotline; see Doi Takeo, *The Psychological World of Natsume Sōseki,* trans. William Jefferson Tyler (Cambridge and London: East Asian Research Center, Harvard University, 1976), pp. 105–107.

12. David Pollack, *Reading against Culture: Ideology and Narrative in the Japanese Novel* (Ithaca, N.Y.: Cornell University Press, 1992), p. 61.

13. Ibid., p. 63.

14. Dennis C. Washburn, *The Dilemma of the Modern in Japanese Fiction* (New Haven, Conn., and London: Yale University Press, 1995), pp. 171, 178.

15. Fujii, *Complicit Fictions*, p. 135. In contrast to Fujii's critique of Sōseki's silence on Japanese colonialism, Sharalyn Orbaugh's postmodernist critique focuses on Sōseki's failure in *Kokoro* to address gender imbalances in late Meiji society. Sharalyn Orbaugh, "General Nogi's Wife: Representations of Women in Narratives of Japanese Modernization," in Xiaobing Tang and Stephen Snyder, eds., *In Pursuit of Contemporary East Asian Culture* (Boulder, Colo.: Westview Press, 1996), pp. 7–31.

16. Nishi Masahiko, "Ōgai to Sōseki: Nogi Maresuke no 'junshi' o meguru futatsu no bungaku," in Tamai Takayuki and Fujii Hidetada, eds., *Kokoro*, Sōseki sakuhin ronshūsei, vol. 10 (Ōfūsha, 1991), p. 329.

17. Ibid., p. 332. Nishi's article was first published in *Hikaku bungaku* 28 (March 1986). He discerns "assujetissement" in the Japanese context of junshi and confession as a pivot word *(kakekotoba)* for "loyal retainer" *(chūshin)* and "subject" *(shutai).*

18. Ibid., p. 330.

19. Compared to the precise historical dates leading up to Nogi's junshi, the fictional chronology of *Kokoro* is so vague that readers are compelled continually to order the novel's events by reference to their historical correlates. The text demands a detective-like engagement as Sōseki's readers reflect on the relationship between Nogi's junshi and Sensei's suicide. A few clues help to situate the fictional characters in time. If Sensei lost his parents to typhoid in the mid-1890s, when he was not yet twenty, then he must have been born not long before the Satsuma Rebellion. Alan Wolfe notes that "the three generations represented by General Nogi, Sensei, and the student narrator 'I' are linked by suicide, but the clarity of purpose associated with the earlier period is replaced here by an obscurity of purpose and of identity." Wolfe, *Suicidal Narrative in Modern Japan: The Case of Dazai Osamu* (Princeton, N.J.: Princeton University Press, 1990), p. 35. For a discussion of the chronology of *Kokoro*, see Ito, "Writing Time in Sōseki's *Kokoro*," pp. 5–7.

20. It is perhaps ironic that the only major fictional character in *Kokoro* to be known by name, and that only by given name, is Sensei's wife, Shizu.

21. Ōhama Tetsuya, *Meiji no gunshin: Nogi Maresuke* (Yūzankaku, 1970), p. 57; Wada Masao, ed., *Nogi Maresuke nikki* (Kin'ensha, 1970), p. 184. *Yomikudashi* courtesy of Kyoko Selden.

22. It is unclear whether Sōseki is referring to the testament censored by the government or to the entire original text published on the same day, 16 September, by the *Kokumin shinbun*. For more detailed information about the press releases of Nogi's testament, see Robert Jay Lifton, Shūichi Katō, and Michael R. Reich, *Six Lives Six Deaths: Portraits from Modern Japan* (New Haven, Conn.: Yale University Press, 1979), pp. 59–60.

23. See Oketani Hideaki, "Sabishii 'Meiji no seishin'—*Kokoro*," in *Natsume Sōseki ron* (Kawade shobō, 1972), p. 179.

24. Nishi, "Ōgai to Sōseki," p. 331.

25. Oketani uses the terms for sacrifice *(gisei)* and self-sacrifice *(kenshin)* in his discussion of K's pursuit of the "way" *(michi)*. Oketani, "Sabishii 'Meiji no seishin'—*Kokoro*," pp. 187, 190.

26. Nishi, "Ōgai to Sōseki," pp. 333–334.

27. The line is from Wilde's *The Ballad of Reading Gaol* (1898). It is not certain that Sōseki was thinking of this line when he wrote *Kokoro*, but it was widely read and frequently quoted during his sojourn in Britain (1900–1902).

28. Doi, *The Psychological World of Natsume Sōseki*, pp. 125, 126.

29. See Stephen Dodd, "The Significance of Bodies in Sōseki's *Kokoro*," *Monumenta Nipponica* 53.4 (Winter 1998): 475.

30. Ibid., p. 474.

31. See ibid., p. 483.

32. Not surprisingly, Sōseki's library contained works by Havelock Ellis; see ibid., p. 475.

33. Is his writing, like Sensei's, intimately linked to voluntary death? If Watakushi's opus (his two autobiographical parts tied to Sensei's testament) can be construed as his legacy to the general reader, are we to assume that Watakushi went to Tōkyō in order to follow Sensei in death out of loyalty while simultaneously atoning for abandoning his father?

34. Sōseki places the fused historical events in a pivotal position in his fiction, splitting Sensei's story into the story of his past with K, and the story of his present with Watakushi.

35. Nishi Masahiko cites a passage from Ōgai's "Abe ichizoku" that highlights the potential for "sophistry" *(kiben)* in the struggle for honorable junshi as opposed to a "dog's death" *(inujini)*; see Nishi, "Ōgai to Sōseki," p. 330.

36. Orbaugh links K's "spurt" of blood to Nogi's; see "General Nogi's Wife," pp. 16–17.

37. Nancy Jay, "From *Throughout your Generations Forever: Sacrifice, Religion, and Paternity*," in Jeffrey Carter, ed., *Understanding Religious Sacrifice: A Reader* (London and New York: Continuum, 2003), pp. 374, 375.

38. I appreciate one anonymous reader's reference to a critic who has argued that Sensei looks upon General Nogi's suicide as an event he can use for his own purposes. See Shimada Masahiko, *Sōseki o kaku* (Iwanami shoten, 1993), p. 155.

39. There may never have been much of a "gap" between Sensei's suicide and Watakushi's writing potentially leading to his suicide and thus continuing the toppling domino effect set into motion by K. Ito notes that Watakushi's writing occurs at an "unspecified" time, and that "there is a temptation to assume that its narrating coincides with the serialization of the novel in 1914." However, Ito senses an even greater temporal distance than that in Watakushi's narrating the past, "because the younger narrator so often sounds as though he is describing events of the distant rather than the relatively recent past"; Ito, "Writing Time in Sōseki's *Kokoro*," p. 6. Ito's impression can perhaps be understood in the context of the relative recentness of the events Watakushi's relates, events so dense that they may, to him in his youth, seem to occupy more than only four years at most. Another argument for situating Watakushi's narration closer in time to the tumultuous fall of 1912 is his more spontaneous and less pre-

meditated, lively style that, in Ito's eyes, follows "a form of organization more dependent upon association than upon chronological progression" (ibid., p. 20, n. 6). By contrast, Sensei's epistolary style is drier, even didactic at times, and his arrangement of points and episodes gives the impression of having been meticulously planned well in advance.

40. Like Sensei's missed opportunity to confess his betrayal to K, Watakushi's confession is made too late to reach the person it was intended for and must therefore be redirected to a spiritual heir. For Sensei, that heir was Watakushi. Since Watakushi has no fictional "narratee" (Ito's term; see Ito, "Writing Time in Sōseki's *Kokoro,*" p. 15) or successor of the kind he represented to Sensei, there can only be Sensei's wife or the reader outside the narrative to witness his conflict and vicariously to experience his past while interpreting it without assistance, that is, without the possibility of dialogue with Watakushi.

In *Kokoro,* the historical event of Nogi's junshi is presented without any exploration of the private conflict that led up to the drama played out on the public stage of history. By contrast, Sōseki's fictional characters experience their conflict as a private drama heavily influenced by public events. In an inversion of the pattern of public over private emphasis in Nogi's historical junshi, the private, fictional drama manages to transcend its boundaries only when Watakushi's account cum Sensei's testament is published. On the fictional plane, we cannot assume publication at all, for Watakushi might have simply composed his account, attached Sensei's, and left it at that. Conversely, he might have done what the author of *Kokoro* did, thereby establishing a persona-like link between author Natsume Sōseki and fictional character Watakushi. We cannot be sure about what Watakushi did, but we do know that in 1914 Natsume Sōseki made *Kokoro* available to a wide audience through newspaper serialization.

While in *Kokoro* the fictional and nonfictional planes are linked through the contemporary newspaper medium that reports the deaths of Emperor Meiji and Nogi Maresuke and his wife, the author of *Kokoro* seems to challenge his readers, via the persona of Watakushi, to link themselves to his fiction by reflecting about its meaning. It is through this process of engaging the reader with fictional subjects that Natsume Sōseki allows readers of all time periods to get a feel for the *mentalité* of his times so divided by the junshi of Nogi and his wife.

41. Shizu tells Watakushi about her husband's alteration after his friend's death, and Watakushi immediately associates this connection with Sensei's visits to Zōshigaya. The historical Shizuko also witnessed a change in her husband. In the early days of their marriage he had been notorious for his womanizing and heavy drinking, proverbially known as "Nogi's living it up" (Nogi *no gōyū*). Later, Nogi's lifestyle became Spartan. Shizuko had to adjust to these extremes as she bore her husband children and suffered their loss with him. Unlike Sōseki's Shizu, she lived a Meiji woman's role as good wife and wise mother *(ryōsai kenbo).* Nogi's attitude toward his wife has been criticized as misogynistic, but there are signs of his attachment to her in the gifts he gave her, some of which were purchased during his stay in Germany. These gift items are preserved in the Nogi Shrine Museum in Chōfu.

42. How did Sensei, who in a reproductive sense failed to replace K, manage to replace Watakushi's dying father? In his testament Sensei confirms his symbolic paternity in a striking image whose physicality resembles that of childbirth. Howard S.

Hibbett has pointed to the "futility of a substitution which will only lead to another estrangement and loss: the student's development as an individual . . . can only come with freedom from this seemingly beneficial dependency. And Sensei's caution reflects fear of what he himself will lose." "Natsume Sōseki and the Psychological Novel," in Donald H. Shively, ed., *Tradition and Modernization in Japanese Culture* (Princeton, N.J.: Princeton University Press, 1971), p. 340.

43. Ito, "Writing Time in Sōseki's *Kokoro,*" p. 4.

44. Gayle Rubin, "The Traffic in Women," in Rayna Reiter, ed., *Toward an Anthropology of Women* (New York: Monthly Review Press, 1975), pp. 157–210; Orbaugh, "General Nogi's Wife," p. 13.

45. Orbaugh, "General Nogi's Wife," p. 15.

46. Ibid., p. 17.

47. Ibid.

48. It is important to recall that Shizuko's maiden name was spelled with the kanji for "will," "determination," "kindness" *(kokorozashi),* "harbor" *(tsu),* and "child" *(ko).*

49. Tanaka Minoru "points out that Sensei's testament has been edited by its primary reader, *watakushi,* in the act of copying it"; Sakaki, *Recontextualizing Texts,* p. 39. Sakaki refers to Tanaka Minoru, "*Kokoro* to iu kakehashi," *Nihon bungaku* 35.12 (December 1986): 4.

50. Ito, "Writing Time in Sōseki's *Kokoro,*" p. 19.

51. Fujii, *Complicit Fictions,* p. 148.

52. Ito, "Writing Time in Sōseki's *Kokoro,*" p. 15.

53. See Sakaki, *Recontextualizing Texts,* pp. 31, 34.

54. Nishi, "Ōgai to Sōseki," p. 331.

55. Ibid. If the lord had granted a subject his "tacit understanding" *(mokkei),* then seppuku could be honored as junshi after all. Whether this is mere "sophistry" *(kiben),* as Nishi argues, or an "expedient device" *(hōben)* in the best Buddhist fashion must be left to the individual case.

56. Sakaki, *Recontextualizing Texts,* p. 40.

57. Many critics take Shizu to be alive when Watakushi makes his and Sensei's texts public because of the following line in Watakushi's recollections: "I could not know that there had been in Sensei's life a frightening tragedy, inseparable from his love for his wife. Nor did his own wife know how wretched this tragedy had made him. To this day she does not know. Sensei died keeping his secret from her. Before he could destroy his wife's happiness, he destroyed himself" (24–25/ 9:34). However, Orbaugh has correctly pointed out that writing and publication are not concurrent: ". . . Shizu was still alive and still in ignorance at the time of the student's *writing* of this passage, his assembling of the narrative, but indicates nothing about the putative time of the student's *dissemination* of the narrative." Orbaugh, "General Nogi's Wife," p. 29, n. 36.

58. It may be that Shizu died in the interval between Watakushi's writing and the publication. It may also be that Shizu survived her husband by many years and died of old age, in which case Watakushi may have quietly assumed that her death was not worthy of special note. For the latter hypothesis, one has to assume that the rules of fiction do not forbid Watakushi from publishing his text anytime after October 1912, or even after 1914, when *Kokoro* was published.

59. Whether or not Shizu committed suicide depends on whether one believes that she wanted to die proudly insisting on atoning for her complicity in K's suicide or whether one thinks of Shizu as less engaged emotionally than Sensei and less articulate than either of the two narrators. Surely, Nogi Shizuko's example is difficult for any woman to emulate, but no more so than for any man. Sensei does not hesitate to take an easier, less bloody path to death than Nogi. He is already a latter-day Meiji man, as Nogi was not, and his softer approach to voluntary death foreshadows the Taishō mode, which culminated in Akutagawa Ryūnosuke's suicide by drugs in 1927. "His suicide was no less significant than that of General Nogi, whom he disliked, for it heralded the end of the Taishō period just as Nogi's suicide did that of the Meiji period (1868–1912)." Nakamura Mitsuo, *Modern Japanese Fiction 1926–1968* (Kokusai Bunka Shinkōkai, 1969), pt. 2, p. 54; cited from Wolfe, *Suicidal Narrative in Modern Japan,* p. 36.

60. Since it was widely believed that Nogi Shizuko had followed her husband into death according to samurai custom (although in fact she died before him), Shizu might also be seen to follow Sensei into death.

61. As he observes his newly wed wife at K's grave, Sensei blames himself, but it is not clear whether it is for having suspected her and K of romantic feelings for one another or whether for having claimed her for himself (see 236/ 286).

62. Sakaki cites Komori's 1985 controversial theory of Watakushi's affair with Shizu after Sensei's suicide: "by the time the narrator begins to narrate the story, he has established a fulfilling relationship with Sensei's widow, based upon physical consummation and the fathering of a child, which Sensei could not do." Sakaki, *Recontextualizing Texts,* p. 34.

Coda: Last Stands in Ancient Rome and Modern Japan

1. See Manfred Fuhrmann, *Cicero und die römische Republik: Eine Biographie* (1989; München: Piper, 1992), p. 307.

2. See Christian Habicht, *Cicero the Politician* (Baltimore and London: Johns Hopkins University Press, 1990), p. 48.

3. Thomas H. Johnson, ed., *The Poems of Emily Dickinson,* 3 vols. (Cambridge, Mass.: The Belknap Press of Harvard University, 1958), poem 241, 1:174. The poem reads in its entirety: "I like a look of Agony,/ Because I know it's true—/ Men do not sham Convulsion,/ Nor simulate, a Throe—/ The Eyes glaze once—and that is Death—/ Impossible to feign/ The Beads upon the Forehead/ By homely Anguish strung."

4. Habicht, *Cicero the Politician,* p. 34.

5. For Cicero's uncertainties, see Fuhrmann, *Cicero und die römische Republik,* p. 114.

6. See ibid., pp. 133–134, 174–175.

7. Habicht, *Cicero the Politician,* p. 49.

8. There are many sources; see Fuhrmann, *Cicero und die römische Republik,* p. 204.

9. Habicht, *Cicero the Politician,* p. 72.

10. *Cicero: Letters to Friends,* ed. and trans. D. R. Shackleton Bailey, 3 vols. (Cambridge, Mass.: Harvard University Press, 2001), 2:311 (*Fam.* IV.13.2); *Cicero: Letters to*

Atticus, ed. and trans. D. R. Shackleton Bailey, 4 vols. (Cambridge, Mass.: Harvard University Press, 1999), 4:31 (*Att.* XIII.28.2).

11. Paul Plass, *The Game of Death in Ancient Rome: Arena Sport and Political Suicide* (Madison: University of Wisconsin Press, 1995), p. 90.

12. Yoshihito was the third son of Emperor Meiji; his mother was an imperial concubine by the name of Yanagihara Naruko (1855–1943). Soon after his birth, it appears that Yoshihito contracted meningitis and, although deemed competent to succeed his father to the throne, he was never physically or mentally fully engaged in performing his duties. In 1921, Crown Prince Hirohito (1901–1989) became regent *(sesshō)* for his father and succeeded him upon his death in 1926.

13. Habicht, *Cicero the Politician,* p. 98.

14. Plass adds that Mark Antony "is said to have kept Cicero's head in sight of his dining table (App. *BCiv.* 4.4.20; cf. Sen. *Ep.* 83.25), perhaps for reasons having something to do with the Italian practice of including gladiatorial matches in entertainment at banquets." Plass, *The Game of Death in Ancient Rome,* p. 144.

15. *Seneca: Moral Essays,* trans. John W. Basore, 3 vols. (1928; rpt. Cambridge, Mass.: Harvard University Press, 1963), 1:13 (*Prov.* II.12).

16. Robert J. Goar, *The Legend of Cato Uticensis from the First Century B.C. to the Fifth Century A.D.: With an Appendix on Dante and Cato* (Bruxelles: Latomus Revue d'Études Latines, 1987), p. 40.

17. *Plutarch's Lives,* trans. Bernadotte Perrin, 11 vols. (New York: G. P. Putnam's Sons, 1919), 8:405, 407 (*Cat. Min.* LXX.1, 5–6).

18. Goar, *Legend of Cato,* p. 41.

19. Carlin A. Barton, *The Sorrows of the Ancient Romans: The Gladiator and the Monster* (Princeton, N.J.: Princeton University Press, 1993), pp. 37, 39.

20. Sharalyn Orbaugh, "General Nogi's Wife: Representations of Women in Narratives of Japanese Modernization," in Xiaobing Tang and Stephen Snyder, eds., *In Pursuit of Contemporary East Asian Culture* (Boulder, Colo.: Westview Press, 1996), p. 13. Orbaugh cites Ōhama Tetsuya's listing in *Meiji no gunshin: Nogi Maresuke* (Yūzankaku, 1970) of "44 monographs published on the subject [of Nogi's suicide] by the end of 1913, and more than 120 published by 1960"; ibid., p. 27, n. 12. Mark R. Peattie counts 152 books written about Nogi between 1912 and 1942; see Peattie, "The Last Samurai: The Military Career of Nogi Maresuke," *Princeton Papers in East Asian Studies* 1 (1972): 89.

21. All quotations from the *Suasoriae* are from Michael Winterbottom, trans., *The Elder Seneca: Declamations,* 2 vols. (Cambridge, Mass.: Harvard University Press, 1974).

22. Unless otherwise noted, names refer to declaimers, many of whose dates are unknown.

23. See John W. Dower, *Embracing Defeat: Japan in the Wake of World War II* (New York: W. W. Norton and Company, 1999), pp. 38–39 and 569, n. 6. For specifics on the group of fourteen who committed suicide on 25 August, see Ōkuma Miyoshi, *Seppuku no rekishi* (Yūzankaku, 1995), pp. 259–266.

24. In addition to tears of sadness and tears of joy there was anger. Richard B. Frank registers Dr. Hachiya's Hiroshima patients' reaction to the imperial broadcast as

one of revulsion and anger at the emperor's acceptance of the Potsdam Declaration; see Frank, *Downfall: The End of the Imperial Japanese Empire* (1999; Harmondsworth: Penguin Books, 2001), pp. 320–321.

25. Dower, *Embracing Defeat*, p. 36. The official English translation of "The Imperial Rescript of August 14, 1945" is less graphic in depicting the emperor's feeling for his subjects that "pains Our heart night and day." Robert J. C. Butow, *Japan's Decision to Surrender* (Stanford, Calif.: Stanford University Press, 1954), p. 248.

26. John W. Dower notes that General MacArthur "feared that, under the strain of the impending military tribunal judgments, Hirohito might consider not merely abdicating but even committing suicide"; *Embracing Defeat*, p. 328. However, Dower considers this "a strange reading of Emperor Hirohito's personality" (ibid., p. 329).

27. For the diplomatic intricacies surrounding Emperor Hirohito's "Becoming Human," see ibid., pp. 308–318.

28. Mark R. Peattie, "Nogi Maresuke," *Kodansha Encyclopedia of Japan* (New York and Tokyo: Kodansha, 1983), 6:31.

29. Marius B. Jansen, *The Making of Modern Japan* (Cambridge, Mass.: The Belknap Press of Harvard University Press, 2000), p. 223.

30. Kojin Karatani, "The Discursive Space in Modern Japan," trans. Seiji M. Lippit, in *Japan in the World*, special issue of *Boundary 2*, ed. Masao Miyoshi and H. D. Harootunian, 18.3 (Fall 1991): 196.

31. Ibid., p. 210.

32. Ibid., p. 209.

33. Ibid., p. 210.

34. Ibid., p. 216.

35. Ibid., p. 215.

36. Mishima's novel *Honba* (1969; Runaway horses 1973), the second volume of his tetralogy *Hōjō no umi* (The sea of fertility, completed in 1970), contains a story within the story about the Shinpūren.

37. For a translation, see Geoffrey W. Sargent, trans., "Patriotism," in *Death in Midsummer and Other Stories by Yukio Mishima* (New York: New Directions, 1966), pp. 93–118.

38. "Shisei" (aiming for sincerity) was the motto written on the calligraphy scroll in front of which the actor Mishima enacted the seppuku of Lieutenant Shinji Takeyama on 28 February 1936 in order to prove his sincere commitment to the rebels' cause. Mishima was the film's producer and director, the screenwriter (subtitles in English, French, and German) and lead actor.

39. Karatani, "The Discursive Space in Modern Japan," p. 217.

BIBLIOGRAPHY

The city of publication of all works in Japanese is Tōkyō unless otherwise indicated.

Addiss, Stephen. *The Art of Zen: Paintings and Calligraphy by Japanese Monks, 1600–1925.* New York: Harry N. Abrams, 1989.

Adolphson, Mikael S. *The Gates of Power: Monks, Courtiers, and Warriors in Premodern Japan.* Honolulu: University of Hawai'i Press, 2000.

Aigner, Heribert. *Der Selbstmord im Mythos: Betrachtungen über die Einstellung der Griechen zum Phänomen Suizid von der homerischen Zeit bis in das ausgehende 5. Jahrhundert v. Chr.* Graz: Publikation des Instituts für Alte Geschichte und Altertumskunde der Karl-Franzens-Universität Graz, 1982.

Akiyama Kenzō. *The History of Nippon.* Trans. Toshirō Shimanouchi. Tōkyō: Kokusai Bunka Shinkokai, 1941.

Akutagawa. *See* Norman, W. H. H.

Akutagawa Ryūnosuke. "Shōgun." In *Akutagawa Ryūnosuke shū,* ed. Nakamura Shin'ichirō. Nihon bungaku zenshū 22, pp. 335–354. Shinchōsha, 1959. Originally published in the journal *Kaizō* in January 1922.

Allan, James. *Under the Dragon Flag: My Experiences in the Chino-Japanese War.* London: William Heinemann, 1898; rpt. Wilmington, Del.: Scholarly Resources, Inc., 1973.

Aoki, Michiko Y. *Records of Wind and Earth: A Translation of Fudoki with Introduction and Commentaries.* Monograph and Occasional Paper Series, No. 53. Ann Arbor, Mich.: Association for Asian Studies, 1997.

Aoyama, Tomoko. "Japanese Literary Responses to the Russo-Japanese War." In David Wells and Sandra Wilson, eds. *The Russo-Japanese War in Cultural Perspective, 1904–05,* pp. 60–85. London; New York: Macmillan; St. Martin's Press, 1999.

Assmann, Jan. *Das kulturelle Gedächtnis: Schrift, Erinnerung und politische Identität in frühen Hochkulturen.* München: C. H. Beck, 1997.

Aston, William George, trans. *Nihongi: Chronicles of Japan from the Earliest Times to A.D. 697.* Rutland, Vt., and Tokyo: Charles E. Tuttle, 1972. Originally published in two volumes by the Japan Society in 1896; reissued in London in 1924.

Baelz, Toku, ed. *Awakening Japan: The Diary of a German Doctor: Erwin Baelz.* 1932; rpt. Bloomington: Indiana University Press, 1974. Originally published in German: Erwin Baelz, *Das Leben eines deutschen Arztes im erwachenden Japan.* Stuttgart: J. Engelhorns Nachf., 1931.

Bakumatsu ishin jinmei jiten. See Miyazaki Tomihachi and Yasuoka Akio, eds.

Barnes, Gina L. *The Rise of Civilization in East Asia: The Archaeology of China, Korea and Japan.* 1993; rpt. London: Thames and Hudson, 1999.

Barry, Richard. "Nogi—Seer, Statesman, and Soldier." *Harper's Weekly,* 28 September 1912, p. 20.

———. "The Suicide of a True Shintoist: Richard Barry Defends His Belief That Nogi Wished to Die for His Ideals." *New York Times,* 19 September 1912, p. 10.

Barthes, Roland. *Empire of Signs.* Trans. Richard Howard. New York: Hill and Wang, 1982. Originally published in French as *L'empire des signes.* Genève: Éditions d'Art Albert Skira S.A., 1970.

Barton, Carlin A. *The Sorrows of the Ancient Romans: The Gladiator and the Monster.* Princeton, N.J.: Princeton University Press, 1993.

———. *Roman Honor: The Fire in the Bones.* Berkeley: University of California Press, 2001.

———. "The Emotional Economy of Sacrifice and Execution in Ancient Rome." *Historical Reflections/Réflexions Historiques* 29.2 (Summer 2003): 341–360.

Benedict, Ruth. *The Chrysanthemum and the Sword: Patterns of Japanese Culture.* 1946; rpt. New York: World Publishing, 1967.

Benfey, Christopher. *The Great Wave: Gilded Age Misfits, Japanese Eccentrics, and the Opening of Old Japan.* New York: Random House, 2003.

Bitō Masahide. "Junshi." In *Kodansha Encyclopedia of Japan,* 1st ed., 4: 84–85. Tokyo and New York: Kodansha, 1983.

———. "The Akō Incident, 1701–1703." Trans. Henry D. Smith II. *Monumenta Nipponica* 58.2 (Summer 2003): 149–170.

Bix, Herbert P. *Hirohito and the Making of Modern Japan.* New York: HarperCollins, 2000.

Black, John R. *Young Japan: Yokohama and Yedo 1858–79.* With an introduction by Grace Fox. Oxford in Asia Historical Reprints. 2 vols. 1883; rpt. Tokyo: Oxford University Press, 1968.

Booth, James. "Self-Sacrifice and Human Sacrifice in Soyinka's *Death and the King's Horseman.*" In James Gibbs and Bernth Lindfors, eds., *Research on Wole Soyinka,* pp. 127–147. Trenton, N.J.: Africa World Press, 1993.

Bowring, Richard John. *Mori Ōgai and the Modernization of Japanese Culture.* Cambridge: Cambridge University Press, 1979.

———, trans. "Okitsu Yagoemon no isho" (First Version). In David Dilworth and J. Thomas Rimer, eds., *The Historical Fiction of Mori Ōgai,* pp. 45–52. Rpt. Honolulu: University of Hawai'i Press, 1991. Originally published in 1977.

Brandt, Max von. *Dreiunddreissig Jahre in Ost-Asien: Erinnerungen eines deutschen Diplomaten.* 3 vols. Leipzig: Georg Wigand, 1901.

Brazell, Karen, ed. *Traditional Japanese Theater: An Anthology of Plays.* New York: Columbia University Press, 1998.

Breen, John. "The Imperial Oath of April 1868: Ritual, Politics, and Power in the Restoration." *Monumenta Nipponica* 51.4 (Winter 1996): 407–429.

Broda, Johanna. "Templo Mayor as Ritual Space." In Johanna Broda, Davíd Carrasco, and Eduardo Matos Moctezuma. *The Great Temple of Tenochtitlan:*

Center and Periphery in the Aztec World, pp. 61–123. Berkeley: University of California Press, 1987.

Broda, Johanna, Davíd Carrasco, and Eduardo Matos Moctezuma. *The Great Temple of Tenochtitlan: Center and Periphery in the Aztec World.* Berkeley: University of California Press, 1987.

Brown, Delmer M., and Ichirō Ishida, trans. and study. *The Future and the Past: A Translation and Study of the Gukanshō, an Interpretative History of Japan Written in 1219.* Berkeley: University of California Press, 1979.

———. "The Early Evolution of Historical Consciousness." In Delmer M. Brown, ed., *Cambridge History of Japan, Volume I: Ancient Japan,* pp. 504–548. Cambridge: Cambridge University Press, 1993.

Brown, Sidney Devere, and Akiko Hirota, trans. *The Diary of Kido Takayoshi.* 3 vols. Tokyo: University of Tokyo Press, 1986.

Buck, James H. "The Satsuma Rebellion of 1877. From Kagoshima through the Siege of Kumamoto Castle." *Monumenta Nipponica* 28.4 (Winter 1973): 427–446.

———, trans. *The True Story of* THE SIEGE OF KUMAMOTO CASTLE: *Kumamoto Rojo no Jikkyo by Takehiko Ideishi.* New York: Vantage Press, 1976.

Butow, Robert J. C. *Japan's Decision to Surrender.* Stanford, Calif.: Stanford University Press, 1954.

Calman, Donald. *The Nature and Origins of Japanese Imperialism: A Reinterpretation of the Great Crisis of 1873.* London and New York: Routledge, 1992.

Carney, Elizabeth. "Macedonicans and Mutiny: Discipline and Indiscipline in the Army of Philip and Alexander." *Classical Philology* 91 (1996): 19–44.

Carrasco, Davíd. *Religions of Mesoamerica: Cosmovision and Ceremonial Centers.* New York: HarperCollins [HarperSanFrancisco], 1990.

———, ed. *To Change Place: Aztec Ceremonial Landscapes.* Niwot: University Press of Colorado, 1991.

———. *City of Sacrifice: The Aztec Empire and the Role of Violence in Civilization.* Boston: Beacon Press, 1999.

Carter, Jeffrey, ed. *Understanding Religious Sacrifice: A Reader.* London: Continuum, 2003.

Chaïkin, Nathan. *The Sino-Japanese War (1894–1895): The Noted Basil Hall Chamberlain Collection and a Private Collection.* Venthône, Switzerland: Nathan Chaïkin, 1983.

Challaye, Félicien. *Le Japon illustré.* Paris: Librairie Larousse, 1915.

Chamberlain, Basil Hall. *Things Japanese: Notes on Various Subjects Connected with Japan.* 4th ed. Revised and enlarged. London: John Murray, 1902. Originally published in 1890.

Chiba Tokuji. *Nihonjin wa naze seppuku suru no ka.* Tōkyōdō, 1994.

Chikano Shigeru. *Nihon kamon sōkan.* Kadokawa shoten, 1993.

———. *Tanbō Edo Meiji meishi no haka.* Shinjinbutsu ōraisha, 1993.

Cicero: Letters to Atticus. Ed. and trans. D. R. Shackleton Bailey. 4 vols. Cambridge, Mass.: Harvard University Press, 1999.

Cicero: Letters to Friends. Ed. and trans. D. R. Shackleton Bailey. 3 vols. Cambridge, Mass.: Harvard University Press, 2001.

Cleary, Thomas, trans. *The Art of War.* Boston: Shambala, 1998.

———. *Code of the Samurai: A Modern Translation of the* Bushido Shoshinsu *[sic].* Boston, Rutland, Vt., and Tokyo: Tuttle Publishing, 1999.

Connaughton, Richard Michael. *The War of the Rising Sun and Tumbling Bear: A Military History of the Russo-Japanese War 1904–5.* London: Routledge, 1988.

Cooper, Michael, ed. *They Came to Japan: An Anthology of European Reports on Japan, 1543–1640.* Berkeley: University of California Press, 1965.

Cortazzi, Hugh. "The Pestilently Active Minister: Dr. Willis's Comments on Sir Harry Parkes." *Monumenta Nipponica* 39.2 (1984): 147–161.

———, ed. *Mitford's Japan: The Memoirs and Recollections, 1866–1906, of Algernon Bertram Mitford, the first Lord Redesdale.* London and Dover, N.H.: The Athlone Press, 1985.

Craig, Albert M. *Chōshū in the Meiji Restoration.* Harvard Historical Monographs, vol. 47. Cambridge, Mass.: Harvard University Press, 1961.

Cranston, Edwin A., trans., with commentary and notes. *A Waka Anthology, Volume One: The Gem-Glistening Cup.* Stanford, Calif.: Stanford University Press, 1993.

Daniels, Gordon. "The British Role in the Meiji Restoration: A Re-Interpretive Note." *Modern Asian Studies* 2.4 (1968): 291–313.

Dilworth, David, trans. "The Abe Family." In David Dilworth and J. Thomas Rimer, eds., *The Historical Fiction of Mori Ōgai,* pp. 65–99. 1977; rpt. Honolulu: University of Hawai'i Press, 1991.

———. "The Incident at Sakai." In David Dilworth and J. Thomas Rimer, eds., *The Historical Fiction of Mori Ōgai,* pp. 129–151. 1977; rpt. Honolulu: University of Hawai'i Press, 1991.

Dilworth, David, and J. Thomas Rimer, eds. *The Historical Fiction of Mori Ōgai.* 1977; rpt. Honolulu: University of Hawai'i Press, 1991.

Documents Diplomatiques. 1869. No. XI (Janvier 1869). Paris: Imprimerie Impériale, 1869.

Dodd, Stephen. "Different Feelings: The Intellectual Shift between Meiji and Taishō." In Amy Vladeck Heinrich, ed., *Currents in Japanese Culture: Translations and Transformations,* pp. 263–277. New York: Columbia University Press, 1997.

———. "The Significance of Bodies in Sōseki's *Kokoro.*" *Monumenta Nipponica* 53.4 (Winter 1998): 473–498.

Doi Takeo. *The Psychological World of Natsume Sōseki.* Trans. William Jefferson Tyler. Cambridge and London: East Asian Research Center, Harvard University, 1976.

Dower, John W. *Embracing Defeat: Japan in the Wake of World War II.* New York: W. W. Norton and Company, 1999.

Durkheim, Emile. *Suicide: A Study in Sociology.* Trans. John A. Spaulding and George Simpson. Glencoe, Ill.: The Free Press, 1951. Originally published in 1897 as *Le Suicide.*

Eastlake, F. Warrington, and Yamada Yoshiaki. *Heroic Japan: A History of the War Between China and Japan.* London: Sampson, Low, Marston and Company, 1897; rpt. Washington, D.C.: University Publications of America, 1979.

Ebersole, Gary L. *Ritual Poetry and the Politics of Death in Early Japan.* Princeton, N.J.: Princeton University Press, 1989.

Edwards, Walter. "In Pursuit of Himiko: Postwar Archaeology and the Location of Yamatai." *Monumenta Nipponica* 51.1 (Spring 1996): 53–79.

Eliade, Mircea, ed. *Encyclopedia of Religion.* 16 vols. New York: Macmillan, 1987.

Elison, George. *Deus Destroyed: The Image of Christianity in Early Modern Japan.* 1973; rpt. Cambridge, Mass.: Council on East Asian Studies, Harvard University, 1991.

Elison, George, and Bardwell L. Smith, eds. *Warlords, Artists, and Commoners: Japan in the Sixteenth Century.* Honolulu: University of Hawai'i Press, 1981.

Emery, Walter B. *Archaic Egypt.* Harmondsworth: Penguin, 1961.

Ericson, Mark David. "The Tokugawa *Bakufu* and Léon Roches." Ph.D. diss., University of Hawai'i, 1978.

Farris, William Wayne. *Sacred Texts and Buried Treasures: Issues in the Historical Archaeology of Ancient Japan.* Honolulu: University of Hawai'i Press, 1998.

Faure, Bernard. *Visions of Power: Imagining Medieval Japanese Buddhism.* Trans. from the French by Phyllis Brooks. Princeton, N.J.: Princeton University Press, 1996.

Feldherr, Andrew. *Spectacle and Society in Livy's* History. Berkeley: University of California Press, 1998.

Finn, Dallas. *Meiji Revisited: The Sites of Victorian Japan.* New York: Weatherhill, 1995.

Fox, Grace. *Britain and Japan, 1858–1883.* Oxford: Clarendon Press, 1969.

Frank, Richard B. *Downfall: The End of the Imperial Japanese Empire.* 1999; rpt. Harmondsworth: Penguin Books, 2001.

Frankfort, Henri. *Kingship and the Gods: A Study of Ancient Near Eastern Religion as the Integration of Society and Nature.* 1948; rpt. Chicago and London: University of Chicago Press, 1978.

Freed, Rita E., Yvonne J. Markowitz, and Sue H. D'Auria, eds. *Pharaohs of the Sun: Akhenaten, Nefertiti, Tutankhamen.* Boston: Museum of Fine Arts with Bulfinch Press / Little, Brown and Company, 1999.

Friday, Karl F. *Hired Swords: The Rise of Private Warrior Power in Early Japan.* Stanford, Calif.: Stanford University Press, 1992.

Fuhrmann, Manfred. *Cicero und die römische Republik: Eine Biographie.* 1989; München: Piper, 1992.

———. *Seneca und Kaiser Nero: Eine Biographie.* 1997; rpt. Frankfurt am Main: Fischer, 1999.

Fujii, James A. *Complicit Fictions: The Subject in the Modern Japanese Prose Narrative.* Berkeley: University of California Press, 1993.

———. "Death, Empire, and the Search for History in Natsume Sōseki's *Kokoro.*" In James A. Fujii, *Complicit Fictions: The Subject in the Modern Japanese Prose Narrative,* pp. 126–150. Berkeley: University of California Press, 1993.

Fujita Satoru. "Kaidai," 2: 443–468. In *Ōgai rekishi bungaku shū.* 13 vols. Iwanami shoten, 2000.

Fujitani, Takashi. *Splendid Monarchy: Power and Pageantry in Modern Japan.* Berkeley: University of California Press, 1996.

Fukuchi, Isamu. "*Kokoro* and 'the Spirit of Meiji.'" *Monumenta Nipponica* 48.4 (Winter 1993): 469–488.

Fukumoto Akira. "*Iji:* bihō no 'seiri' ni koraeeru fukashigi na shōhakusei." In *Mori Ōgai.* Issatsu no kōza. Nihon no kindai bungaku, 5: 113–126. Yūseidō, 1984.

Gaikoku shinbun ni miru Nihon. See Kokusai nyūsu jiten shuppan iinkai, ed.

Gennep, Arnold van. *The Rites of Passage.* Trans. Monika B. Vizedom and Gabrielle L. Caffee. Chicago: University of Chicago Press, 1960. Originally published in 1909.

Gernet, Jacques. *A History of Chinese Civilization.* Trans. J. R. Foster and Charles Hartman. Cambridge: Cambridge University Press, 1996. Originally published as *Le monde chinois.* Paris: Librairie Armand Colin, 1972.

Gilday, Edmund T. "Bodies of Evidence: Imperial Funeral Rites and the Meiji Restoration." *Japanese Journal of Religious Studies* 27.3–4 (Fall 2000): 273–296.

Girard, René. *Violence and the Sacred.* Trans. Patrick Gregory. Baltimore and London: Johns Hopkins University Press, 1977. Originally published as *La violence et le sacré.* Paris: Éditions Bernard Grasset, 1972.

Gluck, Carol. *Japan's Modern Myths: Ideology in the Late Meiji Period.* Princeton, N.J.: Princeton University Press, 1985.

Goar, Robert J. *The Legend of Cato Uticensis from the First Century B.C. to the Fifth Century A.D.: With an Appendix on Dante and Cato.* Bruxelles: Latomus Revue d'Études Latines, 1987.

Godolphin, Francis R. B., ed. *The Greek Historians: The Complete and Unabridged Historical Works of Herodotus, Thucydides, Xenophon, Arrian.* 2 vols. New York: Random House, 1942.

Graf E. zu Reventlow. *See* Reventlow, Graf E. zu

Guttmann, Allen. *Sports: The First Five Millennia.* Amherst and Boston: University of Massachusetts Press, 2004.

Guttmann, Allen, and Lee Thompson. *Japanese Sports: A History.* Honolulu: University of Hawai'i Press, 2001.

Habicht, Christian. *Cicero the Politician.* Baltimore: Johns Hopkins University Press, 1990.

Hackett, Roger F. *Yamagata Aritomo in the Rise of Modern Japan, 1838–1922.* Cambridge, Mass.: Harvard University Press, 1971.

Haider, Peter. "Gefolgschaftsbestattungen in universalhistorischer Sicht." In Franz Hampl and Ingomar Weiler, eds., *Kritische und vergleichende Studien zur Alten Geschichte und Universalgeschichte.* Innsbrucker Beiträge zur Kulturwissenschaft, 18: 89–120. Innsbruck: Institut für Sprachwissenschaft der Universität Innsbruck, 1974.

Hamerton-Kelly, Robert G., ed. *Violent Origins: Walter Burkert, René Girard, and Jonathan Z. Smith on Ritual Killing and Cultural Formation,* with an introduction by Burton Mack and a commentary by Renato Rosaldo. Stanford, Calif.: Stanford University Press, 1987.

Hampl, Franz, and Ingomar Weiler, eds. *Kritische und vergleichende Studien zur Alten Geschichte und Universalgeschichte.* Innsbrucker Beiträge zur Kulturwissenschaft, vol. 18. Innsbruck: Institut für Sprachwissenschaft der Universität Innsbruck, 1974.

Handel, Michael I. *Sun Tzu and Clausewitz: The Art of War and On War Compared.* Carlisle Barracks, Pa.: Strategic Studies Institute, U.S. Army War College, 1991.

Hardacre, Helen, with Adam L. Kern, eds. *New Directions in the Study of Meiji Japan.* Brill's Japanese Studies Library, vol. 6. Leiden, New York and Köln: Brill, 1997.

Hargreaves, Reginald. *Red Sun Rising: The Siege of Port Arthur.* Philadelphia and New York: J. B. Lippincott, 1962.

Harrison, Jane Ellen. *Prolegomena to the Study of Greek Religion.* 1903; rpt. Princeton, N.J.: Princeton University Press, 1991.

Hasegawa, Izumi. "The Significance of the Meiji Period in Mori Ōgai's Literature." *Acta Asiatica* 40 (1981): 1–21.

Hashimoto, Mitsuru. "Collision at Namamugi." Trans. Betsey Scheiner. *Representations* 18 (Spring 1987): 69–90.

Heinrich, Amy Vladeck, ed. *Currents in Japanese Culture: Translations and Transformations.* New York: Columbia University Press, 1997.

Henderson, John S. *The World of the Ancient Maya.* 1981; 2nd edition, Ithaca, N.Y., and London: Cornell University Press 1997.

Henshall, Kenneth G., trans. *Literary Life in Tōkyō 1885–1915: Tayama Katai's Memoirs ('Thirty Years in Tōkyō').* Leiden: E. J. Brill, 1987.

Hesselink, Reinier. "The Assassination of Henry Heusken." *Monumenta Nipponica* 49.3 (Autumn 1994): 331–351.

Heuvers, Hermann. "Kaiser Meiji als Dichter." *Monumenta Nipponica* 2.2 (July 1939): 333–348.

Heyden, Doris. "Dryness before the Rains: Toxcatl and Tezcatlipoca." In Davíd Carrasco, ed., *To Change Place: Aztec Ceremonial Landscapes,* pp. 188–202. Niwot: University Press of Colorado, 1991. (Electronic book version 1999.)

Hibbett, Howard S. "Natsume Sōseki and the Psychological Novel." In Shively, Donald H., ed., *Tradition and Modernization in Japanese Culture,* pp. 305–346. Princeton, N.J.: Princeton University Press, 1971.

Hobsbawm, Eric, and Terence Ranger, eds. *The Invention of Tradition.* Cambridge: Cambridge University Press, 1983.

Hopper, Helen M. "Mori Ōgai's Response to Suppression of Intellectual Freedom, 1909–12." *Monumenta Nipponica* 29.4 (Winter 1974): 381–413.

Huber, Thomas M. *The Revolutionary Origins of Modern Japan.* Stanford, Calif.: Stanford University Press, 1981.

Hubert, Henri, and Marcel Mauss. *Sacrifice: Its Nature and Function.* Trans. W. D. Hall. Chicago: University of Chicago Press, 1969. Originally published as "Essai sur la nature et la fonction du sacrifice," *L'Année sociologique*. 1898.

Idota Hirofumi. *Nogi Maresuke junshi—igo: hakushaku kasaikō o megutte.* Shinjinbutsu ōraisha, 1989.

Ikegami, Eiko. *The Taming of the Samurai: Honorific Individualism and the Making of Modern Japan.* Cambridge, Mass., and London: Harvard University Press, 1995.

Inagaki Tatsurō, ed. *Mori Ōgai hikkei.* Gakutōsha, 1968.

Inoue Haruki. *Ryojun gyakusatsu jiken.* Chikuma shobō, 1995.

Irokawa Daikichi. *The Culture of the Meiji Period.* Trans. and ed. Marius B. Jansen. Princeton, N.J.: Princeton University Press, 1985. Originally published as *Meiji no bunka,* 1970.

Ishii Ryōsuke, ed. *Tokugawa kinreikō.* 11 vols. Sōbunsha, 1959.

Ishii Takashi. *Meiji ishin no kokusaiteki kankyō.* Yoshikawa kōbunkan, 1966.

Ito, Ken K. "Writing Time in Sōseki's *Kokoro.*" In Dennis Washburn and Alan Tansman, eds., *Studies in Modern Japanese Literature: Essays and Translations in Honor of Edwin McClellan*, pp. 3–21. Ann Arbor: University of Michigan, Center for Japanese Studies, 1997.

Itō Kōsaku. *Monshō: Chōjūgyo, katachi, shirushi, ji, gu.* 2 vols. Bijutsu shuppansha, 1969.

James, David H. *The Rise and Fall of the Japanese Empire.* London: George Allen and Unwin, 1951.

Jansen, Marius B. *Sakamoto Ryōma and the Meiji Restoration.* 1961; rpt. New York: Columbia University Press, 1994.

———, ed. *The Emergence of Meiji Japan.* Cambridge: Cambridge University Press, 1995.

———. *The Making of Modern Japan.* Cambridge, Mass., and London: The Belknap Press of Harvard University Press, 2000.

Janssen, L. F. "Some Unexplored Aspects of the *Devotio Deciana.*" *Mnemosyne* 4.34 (1981): 357–381.

Japan National Tourist Organization, ed. *The New Official Guide: Japan.* Tokyo: Japan Travel Bureau, 1975.

Jay, Nancy. "From *Throughout your Generations Forever: Sacrifice, Religion, and Paternity.*" In Jeffrey Carter, ed., *Understanding Religious Sacrifice: A Reader*, pp. 370–383. London and New York: Continuum, 2003.

Johnson, Eric W. "The Historical Fiction and Biography of Mori Ogai." *The Journal of the Association of Teachers of Japanese* 8.1 (November 1972): 7–25.

———. "Mori Ōgai: The Fiction from 1909 to Early 1914." Ph.D. diss., University of Chicago, 1973.

Johnson, Samuel. *The History of the Yorubas.* Ed. O. Johnson. 1921; rpt. Lagos, Nigeria: CSS Limited, 2001.

Johnson, Thomas H., ed. *The Poems of Emily Dickinson.* 3 vols. Cambridge, Mass.: The Belknap Press of Harvard University, 1958.

Jolly, Mark E. "Nogi's Last Lesson." Senior Honors thesis, University of Massachusetts at Amherst, Department of Asian Languages and Literatures. May 2000.

Kamei Koreaki. *Nisshin sensō jūgun shashinchō.* Hakushobō, 1992.

Karatani, Kōjin. "The Discursive Space in Modern Japan." Trans. Seiji M. Lippit. In *Japan in the World.* Special issue of *Boundary 2*, ed. Masao Miyoshi and H. D. Harootunian. 18.3 (Fall 1991): 190–219.

———. *Origins of Japanese Literature.* Translation edited by Brett de Bary. Durham, N.C., and London: Duke University Press, 1993.

Katsukura Toshikazu. "Mori Ōgai 'Sahashi Jingorō' shiron: ekken no ba no kōzu to Nikkan heigō mondai ni tsuite." *Fukushima Daigaku kyōiku gakubu ronshū* 63 (December 1997): 84–69; reverse pagination.

Kawahara, Toshiaki. *Hirohito and His Times: A Japanese Perspective.* Tokyo and New York: Kodansha International, 1990.

Keene, Donald, trans. *Major Plays of Chikamatsu.* New York: Columbia University Press, 1961.

———. "Hagi." In Donald Keene, *Travels in Japan: Nihon saiken*, pp. 97–106. Gakueisha, 1981.

———. *Emperor of Japan: Meiji and His World, 1852–1912.* New York: Columbia University Press, 2002.

Keitel, Elizabeth. "Otho's Exhortations in Tacitus' *Histories.*" *Greece & Rome* 34.1 (April 1987): 73–82.

Kenney, Elizabeth. "Shinto Funerals in the Edo Period." *Japanese Journal of Religious Studies* 27.3–4 (Fall 2000): 239–271.

Ketelaar, James Edward. *Of Heretics and Martyrs in Meiji Japan: Buddhism and Its Persecution.* Princeton, N.J.: Princeton University Press, 1990.

Kiyota, Minoru. *Kendō: Its Philosophy, History and Means to Personal Growth.* London and New York: Kegan Paul International, 1995.

Kodansha Encyclopedia of Japan. 9 vols. 1st ed. Tokyo and New York: Kodansha International, 1983.

Kokusai nyūsu jiten shuppan iinkai, ed. *Gaikoku shinbun ni miru Nihon 1852–1873.* 4 vols. in 10 parts. Mainichi Communications, 1989.

Kono, Shion. "Self-Commentary in Mori Ōgai's Historical Fiction and the Rhetoric of Annotation in Modern Japan." Forthcoming in the *Journal of Japanese Studies* (Summer 2006).

Kumakura Isao. "Kan'ei Culture and *Chanoyu,*" trans. Paul Varley. In Paul Varley and Kumakura Isao, eds., *Tea in Japan: Essays on the History of* Chanoyu, pp. 135–160. Honolulu: University of Hawai'i Press, 1989.

Kunaichō, ed. *Meiji tennō ki.* 13 vols. Yoshikawa kōbunkan, 1968–1975.

Kuwahara Takeshi and Sugahara Kazutora, eds. *Nogi Maresuke no sekai.* Shinjinbutsu ōraisha, 1992.

Kyle, Donald G. *Spectacles of Death in Ancient Rome.* London and New York: Routledge, 1998.

Lane-Poole, Stanley, and Frederick Victor Dickins. *The Life of Sir Harry Parkes.* 2 vols. 1894; rpt. Wilmington, Del.: Scholarly Resources, 1973.

Lattimore, Richmond, trans. *The Iliad of Homer.* Chicago: University of Chicago Press, 1951.

Lebra, Takie Sugiyama. *Above the Clouds: Status Culture of the Modern Japanese Nobility.* Berkeley: University of California Press, 1993.

Lehmann, Jean-Pierre. "Léon Roches—Diplomat Extraordinary in the Bakumatsu Era: An Assessment of His Personality and Policy." *Modern Asian Studies* 14.2 (1980): 273–307.

Lewis, Mark Edward. *Sanctioned Violence in Early China.* Albany: State University of New York Press, 1990.

Lifton, Robert Jay, Shūichi Katō, and Michael R. Reich. *Six Lives Six Deaths: Portraits from Modern Japan.* New Haven, Conn.: Yale University Press, 1979.

Lincoln, Bruce. *Death, War, and Sacrifice: Studies in Ideology and Practice.* Chicago and London: University of Chicago Press, 1991.

Lone, Stewart. *Japan's First Modern War: Army and Society in the Conflict with China, 1894–95.* New York: St. Martin's Press, 1994.

———. *Army, Empire and Politics in Meiji Japan: The Three Careers of General Katsura Tarō.* London: Macmillan Press, 2000.

Marcus, Marvin. "Mori Ōgai and the Biographical Quest." *Harvard Journal of Asiatic Studies* 51.1 (June 1991): 233–262.

———. *Paragons of the Ordinary: The Biographical Literature of Mori Ōgai.* Honolulu: University of Hawai'i Press, 1993.

Matos Moctezuma, Eduardo. *The Great Temple of the Aztecs: Treasures of Tenochtitlan.* Translated from the Spanish by Doris Heyden. London: Thames and Hudson, 1988.

Matsui Toshihiko. *Gun'i Mori Ōgai: tōsuiken to bungaku.* Ōfūsha, 1989.

Matsushima Ei'ichi. "Ōgai to Nogi Taishō." *Kokubungaku kaishaku to kanshō* 49.2 (January 1984): 180–185.

Matsushita Yoshio. *Nogi Maresuke.* 1960; rev. 4th ed. Jinbutsu sōsho series. Yoshikawa kōbunkan, 1997.

Mauss, Marcel. *The Gift: Forms and Functions of Exchange in Archaic Societies.* Trans. Ian Cunnison. New York: W. W. Norton, 1967. Originally published as *Essai sur le don: Forme archaïque de l'échange,* 1925.

McCullough, Helen Craig, trans. *"A Tale of Mutsu." Harvard Journal of Asiatic Studies* 25 (1964–1965): 178–211.

———, trans. *The Taiheiki: A Chronicle of Medieval Japan.* 1959; rpt. Rutland, Vt.: Charles E. Tuttle, 1979.

———, trans. *The Tale of the Heike.* Stanford, Calif.: Stanford University Press, 1988.

Medzini, Meron. *French Policy in Japan during the Closing Years of the Tokugawa Regime.* Harvard East Asian Monographs 41. Cambridge, Mass.: Harvard University Press, 1971.

Meech-Pekarik, Julia. *The World of the Meiji Print.* New York: Weatherhill, 1986.

Meguro Masumi, trans. *Nogi Taishō to Nihonjin.* Kōdansha gakujutsu bunko, 1980.

"Meiji period." In *Kodansha Encyclopedia of Japan,* 5:155. 9 vols. 1st ed.; Tokyo and New York: Kodansha International, 1983.

Meiji tennō ki. See Kunaichō, ed.

Meuli, Karl. *Der Griechische Agon: Kampf und Kampfspiel im Totenbrauch, Totentanz, Totenklage und Totenlob.* Köln: Sporthochschule Köln, 1968.

Minamoto Ryōen. "Nogi taishō no jisatsu to sono seishin shiteki haikei." *Kokoro* 16 (December 1963): 11–20.

Minear, Richard H. *Japanese Tradition and Western Law: Emperor, State, and Law in the Thought of Hozumi Yatsuka.* Cambridge, Mass.: Harvard University Press, 1970.

Minichiello, Sharon A., ed. *Japan's Competing Modernities: Issues in Culture and Democracy 1900–1930.* Honolulu: University of Hawai'i Press, 1998.

Minois, Georges. *History of Suicide: Voluntary Death in Western Culture.* Trans. Lydia G. Cochrane. Baltimore and London: Johns Hopkins University Press, 1999. Originally published in French as *Histoire du suicide: La société occidentale face à la mort volontaire.* Paris: Librairie Arthème Fayard, 1995.

Mitchell, Thomas N. *Cicero: The Ascending Years.* New Haven, Conn., and London: Yale University Press, 1979.

———. *Cicero: The Senior Statesman.* New Haven, Conn., and London: Yale University Press, 1991.

Miyazaki Tomihachi and Yasuoka Akio, eds. *Bakumatsu ishin jinmei jiten.* Shinjinbutsu ōraisha, 1994.

Mori Ōgai. *Doitsu nikki, Kokura nikki.* In *Mori Ōgai zenshū.* Vol. 13. Chikuma shobō, 1996.

———. "Saigo no ikku," 3: 219–240. In *Ōgai rekishi bungaku shū,* ed. Suda Kiyoji. 13 vols. Iwanami shoten, 1999.

———. "Tsuge Shirōzaemon," 3: 127–173. In *Ōgai rekishi bungaku shū,* ed. Suda Kiyoji. 13 vols. Iwanami shoten, 1999.

———. *Ōgai rekishi bungaku shū.* 13 vols. Iwanami shoten, 1999–2002.

———. "Abe ichizoku," 2: 23–82. In *Ōgai rekishi bungaku shū,* ed. Fujita Satoru. 13 vols. Iwanami shoten, 2000.

———. "Okitsu Yagoemon no isho," 2: 379–384 (1st version). In *Ōgai rekishi bungaku shū,* ed. Fujita Satoru. 13 vols. Iwanami shoten, 2000.

———. "Okitsu Yagoemon no isho," 2: 1–22 (2nd version). In *Ōgai rekishi bungaku shū,* ed. Fujita Satoru. 13 vols. Iwanami shoten, 2000.

———. "Ōshio Heihachirō," 2: 155–263. In *Ōgai rekishi bungaku shū,* ed. Fujita Satoru. 13 vols. Iwanami shoten, 2000.

———. "Sahashi Jingorō," 2: 83–99. In *Ōgai rekishi bungaku shū,* ed. Fujita Satoru. 13 vols. Iwanami shoten, 2000.

———. "Sakai jiken," 2: 265–307. In *Ōgai rekishi bungaku shū,* ed. Fujita Satoru. 13 vols. Iwanami shoten, 2000.

Morris, Ivan. *The World of the Shining Prince: Court Life in Ancient Japan.* 1964; rpt. Harmondsworth: Penguin, 1979.

———. *The Nobility of Failure: Tragic Heroes in the History of Japan.* New York: Holt, Rinehart and Winston, 1975.

Morris, V. Dixon. "The City of Sakai and Urban Autonomy." In George Elison and Bardwell L. Smith, eds., *Warlords, Artists, and Commoners: Japan in the Sixteenth Century,* pp. 23–54. Honolulu: University of Hawai'i Press, 1981.

Mounsey, Augustus H. *The Satsuma Rebellion: An Episode of Modern Japanese History.* London: John Murray, Albemarle Street, 1879; rpt. Washington, D.C.: University Publications of America, 1979.

Murray, Darcy, trans. "History as It Is and History Ignored." In David Dilworth and J. Thomas Rimer, eds., *The Historical Fiction of Mori Ōgai,* pp. 179–184. 1977; rpt. Honolulu: University of Hawai'i Press, 1991.

Nakai, Yoshiyuki. "The Young Mori Ōgai (1862–1892)." Ph.D. diss., Harvard University, 1974.

Nakanishi Susumu. *Jisei no kotoba.* Chūō kōron shinsha, 1995.

Nakayama Gishū. "Tosa hei no yūkan na hanashi." In *Nakayama Gishū.* Nihon no bungaku 61, pp. 474–485; 499–500. Chūō kōronsha, 1967. Originally published in 1965.

Nakazawa Shōji. *Ozannen-san.* 2 vols. Orijin shobō, 1977.

Natsume Kinnosuke. *Kokoro: Sensei no isho.* Vol. 9. of *Sōseki zenshū.* 28 vols. 1994; rpt. Iwanami shoten, 2002.

Natsume Sōseki. *Kokoro.* Trans. Edwin McClellan. Washington, D.C.: Regnery Gateway, 1957.

Nihon Kokugo Daijiten Dainihan Henshū Iinkai, ed. *Nihon kokugo daijiten.* 14 vols. Shōgakukan, 2002.

Nihon shiryō shūsei hensankai, ed. *Chūgoku, Chōsen no shiryō ni okeru Nihon shiryō shūsei,* vol. 1: *Seishi.* Kokusho kankōkai, 1975.

Nish, Ian H. *The Origins of the Russo-Japanese War.* London: Longman, 1985.

Nishi Masahiko. "Ōgai to Sōseki: Nogi Maresuke no 'junshi' o meguru futatsu no bungaku." In Tamai Takayuki and Fujii Hidetada, eds., *Kokoro.* Sōseki sakuhin ronshūsei, 10: 329–336. Ōfūsha, 1991.

Nogi jinja shamusho, ed. *Nogi Maresuke zenshū.* 4 vols. Kokusho kankōkai, 1994.

Nogi Maresuke zenshū. See Nogi jinja shamusho, ed.

Norman, W. H. H., trans. "The General." In *Hell Screen ("Jigoku Hen") and Other Stories by Ryunosuke Akutagawa,* pp. 135–167. Printed in Occupied Japan; The Hokuseido Press, 1948.

Notehelfer, F. G., ed. *Japan through American Eyes: The Journal of Francis Hall, Kanagawa and Yokohama, 1859–1866.* Princeton, N.J.: Princeton University Press, 1992.

Ōgai. *See* Mori Ōgai.

Ogata Tsutomu. "Sahashi Jingorō: iji." In Ogata Tsutomu. *Mori Ōgai no rekishi shōsetsu: shiryō to hōhō,* pp. 115–133. Chikuma shobō, 1979. Originally published as " 'Sahashi Jingorō' no tenkyo to hōhō," in *Bungaku* 32 (October 1964).

———. *Mori Ōgai no rekishi shōsetsu: shiryō to hōhō.* Chikuma shobō, 1979.

———. "The Charm of Mori Ōgai's Literature: His Historical Novella, *Gojiingahara no Katakiuchi.*" *Acta Asiatica* 40 (1981): 37–56.

Ogawa Mariko. *Robert Koch's 74 Days in Japan.* Kleine Reihe 27. Berlin: Mori-Ōgai-Gedenkstätte, 2003.

Ogawa Masa'ichi, ed. *Rekkyo: Meiji ishin Senshū Sakai Tosa-hanshi kappuku jiken jikki.* Ōsaka: Resshi Kappuku Chūkonhi Kensetsukai, 1929.

Ōhama Tetsuya. *Meiji no gunshin: Nogi Maresuke.* Yūzankaku, 1970.

Ohnuki-Tierney, Emiko. *Kamikaze, Cherry Blossoms, and Nationalisms: The Militarization of Aesthetics in Japanese History.* Chicago and London: University of Chicago Press, 2002.

Okabayashi Kiyomi. " 'Rekkyo jikki' to 'Sakai jiken.' " In Tosa shidankai, ed., *Senshū: Sakai do hanshi rekkyo jikki: Myōkokuji no seppuku,* pp. 29–34. Tosa shidan fukkoku sōsho 3. Kōchi: Tosa shidankai, 1979.

Okada Mikihiko. *Nogi Maresuke: kōki naru Meiji.* Tentensha, 2001.

Okamoto, Shumpei. *The Japanese Oligarchy and the Russo-Japanese War.* New York: Columbia University Press, 1970.

Oketani Hideaki. "Sabishii 'Meiji no seishin'—*Kokoro.*" In *Natsume Sōseki ron,* pp. 176–206. Kawade shobō, 1972.

Ōkuma Miyoshi. *Seppuku no rekishi.* Yūzankaku, 1995.

Ōoka Shōhei. " 'Sakai jiken' no kōzu: Mori Ōgai ni okeru kirimori to netsuzō." In Ōoka Shōhei. *Bungaku ni okeru kyo to jitsu,* pp. 9–57. Rpt. Kōdansha, 1976. Originally published in 1975.

———. *Sakai-kō jōi shimatsu.* Chūō kōronsha, 1989. Originally published in *Chūō kōron bungei tokushū* (Winter 1984–Winter 1988).

Orbaugh, Sharalyn. "General Nogi's Wife: Representations of Women in Narratives of Japanese Modernization." In Xiaobing Tang and Stephen Snyder, eds., *In Pursuit of Contemporary East Asian Culture*, pp. 7–31. Boulder, Colo.: Westview Press, 1996.

Paine, S. C. M. *The Sino-Japanese War of 1894–1895: Perceptions, Power, and Primacy.* Cambridge: Cambridge University Press, 2003.

Papers Relating to Foreign Affairs 1868. Third Session of the Fortieth Congress, 1868. Part 1, 1869. Rpt. New York: Kraus Reprint, 1965.

Peattie, Mark R. "The Last Samurai: The Military Career of Nogi Maresuke." *Princeton Papers in East Asian Studies* 1 (1972): 87–121.

———. "Nogi Maresuke." In *Kodansha Encyclopedia of Japan,* 6: 31. 9 vols. 1st ed. New York and Tokyo: Kodansha, 1983.

Pflugfelder, Gregory M. *Cartographies of Desire: Male-Male Sexuality in Japanese Discourse, 1600–1950.* Berkeley: University of California Press, 1999.

Philippi, Donald L., trans. *Kojiki.* University of Tokyo Press, 1968.

Piggot, Joan R. *The Emergence of Japanese Kingship.* Stanford, Calif.: Stanford University Press, 1997.

Pinguet, Maurice. *Voluntary Death in Japan.* Trans. Rosemary Morris. Cambridge: Polity Press, 1993. Originally published as *La mort volontaire au Japon.* Paris: Éditions Gallimard, 1984.

Plass, Paul. *The Game of Death in Ancient Rome: Arena Sport and Political Suicide.* Madison: University of Wisconsin Press, 1995.

Plutarch's Lives. Trans. Bernadotte Perrin. 11 vols. New York: G. P. Putnam's Sons, 1914–1926.

Pollack, David. *Reading against Culture: Ideology and Narrative in the Japanese Novel.* Ithaca, N.Y.: Cornell University Press, 1992.

Presseisen, Ernst L. *Before Aggression: Europeans Prepare the Japanese Army.* The Association for Asian Studies: Monographs and Papers, No. 21. Tucson: University of Arizona Press, 1965.

Rabson, Steve. "Shimazaki Tōson on War." *Monumenta Nipponica* 46.4 (Winter 1991): 453–481.

Ratti, Oscar, and Adele Westbrook. *Secrets of the Samurai: A Survey of the Martial Arts of Feudal Japan.* Rutland, Vt.: Charles E. Tuttle, 1973.

Rawson, Elizabeth. *Cicero: A Portrait.* 1975; rpt. Ithaca, N.Y.: Cornell University Press, 1983.

Redesdale, Lord [Algernon Bertram Freeman-Mitford]. *Memories.* 2 vols. 1915; rpt. New York: E. P. Dutton, n.d.

Reiter, Rayna, ed. *Toward an Anthropology of Women.* New York: Monthly Review Press, 1975.

Reventlow, Graf E. zu. *Der Russisch-Japanische Krieg: Nebst einer Beschreibung von Japan, Korea, Russisch-Asien u. einer Geschichte dieser Länder, von Dr. H. Döring.* 3 vols. Berlin-Schöneberg: Internationaler Welt-Verlag, 1906.

Rimer, J. Thomas. *Mori Ōgai.* Boston: Twayne Publishers, 1975.

———. "The Last Phrase." In David Dilworth and J. Thomas Rimer, eds., *The Historical Fiction of Mori Ōgai,* pp. 209–221. 1977; rpt. Honolulu: University of Hawai'i Press, 1991.

———, trans. "Sahashi Jingorō." In David Dilworth and J. Thomas Rimer, eds., *The Historical Fiction of Mori Ōgai*, pp. 245–254. 1977; rpt. Honolulu: University of Hawai'i Press, 1991.

———, ed. *Not a Song Like Any Other: An Anthology of Writings by Mori Ōgai.* Honolulu: University of Hawai'i Press, 2004.

Rogers, John M. "Divine Destruction: The Shinpūren Rebellion of 1876." In Helen Hardacre, with Adam L. Kern, eds., *New Directions in the Study of Meiji Japan*, pp. 408–439. Brill's Japanese Studies Library, vol. 6. Leiden, New York, and Köln: Brill, 1997.

Rosenstein, Nathan. "Sorting out the Lot in Republican Rome." *American Journal of Philology* 116.1 (1995): 43–75.

Roussin, Alfred. "Une révolution au Japon." *Revue des Deux Mondes* 80, 1 April 1869, pp. 673–701.

Rubin, Gayle. "The Traffic in Women." In Rayna Reiter, ed., *Toward an Anthropology of Women*, pp. 157–210. New York: Monthly Review Press, 1975.

Rubin, Jay. "Sōseki on Individualism: *Watakushi no Kojinshugi.*" *Monumenta Nipponica* 34.1 (1979): 21–48.

Sabbatucci, Dario. "Ordeal." Trans. Miriam Friedman. In Mircea Eliade, ed., *Encyclopedia of Religion.* 16 vols., 11: 92–97. New York: Macmillan, 1987.

Sakaki, Atsuko. *Recontextualizing Texts: Narrative Performance in Modern Japanese Fiction.* Cambridge, Mass.: Harvard University Asia Center, 1999.

Sakamoto Tarō et al., eds. *Nihon shoki.* Nihon koten bungaku taikei 67 and 68. Iwanami shoten, 1967.

Sakurai Tadayoshi. *Human Bullets: A Soldier's Story of Port Arthur.* Trans. Masujiro Honda. Ed. Alice Mabel Bacon. Boston and New York: Houghton, Mifflin and Company, 1907. Originally published in Japanese as *Nikudan: Ryojun jissenki*, 1906.

Sansom, George. *A History of Japan: 1615–1867.* Stanford, Calif.: Stanford University Press, 1963.

Sargent, Geoffrey W., trans. "Patriotism." In *Death in Midsummer and Other Stories by Yukio Mishima*, pp. 93–118. New York: New Directions, 1966.

Sasaki Hideaki. *Nogi Maresuke: yo wa shokun no shitei wo.* Kyōto: Mineruba shobō, 2005.

Sasaki Kōzō. *Senshū: Sakai rekkyo shimatsu.* 1893; rpt. Tosa shidankai, ed., *Senshū: Sakai do hanshi rekkyo jikki: Myōkokuji no seppuku.* Kōchi: Tosa shidankai, 1979.

Sato, Hiroaki, trans. "'The Abe Family' by Mori Ōgai." In Hiroaki Sato, *Legends of the Samurai*, pp. 341–379. Woodstock, N.Y.: The Overlook Press, 1995.

———. *Legends of the Samurai.* Woodstock, N.Y.: The Overlook Press, 1995.

———, trans. "General Nogi." In J. Thomas Rimer, ed. *Not a Song Like Any Other: An Anthology of Writings by Mori Ōgai*, pp. 295–296. Honolulu: University of Hawai'i Press, 2004.

Satow, Sir Ernest. *A Diplomat in Japan.* 1921; rpt. New York, Tokyo, Osaka, and London: ICG Muse, 2000.

Schele, Linda. "Bloodletting and the Vision Quest." In Linda Schele and Mary Ellen Miller, photographs by Justin Kerr, *The Blood of Kings: Dynasty and Ritual in*

Maya Art, pp. 175–185. New York: George Braziller in association with Kimbell Art Museum, Fort Worth, Tex. 1986.

Schellendorff, Bronsart von. *Sechs Monate beim Japanischen Feldheer.* Berlin: Ernst Siegfried Mittler und Sohn, 1906.

Schöche, Heike, ed. and trans. *Mori Ōgai: Deutschlandtagebuch 1884–1888.* Tübingen: konkursbuchverlag, 1992.

Schulz, Regine, and Matthias Seidel, eds. *Egypt: The World of the Pharaohs.* Cairo: The American University in Cairo Press, 2001. Originally published in German as *Ägypten: Die Welt der Pharaonen.* Köln: Könemann, 1998.

Schwenn, Friedrich. *Die Menschenopfer bei den Griechen und Römern.* Religionsgeschichtliche Versuche und Vorarbeiten, 15.3. 1915; rpt. Berlin: Alfred Töpelmann [vormals J. Ricker], 1966.

Seidensticker, Edward, trans. *The Tale of Genji.* 2 vols. New York: Alfred A. Knopf, 1976.

———. *Low City, High City: Tokyo from Edo to the Earthquake.* New York: Alfred A. Knopf, 1983.

Seidlmayer, Stephan. "The Rise of the State to the Second Dynasty." In Regine Schulz and Matthias Seidel, eds., *Egypt: The World of the Pharaohs*, pp. 25–39. Cairo: The American University in Cairo Press, 2001. Originally published in German as *Ägypten: Die Welt der Pharaonen.* Köln: Könemann, 1998.

Seita Fumitake. "Mori Ōgai no rekishi shōsetsu ni okeru ningenzō no keisei: 'matsu' 'taeru' to iu keiki o chūshin ni." In Nihon bungaku kenkyū shiryō kankōkai, ed., *Mori Ōgai II*, pp. 192–202. Nihon bungaku kenkyū shiryō sōsho. 100 vols. Yūseidō, 1979; 4th rpt. 1991.

Seneca the Elder. *See* Winterbottom, Michael.

Seneca: Moral Essays. Trans. John W. Basore. 3 vols. 1928; rpt. Cambridge, Mass.: Harvard University Press, 1963.

Seward, Jack. *Hara-kiri: Japanese Ritual Suicide.* Rutland, Vt.: Charles E. Tuttle, 1968.

Sharf, Frederic A., Anne Nishimura Morse, and Sebastian Dobson. *A Much Recorded War: The Russo-Japanese War in History and Imagery.* Boston: Museum of Fine Arts, 2005.

Shiba Ryōtarō. *Junshi.* 1978; rpt. Bungei shunjū, 1999.

Shibata Mitsuhiko. "Kamon no hanashi: Natsume Sōseki to Mori Ōgai." In Yoshinari Isamu, ed., *Bessatsu rekishi tokuhon: Nihon 'kamon yurai' sōran*, pp. 228–231. Shinjinbutsu ōraisha, 1997.

Shibusawa Hideo, Enchi Fumiko, and Yoshida Sei'ichi. "Onna daigaku no saininshiki: 'Haha no oshie' o yonde." *Bungei shunjū* 40.4 (April 1962), pp. 211–215.

Shimada Masahiko. *Sōseki o kaku.* Iwanami shoten, 1993.

Shimana Masao. *Nogi 'shinwa' to Nis-Shin, Nichi-Ro.* Ronsōsha, 2001.

Shimazaki, Chifumi. *Warrior Ghost Plays from the Japanese Noh Theater: Parallel Translations with Running Commentary.* Cornell East Asia Series 60. Ithaca, N.Y.: Cornell University East Asia Program, 1993.

Shimazaki Tōson. *Before the Dawn.* Trans. William E. Naff. Honolulu: University of Hawai'i Press, 1987.

Shively, Donald H., ed. *Tradition and Modernization in Japanese Culture.* Princeton, N.J.: Princeton University Press, 1971.

Singer, Robert T., with contributions by Herman Ooms et al. *Edo: Art in Japan 1615–1868.* Exh. cat., National Gallery of Art, Washington, D.C. New Haven, Conn.: Yale University Press, 1998.

Smith, Leonard V. *Between Mutiny and Obedience: The Case of the French Fifth Infantry Division during World War I.* Princeton, N.J.: Princeton University Press, 1994.

Smith, Robert J. *Ancestor Worship in Contemporary Japan.* Stanford, Calif.: Stanford University Press, 1974.

Snyder, Stephen. "Ōgai and the Problem of Fiction: *Gan* and Its Antecedents." *Monumenta Nipponica* 49.3 (Autumn 1994): 353–373.

Sōseki. *See* Natsume Kinnosuke or Natsume Sōseki.

Soyinka, Wole. *Death and the King's Horseman.* New York: Hill and Wang, Noonday Press, 1987.

Spencer, Herbert. "From *The Principles of Sociology.*" In Jeffrey Carter, ed., *Understanding Religious Sacrifice: A Reader,* pp. 41–52. London: Continuum, 2003.

Starrs, Roy. "Writing the National Narrative: Changing Attitudes toward Nation-Building among Japanese Writers, 1900–1930." In Sharon A. Minichiello, ed., *Japan's Competing Modernities: Issues in Culture and Democracy 1900–1930,* pp. 206–227. Honolulu: University of Hawai'i Press, 1998.

Suenaga Katsusuke. "Nogi Taishō fujin no 'Haha no oshie.'" *Bungei shunjū* 40.4 (April 1962), pp. 204–210.

Tamai Takayuki and Fujii Hidetada, eds. *Kokoro.* Sōseki sakuhin ronshūsei. Vol. 10. Ōfūsha, 1991.

Tang, Xiaobing, and Stephen Snyder, eds. *In Pursuit of Contemporary East Asian Culture.* Boulder, Colo.: Westview Press, 1996.

Togawa Yukio. "Meiji no bujin." In Tsubota Itsuo, ed., *Meiji no itsuzai,* pp. 124–134. Jinbutsu tanbō, Nihon no rekishi 18. Akatsuki kyōiku tosho, 1975.

———. *Ningen Nogi Maresuke.* Kōjinsha, 1988.

Tōson. *See* Shimazaki Tōson.

Totman, Conrad. *The Collapse of the Tokugawa Bakufu, 1862–1868.* Honolulu: University of Hawai'i Press, 1980.

———. *Early Modern Japan.* Berkeley: University of California Press, 1993.

Tsubota Itsuo, ed. *Meiji no itsuzai.* Jinbutsu tanbō, Nihon no rekishi 18. Akatsuki kyōiku tosho, 1975.

Tsunoda Ryūsaku, trans., and L. Carrington Goodrich, ed. *Japan in the Chinese Dynastic Histories: Later Han through Ming Dynasties.* Perkins Asiatic Monographs, No. 2. South Pasadena, Calif.: P. D. and Ione Perkins, 1951.

Tsunoda Ryusaku, Wm. Theodore de Bary, and Donald Keene, eds. *Sources of Japanese Tradition.* New York: Columbia University Press, 1958. Rpt. in 2 vols. 1964.

Turnbull, Stephen. *Samurai Invasion: Japan's Korean War 1592–1598.* London: Cassell, 2002.

Turner, Victor. *Dramas, Fields, and Metaphors: Symbolic Action in Human Society.* Ithaca, N.Y., and London: Cornell University Press, 1974.

———. "Hidalgo: History as Social Drama." In Victor Turner, *Dramas, Fields, and*

Metaphors: Symbolic Action in Human Society, pp. 98–155. Ithaca, N.Y., and London: Cornell University Press, 1974.

———. *The Forest of Symbols: Aspects of Ndembu Ritual*. Ithaca, N.Y.: Cornell University Press, 1981. Originally published in 1967.

Tyler, William Jefferson. "The Art and Act of Reflexivity in *The Bodhisattva*." In William Jefferson Tyler, trans., *The Bodhisattva or Samantabhadra: A Novel by Ishikawa Jun*, pp. 139–174. New York: Columbia University Press, 1990.

———, trans. *The Bodhisattva or Samantabhadra: A Novel by Ishikawa Jun*. New York: Columbia University Press, 1990.

Tylor, Edward Burnett. "From *Primitive Culture: Researches in the Development of Mythology, Philosophy, Religion, Language, Arts, and Custom*." In Jeffrey Carter, ed., *Understanding Religious Sacrifice: A Reader*, pp. 14–38. London: Continuum, 2003.

Ubukata Toshirō. *Meiji Taishō kenbun shi*. Chūkō bunko series. Chūō kōronsha, 1978.

van Gennep, Arnold. *See* Gennep, Arnold van.

Varley, Paul. *Japanese Culture*. 1973. 4th ed. Honolulu: University of Hawai'i Press, 2000.

———. *Warriors of Japan as Portrayed in the War Tales*. Honolulu: University of Hawai'i Press, 1994.

Varley, Paul, and Kumakura Isao, eds. *Tea in Japan: Essays on the History of* Chanoyu. Honolulu: University of Hawai'i Press, 1989.

Versnel, H. S. "Two Types of Roman *Devotio*." *Mnemosyne* 29 (1976): 365–410.

———. "Destruction, *devotio* and Despair in a Situation of Anomy: The Mourning for Germanicus in Triple Perspective." In Giulia Piccaluga, ed., *Perennitas: Studi in Onore di Angelo Brelich*, pp. 546–618. Rome: Ateneo, 1980.

———. "Beyond Cursing: The Appeal to Justice in Judicial Prayers." In Christopher A. Faraone and Dirk Obbink, eds., *Magika Hiera: Ancient Greek Magic and Religion*, pp. 60–106. New York and Oxford: Oxford University Press, 1991.

Victoria, Brian (Daizen) A. *Zen at War*. New York: Weatherhill, 1997.

von Brandt, Max. *See* Brandt, Max von.

Wada Masao, ed. *Nogi Maresuke nikki*. Kin'ensha, 1970.

Walder, David. *The Short Victorious War: The Russo-Japanese Conflict 1904–5*. London: Hutchinson, 1973.

Wallace, Anthony F. C. With the assistance of Sheila C. Steen. *The Death and Rebirth of the Seneca*. New York: Alfred A. Knopf, 1970.

Walthall, Anne. "Off with Their Heads! The Hirata Disciples and the Ashikaga Shoguns." *Monumenta Nipponica* 50.2 (Summer 1995): 137–170.

Wang Ping. *Aching for Beauty: Footbinding in China*. Minneapolis: University of Minnesota Press, 2000; rpt. New York: Anchor Books, 2002.

Warner, Denis, and Peggy Warner. *The Tide at Sunrise: A History of the Russo-Japanese War, 1904–1905*. New York: Charterhouse, 1974.

Washburn, Dennis C. *The Dilemma of the Modern in Japanese Fiction*. New Haven, Conn.: Yale University Press, 1995.

Washburn, Dennis, and Alan Tansman, eds. *Studies in Modern Japanese Literature:*

Essays and Translations in Honor of Edwin McClellan. Ann Arbor: University of Michigan, Center for Japanese Studies, 1997.

Washburn, Stanley. *Nogi.* London: Andrew Melrose, 1913.

Watson, Burton, trans. *Kanshi: The Poetry of Ishikawa Jōzan and Other Edo-Period Poets.* Berkeley, Calif.: North Point Press, 1990.

Wells, David, and Sandra Wilson, eds. *The Russo-Japanese War in Cultural Perspective, 1904–05.* London: Macmillan; New York: St. Martin's Press, 1999.

Williams, Yoko. Tsumi—*Offence and Retribution in Early Japan.* London and New York: RoutledgeCurzon, 2003.

Wilson (Mitchell), Elizabeth A. "Reading Ōgai's 'Sakai Jiken': An Exercise in Disclosing Meanings." Unpublished paper. University of Michigan, Ann Arbor. Department of Asian Languages and Cultures. 11 September 1989.

Wilson, George M. *Patriots and Redeemers in Japan: Motives in the Meiji Restoration.* Chicago: University of Chicago Press, 1992.

———. "Murder at the Shogun's Gate: The Sakuradamongai Incident in Meiji Restoration History." Unpublished manuscript, 1999.

Wilson, William R., trans. *Hōgen monogatari: Tale of the Disorder in Hōgen.* Cornell East Asia Series No. 99, 1971; rpt. Ithaca, N.Y.: East Asia Program, Cornell University, 2001.

———. "Okitsu Yagoemon no isho" (2nd version). In David Dilworth and J. Thomas Rimer, eds., *The Historical Fiction of Mori Ōgai,* pp. 53–63. 1977; rpt. Honolulu: University of Hawai'i Press, 1991.

Wilson, William Scott, trans. *Hagakure: The Book of the Samurai.* 1979; rpt. Tokyo, New York, and London: Kodansha International, 1983.

Winterbottom, Michael, trans. *The Elder Seneca Declamations.* 2 vols. Cambridge, Mass.: Harvard University Press, 1974.

Wolfe, Alan. *Suicidal Narrative in Modern Japan: The Case of Dazai Osamu.* Princeton, N.J.: Princeton University Press, 1990.

Wunner, Rosa. "Mori Ōgai—Studies and Translations in Western Languages: A Bibliography." *Japonica Humboldtiana* 2:195–244. Wiesbaden: Harrassowitz, 1998.

Yamamoto Hirofumi. *Junshi no kōzō.* Kōbundō, 1994.

———. *Seppuku: Nihonjin no sekinin no torikata.* Kōbunsha, 2003.

Yamamoto Takeshi. "'Rekkyo jikki' no jisshō shugi ni tsuite." In Sasaki Kōzō, *Senshū: Sakai rekkyo shimatsu.* 1893; rpt. Tosa shidankai, ed., *Senshū: Sakai do hanshi rekkyo jikki: Myōkokuji no seppuku,* pp. 1–5. Kōchi: Tosa Shidankai, 1979.

Yamamoto, Tomoko, trans. With corrections by Veronica M. Jeffers. *The Abe Family, by Mori Ōgai.* Tokyo: Personal Publishing Service of Asahi Shimbun, 1990.

Yanaga, Chitoshi. *Japan since Perry.* 1949; rpt. Hamden, Conn.: Archon Books, 1966.

Yanagita Izumi. "Hakushaku Kamei Koreaki no bijutsu kenkyū oyobi bijutsuron." In Kamei Koreaki, *Nisshin sensō jūgun shashinchō,* pp. 305–325. Hakushobō, 1992.

Yates, Charles L. *Saigō Takamori: The Man behind the Myth.* London and New York: Kegan Paul International, 1995.

Yiu, Angela. *Chaos and Order in the Works of Natsume Sōseki.* Honolulu: University of Hawai'i Press, 1998.

Yoshikawa Torajirō. "Shōnen jidai no Nogi Maresuke." In Kuwahara Takeshi and Sugawara Kazutora, eds., *Nogi Maresuke no sekai*, pp. 56–69. Shinjinbutsu ōraisha, 1992.

Zöllner, Reinhard. "The Sun Also Rises: Go-Daigo in Revolt." Review of *Kenmu: Go-Daigo's Revolution*, by Andrew Edmund Goble (Cambridge, Mass.: Harvard University Press, 1996), *Monumenta Nipponica* 53.4 (Winter 1998): 517–527.

INDEX

Boldface type refers to illustrations.

ABOUT THE AUTHOR

Doris G. Bargen is professor of Japanese Literature and Culture and director of Asian Languages and Literatures at the University of Massachusetts Amherst. Her essays on *The Tale of Genji* have appeared in *Mosaic* (1986), *The Harvard Journal of Asiatic Studies* (1988 and 1991), *Approaches to Teaching Murasaki Shikibu's* The Tale of Genji (1993), and *Genji kenkyū* (1999). The 1991 article from *The Harvard Journal of Asiatic Studies* was recently reprinted in Harold Bloom's collection of essays on *The Tale of Genji* (2004). Bargen's publications on Heian culture culminated in her interdisciplinary study, *A Woman's Weapon: Spirit Possession in* The Tale of Genji (University of Hawai'i Press, 1997). She has also published essays on modern Japan, including one on Kawabata Yasunari in the *Japanese Journal of Religious Studies* (1992), and two on Enchi Fumiko—in *Monumenta Nipponica* (1991) and in *The Woman's Hand: Gender and Theory in Japanese Women's Writing*, edited by Paul Gordon Schalow and Janet A. Walker (1996). In *Suicidal Honor*—a study of General Nogi's *junshi* and its influence on the fiction of Mori Ōgai and Natsume Sōseki—Bargen explores and interprets the national crises that exposure to the West triggered during the Bakumatsu and Meiji-Taishō periods.